The Making of Christianity

CB

CONIECTANEA BIBLICA
NEW TESTAMENT SERIES

47

ISSN 0069-8946
Editor:
Samuel Byrskog

The Making of Christianity

Conflicts, Contacts, and Constructions:
Essays in Honor of
Bengt Holmberg

Edited by
Magnus Zetterholm and Samuel Byrskog

Winona Lake, Indiana
Eisenbrauns
2012

Library of Congress Cataloging-in-Publication Data

The making of Christianity : conflicts, contacts, and constructions ; essays in honor of
  Bengt Holmberg / edited by Magnus Zetterholm and Samuel Byrskog.
       p. cm. — (Coniectanea Biblica. New Testament series, ISSN 0069-8946 ; 47)
    Includes bibliographical references (p.   ) and index.
    ISBN 978-1-57506-817-6 (pbk. : alk. paper)
    1. Church history—Primitive and early church, ca. 30–600.   I. Holmberg, Bengt,
  1942–   II. Zetterholm, Magnus, 1958–   III. Byrskog, Samuel.
    BR162.3.M35   2012
    270.1—dc23
                                                                  2012041602

Contents

Editors' Preface

We are delighted to present this volume to Bengt Holmberg in honor of his important contribution to the international field of New Testament scholarship and of his service to New Testament studies at the Faculty of Theology, Lund University, Sweden. The essays in this volume have been authored by colleagues who have benefited from his work, not least from his development and discussion of the sociological study of the New Testament, or in other ways interacted with him during his long career.

Bengt is widely known and respected for introduction of sociology into the study of the New Testament. He was one of the pioneers. His dissertation *Paul and Power*, published both by CWK Gleerup in 1978 and by Fortress Press in 1980, was among the first studies using sociological theory on Pauline letters and set the agenda for much future research. Partly on the basis of his conviction that the ultimate reality at the end escapes scholarly analytical categories, Bengt always sensed both the advantages and the dangers of sociological approaches to the study of religious phenomena and discussed them with much insight in his second monograph *Sociology and the New Testament* published by Fortress Press in 1990.

Later on he received a large grant for a project dealing with Christian identity during the first century c.e. and generously involved colleagues and doctoral students from different Swedish universities to investigate various dimensions of the topic. Several studies have emerged from the project. Bengt himself wrote an insightful article which he included in the project volume *Exploring Early Christian Identity* published by Mohr Siebeck in 2008. It is therefore as it should that this celebration of his international scholarly activity focuses on the making of Christianity in terms of its conflicts, contacts and constructions.

This volume is also a tribute to Bengt's service to New Testament studies at the Faculty of Theology at Lund University. Bengt remained faithful to Lund University from his young age as a graduate student until his retirement in 2007. His dissertation immediately received

much and well-deserved attention. The Faculty was proud of its new
scholar of the highest international standard. He subsequently served
the Faculty as Docent, senior lecturer and Professor of New Testament studies, with interruptions for assignments in the church and at
seminaries in Norway, Tanzania and Israel. He was Dean of the Faculty 2003–2005. Bengt strenuously and with much integrity stood up
for what he believed to be right for our discipline and for the Faculty.

It is with a special sense of pleasure that two of the present members
of the Faculty, one of which was Bengt's doctoral student, now can present this book to his honor as a token of our appreciation for his long service to New Testament studies and to the Faculty of Theology in Lund.

Spring 2012
Magnus Zetterholm and Samuel Byrskog

List of Contributors

Samuel Byrskog
Professor of New Testament Studies, Lund University, Sweden

William S. Campbell
Reader in Biblical Studies, University of Wales, Lampeter, Trinity Saint David, United Kingdom

Adela Yarbro Collins
Buckingham Professor of New Testament Criticism and Interpretation, Yale University, USA

James D. G. Dunn
Lightfoot Professor of Divinity Emeritus, Durham University, United Kingdom

Birger Gerhardsson
Professor Emeritus of New Testament Studies, Lund University, Sweden

Judith Lieu
Lady Margaret's Professor of Divinity, University of Cambridge, United Kingdom

Dieter Mitternacht
Associate Professor of New Testament Studies, Lutheran Theological Seminar, Hong Kong, S.A.R., China

Halvor Moxnes
Professor of New Testament Studies, University of Oslo, Norway

Birger Olsson
Professor Emeritus of New Testament Studies, Lund University, Sweden

Anders Runesson
Associate Professor of Early Christianity and Early Judaism, McMaster University, Canada

Karl Olav Sandnes
Professor of New Testament Studies, MF Norwegian School of Theology, Oslo, Norway

Mikael Tellbe
Associate Professor of New Testament Studies, Örebro School of Theology, Sweden

Gerd Theissen
Professor Emeritus of New Testament Theology, University of Heidelberg, Germany

Tommy Wasserman
Researcher at the Norwegian School of Leadership and Theology, Norway

Stephen Westerholm
Professor of Biblical Studies, McMaster University, Canada

Magnus Zetterholm
Associate Professor of New Testament Studies, Lund University, Sweden

Abbreviations

Primary Sources

1 Apol.	*Apologia i* (Justin Martyr)
1 En.	*1 Enoch* (Pseudepigrapha)
1QpHab	*Pesher Habakkuk* (Qumran)
1QS	*Serek Hayaḥad* (Qumran)
1QSb	Rule of the Blessing (Qumran)
2 Apol.	*Apologia ii* (Justin Martyr)
2 Clem.	*2 Clement* (Apostolic Fathers)
4 Macc	4 Maccabees (Apocrypha and Septuagint)
A.J.	*Antiquitates judaicae* (Josephus)
Adfin.	*De adfinium vocabulorum differentia* (Ammonius Grammaticus)
Adv. Jud.	*Adversus Judaeos* (John Chrysostom)
Agr.	*Agricola* (Tacitus)
Ann.	*Annales* (Tacitus)
Apoc. Ab.	*Apocalypse of Abraham* (Pseudepigrapha)
Apol.	*Apologeticus* (Tertullian)/Apology (Aristides)
Apos. Con.	*Apostolic Constitutions and Canons*
Ascen. Isa.	*Ascension of Isaiah* (Pseudepigrapha)
Att.	*Epistulae ad Atticum* (Cicero)
Autol.	*Ad Autolycum* (Theophilus of Antioch)
B.J.	*Bellum judaicum* (Josephus)
Bar	Baruch (Apocrypha and Septuagint)
Ber.	*Berakhot* (Mishnah, Talmud)
C. Ap.	*Contra Apionem* (Josephus)
CD	Damascus Document (Qumran)
Cels.	*Contra Celsum* (Origen)
Civ.	*De civitate Dei* (Augustine)
Claud.	*Divus Claudius* (Suetonius)
Comm. Jo.	*Commentarii in evangelium Joannis* (Origen)

Conf.	*Confessiones* (Augustine)
Contempl.	*De vita contemplativa* (Philo)
Contr.	*Controversiae* (Seneca the Elder)
Decal.	*De decalogo* (Philo)
Deut. Rabb.	*Deuteronomy Rabbah* (Midrash)
Dial.	*Dialogus cum Tryphone* (Justin Martyr)
Diatr.	*Diatribai* (Epictetus)
Did.	*Didache* (Apostolic Fathers)
Diogn.	*Diognetus* (Apostolic Fathers)
Disc.	*Discourses* (Musonius Rufus)
Dom.	*Domitianus* (Suetonius)
Eccl. Rabb.	*Ecclesiastes Rabbah* (Midrash)
Ecl.	*Eclogae propheticae* (Clement of Alexandria)
Ep.	*Epistulae* (Pliny the Younger)/ *Epistulae morales* (Seneca the Younger)
Epist.	*Epistulae* (Jerome)
Exod. Rabb.	*Exodus Rabbah* (Midrash)
Flacc.	*In Flaccum* (Philo)
Fug.	*Fugitivi* (Lucian)
Gen. Rabb.	*Genesis Rabbah* (Midrash)
Geogr.	*Geographica* (Strabo)
Haer.	*Adversus haereses* (Irenaeus)
Hell.	*Hellenica* (Xenophon)
Hist.	*Historiae* (Tacitus)
Hist. eccl.	*Historia ecclesiastica* (Eusebius)
Hist. Rom.	*Historiae Romanae* (Velleius Paterculus)
Hom. Lev.	*Homiliae in Leviticum* (Origen)
Ign. Eph.	*To the Ephesians* (Ignatius)
Ign. Magn.	*To the Magnesians* (Ignatius)
Ign. Phld.	*To the Philadelphians* (Ignatius)
Ign. Rom.	*To the Romans* (Ignatius)

Ign. Smyrn.	*To the Smyrnaeans* (Ignatius)
Ign. Trall.	*To the Trallians* (Ignatius)
Inst.	*Institutio oratoria* (Quintilian)
Jdt	Judith (Apocrypha and Septuagint)
Jub.	*Jubilees* (Pseudepigrapha)
Leg.	*Legatio pro Christianis* (Athenagoras)/*Leges* (Plato)
Legat.	*Legatio ad Gaium* (Philo)
Lept.	*Adversus Leptinem* (Demosthenes)
Let. Aris.	*Letter of Aristeas* (Pseudepigrapha)
LSAM	Sokolowski, F. Lois sacrées de l'Asie Mineure. Paris: Boccard, 1955
Mart. Pol.	*Martyrdom of Polycarp* (Apostolic Fathers)
Mor.	*Moralia* (Plutarch)
Nat.	*Ad nationes* (Tertullian)/*Naturalis historia* (Pliny the Elder)
Ned.	*Nedarim* (Mishnah, Talmud)
Num. Rabb.	*Numbers Rabbah* (Midrash)
Oct.	*Octavius* (Minucius Felix)
Or.	*Oratio* (Dio Chrysotom)
Orat.	*Oratio ad Graecos* (Tatian)
Pan.	*Panarion* (Epiphanius)
Pesaḥ.	*Pesahim* (Mishnah, Talmud)
Phaedr.	*Phaedrus* (Plato)
Praep. ev.	*Praeparatio evangelica* (Eusebius)
Pss. Sol.	*Psalms of Solomon* (Pseudepigrapha)
Res.	*De resurrectione* (Athenagoras)
Šabb.	*Shabbat* (Mishnah, Talmud)
Sanh.	*Sanhedrin* (Mishnah, Talmud)
Sat.	*Satirae* (Juvenal)
Sel. Exod.	*Selecta in Exodum* (Origen)
Sib. Or.	*Sibylline Oracles* (Pseudepigrapha)
SIG	*Sylloge inscriptionum graecarum.* Edited by W. Dittenberger. 4 vols. 3d

	ed. Leipzig, 1915–1924.
Sir	Sirah/Ecclesiasticus (Apocrypha and Septuagint)
Spec.	*De specialibus legibus* (Philo)
Superst.	*De superstitione* (Plutarch)
T. Mos.	*Testament of Moses* (Pseudepigrapha)
Tib.	*Tiberius* (Suetonius)
Trad. ap.	*Traditio apostolica* (Hippolytus)
Vit. Apoll.	*Vita Apollonii* (Philostratus)
Vitae	*Vitae philosophorum* (Diogenes Laertius)
Wis	Wisdom of Solomon (Apocrypha and Septuagint)

Secondary Sources

AJSR	*Association for Jewish Studies Review*
ANRW	*Aufstieg und Niedergang der römischen Welt: Geschichte und Kultur Roms im Spiegel der neueren Forschung.* Edited by H. Temporini and W. Haase. Berlin, 1972–
ASTI	*Annual of the Swedish Theological Institute*
BASOR	*Bulletin of the American Schools of Oriental Research*
BBR	*Bulletin for Biblical Research*
BDAG	Bauer, W., F. W. Danker, W. F. Arndt, and F. W. Gingrich. *Greek-English Lexicon of the New Testament and Other Early Christian Literature.* 3d ed. Chicago, 1999

Bib	*Biblica*
BJRL	*Bulletin of the John Rylands University Library of Manchester*
BR	*Biblical Research*
BTB	*Biblical Theology Bulletin*
BZ	*Biblische Zeitschrift*
CBQ	*Catholic Biblical Quarterly*
CRBR	*Critical Review of Books in Religion*
DTT	*Dansk teologisk tidsskrift*
ExpTim	*Expository Times*
HTR	*Harvard Theological Review*
JBL	*Journal of Biblical Literature*
JECS	*Journal of Early Christian Studies*
JETS	*Journal of the Evangelical Theological Society*
JIWE	*Noy, D. Jewish Inscriptions of Western Europe. 2 vols. Cambridge: Cambridge University Press, 1993–1995.*
JQR	*Jewish Quarterly Review*
JRH	*Journal of Religious History*
JRS	*Journal of Roman Studies*
JSHJ	*Journal for the Study of the Historical Jesus*
JSJ	*Journal for the Study of Judaism in the Persian, Hellenistic, and Roman Periods*
JSNT	*Journal for the Study of the New Testament*
JSOT	*Journal for the Study of the Old Testament*
JSSR	*Journal for the Scientific Study of Religion*
JTS	*Journal of Theological Studies*
LumVie	*Lumière et vie*

NovT	*Novum Testamentum*
NTS	*New Testament Studies*
OLD	*The Oxford Latin Dictionary*
OTP	*Old Testament Pseudepigrapha.* Edited by J. H. Charlesworth. 2 vols. New York, 1983
ProEccl	*Pro ecclesia*
RB	*Revue biblique*
SEÅ	*Svensk exegetisk årsbok*
SR	*Studies in Religion*
TTKi	*Tidsskrift for Teologi og Kirke*
TynBul	*Tyndale Bulletin*
TZ	*Theologische Zeitschrift*
ZAW	*Zeitschrift für die alttestamentliche Wissenschaft*
ZKG	*Zeitschrift für Kirchengeschichte*
ZNW	*Zeitschrift für die neutestamentliche Wissenschaft und die Kunde der älteren Kirche*
ZTK	*Zeithschrift für Theologie und Kirche*
ZWT	*Zeitschrift für wissenschaftliche Theologie*

From Memory to Memoirs
Tracing the Background of a Literary Genre

Samuel Byrskog
Lund University

> Great is this force of memory, exceedingly great,
> O my God – a large and boundless chamber!
> Who has plumbed the depth of it?
> Augustine, *Confessions* 10.8.15

Introduction

During the course of several seminars directed by Bengt Holmberg, I had the opportunity to discuss with him the importance of memory for understanding the formation of early Christian identity.[1] Holmberg was encouraging and positive to my ideas and endorsed the notion of the mnemonic identity of the early Christ-believers. As a small token of gratitude for years of scholarly collaboration and friendship, I wish to discuss the remarkable fact that one of the first literary designations of the Gospels focused precisely on their mnemonic character. My basic question is: to what extent and in what sense does this designation indicate a broader trajectory fostering the idea that the Gospels were memoirs?

---

[1] The project was entitled "Early Christian Identity – the First Hundred Years." The participants in the project present articles on each of their individual topics in *Exploring Early Christian Identity* (ed. Bengt Holmberg; Tübingen: Mohr Siebeck, 2008).

The Memoirs of Justin Martyr

In the second century c.e. the narratives telling the story about Jesus Christ had not yet received a literary designation that was generally accepted. The Christian philosopher and apologist Justin Martyr knows these stories well. Only in *1 Apol.* 66.3 does he call them "gospels." Discussing the Eucharist he refers to the memoirs of the apostles and points out that they "are called gospels" (καλεῖται εὐαγγέλια). Justin's comment, which probably served as a clarification for the Gentile audience, implies that some people had already recognized them as "gospels." Yet we have no earlier texts using this term as a literary designation. Justin employs it twice in the singular in order to point to individual narratives (*Dial.* 10.2; 100.1), but mostly he prefers not to use it at all.

The term "gospels," in the plural, could easily be misunderstood. Perhaps Justin realized that it would have reminded the Gentile audience too much about news concerning the emperor. On such occasions the plural was regularly employed, from early on. Most well-known is the inscription in Priene (south of Ephesus) dated to 9 b.c.e., which tells about the birthday of Augustus as the beginning of the "gospels" (εὐαγγελί[ων]) for the world.[2] Josephus' accounts of Vespasian's acclamation are equally famous. Every city in the East, he says, kept festival for the "gospels" (εὐαγγέλια) on Vespasian's behalf (*War* 4.618). On reaching Alexandria, in the West, Vespasian was greeted by the "gospels from Rome" (τὰ ἀπὸ Ῥώμης εὐαγγέλια) and by embassies from every quarter of the world (*War* 4.656). Justin addressed his *Apology* to the emperor Antoninus Pius and his sons, in addition to the Senate and the people of the Romans, and might for that reason have been anxious that the narratives about Jesus not be confused with political and religious propaganda. This was probably all the more important as the purpose of the *Apology* was to prove to the upright and philosophical minded emperor the injustice of the persecution of the Christians,

---

[2] *Griechische Inschriften als Zeugnisse des privaten und öffentlichen Lebens* (ed. G. Pfohl; München: Heimeran, 1965), no. 118 (pp. 134–5).

whom he regarded as the representatives of true philosophy. He prefers the expression τὰ ἀπομνημονεύματα τῶν ἀποστόλων, the reminiscences or memoirs of the apostles.[3] It appears 15 times, twice in the *Apology* and 13 times in the *Dialogue with Trypho*. The *Apology* was written first. For Justin the expression pointed a literary genre. Most likely he formed it on the basis of Xenophon's famous memoirs of Socrates—the so-called *Memorabilia* or ἀπομνημονεύματα. Justin admired Socrates and quoted from Xenophon's writing in *2 Apol.* 11.3. The decisive difference is of course that Justin added τῶν ἀποστόλων, pointing to eyewitnesses and authors. In doing so, Justin created a hybrid. Nevertheless, by ranking the narratives about Jesus together with Xenophon's work he placed them in the literary family of other similar kinds of writings.

The generic use of the title did not mean that it lost its mnemonic colour. It was not all that common, after all, and it was not entirely stylized.[4] Long ago, the classicist Eduard Schwartz gave it a concise definition:

> **Apomneumoneumata** heißen technisch solche Berichte über Handlungen, merkwürdige Einzelheiten, besonders Aussprüche, welche lediglich auf der persönlichen Erinnerung an Dinge selbst oder an die mündliche Tradition über sie beruhen oder beruhen wollen und bei denen der Erzähler zwar Zeuge, aber nicht das vornehmliche Object des Erzählten ist.[5]

Scholars debate the apologetic and antignostic reasons for Justin's use of the term. Such factors were probably influential. Also the

---

[3] For discussion and literature, see L. Abramowski, "Die 'Erinnerungen der Apostel' bei Justin," in *Das Evangelium und die Evangelien: Vorträge vom Tübinger Symposium 1982* (ed. P. Stuhlmacher; Tübingen: Mohr Siebeck, 1983), 341–53.

[4] See references in M. Hengel, *The Four Gospels and the One Gospel of Jesus Christ* (Harrisburg: Trinity Press International, 2000), 212 n. 13; L. Alexander, "Memory and Tradition in the Hellenistic Schools," in *Jesus in Memory: Traditions in Oral and Scribal Perspectives* (ed. W. H. Kelber and S. Byrskog; Waco: Baylor University Press, 2009), 113–53, esp. 120–41.

[5] E. Schwartz, PW 2 (1896): 170–1, esp. 170. J. Werner gives a similar comment in *Der kleine Pauly: Lexikon der Antike* (5 vols.; ed. K. J. F. Ziegler, W. Sontheimer and H. Gärtner; München: Druckenmüller, 1964–1975), 1:455–6. The term does not have a separate entry in *Der neue Pauly: Enzyklopädie der Antike* (16 vols.; ed. H. Cancik and H. Schneider; Stuttgart: Metzler, 1996–2003).

philosophical connotation might have played a role in view of
Justin's conviction that Christianity was the true philosophy and his
fondness of Jesus as teacher. But we should not forget its mnemonic
implication. According to Schwartz, it communicated the idea that the
writing in question rested or sought to rest on personal reminiscence
of the things themselves or on the oral tradition about them.

If we follow Schwartz, we may assume that when Justin labeled
the narratives about Jesus ἀπομνημονεύματα he indicated that
they had to do with what people remembered. This is confirmed
by his use of mnemonic terminology in relation to the apostles.
He once uses the verb "remember." In *1 Apol.* 33.5 he speaks
about Jesus' birth, adding "as those who remembered everything
about our saviour Jesus Christ taught" (ὡς οἱ ἀπομνημονεύσαντες
πάντα τὰ περὶ τοῦ σωτῆρος ἡμῶν Ἰησοῦ Χριστοῦ ἐδίδαξαν).
The apostles were "those who remembered." Their teaching
was from memory. Accordingly, their own writings and those
of their followers received a generic classification which
integrated their mnemonic character into their literary status.

Theodor Zahn gave a definition which resembles the one proposed
by Schwartz, though emphasizing more strongly that these kinds
of writings deal with a specific person.[6] As Zahn understands the
matter, the ἀπομνημονεύματα are neither remarks to be used only
for one's own purpose nor collections for those who come after—
that would be ὑπομνήματα. They are notes from memory about a
significant person. Zahn stresses also the importance of eyewitnesses
as an element of generic classification, but this element has more
to do with apologetic—and particularly antignostic—tendencies
than genre. The focus on a specific person is, however, interesting.
The ἀπομνημονεύματα are, according to Zahn, mnemonic notes
concerning a person who was considered to be of vital importance.
It is not without reason that such stories about Socrates as the ones
found in the writings of Plato and Xenophon, with their combination

---

[6] T. Zahn, *Geschichte des Neutestamentlichen Kanons* (2 vols.; Erlangen and Leipzig: A.
Deichert'sche Verlagsbuchh, 1889), 1:471–6.

of anecdote and memoir, early stimulated biographical tendencies.[7] The generic use of ἀπομνημονεύματα holds together two aspects of the writing: it is a representation of what was thought to be remembered *and* a literary characterisation focusing on a particular individual.

From Justin's Memoirs to Papias' *chreiai*

Justin was only slightly interested in the individual writings and authors of the New Testament and mentions mostly the narratives about Jesus without distinguishing between them. They are simply memoirs of the apostles. He harmonizes the Jesus-sayings when he quotes from them.[8] Tatian, who composed the *Diatessaron*, was one of his students in Rome.[9]

On one occasion, however, he indicates awareness of something more specific. In *Dial.* 106.3 he points out that Jesus changed the name of an apostle to Peter and the name of the sons of Zebedee to Boanerges, sons of thunder. This is an implicit reference to Mark 3:16–17,[10] one of the few indications of Justin's use of the Markan narrative. He explains that this is what is said "in his memoirs" (ἐν τοῖς ἀπομνημονεύμασιν αὐτοῦ), where "his" refers to Peter. The classicist Miroslav Marcovich, in his 1997 edition of the *Dialogues*,[11] inserts τῶν ἀποστόλων in front of αὐτοῦ, suggesting the reading "in the memoirs of his apostles." This is a feasible conjecture which accords with Justin's way of expressing himself elsewhere. Against Marchovich's proposal stands the fact that the available text does not have this reference to the apostles and that Peter is mentioned in the immediate context. It is also noteworthy that Justin elsewhere names an apostle as the author of a particular New Testament writing. In *Dial.* 81.4 John the apostle is the one

---

[7] R. A. Burridge, *What are the Gospels? A Comparison with Graeco-Roman Biography* (2d ed.; Grand Rapids: Eerdmans, 2004), 69.

[8] A. J. Bellinzoni, *The Sayings of Jesus in the Writings of Justin Martyr* (Leiden: Brill, 1967).

[9] Cf. W. L. Petersen, "Textual Evidence of Tatian's Dependence upon Justin's Apomnemoneumata," *NTS* 36 (1990): 512–34.

[10] C.-J. Thornton, "Justin und das Markusevangelium," *ZNW* 84 (1993): 93–109.

[11] *Dialogus cum Tryphone* (ed. M. Marcovich; Berlin: de Gruyter, 1997).

who prophesised in the book of Revelation. If "his" thus refers to Peter, we have an indication that Justin, when he for once referred to the Markan narrative, specified it as the memoirs of Peter.

This gives us reason move a few decades back in time. Eusebius' quotation from Papias' *Expositions of Oracles of the Lord* includes the first reference to the idea of a connection between Peter and the Markan narrative (*Hist. eccl.* 3.39.15). Papias claims to have this information from the Presbyter. In the extensive debate about the significance of Eusebius' quotation, one rarely pays attention to the double occurrence of mnemonic terminology. It is said twice that Mark wrote down things from memory. Papias employs, first, the verb μνημονεύειν—Mark wrote "as much as he remembered" (ὅσα ἐμνημόνευσεν)—and, secondly, ἀπομνημονεύειν—he wrote down single points "as he remembered" (ὡς ἀπεμνημόνευσεν). The second occurrence accords with Justin's use of the term ἀπομνημονεύματα.

There is no reason quibble about the fact that Justin writes of Peter's memoirs while Papias suggests that Mark is the one who remembers. Justin knew that the apostles themselves as well as their followers composed memoirs (*Dial.* 103.8). Nor should we jump to the conclusion that Justin was himself aware of Papias' statement. Some scholars have claimed that this was the case and assumed that Papias' view in fact caused Justin to define the writings as memoirs. But this is difficult to ascertain. As we have seen, Xenophon's writing about Socrates is likely to have played a decisive role. What is noteworthy, however, is the use of common mnemonic terminology concerning the Gospels in the writings of two— probably independent—authors. For both of them the narratives about Jesus were textual representations of mnemonic processes.

According to Papias, Mark remembered the teaching from Peter in the form of *chreiai*. This is how Josef Kürzinger, and several other recent scholars, understand the expression πρὸς τὰς χρείας ἐποιεῖτο τὰς διδασκαλίας.[12] It does not imply that Peter taught

---

[12] J. Kürzinger, "Die Aussage des Papias von Hierapolis zur literarischen Form des Markusevangeliums," *BZ* 21 (1977): 245–64. Cf. also M. Black, "The Use of Rhetorical Terminology in Papias on Mark and Matthew," *JSNT* 37 (1989): 31–41, esp. 34, 38.

as the need aroused, but rather that his teaching had the form of small memorable anecdotes. Remembering such anecdotes was not difficult. Aelius Theon (circa 50–100 C.E.), the Alexandrian sophist, gave the earliest definition of the *chreia*. It consisted of "a concise statement or action which is well aimed, attributed to a specified character or something analogous to a character" (*Progymnasmata* 5). It could be unprompted or prompted by a specific situation, a statement or a response of varying character, single or double, active or passive (for the "action"-*chreia*). It could be presented according to various rhetorical patterns and expanded or elaborated to function in a variety of discourses and argumentative contexts. What Mark remembered and tried to write down, according to Papias, were thus well aimed sayings or actions attributed to a specific character.[13] Considering the rhetorical quality and elaborative potential of the ancient *chreia*, it must have been natural, in his view, to expand the collection and arrangement of such anecdotes—even if they were not in order—into mnemonic stories of a more literary and hermeneutically profound kind. It was but a short step from a series of memorable anecdotes to memoirs.

From Papias' *chreiai* to Johannine Reminiscences

Granted Papias had his information from the Presbyter, we are back in the 90s when the Johannine tradition was flourishing somewhere in the vicinity of Ephesus. This is where Justin, according to some

---

[13] I am not discussing if this is what really happened. V. Taylor, *The Gospel According to St. Mark* (London: Macmillan, 1952), 102, cautiously defined "the Petrine *chreiai*" in Mark as consisting of 1:21–39; 4:35–5:43; 6:30–56; 7:24–37; 8:27–9:29, and parts of 14:1–16:8. I have discussed them in *Story as History – History as Story: The Gospel Tradition in the Context of Ancient Oral History* (Tübingen: Mohr Siebeck, 2000), 289–92, concluding that while a Petrine influence is likely, Mark in fact incorporated Peter's oral history into his own story by means of an interchange with other material and various hermeneutical factors. The Gospel tradition might have developed partly through argumentative *chreia* elaboration. Cf. B. L. Mack and V. K. Robbins, *Patterns of Persuasion in the Gospels* (FF Literacy Facets; Sonoma, Polebridge Press, 1988); S. Byrskog, "The Early Church as a Narrative Fellowship: An Exploratory Study of the Performance of the *Chreia*," *TTKi* 78 (2007): 207–26; idem, "When Eyewitness Testimony and Oral Tradition Become Written Text," *SEÅ* 74 (2009): 41–53.

scholars, a few decades later converted to Christianity.

Memory plays an important role in the Johannine writings. In John 2:22 the author suddenly opens up the internal story and adds a reference to what the disciples remembered after Jesus was raised from the dead. When Jesus cleanses the temple they remember the Scripture (2:17), but their remembrance of Jesus' own saying after the resurrection causes them to believe the Scripture as well as the word that Jesus had spoken. This seemingly unnecessary excursion into the extradiegetic future points to the mnemonic link between history and faith. A similar venture appears in 12:16. This time the internal flow of the story is interrupted as Jesus triumphantly enters into Jerusalem. The narrator tells the hearers/readers that while the disciples did not at first understand the Scripture, after Jesus was glorified they remembered that these things had been written of him and that they had done these things unto him. Memory was as a means of realizing in light of Jesus' glorification what had essentially happened.

The author validates this mnemonic activity in two ways. Firstly, in 16:4a, when the Johannine Jesus gives his farewell discourses, he points out to the disciples the that he says certain things in order that they shall remember that he told them so when the(ir) hour comes (cf. 15:20). He links back to what he just promised in 16:1, indicating the intentionality of his teaching. Just as he says things to the disciples in order that (ἵνα) they should not be caused to stumble, so he also says things to them in order that (ἵνα) they should remember them. Intersected with this kind of mnemonic determination is, secondly, the reminding and didactic function of the Paraclete. In 14:26 Jesus forecasts that the Holy Spirit will teach the disciples everything and that this teaching, in effect, means that the Spirit will remind them of everything that he had said to them.[14] The future mnemonic activity is a spiritual activity inspired by the teaching of the Paraclete from the Father. It carries a strong theological nuance, which anchors what Jesus says in a divinely and spiritually sanctioned process of traditioning and reconfiguration.

---

[14] The last two lines of verse 26 are in synonymous parallelism. So R. E. Brown, *The Gospel According to John* (2 vols.; Garden City: Doubleday, 1966), 651.

This "mnemonic theology" concerns more than the sayings of Jesus. As is shown by the intricate relationship between remembering and testifying in the Gospel of John, it includes his activity from the beginning. In 14:26 the Spirit reminds the disciples of what Jesus had said, but in 15:26–27 it testifies on Jesus' behalf so that the disciples also will testify. The reason they are to testify is that they have been with Jesus from the beginning, already during his earthly ministry. Their testimony is anchored in and concerns Jesus' entire career from the start.

The interplay between memory and testimony among the disciples corroborates with the author's understanding of the writing itself. Not only do characters within the story give testimony, but the author or someone close to him regarded the finished writing to be in direct continuity with these testimonies. In 21:20–24 Jesus tells Peter that the Beloved Disciple will remain until he comes; and this disciple, the narrator continues, is the one who is testifying to "these things" and has written them. The Beloved Disciple had been with Jesus during all the decisive events. The things that he is testifying to and the things that he has written are one and the same and probably refer to the entire Johannine story of Jesus.[15] Evidently there were people—the text continues with "we"—who looked upon the finished narrative as a reflection of the disciples' inspired reminiscences and testimonies and deliberately shaped it to convey the idea that memory provided the spiritual path from the Jesus of history to the finished Gospel about his life, death and glorification. The "pneumatic memory" was textualized and momentarily frozen, not in terms of a perpetually non-negotiable medium,[16] but as an infusion of the mnemonic history into the writing itself.

If Papias was correct to claim that his information came from the

---

[15] C. H. Dodd believed that they refer only to 21:20–23 or possibly the whole of chapter 21. See his "Note on John 21,24," *JTS* 4 (1953): 212–13. But there is no reason for such a solemn attestation for a few paragraphs added to someone else's writing.

[16] So T. Thatcher, "Why John Wrote a Gospel: Memory and History in an Early Christian Community," in *Memory, Tradition, and Text: Uses of the Past in Early Christianity* (ed. A. Kirk and T. Thatcher; Atlanta: Society of Biblical Literature, 2005), 79–97. I doubt that anyone in the first audience would have regarded the Gospel as a "history book" and appreciated the perpetual character of the written text in the way Thatcher assumes.

Presbyter, we may sense the contours of a trajectory where memory was a formative element in the composition of the first as well as the last of the canonical Gospels. Papias' seemingly random notice that Mark remembered certain things carries perhaps more theological weight than it appears to do at a first glance. Justin brings this mnemonic line one step further as he integrates it into a classical literary category. There exists a trajectory that leads from the perceived testimonies of the Johannine disciples to the memoirs of the apostles.

Lukan Remembrances and Witnesses

Theo K. Heckel has observed that both Justin and Papias use παρακολουθεῖν in order to distinguish between the apostles and their followers.[17] This is also the term used in Luke 1:3. In *Dial.* 103.8 Justin refers to the memoirs which were "put together" (συντετάχθαι; cf. ἀνατάξασθαι in Luke 1:1) by Jesus' apostles and "those who followed them" (τῶν ἐκείνοις παρακολουθησάντων); and according to Eusebius, *Hist. Eccl.* 3.39.4, Papias uses the same participial form as the one in Luke 1:3 for "anyone who had followed the presbyters" (παρηκολουθηκώς τις τοῖς πρεσβυτέροις), whose words he was eager to inquire about. Mark was, according to Papias, one of these followers. The author of Luke-Acts is also a παρηκολουθηκώς. If Heckel is correct, Justin and Papias read the Lukan prologue in a way which not only pointed to the author's ambition to investigate everything thoroughly, but to his desire to identify himself as a follower of the apostles. Although this might not be what the Lukan author had in mind when he employed the term of himself and his activity, it is striking that both Justin and Papias understood it to imply a distinction between those who were with Jesus and those who were not. They realized that the followers of the apostles, including the author of Luke-Acts, knew about Jesus by remembering what others had told them, just as Mark did.

---

[17] T. K. Heckel *Vom Evangelium des Markus zum viergestaltigen Evangelium* (Tübingen: Mohr Siebeck, 1999), 92.

This mnemonic implication comes to the fore in Luke-Acts itself. The prologue, with its emphasis on what had been transmitted from the eyewitnesses and ministers of the word (Luke 1:2), accords with the peculiar accent on the role of memory and witnessing in the ensuing narrative. It is only in the Lukan tradition that the Lord's Supper is to be celebrated in memory of Jesus, as an ἀνάμνησις Χριστοῦ (Luke 22:19; 1 Cor. 11:24–25). It is difficult to know the precise meaning of this memorial act, but it was evidently thought of as a ritual moment when the members of the community jointly recalled and re-experienced the Jesus event.[18] The Jesus of history was Jesus remembered.

From the perspective of the Lukan narrative, this liturgical and Christological dimension of memory relates to the remembrance of the words of Jesus. The author presents the mnemonic activity in a somewhat odd way. At a climactic point in the Gospel, the women are to remember, and do remember, that Jesus, while still in Galilee, said that the Son of Man must be handed over to the sinners, crucified, and on the third day rise again (Luke 24:6-8). The angelic message reproduces what Jesus had said earlier, but we have no indication that the women had actually heard this saying in Galilee. They are assumed to have been with the disciples when Jesus made his prophecy in 9:22, or to have heard it from the disciples. Jesus' call to remember evidently goes beyond the intrinsic development of the narrative.

Later on, when he reports to the church in Jerusalem about what happened in the house of Cornelius, Peter tells how the Holy Spirit fell upon them and how he remembered the programmatic (cf. Acts 1:5) word of the Lord: "John baptized with water, but you will be baptized by the Holy Spirit" (Acts 11:16). The author, who is usually much aware of parallels between his two volumes, must have realized that this idea was uttered by John the Baptist (Luke 3:16).[19] Yet, as in 1:5 he attributes the saying to Jesus and insists

---

[18] In terms of social memory, we may look at this as an act of "mnemonic synchronization" and "co-remembering." See further my article "A New Quest for the *Sitz im Leben*: Social Memory, the Jesus Tradition and the Gospel of Matthew," *NTS* 52 (2006): 319–36.

[19] The only occasion in the synoptic Gospels when Jesus speaks of the Spirit is in Mark 13:11 par., but Luke 21:15 omits the reference to the Spirit.

that the mnemonic activity is focused on what Jesus alone had said.

In Paul's speech to the Ephesian elders the apostle urges them to remember the words of the Lord Jesus as he himself said: "It is more blessed to give than to receive" (Acts 20:35). Again, the author must have realized that he had not recorded any such saying. Evidently he referred to a Greek aphorism with a slight Christian touch and presented it as a Jesus-saying,[20] once more attributing an important utterance to Jesus and directing the mnemonic attention to him exclusively.

The motif of witnessing broadens this mnemonic focus to include more than the sayings. Acts 1:8 is programmatic in that Jesus commissions the apostles to be "his witnesses." This expression is frequent in Acts and usually concerns the witness of Jesus' resurrection before Israel and the Gentile authorities.[21]

However, the resurrection is not seen in isolation from Jesus' words and deeds and what happened to him—his entire ministry. This is evident already when the motif recurs towards the end of chapter 1. As the apostles are to replace Judas with another witness to Jesus' resurrection, the decisive criterion is that this person must have accompanied them during all the time that the Lord Jesus went in and out among them, beginning from the baptism to the day of his ascension (1:21–22). Those persons who came up with him from Galilee to Jerusalem are to be his witnesses (cf. 13:31). Only someone who has been with Jesus for an extended time of his active ministry, one who has seen and heard him regularly, is to qualify as a witness of his resurrection.

Accordingly, when Peter later on testifies about Jesus in front of Cornelius and his household, he rehearses Jesus' entire ministry: what he did in Galilee, the baptism, how he was anointed, how he went about doing good and healing all who were oppressed by the devil. He thus summarizes the apostolic testimony in broad terms: "We are witnesses to all that he did both in Judea and in Jerusalem" (10:39).

To proclaim salvation means therefore, as the angel says, to tell

---

[20] Cf. e.g. Thucydides 2.97.4 (attributing it to the Persians); Plutarch, *Mor*. 173d.

[21] For the apostles as witnesses, cf. also 1:22; 2:32; 3:15; 5:32; 10:39, 41; 13:31; for Paul as a witness, cf. 22:15; 26:16; and for Stephen as a witness, cf. 22:20.

the people "the whole message about this life" (5:20; cf. 13:26). The words that are to be remembered and the resurrection to which they should bear testimony are part of his life and integral to the total impact of his appearance in word and deed. As in the Gospel of John, but with different emphases, memory is connected to the witnessing of Jesus' earthly ministry from the beginning. It does not only reconstruct the past; it re-presents it narratively. It does not merely quote his sayings and report about his deeds; it reconfigures his life.

A Trajectory of Memory

These occurrences of mnemonic terminology and concepts in the writings of Justin and Papias and in the Gospel of John and in Luke-Acts say nothing about how memory in fact worked. Rather, they provide glimpses of an early Christian trajectory regarding the mnemonic facets of the Gospels. This is how some early Christians thought about memory in relation to the narratives about Jesus. Memory was not merely the bridge to the past, but reached into the present and created visions for the future. In that sense it could function as a trajectory of theological and hermeneutical importance. Although there is not sufficient evidence to assume a genetic kind of relationship between the writings discussed above, they betray enough similarities in order for us to assume certain common frames of reference and convictions concerning the Gospels.

As to the characteristics of this trajectory, we may sum up our two major conclusions thus far. First, when Justin for the first time labelled the narratives about Jesus ἀπομνημονεύματα, he applied to them a literary category which harmonizes well with his own and others' understanding of the mnemonic character of the Gospels. There are three arguments pointing in this direction. (a) Justin uses the corresponding verb in a way which shows that he assumed the apostles were in fact teaching from memory, (b) Justin betrays awareness that the Markan narrative was the memoirs of Peter, (c) Papias (the Presbyter) and the Johannine tradition suggest that writings could be regarded as reminiscences and testimonies of certain apostles. Secondly, this literary category indicates a link to narrative aspects and biographical tendencies. Two observations are pertinent to this conclusion. (a) Papias thinks of Peter's teaching recorded in Mark as *chreiai*, that is, as memorable and expandable anecdotes attributed to a specific character. (b) The authors of the Johannine literature and Luke-Acts relate the mnemonic activity to the witnessing about Jesus' earthly ministry from its beginning to its end and thus include the central parts of his *bios*. Memory becomes a theological and hermeneutical category which unites history with the present time in a narrativizing process of interpretation and which reconfigures the life, death and resurrection of Jesus.

Memory and Forgetfulness

How are we, more precisely, to construe this mnemonic trajectory which was theologized and employed as an interpretative forum and steeped into a literary category? Motifs and practices normally become distinguishable trajectories because they are part of a related stream of socio-cultural patterns. Our appreciation of the psychological and social factors of memory needs therefore to go hand in hand with keen sensitivity to what the ancients themselves said and thought about it.

As is well-known, the rabbis accorded an extraordinary importance to it. Some scholars would say they were extreme and did not live up to their own standards. What is rarely noticed is that their discussion of memorization and mnemo-technical advices reflects a deep awareness of human forgetfulness. Precisely in the midst of actualizing midrashic exposition and elaborative haggadic narration it was important to preserve a space for faithful transmission.[22]

The importance of memory was not only a concern of the rabbis. In ancient Greece, at a very early time, we come across a venerated goddess, *Mnemosyne*. She was born when earth and heaven were

---

[22] B. Gerhardsson, *Memory and Manuscript: Oral Tradition and Written Transmission in Rabbinic Judaism and Early Christianity* (Lund: Gleerup, 1964 [1961]).

united and gave herself birth to the Muses (Hesiod, *Theogony* 53–63). Memory had divine sanction and dignity and was exceedingly important for anyone seeking to narrate about the past. She was a guarantee against forgetfulness.[23] This is how her daughters sing for the shepherding Hesiod: "We know how to speak many false things like real things, and we know, when we wish, to utter true things" (*Theogony* 27–28). In an oral culture everything depends on memory and truth and falsehood are intrinsically related to it. Already at the prehistoric Olympus or Helicon, long before the notion of fiction existed, the daughters of *Mnemosyne* knew how to distinguish between what was true and what was false; and Hesiod, it is implied, did not believe everything that was told.

A few centuries later, in Athens, Plato produced his famous dialogues, making Socrates ask Phaedrus if he knows how to speak and act in order to please the gods. When Socrates tells Phaedrus of Teuth's invention of the alphabet, he points out how the Egyptian king Thamus complained about the distortion of memory and the forgetfulness that this invention will create:

> For this invention will produce forgetfulness in the minds of those who learn to use it, because they will not practice their memory. Their trust in writing, produced by external characters which are no part of themselves, will discourage the use of their own memory within them [οὐκ ἔνδοθεν ... μνησκομένους]. You have invented an elixir not of memory, but of reminding [οὔκουν μνήμης ἀλλὰ ὑπομνήσεως]. *Phaedr.* 275a

Once more memory is mentioned in order to counter forgetfulness. Writing is a threat to memory, according to Plato (Socrates), because it creates an illusion of truth and knowledge. This illusion consists of vague reminiscing and, in fact, equals forgetfulness. True knowledge, which cannot be forgotten, resides inside the students, in their memory.

At a later time, when we come to the the major rhetoricians, the

---

[23] See the much neglected study by M. Simondon, *La mémoire et l'oubli dans la pensée grecque jusqu'à la fin du Vᵉ siècle avant J.-C: Psychologie archaïque, mythes et doctrines* (Paris: Les Belles Lettres, 1983).

wax tablet has become a standard image of memory. We find it
already in the writings of Plato and Aristotle,[24] but now it is employed
more regularly to indicate an idea of memory as something where
word and happenings make a visible imprint. Quintilian rightly says
that many hold this view (*Inst.* 11.2.4).

Memory was exceedingly important to the rhetoricians. Quintilian
would not write anything which he did not intend to memorize (*Inst.*
10.7.32). A persuasive performance could not rely on a manuscript.
Accordingly, they discuss the advanced mnemo-technical repertoire
which, as they thought,[25] could be traced back to Simonides of Ceos
(556–468 B.C.E.) and was further developed by Hippias (5th cent.
B.C.E.), the sophist, and by Theodect (377–336 B.C.E.), the tragedian.[26]
The essential idea was to imagine mental places (*loci*) that could
guarantee the proper remembrance of events (*memoria rerum*) as
well as words (*memoria verborum*). Some rhetoricians were slightly
sceptical of this technique and maintained that people should have
a natural disposition towards memorization. Nevertheless, it reflects
the constant fear of embarrassing forgetfulness and the profound
respect for detailed memorization.

We have come to the turn of the eras. Seneca the Elder (50
B.C.E.–40 C.E.), the father of the famous philosopher carrying the
same name and himself a skilled rhetorician, boasts that in his youth
he was able to repeat two thousand names that were read to him and
that he could recite in reverse order over two hundred verses that his
fellow student told him. To him, this was a true *miraculum* (*Contr.* 1
pref. 2). He exaggerates, to be sure, but his boasting is a reminder
of the vital importance that anyone who wished to speak and write
persuasively attached to a good and accurate memory.

While ancient people could overstate the accuracy of memory to
a considerable extent, they were not naïve and ignorant as to how it

---

[24] References in Byrskog, *Story as History*, 162. See also J. P. Small, *Wax Tablets of the Mind:
Cognitive Studies of Memory and Literacy in Classical Antiquity* (London: Routledge, 1997).

[25] For a possible scenario of its origin and development, cf. S. Goldmann, "Statt Totenklage
Gedächtnis: Zur Erfindung der Mnemotechnik durch Simonides von Keos," *Poetica* 21 (1989): 43–66.

[26] For discussion and literature, see already H. Blum, *Die antike Mnemotechnik* (Hildesheim: Georg
Olms Verlag, 1969), 38–149.

functioned. The well-informed Pliny the Elder (23–79 c.e.) praises in book 7 of his encyclopaedic *Naturalis Historia* memory as the greatest gift of nature and gives several examples of persons with an exceptionally good memory. Cyrus knew the names of all men in his army; Lucius Scipio knew the names of all the Roman people; Cineas repeated the names of all the senators and knights of Rome within a day of arriving there; Mithridates addressed his subjects in 22 different languages; Carmidas recited by heart any book in the libraries (7.24.88–89). Many had gained glory from this "most necessary boon of life," he says (7.24.88). It was a matter of glory and honour, hardly to be dealt with randomly.

Pliny places anecdotes such as these within the context of his interest in anthropology and physiology. He takes them seriously and links them to an account of how memory for various reasons may fail in human beings:

> Also no other human faculty is equally fragile: injuries from, and even apprehensions of, diseases and accident may affect in some cases a single field of memory and in others the whole. A man has been known when struck by a stone to forget how to read and write but nothing else. One who fell from a very high roof forgot his mother and his relatives and friends, another when ill forgot his servants also; the orator Messala Corvinus forgot his own name. Similarly tentative and hesitating lapses of memory often occur when the body even when uninjured is in repose; also the gradual approach of sleep curtails the memory and makes the unoccupied mind wonder where it is. *Nat.* 7.24.90

Pliny had seen many things and noticed both a good and a weak—even a lost—memory. His anecdotes about the exceptional memory of some skilled and well-known persons are exaggerated, but by relating them to a broader discussion of how memory failed to work under certain circumstances he indicates a subtle awareness of the individual act of recall that goes beyond the mere search for praise and glory and reflects sensitivity to the danger of shameful forgetfulness.

In the large context of the ancient Mediterranean world, memory was thus both divinely sanctioned and made into a matter of honour and shame. It was of uttermost importance to Greeks and Romans alike. As with the rabbis, it was a vital factor intended to counteract the danger of forgetfulness in situations where various forms of orality were the crucial modes of communication. Although its divine sanction faded into the background as time went by, its significance as a means of gaining glory increased, especially among the rhetoricians. This comes as no surprise, because ancient rhetoric was essentially a sophisticated outgrowth of ancient orality.

Memory, Narrative and Memoirs

The mnemonic trajectory of early Christianity needs to be measured against this background. Developing its own theological, hermeneutical and literary characteristics, it did not lose the socio-cultural codes of its environment. On the contrary, it was precisely because memory was widely seen as the essential rhetorical ingredient in the combat against embarrassing forgetfulness that it received its own divine and pneumatic sanction and hermeneutical and literary dignity among the early Christians. Regardless of how we estimate the reliability of the tradition, it is evident that there was a concern not to forget the Jesus event in the midst of rhetorical elaborations. Writing was no secure measure against forgetfulness and it was normally integrated into persuasive oral performances. Rather, the Christians took over the mnemonic codes of antiquity and contextualized them into their own discourse as they were to communicate the decisive past into present situations and for new audiences.

As we noticed above, the mnemonic trajectory also had narrative characteristics. Memory was a theological and hermeneutical category which united history with the present time in complex narrativizing processes of interpretation and reconfiguration. New Testament scholarship has often looked at memory in terms of memorization of isolated items, especially Jesus-sayings, producing a strange dichotomy between sayings material and narrative material. But this is not how memory works.[27] Recent studies of social memory have high-lightened that memory is a process of negotiation where the narrative representation of the past plays a crucial role. This "narratization" both tells a story about the past and tells a story about the past's relation to the present, being part of the construction of narrative identity.[28]

We might find a subtle awareness of the way memory navigates narratively between the past and the present already in the earliest systematic and philosophical reflection on memory and recollection in ancient Greece.[29] In his treatise *de Memoria et Reminiscentia*, Aristotle distinguished between μνήμη as the memory of the past—ἡ δὲ μνήμη τοῦ γενομένου (449b.15)—and ἀνάμνησις as the process through which one find one's way by means of association and order among the contents of μνήμη. In his reflection on the way the past interacts with the present, the decisive thing is the notion of time. It not only distinguishes between memory and mere perceptions about the present and expectations for the future, but also defines the process of recollection. Aristotle discusses it in the section dealing with ἀνάμνησις. The first step is to find a starting point for the recollection—he refers to the idea of mnemonic *loci*. This can be done either by means of logic association—e.g. from milk to white, from white to mist, and thence to moist, from which one remembers autumn (the "season of mists")—or by establishing a point in the middle of the events from which one can reach in any direction.[30] He stresses again that above all it is necessary to know the time—τὸ δὲ μέγιστον γνωρίζειν δεῖ τὸν χρόνον (452b.7). Recollection navigates

---

[27] See my critique in the review article of Rudolf Bultmann, *The History of the Synoptic Tradition*, *JBL* 122 (2003): 549–55, and "The Transmission of the Jesus Tradition," in vol. 2 of *The Handbook of the Study of the Historical Jesus* (4 vols.; ed. T. Holmén and S. E. Porter; Leiden: Brill, 2011), 1465–94.

[28] For discussion and literature, see B. A. Misztal, *Theories of Social Remembering* (Maidenhead: Open University Press, 2003) 67–74.

[29] Mainly two philosophers in the Greek and Roman antiquity reflected more extensively on memory, namely Aristotle in the fourth century B.C.E. and the neo-Platonist Plotinus in the third century C.E. For a recent discussion of both of them, see R. A. H. King, *Aristotle and Plotinus on Memory* (Berlin: de Gruyter, 2009).

[30] Cf. Richard Sorabji's discussion of the "technique of midpoints" in *Aristotle on Memory* (2d ed.; London: Duckworth, 2004), 31–34.

between the initial impression and its present return and occurs when the movement between the images or mental copies of the past corresponds with the cognition of time. To remember means, in other words, to recollectively position oneself in time through an intricate mental synopsis of identification and distance and, by implication, to foster a sense of belonging to that present past.

Augustine, whose quotation above about the depth of memory may stand as a challenge to present scholarship, was aware of Aristotle's reflection on memory and recollection. He struggles in book 10 of his *Confessions* with how to understand the nature of his own memory and forgetfulness and resorts at the end, while always lost in wonder, to the idea that what we remember and forget are images of the past. There is always an interpretative element in the process of remembering and memory makes use of metaphors and images.[31] For Aristotle this had to do with time. The recollective process arranges the past according to the sequential structures between the images and in relation to the sense of temporal distance between the past and the present.

With this in mind, it comes as no surprise that narrative entities, which normally relate events to each other according to a sense of time and causality, are part of the mnemonic trajectory of the early Christians. Recent investigations into the narrative and biographical character of the Gospels have tended to separate the question of literary genre from considerations of memory and temporal identity.[32] More work is needed before we understand how the memories of Jesus were transformed into full-blown *bioi*. However, there was no sharp break. The mnemonic signals encoded into the narratives of Luke and John and the appreciation of memory evidenced by Papias' view of the Markan narrative and Justin's labelling of the Gospels as memoirs, indicate sensibility to the remembering process as a narrative kind of mnemonic negotiation. Smaller and larger units were thought to

---

[31] Cf. D. Draaisma, *Metaphors of Memory: The History of Ideas about the Mind* (Cambridge: Cambridge University Press, 2000).

[32] Cf. my discussion in "Performing the Past: Gospel Genre and Identity Formation in the Context of Ancient History Writing," in *History and Exegesis: New Testament Essays in Honor of Dr. E. Earle Ellis for His Eightieth Birthday* (ed. S.-W. Son; New York: T&T Clark, 2006), 28–44.

be intrinsically held together by a certain idea of temporality and causation. The production of extensive literary narratives was not seen as an activity separated from individual and social aspects of memory. Redactional units were testimonies about the narrative past in the present and hence reflections of a way of recalling what one believed had happened; and the use of tradition and sources was not perceived in terms of passive reproduction and copying but appeared as oral and re-oralized moments of remembrance.

From this built-in relationship between memory and narrative, it is possible to understand better the route from memory to memoirs. When Justin adopted the designation ἀπομνημονεύματα for the Gospels, he not only raised them to the level of philosophical and literary pieces of writing, but he also high-lightened the mnemonic trajectory imbedded in early Christianity from early on. The impact of Jesus was so decisive that it shaped the memories of his followers.[33] Such an impact must have been intrinsically narrative, because it remembered an event that was manifested in the life and destiny of an important and venerated person appearing in word and deed. Taking over and contextualizing the strong emphasis on memory in the predominantly rhetorical milieu of the first century c.e., the early Christians made their own mnemonic experiences of that same narrative past and fostered a trajectory which held together mnemonic and narrative aspects within various theological, hermeneutical and literary processes of communication.

---

[33] This is the basic idea behind James Dunn's notion of "traditioning" in *Jesus Remembered* (Grand Rapids: Eerdmans, 2003).

Gentile Identity and Transformation in Christ According to Paul[1]

William S. Campbell
University of Wales, Trinity St David

Origins of Christian Identity?

Paul's policy was that converts should remain as they were when called, his intention being that they would continue to regulate their lives as Jews or as gentiles in Christ. In my book, *Paul and the Creation of Christian Identity*[2] my chief concern was to establish this pattern in the case of Christ-followers who came from Jewish roots, following on the evidence that Paul himself continued to adhere to his Jewish pattern of life. The integral significance of this insight for Paul's generally even-handed dealing with Jews and gentiles in Christ had not been appreciated in earlier research but is now becoming increasingly recognized.[3] Thus the focus of my book was with the identity of Jews who became Christ-followers rather than with gentiles. In this study, however, my focus is on gentiles in Christ and their identity formation.

Bengt Holmberg in his excellent discussion of the nature of identity as proposed in recent scholarship lists six possible definitions of Christian identity, ranging from this being perceived as a textual reality, a post-factum ideological construct, an entrepreneurial rhetorical construction of groups within the movement (and) accepted by it, or the autonomous inner structure of the Christian semiotic system. He finally opts for a definition with high concreteness, i.e., "Christian identity is the evolving self-understanding of the movement, shaped

---

[1] This article is offered in grateful appreciation of Bengt Holmberg's significant contribution to New Testament interpretation especially in relation to the sociological understanding of power and identity.
[2] London: T&T Clark, 2006 (paperback 2008).
[3] See e.g. J. Frey, "Paul's Jewish Identity," in *Jewish Identity in the Greco-Roman World* (ed. J. Frey, D. R. Schwartz, and S. Gripentrog; Leiden: Brill 2007), 285–321.

by a feedback process between its original experience and its evolving history."[4] As a comprehensive and useful definition, this offers an excellent starting point in that it seems to combine twin aspects useful in seeking to understand Paul's contribution to the forming of identity, i.e., those aspects given and those in process of ongoing dynamic change and development. The question arises, however, as to what is meant by "original experience"—to what does this refer? Is it its *originating,* possibly post-resurrection, experience or does this also include elements of pre-conversion culture/experience, as Paul suggests in 1 Cor 7 when he advocates "remain as you were when called"? Since this guidance is repeated no less than three times in the space of 1 Cor 7:17–24, and since Paul claims it as his policy in all his churches, then it must have operated as an important element in Paul's formation of his communities and their ongoing identity construction.

In the case of Christ-followers of Jewish origin, it is easy to see how a strong argument can be made for regarding their faith as originating from a prior group of Jews who were disciples of the historical Jesus. But even if we take this position, then the investigation of identity cannot begin only with the Jesus tradition[5], but must start from the earlier tradition of Israel which gives meaning and significance to the life and death of Jesus for the first community of disciples. As Ben F. Meyer maintains, "From the outset, Christian self-understanding was covenantal, qualified in its earliest moment by the ecclesial and election-historical conception of 'the remnant of Israel'."[6] Meyer goes on to claim that the key issues for Paul were unity and identity, "most, perhaps all, of Paul's battles were rooted in divergent views of what was requisite to the authentic ecclesial identity of Christians."[7] It would appear

---

[4] B. Holmberg, "Understanding the First Hundred Years of Christian Identity," in *Exploring Early Christian Identity* (ed. B. Holmberg; Tübingen: Mohr Siebeck, 2008), 1–32, esp. 6.

[5] According to D. Harink, part from the testimony of Israel's law and prophets, Jesus Christ would be a mere cipher, unrecognizable as the *apokalypsis* of the God of Israel,"Paul and Israel: An Apocalyptic Reading," *ProEccl* 16 (2007): 359–80, esp. 368–-70.

[6] B. F. Meyer, *The Early Christians: Their World Mission and Self-Discovery* (Wilmington: Glazier 1986), 182.

[7] Meyer, *Early Christians,* 183–4.

from this view that Meyer designates the earliest group of Christ-followers as in fact a remnant of Israel, to whom were soon added gentiles who may at first have assumed full incorporation into the commonwealth of Israel as the only option available to them. These particular gentile believers were thus attached to a prior existing group of Jewish Christ-followers and it is beyond dispute that their earliest identity was therefore indebted to a given Jewish source.

What is not so obvious in discussions of gentile identity in Christ is that at a somewhat later date when groups of Christ-followers with a gentile majority and no longer following a Jewish pattern of life emerged, these likewise must have been subject to influence from, and doubtless retained some elements in their identity formation resulting from, the association with previously existing groups of entirely or mainly Jewish Christ-followers. Since gentiles joining the movement at a later date, could not experience the crucial events of the immediate post-resurrection period, they had to be taught about these and inducted into the resulting ethos.[8] A presupposition that needs to be acknowledged is that in the study of identity in Paul, we are operating within the context of a Jewish discourse. The basic division of the world into Jews and non-Jews, i.e, Israel and the nations as held by Jews of the first century continues to operate even in the perspective of Paul and other Christ-following Jews of the earliest days of the Christ-movement. This pattern of thinking is paralleled with the division of humanity into, e.g. Greeks and barbarians, something of which Paul was very much aware, (cf. Rom 1:14). Only in light of the specific identity of Israel as God's covenantal people can some of the early conflicts about the status of gentiles in the movement be understood. Nor should it be overlooked that in and with the narrative of Israel's election there existed also a destiny for gentiles in the purposes of Israel's God, even though their destiny was perceived as bound up inextricably with that of Israel.[9] The God of Israel was acknowledged to be

---

[8] See M. Zetterholm, *The Formation of Christianity in Antioch: A Social Science Approach to the Separation Between Judaism and Christianity* (London: Routledge, 2003), 148.

[9] On this see the view of Frank Crüsemann who maintains that the concept of covenant was not applied to the new community of believers in the New Testament, nor were gentile believers

not just the God of this particular people, but of the entire world, the God of both Jews and the nations.[10] Thus Paul significantly asks in Rom 3:29–30, "is God the God of Jews only? Is he not the God of gentiles also?" Based on the *Shema*, Paul replies to the question he put, "Yes of gentiles also, since God is one."

This acknowledged oneness of God might have led some to claim sameness as the mark of all of God's people, whether Jews or gentiles in Christ, but this is not how Paul argues in Rom 3–4 or elsewhere. To some Jews it might have seemed perfectly reasonable to claim that if gentile Christ-followers wished to share an identity as people of God, they must then share the identity of Israel and accept circumcision and other demands of the Torah. In Paul's reasoning, however, such a demand would mean that God is not God of gentiles also, but of Jews only. The influx of gentiles into the Christ-movement soon led to the formation of an entirely new group of Christ-believers who, whilst acknowledging the heritage of Israel, nevertheless lived as those outside the Torah, though having, via Paul and his fellow-workers, both foundational and on-going links with other Jews, especially the Jerusalem community and its apostolic leaders. It might be legitimate to designate these gentiles in Christ as in some sense a "new creation." There had never been anything similar to this group in the first century. Yet having some links with Jewish Christ-followers, however tenuous, they were related to Israel in certain respects, but the issue that challenges recent scholarship is whether or not these gentile satellite communities, affiliated loosely to Israel, should be described as Israel despite being of gentile origin. We will return to this issue in more detail later.

Our intention in this section has been to draw attention to the fact

---

simply included in the covenant with Israel. This is partly because for Crüsemann covenant is not an ecclesiological but rather a Christological category, *Kanon und Sozialgeschichte: Beiträge zum Alten Testament* (Gütersloh: Chr.Kaiser/Gütersloher Verlaghaus, 2003), 303–5. Cf. also Zetterholm, *Formation of Christianity*, 157.

[10] On this see the useful study of T. L. Donaldson, *Judaism and the Gentiles: Jewish Patterns of Universalism* (Waco: Baylor University Press, 2007), 4–13. On Jewish expectations for gentile conversion and the relevance of these to Paul's missionary activity see J. P. Ware, *The Mission of the Church in Paul's Letter to the Philippians in the Context of Ancient Judaism* (Leiden: Brill, 2005), 285–92.

that there was differentiation within the Christ-movement that had existed from quite early days. Diversity was normal and increased as gentiles joined the movement, and yet equality of access to salvation did not necessarily demand conformity in every aspect of life. The formation of the Pauline gentile communities was a radical new step, though not so new as to merit the designation "new creation," in that even these groups were themselves an extension of a previously existing Jesus-movement. Taking these factors into account, we will now seek to understand how gentile identity was perceived and formed within the Pauline communities.

Identity in Christ as the Overcoming of Difference

In its most conspicuous form the view that distinctions between Jew and Greek are overcome in Christ led to the concept of a "third race," a people beyond the Jew/gentile divide thus overcoming, in theory at least, the divisive tendencies of ethnic differences.[11] It has seemed to many that this image of a new people is the most fitting identity marker for the followers of Christ. It is already apparent in the repeated claim of the martyr Lucian to describe himself only as a Christian.[12] It has become increasingly recognized however that this convenient label of a third race carries with it implications that are not warranted. Despite its preliminary formulation early in the history of the church, its maturation in modern times is dependant on a Hegelian scheme of development long since carrying no conviction. The overcoming of ethnic distinctions and particularism is not the focus of the Christ-movement, however real the danger of ethnic divisiveness may be; and again, how can there exist in everyday

---

[11] One of the best treatments of this issue in an historical overview is William Rader's Basel doctoral thesis written under the supervision of O. Cullmann, *The Church and Racial Hostility: A History of Interpretation of Ephesians 2:11-22* (Tübingen: Mohr Siebeck, 1978), see esp. chs. 7–8.

[12] Chrysostom relates how the martyr Lucian at his trial answered each inquiry as to fatherland, vocation, or ancestor by simply repeating, "I am a Christian," see M. Mitchell, *The Heavenly Trumpet: John Chrysostom and the Art of Pauline Interpretation* (Tübingen: Mohr Siebeck, 2000), 233.

life, as distinct from idealism, a people without any geographical or ethnic affiliation?

Several scholars have argued that it is not ethnicity that Paul opposes but the hostility and enmity that frequently results from the recognition of difference. [13] A closer investigation of ethnicity and identity issues in the Pauline letters confirms this. Over a period of years, I became increasingly aware that a crucial text in relation to this issue in Paul is 1 Cor 7:17–21. Here Paul, as noted above, no less than three times in the space of several verses advocates that everyone remains in the calling or state in which they were called.[14] He does use the theological terminology of calling, so frequent in 1 Corinthians, but it is not simply a theology divorced from social reality that Paul proposes, as is evidenced by the fact that he tells those in a circumcised state not to seek to remove the marks of circumcision, and those in a state of uncircumcision not to seek circumcision.[15] His conclusion that circumcision is nothing and likewise uncircumcision (7:19) reveals that he is revaluing both Jewish and gentile ethnicity in Christ, but by no means calling for its abolition or opposing the recognition of its existence. I have reached the conclusion that it is not the elimination of difference that Paul seeks but rather the reconciliation of those who are different despite their continuing differences as is clear e.g. in Rom 15:1–7.

Recently Philip Esler has acknowledged in Pauline thought the ongoing validity of what remains of the prior identities of Christ-

---

[13] Rader was one of the first in recent scholarship to recognize that in Pauline thought, unity does not demand uniformity: "This is why Eph. 2:11 explicitly calls on gentiles to remember their history. Since the identity of both gentiles and Jews depends on their remembering their history, this means that they do not simply lose their identities in the body of Christ," *Racial Hostility,* 248.

[14] For a fuller discussion of this passage, see my *Christian Identity,* 86–103. It should be noted that the title of this work does not imply that Paul created what emerged as the dominant identity of Christianity, but only that he was active in a process of which this was the outcome. I see Paul as construing as well as creating identity for gentiles in Christ. I oppose the eradication of difference-what Harink terms "a false, idolatrous first principle of identity or sameness" ("Paul and Israel," 378).

[15] Following T. Martin's view that the verb περιτέμνω and the noun περιτομή "refer either to an act, a state or a practice. As an act circumcision relates to the physical operation itself. But … circumcised persons … must still decide if they will practise the distinctions associated with the covenant of circumcision," see "Apostasy to Paganism: The Rhetorical Stasis of the Galatian Controversy," in *The Galatians Debate: Contemporary Issues in Rhetorical and Historical Interpretation* (ed. M. D. Nanos; Peabody: Hendrickson, 2002), 73–94, esp. 85.

believers.[16] I have developed this argument further in my *Paul and the Creation of Christian Identity,* contending that Paul's target is not ethnicity or difference as such, but that he continuously opposes boasting in one's difference, whether as Jew or gentile, and thus destroying unity in Christ. *It is boasting in difference but not difference as such that Paul opposes so fiercely.* The correlative of this must be that the earlier tendency to equate equality in Christ with sameness should now be recognized to be a misrepresentation of Paul's position. As is argued elsewhere in this essay, acknowledgement of oneness within diversity is a better understanding of Paul's stance on ethnicity and identity. [17]

The tendency in Pauline interpretation of the last century to argue for sameness in Christ may seem to promote equality for Jews and gentiles alike, and thus to be eminently "Pauline." But the problem with this proposed goal of equality is that it is normally only to be achieved at the expense of the obliteration of Jewish identity as such. As Magnus Zetterholm has recognized, "Paul was not involved in a process of creating a new religion where the Torah was no longer valid for Jews."[18] The viewpoint, which he criticizes, regards Paul as creating a new Israel, spiritual and non- ethnic to replace the "old Israel," with what is essentially a gentile "Israel." This offers a parallel to the desire of some Jews in the earliest days of the Christ-movement to impose Jewish circumcision and obedience to the law upon everyone without exception, thus effectively regarding Christ-following gentiles as no longer gentiles but proselytes to Judaism. In both of these instances one or other of the previous identities borne by those in Christ was destined for eventual obliteration. Inasmuch as this evidently produces inequality in outcome for one or other of the two groups involved, it requires strong justification

---

[16] P. F. Esler, *Conflict and Identity in Romans: The Social Setting of Paul's Letter* (Minneapolis: Fortress, 2003), 140.

[17] As Meyer notes, "Paul cherished the unity of the church in the full consciousness that uniformity for Jewish and gentile spheres was out of the question," *Early Christians,* 184.

[18] As Zetterholm asserts, "His [Paul's] mission was rather to emphasize that the torah was not for Jesus-believing gentiles. To state ... that Paul thought it not possible to live at the same time 'in Christ' and 'in accordance with the law' is to invert the set of problems," *Formation of Christianity,* 158–9.

if it is to be affirmed. Probably the most common form of viewing Paul as abolishing ethnic and other kinds of difference appears under the label of what I would term, Christianity as a third entity.[19]

The view claims not just that Jewish identity as such is rendered obsolete but that of gentiles also. Rooted, apparently, in a particular understanding of apocalyptic theology, this perspective stresses the newness of being in Christ, its "new creation" aspect. Thus John Barclay asserts that

> Paul makes it as clear as possible that he no longer regards himself as living within 'Judaism'. But this is not because he has entered some other cultural medium, with its own rules of human tradition, but because he now sees with utterly different eyes, from a perspective that radically relativises, if it does not wholly obliterate, all social and historical categories.[20]

Anthony Thiselton's views similarly border on obliteration of previous distinctions such as the law, ethnicity and all other human distinctions, which can never again be regarded as absolute since they have been transcended, or annulled in Christ. For Thiselton, "in the terminology of Pauline studies new creation terminology affirms an eschatological status for believers on the basis of which issues of circumcision and 'Jewishness' have become obsolete."[21] Surprisingly he retracts somewhat from his stated view by adding that "although these things have now been rendered obsolete, they

---

[19] The term "third entity" comes from a well-known citation by E. P. Sanders, "we must recognize the extent to which the church constituted, in Paul's view, a third entity, which stood over against both the obdurate part of Israel and unconverted gentiles. If conceptually Paul, despite himself, had to make the church a third entity, it was all the more the case that it was a third entity in concrete sociality reality," *Paul, the Law, and the Jewish People* (Philadelphia: Fortress, 1983), 176. Sanders's description comes close to the concept of the church as a "third race," though he himself opposed such an anti-Jewish depiction.

[20] J. M. G. Barclay, "Paul's Story: Theology as Testimony," in *Narrative Dynamics in Paul: A Critical Assessment* (ed. B. W. Longenecker; Louisville: Westminster John Knox Press, 2002), 133–56, esp. 139–40.

[21] A. C. Thiselton, *The First Epistle to the Corinthians* (Grand Rapids: Eerdmans, 2000), 550–2. Despite Thiselton's claim to speak in the terminology of Pauline studies, it is entirely foreign to Paul to write critically of "circumcision and Jewishness" within the same phrase. For Paul it would more likely have been "circumcision and uncircumcision"!

are not abrogated wholesale."[22] For a definite statement concerning obliteration of the past we turn to a recent comment by Beverly Gaventa: "The new creation results in the nullification of previous identifications, whether these come from within the law (Gal 1:11–17) or from outside it (Gal 4:8–11)."[23] She asserts:

> The gospel's invasion *necessarily obliterates worlds,* including particularly the world of the law. … It also obliterates those other "places" with which people identify themselves, even the most fundamental places of ethnicity, economic and social standing and gender. The only location available for those grasped by the gospel is "in Christ."[24]

Here there is no doubt that "obliteration" of previous worlds is definitely intended (however these are to be understood considering the diverse options offered by the term "world"[25]). This should mean that all previous identities whether Jewish or gentile are equally subject to annihilation.

This equalizing effect is one of the few constructive qualities of this extreme perspective. However, in terms of social reality, how one's past locations of identity can be obliterated requires more clear exegetical and sociological foundation and raises huge theological questions. It is certainly not consistent with the Jewish and Christian understanding of creation to speak of such obliteration. David Flusser claims that

> neither the scrolls nor the New Testament can promote an absolute negation of the world, since both believe in a good and

---

[22] Ibid., 551.

[23] B. R. Gaventa, *Our Mother Saint Paul* (Louisville: Westminster John Knox Press, 2007), 103. Gaventa does recognize that "the governing theological antithesis in Galatians is between Christ or the new creation and the cosmos" and that "the antithesis between Christ and the law and between the cross and circumcision are not the equivalent of this central premise but follow from it." How these follow from it is the issue, especially as Gaventa acknowledges that the real opposition is between Christ and all things, i.e., not just the law and circumcision.

[24] Gaventa, *Our Mother Saint Paul*, 63–75, esp. 68–9.

[25] As I recall, the term "world" was used first in this way by William James in 1903 in his *Varieties of Religious Experience* (London: Fontana, 1960), but I do not find it useful, especially taken along with "obliteration," the two terms together resonate too closely with contemporary terrorist threats (though this was far from this author's intention).

beneficent God. Thus the flesh/spirit dualism is an ethical dualism in which man is purified by the Spirit rather than an ontological matter-spirit dualism in the vein of Hellenism or Gnosticism.[26]

What is common to the examples noted above is a tendency to exaggerate in the direction of an over-realized eschatology. In my reading of Paul, "new creation" begins with Christ but cannot become a complete reality until the world to come, which includes a transformation rather than obliteration of creation. Paul rebuked the Corinthians for their presumptuous eschatology, ironically telling them, "Already you are filled! Already you have become rich! Without us you have become kings!" (1 Cor 4:8). Also realized judgment for Jews is often the reverse side of a coin that posits over-realized grace for Christians.[27] But the transformation offered in and by the new creation is a transformation in process rather than realized. If it is the case that Paul ruled that gentiles in Christ remain as they were, this involves an affirmation of Hellenistic culture, not its total annihilation. Whilst it may be claimed that the past may be rendered theologically obsolete it is not powerless and not simply a point in one's memory but a present force in accordance, competition or conflict with the indwelling Spirit. Thus transformation for gentiles according to Paul involves real cultural and social conflicts of values as e.g., 1 Corinthians demonstrates, but he should not be viewed as being simply counter-cultural. What we wish to deny here is the claim that being in Christ does not allow the retention of either Jewish or gentile identity, whether this is prohibited because of a conception such as viewing Christians as a "third race," or because of a perception that previous worlds of identity can somehow altogether be obliterated, thereby creating of Christ-followers what may be termed a "third entity."

The problem we have identified in this section is that of viewing

---

[26] D. Flusser, *Judaism of the Second Temple Period: Vol. 1: Qumran and Apocalypticism* (Grand Rapids: Eerdmans, 2007), 284–7. Flusser is confident that "the notion that it is the holy spirit that turns the carnal man into one of the elect is theologically autocratic; there is no need to resort to Hellenistic (and Gnostic) matter-spirit dualism to explain it" (p. 287).

[27] See my *Christian Identity*, 134 and 171–3.

being in Christ as a means of overcoming difference, rather than of overcoming the discrimination that results from boasting in difference, and thereby destroying or preventing unity in Christ. We will now consider another option, which allows for, and recognizes the significance of, the continuation of difference in Christ.

In Christ as Overarching Identity

Esler views Paul as reusing traditions in the interests of bringing "Judeans" and "Greeks" together, being thus re-categorized into what he envisages as an overarching identity of the Christ-movement at Rome.[28] Instead of advocating that Jews give up their Jewish way of life, what might be viewed as an example of "decategorization," Paul acknowledges the validity of living Jewishly even in their "recategorization" along with fellow gentile Christ-followers,[29] as belonging together in Christ. Paul thus recognizes the validity of both Jewish and gentile subgroup identities in Christ.

However, though belonging to this new overarching grouping that straddles (ethnic) boundaries requires that it has a distinct identity, one that will be lodged as social identity in the minds and hearts of its members, meaning that of who they are as individuals that derives from belonging to this group, "yet such identity will need to co-exist with whatever remains of the member's original Judean and Greek identities."[30] Esler regards Paul as essentially an entrepreneur in the identity creation and reconciliation of the Christ-followers at Rome.[31] In my opinion, he rightly diagnoses that the mutual hostility of Judean and Greek Christ-following groups at Rome requires a reinforcement of what they already share in relation to Christ,

---

[28] Following Esler's suggested terminology of "Judean" rather than Jew. In this article I try to follow the terminology of the author under discussion. For a good overview of this complicated issue see P. F. Esler, *Conflict and Identity*, 63–74 and C. Johnson Hodge, *If Sons, Then Heirs: A Study of Kinship and Ethnicity in the Letters of Paul* (Oxford: Oxford University Press, 2007), 11–15.

[29] For a full discussion of Esler's preferred model for reducing conflict between groups (or subgroups) see *Conflict and Identity*, 27–39.

[30] Ibid., 130–41, cf. also 49–50, 60–61.

[31] Cf. ibid., 32–33 and 38–39.

despite differences originating from differing relations to Torah.[32] In this sense, Paul certainly was an identity entrepreneur, but the question arises as to whether his creative efforts were successful in Rome. Did he, in fact, not merely construe or simply clarify Christian identity rather than create it? Holmberg is somewhat skeptical about designating Paul an "entrepreneur of identity." He reminds us that Paul's powerful arguments were only one input into the process of identity construction and self-categorization that was going on in Rome. The strong opposition from both Judean and gentile Christ-followers may indeed have prevented Paul's creative vision for both from being realized in Rome.[33] In view of the recognition of this possible failure, we may need to limit the conception of Paul as an actual creator of Christian identity not only in Rome but elsewhere. There is not much real evidence for Paul's success in Rome, and the possibility that the letter to the Hebrews has a Roman provenance may also indicate Paul's lack of success.[34] But Paul's lack of (complete) success in Rome in this instance does not mean that his teaching and activity on behalf of the gospel was not designed to change the life of those in his communities. By means of his letters, visits by himself and in company with his fellow workers, his own example, the use of scripture and earlier traditions, Paul certainly had in view an-going transformation of all within the communities he addressed.[35] But this followed from what the communities had brought with

---

[32] Cf. ibid., 109. Esler notes that "both Jewish and Greek converts brought heavy loads of ethnic prejudice with them" (p. 76), with resultant disunity between the groups; he notes especially the disdain towards those who still observe Torah.

[33] "We need some weighty arguments not supplied by Esler for believing that the apostle's theologizing in this letter effected such a transformation," see Holmberg "Understanding the First Hundred Years," 17–18.

[34] On this see K. P. Donfried and P. Richardson, eds., *Judaism and Christianity in First Century Rome* (Grand Rapids: Eerdmans, 1998); B. M. Fisk, "Synagogue Influence and Scriptural Knowledge among the Christians of Rome," in *As It Is Written: Studying Paul's Use of Scripture* (ed. S. E. Porter and C. D. Stanley; Atlanta: Society of Biblical Literature, 2008), 157–85.

[35] Esler points to Paul's leadership in writing to Rome, his planned visit there and the intended effects of these on the Christ-following groups. As their leader, he can expect them to be willing to accept his conception of the identity of the Christ-movement and its relation to Israel, the covenant and the scriptures. Paul is thus involved in what may be termed an effort to control a group's past and hence its present identity, which frequently involves a struggle for the possession and control of a group's collective memory (p. 137). Holmberg is somewhat skeptical that Paul could have succeeded in this project, even if it is useful to view him as an "entrepreneur of identity" (see n. 31 above).

them and which was in process of being transformed, in the case of gentiles, to a gentile identity in Christ. He sought to achieve this in several ways, but chiefly through building them up in solidarity and common conviction in accordance with the gospel passed on to him by revelation and those in Christ prior to himself. He envisaged a radical re-evaluation of all things as a result of being in Christ so that this new priority in values conformed to the life and death of Christ rather than being conformed to the Greco-Roman values of this world, (Rom 12:1–2).[36] Even in Romans, Paul is able to refer back to "the form of teaching" (6:17) to which the Roman Christ-followers had earlier been introduced, i.e., to relate back to the identity forming traditions operative in their first introduction to the faith.[37]

Meyer sees the development of the Christ-movement as a learning process in which the movement gradually changed its self-understanding and ways of manifesting its identity. This identity grew out of what he terms "the Easter experience." The latter consisted of a life-transforming faith relation to the risen Christ Jesus, shared by all Christ-followers, including those who had not personally met the risen Jesus. This was by virtue of the fact that the closest circle of disciples and witnesses shared a common memory, anamnesis, of his life and person, including his resurrection, which formed and shaped the basic content of their preaching, teaching and worship, being nurtured and celebrated in community. Thus institutionalized in the rites of baptism and the Lord's supper, behavior patterns, *ethos* and traditions, this embodiment of the founding Easter experience rendered it continuously accessible to new members as a memory or internal history of the group. Holmberg thus defines (this aspect of) identity as the "feedback-shaped self-understanding of the Christ-movement."[38] Meyer recognizes that even allowing for

---

[36] Cf. Zetterholm's comment, "the fact that the Jesus movement did not allow the gentile adherents to maintain their cultic obligations towards the polis created a complex social and identity problem for the Jesus-believing gentiles," *Formation of Christianity*, 231. Cf. also P. F. Esler, "Paul and Stoicism: Romans 12 as a Test Case," *NTS* 50 (2004): 106–24.

[37] For a good discussion of the "teaching" referred to in this verse see M. D. Nanos *The Mystery of Romans: The Jewish Context of Paul's Letter* (Minneapolis: Fortress 1996), 25–26.

[38] Cf. Holmberg, "Understanding the First Hundred Years, 24.

the wholly legitimate diversity between the life of Jewish Christianity in Palestine and that of gentile Christianity in the diaspora, Christian identity, the subjective correlative of the gospel, lay open to diversity of self-definition (i.e. diverse horizons, self-understanding and self-shaping).[39]

Samuel Byrskog also uses the concept of an over-arching element in identity i.e. in the mnemonic and narrative activity in which the early Christians were involved. Following a social memory approach to identity formation, Byrskog notes how groups usually rely on shared memory to claim and negotiate identity.[40] Being socialized into a group's memories and thereby identifying with its collective past is part of the process of acquiring social identity. The new awareness of how social memory works in creating a particular sense of belonging in the present to a certain narrative past, challenges particularly those scholars who focus on the identity of the gospel communities only as part of their relationship to contemporaneous ethnic, religious and political groups.[41] By pointing to the over-arching mnemonic and narrative activity in which the early Christians were involved, we are made aware of commonality in early Christian traditions which was not limited to Christ-followers of Jewish descent, but must also have influenced gentiles as well.

It would be somewhat surprising if a similar process to that identified for the Gospels did not shape the Pauline gentile communities despite their differing period and character.[42] These, no less than the addressees of the Gospels, are linked back to the life and death of Christ and its significance for them as well as for Jewish Christ-

---

[39] Meyer, *Early Christians,* 186.

[40] S. Byrskog, "Memory and Identity in the Gospels: A New Perspective," in *Exploring Early Christian Identity* (ed. B. Holmberg; Tübingen: Mohr Siebeck), 33–57, esp. 57. Cf. also his essay, "Christology and Identity in the Gospels: The Glory of Adam in the Narrative Substructure of Paul's Letter to the Romans," in *Identity Formation in the New Testament* (ed. B. Holmberg and M. Winninge; Tübingen: Mohr Siebeck, 2008), 1–18, esp.16–18.

[41] Byrskog, "Memory and Identity," 56.

[42] Paul's repetition of phrases such as "Do you not know" etc., point to such a process, see K. Ehrensperger, *Paul and the Dynamics of Power: Communication and Interaction in the Early Christ-Movement* (London, New York: T&T Clark, 2007), esp. ch. 7, "Power in Interaction—Paul and the Discourse of Education," 117–36.

followers. By this, the sense of being a "new creation" is thereby qualified so that the roots of Paul's gentile communities are clearly similar in certain ways to those of Jewish Christ-followers, in that in neither case is a community formed without specific inculcation into and adoption of narratives of redemption linking back both to the life and death of Christ, and also to his attributed role in the narrative of Abraham's promises and posterity. Nor is it legitimate, in light of this renegotiation of contemporary issues in relation to group identity to view the ongoing identity formation as if this is the sole result of influences from a gentile society. However large the gentile majority in the Pauline communities, even with these there was always a prior link back to the Jesus tradition[43] via earlier Jewish Christian Christ-followers or perhaps in some instances only via Paul himself.

Without in any way minimizing or ignoring the process of social memory as outlined above, the concept of an overarching Christian identity may not in practice prove to be without problems, or may at least require clarification. The value of Esler's careful development of a model to overcome interethnic conflict by establishing a common identity while simultaneously maintaining subgroup identities must be acknowledged.[44] However, though it seems perfectly reasonable to speak of being in Christ as an overarching identity straddling sub-group identities whether as Judean or gentile, perhaps such a perspective does not sufficiently recognize that "in Christ" is itself an abstraction not to be concretely observed except in an enculturated form. As such it is certainly a strong component of identity, but always existing in an ethically, geographically and politically influenced state as, for example, in the case of European identity today which includes particular regional identities (there is no one region that can claim to be European as such or by itself,

---

[43] As J. H. Schütz states, "This newness of life so bears the contours of Christ's death and resurrection that it is never to be understood in isolation from those events. When one is in Christ, he lives in that particular confluence of past, present and future," see *Paul and the Anatomy of Apostolic Authority* (Louisville: Westminster John Knox, 2007), 208.

[44] Cf. Esler, *Conflict and Identity*, 144. Esler likewise notes that negatively "Paul knocks away the respective foundations each group has for harboring feelings of ethnic superiority over the other that would get in the way of the new common ingroup identity on offer" (p. 144).

it is only in concrete relation with other regions that this title is warranted). To describe this overarching "in Christ" component as if it were a free-standing entity is theoretically useful, but to recognize its influence in social reality is more difficult in practice than it appears in theory. The concept of being in Christ whilst distinctively Christian is nevertheless not a completely new idea. The Messiah and the role of those to be associated with him in his kingdom (however varied the understanding of this might be) had a long gestation period in Israelite tradition much of which was revitalized in the new situation arising with the dawn of the Christ-movement. We will return to this aspect of being "in Christ" in a later section.

It would seem that the best way to describe this Christ element is not as something that exists freely as an overarching entity but as something that is inevitably intertwined with ethnic and cultural components to the extent that we can speak of Christian existence only contextually, rather than in some envisaged pure form impinging on society from above. In this sense it might be wiser to speak of trans-ethnic existence in Christ (or in Europe) rather than of a non-ethnic Christianity or a third race/third entity, using trans-ethnic not in the sense of fusion or of rising above, but in the sense of including more than one entity without dissolution or assimilation. Thus we conclude that "in Christ" identity however significant and essential, nowhere exists except in tandem with other identities such as Greek or Judean. Thus there can be no Christ-followers who are not simultaneously Roman, Greek etc. Christ identity as such does not actually exist as an isolated or free-standing identity. In view of this, overarching identity in Christ is not fundamentally or necessarily in opposition to other specific forms of identity, but in fact presupposes these. "In Christ" identity is therefore no more incompatible with a Judean identity than with an English or American identity.

It follows from the discussion of in Christ as an over-arching identity that this may help to clarify whether or not gentiles in Christ may be regarded as fully incorporated into Israel as e.g. some readings of Gal 6:16 propose.[45] However, to be in Israel cannot be

---

[45] J. D. G. Dunn, *The Theology of Paul, the Apostle* (Grand Rapids: Eerdmans, 1998), 506–9.

used as equivalent to being in Christ. To be in Israel, or of Israel, is already a designation in which the religious cannot be separated from the ethnic dimension, and so must of necessity apply to Jews only. This means that another application of the concept of an overarching identity is also ruled out. If "in Christ" identity is emphasized so as to suggest that identity as Greek, Judean or Roman is really of no lasting significance, then this represents a deterioration that in practice results in a de-facto doctrine of Christians as a "third race"/"third entity." Thus one's identity prior to being in Christ, and the lasting significance of this "in Christ," cannot be ignored nor should it become a target for a policy of gradual elimination as if such a practice could be christologically or otherwise justified. If being in Christ is to be truly regarded as an overarching identity, it cannot simultaneously be held to be an instrument for the diminishment of that part of one's identity, which it "overarches."

It should be acknowledged that there is both truth and merit in the concept of being in Christ as an overarching identity for all. But because in the history of Christianity it has been associated with a down-playing of one's contextual and historical existence, care now needs to be taken in its use to avoid any suggestion that the recognition of ethnicity as such or even of difference is necessarily in opposition to being in Christ.

Some scholars, such as James Dunn, claim that there are boundary markers integral to Judaism that are incompatible with being in Christ.[46] But the only incompatible element for Jews could be a failure to recognize gentiles in Christ as fellow citizens of the kingdom. Here as with any other identity it is not the identity as such that is incompatible but only aspects of it. Each identity as Greek or Roman, like Jewish, has to be evaluated as is the case with all value systems. In the light of Christ some elements are thus displaced and others reaffirmed,[47] but not simply an identity en bloc (and we

---

[46] On this see my *Christian Identity*, 42–46. One of my criticisms of Dunn is his use of the term "antithesis" in relation to Jewish identity markers in his essay "The New Perspective on Paul." See *Jesus, Paul and the Law: Studies in Mark and Galatians* (Louisville: Westminster John Knox Press, 1990), 183–206, esp. 196–8.

[47] Cf. W. S. Campbell, "I Rate All Things as Loss: Paul's Puzzling Accounting System: Judaism as

need to be careful here in claiming incompatibility between being in Christ with Greco-Roman identity as such). It is Roman imperialism that Paul opposes, not necessarily the whole of its life and culture.[48]

The Formation of Gentile Identity in Christ.

"Remain as you were" as this has been interpreted earlier in this essay is certainly affirmation of gentile culture to some extent. It would not be possible to advocate remaining as you were when called if all of one's previous existence had to be denied or counteracted, hence our critique of phrases such as "obliteration of previous worlds." These must be regarded as exaggerations, even if such proposals could be shown to be in any sense a realistic option in terms of actual human society.[49]

Our basic concern in this discussion of identity in Christ is to take seriously Paul's goal in advocating "remain as you were when called." I take this to mean that one's identity is thus affirmed in Christ, even though all aspects of human existence/life are also likewise judged in coming to Christ.[50] Thus I argued in my book that Paul affirms Jewish identity in Christ, rather than negating it or proposing a gradual diminishment of it. This was because the prevalent attitude in New Testament scholarship for the last two centuries at least has been that Jewish identity cannot co-exist with being in Christ. But I do not wish to suggest that gentile identity in Christ was not also equally important to Paul. It is no less unacceptable to denigrate gentile identity in Christ, particularly since it was something to

---

Loss or the Re-Evaluation of All Things in Christ," in *Celebrating Paul: Festschrift in Honour of J. A. Fitzmyer and J. Murphy-O'Connor* (ed. P. Spitaler; Washington: Catholic Biblical Association of America, 2012), 39–61.

[48] Greek and Roman identity may actually appear to be more compatible with in Christ identity because these are viewed in a merely cultural way in a contemporary sense which may not necessarily include a religious dimension. But in as much as the religious element is inseparable from Jewish identity so was it also from all other ethnic identities in the ancient world.

[49] On what transformation means in Rom 12, see Esler, "Paul and Stoicism," 106–24 and the response from T. Engberg-Pedersen, "The Relationship with Others: Similarities and Differences Between Paul and Stoicism," *ZNW* 85 (2004): 36–60.

[50] As Nanos notes, "Gentiles turning to faith in the Christ of Israel need not (must not!) become Jews; however, *equally important*, they must not remain pagans," see *Mystery of Romans,* 197.

which Paul in his life and mission was so committed. It will not do therefore to assert one identity and to ignore the other, nor to emphasize one at the expense of another, so that instead of one form of bias, we are left with its opposite! What we are concerned to consider here is how both gentile and Jewish self-understanding can co-exist without opposition in Christ. We are also concerned to avoid a model of group understanding that presupposes out-group and in-group mentality as normative based on the recognized difference between them, implying that the very existence of differing sub-groups is already a failure.[51] As Meyer has argued, "Paul cherished the unity of the church in the full consciousness that uniformity for Jewish and gentile spheres was out of the question."[52]

The major incompatibility for gentiles arose from the exclusive loyalty claim of the God of Israel, continued in Christ. This involved an absolute incompatibility with the worship of idols and associated festivals, which of course was a much greater issue for gentile Christ-followers, since this exclusive loyalty was self-evident for Jews including those in Christ. Other elements in Greek and Roman identity were not necessarily as such seen to be in opposition to Christ. Thus Paul while fundamentally opposed to Roman imperial domination, was by no means opposed to every aspect of Greek and Roman culture as such, as may be argued from the fact of the numerous Roman names mentioned in his letters.[53]

Though it may be disputed whether Paul was a Roman citizen, as Luke presents him,[54] this conclusion however, by itself, is not the basis for, nor does it determine, our view that Paul was not simply counter cultural in his attitude even to Rome.

---

[51] On this, see S. Reicher, "The Context of Social Identity: Domination, Resistance and Change," *Political Psychology* 6 (2004): 921–45, esp. 930.

[52] See Meyer, *Early Christians,* 184.

[53] Cf. E. A. Judge, "The Roman Base of Paul's Mission," in *The First Christians in the Roman World: Augustan and New Testament Essays* (ed. J. R. Harrison; Tübingen: Mohr Siebeck, 2008): 553–67.

[54] Cf. E. W. Stegemann and W. Stegemann, *The Jesus Movement: A Social History of Its First Century* (Edinburgh: T&T Clark, 1999), who maintain that the evidence from Paul's letters, in opposition to Luke's picture in Acts, presents Paul as a citizen of neither Rome nor Tarsus (pp. 297–302).

Nevertheless, gentiles in Christ were in a difficult situation in that they were alienated from the worship of ancestral gods and with the cultural and religious elements associated with these that were such a fundamental aspect of their existence. In being in Christ these gentiles were also being incorporated into an Israelite symbolic universe and affiliated into Jewish social life, yet denied the option of converting to Judaism. Moreover, as fictive children of Abraham they were closely associated with the meta-narrative of Jewish tradition which made their continuance as gentiles even more complicated.

In a recent study Caroline Johnson Hodge argues that Paul interweaves various forms of kinship construction "so that gentiles … are now adopted into the lineage of Abraham" via a new kinship of the spirit brought about through baptism into Christ.[55] Paul uses a discourse of kinship and ethnicity, both understood as social constructions, to construct a composite social identity for gentiles. This is sourced in an already existing Jewish identity, but does not, however, result in a fusion or blending of the two identities into one undifferentiated universal identity.[56] The presupposition of Paul's argument lies in his perception of gentile alienation from the God of Israel.

Paul views Christ as the solution to this problem and sets out to construct a kinship that relates gentiles in a lineage of patrilineal descent to Abraham, thus granting them a new inheritance and a relationship with the God of Israel.[57] Although we do not have space in this essay to deal in more detail with Johnson Hodge's proposals, it is important to note certain aspects of her work that resonate or jar

---

[55] Johnson Hodge, *If Sons, Then Heirs*, 41.

[56] Johnson Hodge rightly notes that Gal 3:28 is not an argument for the obliteration of difference, but an "effort to recalibrate the priorities of these baptized gentiles, so that their ethnically specific identity as being in Christ comes first," *If Sons, Then Heirs*, 129.

[57] Johnson Hodge notes that in the ancient world, "constructs of both kinship and ethnicity often support arguments for self-authorization and self-definition. They are well suited to such arguments, for at the same time that they present themselves as natural and fixed, they are also open to negotiation and reworking," *If Sons, Then Heirs*, 17 (also 116–18), following Esler, who used this term, "entrepreneur of identity," in association with S. A. Haslam's and M. J. Platow's description of the qualities of leaders, see "Your Wish is Our Command: The Role of Shared Identity in Translating a Leader's Vision into Followers' Action," in *Social Identity Processes in Organizations* (ed. M. A. Hogg and D. J. Terry; New York: Psychology Press, 2001), 213–28.

with the stance taken here.

Firstly, it is significant that Johnson Hodge's focus is on the creation/construction of gentile identity.[58] She concludes that an ethnic reading of Paul necessarily leads to the conclusion that although *Ioudaioi* and Greeks receive equally impartial treatment from God, "the *Ioudaioi* are marked by ethnic continuity and the Greeks by ethnic disruption and rearranging."[59] We can at least agree that Paul's view of Jews and gentiles though even-handed and laying the basis for equality of opportunity for both, is in the end best described as involving a degree of asymmetry. It is not surprising then that Paul devoted so much effort to assist the gentiles in finding a solution to their plight, and to ensure that they were treated as equal in Christ, even though salvation is first to the Jew and only then to the gentile. But for Paul gentiles remain gentiles in Christ, despite discontinuity and a lack of symmetry with Jews in Christ. Johnson Hodge holds that a complete ethnic reading of Paul results in ethnic ranking with the higher status being accorded to Jews. According to the olive tree image of Rom 9–11 the ethnic identity of gentiles in Christ is a hybrid identity.

Though agreeing generally that gentiles in Christ must be strongly influenced by Jewish faith and tradition, and that "the kinship created through baptism into Christ establishes a tie to Israel and its God," I cannot concur with the view that they actually have a hybrid identity.[60] Whether we use this term or others such as nested or multiple identities, there are still problems with such designations. As Holmberg has noted in relation to a "hierarchy of nested identities":

---

[58] This is partly because she views Paul's letters as addressed to communities of gentiles, though her understanding of Christ's faithfulness (and that of Abraham) offers a lineage also for Jews, see Johnson Hodge, *If Sons, Then Heirs*, ch. 4, "Descendants of a Faithful Ancestor: *Hoi Ek Pisteōs*," esp. 88–91.

[59] See *If Sons, Then Heirs*, 140–1. Johnson Hodge asserts that "Paul never says, for example, that the *Ioudaioi* have to give up any portion of their ethnic and religious identity. Their God, their practices, their scriptures are all intact. The gentiles, by contrast, must give up goods that are central to their identity: their gods, religious practices, myths of origin, epic stories of their ancestors and origins. To receive the same judgment and mercy as the *Ioudaioi*, the gentiles must adopt the God of Israel and Jewish narratives of origin and ancestry" (pp.140–1).

[60] See Johnson Hodge, *If Sons, Then Heirs*, 150–1. Johnson Hodge also asserts, "although Jewish identities themselves may have been multiple and hybrid, as all identities are, being-in Christ requires a more radical *blending* for gentiles" (emphasis mine), 150.

[I]n the case of an individual, the different identities hang together by the fact of belonging to that specific human being. His or her continuous person is an actual reality that holds together all the different partial identities. When talking about the identity of a movement, it is not so easy to see a distinct and continuous core, i.e. an actual reality that "naturally" holds it together.[61]

Although he does also discuss analogies between the group and individual experience, Holmberg remains critical concerning nested identities just as he does also in relation to identity as a textual phenomenon.[62] This suggests to some scholars that our contemporary individualism is anachronistically being read back into ancient societies where group dynamics and rituals were the more powerful determinants.

Granted, Johnson Hodge does also claim a hybrid identity for Jews in Christ, but I am not convinced that the concept of hybrid identity for gentiles does not somehow diminish Paul's stress on distinct peoples. Despite critical opposition to what she terms the "fusion theory" and denials to the contrary,[63] this stance, because based on hybridity, is similar to the view of those who maintain that gentiles in Christ may legitimately be termed Israel. But such a designation destroys Paul's abiding emphasis on the distinction between Jew

---

[61] Holmberg, "Understanding the First Hundred Years," 28. In an example from a novel by Tagore, offered by A. K. Sen, the role of reason and choice in discovering identity is noted, but the example given of a conservative Hindu who finds out that he is an Irishman is relevant only for an individual's identity, not for a group. It would seem unlikely that such a discovery would happen to a group, see A. K. Sen, *Reason Before Identity* (Oxford: Oxford University Press, 1999), 18.

[62] Thus Holmberg in discussing the contribution to identity research by Judith Lieu, is not in agreement with her conclusion in *Image and Reality: The Jews in the World of the Christians in the Second Century* (Edinburgh: T&T Clark, 1996), that the image of Jews in certain writings was created by the need of Christians to make them into their Other, the counter image that the Christians need in order to confirm and explain themselves. He states, "As can be expected, that image is antagonistic and polemical, and to a large extent a rhetorical construct that reflects the needs of 'othering' the Jews much more than it reflects historical experiences," see Holmberg, "Understanding the First Hundred Years," 6. See also his comment that "if the material is approached from the direction of rhetorical analysis (as Lieu and others do) identity appears to be, at least in extreme cases, something floating in the air at a distance from the earth. It is so hard to know whether it floats above the earth, like a balloon that is tied to the earthly terrain, or like a cloud that is not, it is tempting to leave it floating up there in the thin air of ideas," (p. 29).

[63] Johnson Hodge, *If Sons, Then Heirs*, 127–31. Johnson Hodge claims that "Paul and these gentiles share a common component of their identity, in-Christness, even as they remain otherwise separate" (p. 125).

and gentile. If Paul fought so strongly to prevent gentiles in Christ being forced to accept circumcision and to keep the law, it seems strange that they still receive a hybrid Jewish/gentile identity nevertheless. This might suggest that circumcision and the keeping of the law are evils in themselves, whereas most scholars would regard the problem as arising from the fact of their imposition upon gentiles.[64] The problem arises partly from the claim that "being-in-Christ does not involve shifting or mixing for Jews; it is already a Jewish identity."[65] In my view whilst being very sympathetic to the emphasis on Jewish roots, I do not regard "in Christ" as being in itself a Jewish identity, or that it constitutes an ethnic designation.[66] This issue is very much related to our previous discussion of being in Christ as an overarching identity. If, for Jews, "in Christ" which is one's primary identity,[67] is perceived as a Jewish identity, then it cannot easily serve as an overarching identity, since in my view it should serve in the same way as an overarching identity for all those in Christ. To operate, as Paul does in relation to gentiles being in Christ, within the context of a Jewish discourse does not necessarily constitute a basis for claiming "in Christ" as an ethnic designation.

Respect for Difference in Christ— a Source of Conflict or a Rule in All the Churches?

In the earliest days of his mission especially, Paul's task was not an easy one. He had to seek to give his communities an induction into the Jewish roots of their faith without actually becoming Jewish themselves. If only Paul could have accepted the easier solution of

---

[64] On this see M. Bachmann, "Neutestamentliche Hinweise auf halakhische Regelungen," in *Nuovo Testamento: Teologie in dialogo culturale: Scritti in onore di Romano Penna nel suo 70° compleanno* (ed. N. Ciola and G. Pulcinelli; Bologna: Edizioni Dehoniane, 2008), 449–62, esp. 454.

[65] Johnson Hodge, *If Sons, Then* Heirs, 150.

[66] Cf. ibid., 132. Cf. Johnson Hodge's comment, "In explaining to the baptized gentiles what it means to be in Christ, he (Paul) marks their experience as ethnically specific." Whilst concurring with much of Hodge's excellent understanding of how gentiles become kin of Abraham, I see this claim as exaggerating what it means for gentile Christ-followers to be affiliated to Israel.

[67] Cf. ibid., 125.

assimilating gentiles into Judaism, the task would have been so much simpler, and the apostle would not have been so much in the forefront of battles about their ongoing identity and corresponding way of life. This determination on Paul's part, to retain gentile identity in Christ alongside his own ongoing commitment to Jewish identity, illustrates just how important an issue this diversity constituted for him (what I have termed Paul's Peculiar Problem[68]). The God of Israel could not be reduced to being the God of either Jews or gentiles, since he is God of all creation, both of Jews and the nations. It is this recognition that predisposes me to view Gal 6:16 as fitting into the pattern of retaining a clear distinction between Jew and gentile even in Christ. Since Paul has argued fiercely in this letter that gentiles must not conform or yield to the imposition of Jewish life patterns and practices, it would seem most foolish on Paul's part to encourage the view that gentiles are Israel, despite his arguments to forbid them accepting circumcision throughout the letter. This would offer a conclusion that weakened rather than climaxed the argument. Thus our reading of Gal 6:16 relates it to the overall context of the letter, and especially to the preceding verse.[69]

When the ethnic origin of a group is recognized and affirmed, some may see here a risk that unity in Christ will be marred by conflicting identities, which may thus be perceived to represent an ongoing threat to oneness in Christ,[70] unless these are gradually diminished in importance to allow commonality rather than difference to be expressed. But, alternatively, even when being in Christ is viewed in terms of an overarching identity, this can also have a dangerous tendency in that it might suggest to some that this overarching identity somehow in itself offers a solution that actually overcomes difference, a panacea for an illness, as if difference itself were the

---

[68] See my *Christian Identity,* 56–67.

[69] Similarly M. Bachmann, *Antijudaismus im Galaterbrief? Exegetische Studien zu einem polemischen Schreiben und zur Theologie des Apostels Paulus* (Göttingen: Vandenhoeck & Ruprecht, 1999), 159–89. Bachmann agues that the entire argument of Galatians (as does Paul's use of Israel generally) does in no way force us to the conclusion that the church of Jews and gentiles is Israel (pp. 164–8).

[70] Cf. Holmberg's query concerning awareness of one's past as *threat* to Christian identity, see "Understanding the First Hundred Years," 19, also Esler, *Conflict and Identity,* 32.

problem. Paul makes it clear however that when the peace of Christ and reign of God are at risk, circumcision and uncircumision are nothing, compared with being in Christ (1 Cor 7:17–24, Gal 6:15). This assertion occurs in 1 Corinthians in a context where remaining as you were when called is stressed and where Paul claims this is his rule not just for Corinth but also in all his communities. Is there any evidence that this rule applies also in Galatians? Interestingly we find not only the same words in Gal 6:15 concerning circumcision/ uncircumcision, but also in the following verse a parallel reference to Paul's advocated pattern for all his churches "peace and mercy be upon all who walk by this rule" (ὅσοι τῷ κανόνι τούτῳ στοιχήσουσιν)[71]. It would appear that it is not a coincidence that the requirement for a repositioning of circumcision/uncircumcision in the communities' value-system is followed by a reference to a ruling pattern for all the communities. This indicates that here we have evidence of a significant and universal rule operated by the apostle.[72] The attitude towards ethnic origin/affiliation is so important that far from its being ignored, one's attitude to it can be determinative for the receipt of Paul's and his colleagues' approval and blessing. It seems clear that Paul's blessing is on all those who live a life of reconciliation amidst the diversity of groups of Jews and gentiles in Christ, who recognize their differing origins within their commonality in Christ. Yet he does not stop there, but also offers a prayer for "the Israel of God," another group not included among those already mentioned, as indicated by the καί differentiating them. It seems clear from this that Paul in this particular passage, did not mean to state or even to imply that gentiles in Christ can be termed Israel.

Moreover, if Paul in Galatians had achieved a theological depiction of gentiles in Christ as Israel, we would anticipate that there would be evidence of such when similar topics are under discussion in Romans. But here again, the distinction between the two peoples is consistently adhered to. We maintain this in spite of some debate about Rom 9:19–

---

[71] See Campbell, "I Rate All Things as Loss."

[72] We are aware that this interpretation of "rule" in Pauline theology and the mere fact of Paul ruling or operating a "rule" may seem inconsistent with certain portraits of the apostle, but see Ehrensperger's approach in *Paul and the Dynamics of Power*.

29. In a recent analysis of Paul's use of Israel in Romans, I concluded:

> what is most significant from our analysis of Paul's use of Israel
> terminology is that having made a distinction within 'Israel' between
> the 'remnant' and the 'rest' (11.7), he does not disinherit either group
> by employing the term to refer exclusively to one party or the other.[73]

Similarly, I noted that "there is a degree of precision in chs. 9–11 in
his designation of his own people as Israel."[74] We maintain therefore
that Paul is very much aware of his terminology and careful in his
use of it, making it more likely that Israel in Gal 6:16 does not refer
to gentiles and Jews in Christ but only to those Jews who as yet
do not respond in the affirmative to the gospel. We cannot agree
with Dunn's statement that "it might be possible to include 'gentiles'
within 'Israel'. And this is in effect what Paul attempts to do in
Romans 9–11."[75] Israel retains its distinct identity in Pauline usage
both in Galatians and Romans. Indeed the development in Paul's
terminology in Romans is such that the probability of Paul equating
"Israel" with the church of Jews and gentiles in Gal 6:16 remains
most unlikely. Both gentile Christ-followers and Jews are children of
Abraham and of the promise, but gentiles do not become children of
Israel, since Jacob/Israel's progeny can only be Jews. This lineage of
descent would have been fundamental to Paul's thinking as evidenced
in his claim to be a Benjamite. Non-Jews therefore are not required to
adhere to the Torah, which is essentially Israel's law in that it was to
them that the Torah was given at Sinai. To designate gentiles in Christ
as Israel simply confuses Israel's identity with that of the nations.

Probably the most significant passage to add to and thus to
conclude our discussion is Rom 15:7–13, regarded by many as
the concluding summary of Paul's letter to the Romans.[76] Whilst

---

[73] Campbell, *Christian Identity*, 123.

[74] Ibid., 124.

[75] Dunn, *Theology of Paul*, 506. Dunn also argues that "if church is not defined by differentiation *from* Israel, but rather by inclusion *in* Israel and identification with Israel's blessings, then Christianity's self-understanding is at issue" (p. 507, cf. also p. 525).

[76] See esp. B. Schaller, "Christus, 'der Diener der Bescheidung…, auf ihn werden die Völker hoffen': Zu Charakter und Funktion der Schriftzitate in Röm 15,7–13," in *Das Gesetz im frühen Judentum und*

scholars have disputed to what degree the issue of the weak and the strong, and the context implicit in this discussion represent a focal point in Romans, there has been much agreement that the conclusion to these issues in Rom 15:7–9, provides a suitable conclusion not only to such issues, but also to the entire letter. In 15:7, two groups (or more) of Christ-followers are exhorted to welcome one another as Christ welcomed them. The verb προσλαμβάνω means, as Fitzmyer has noted, to "take to oneself ... take into one's household ... accept with an open heart."[77] Groups divided over issues that involved, or perhaps even primarily concerned, Jewish identity in relations between Christ-followers, are advised by Paul to look to the example of Christ who is significantly depicted here in a quite spectacular phrase as "servant to the circumcision" (15:8). As I have noted elsewhere, Paul has been speaking of Jews and gentiles throughout Romans, except where he deliberately uses the terms Israel/Israelite,[78] and it is surprising that he should in the climax of this discussion coin such an apparently provocative designation for the mission of Christ.[79] Also as apostle to the gentiles, whilst gentiles are one party amongst those who are to welcome one another, and whilst they are to join together in an eschatological hymn of praise with the historic people of God, Christ's mission is radically represented as being to the circumcision. Nothing could make it clearer than at the very end of Romans Paul still thinks in terms of differentiated groups with differing identities in terms of Jews and gentiles, rather than in a church where there is neither Jew nor gentile.

Also, at a concluding point in his argument where it might seem politic for Paul to appear to be very even-handed in speaking of Jews and gentiles, especially with reference to a situation where there is obviously dissension, it is all the more surprising that he gives such

---

im Neuen Testament: Festschrift für Christoph Burchard zum 75. Geburtstag (ed. D. Sänger and M. Konradt; Fribourg: Vandenhoeck & Ruprecht, 2006), 261–85; J. R. Wagner, *Heralds of the Good News: Isaiah and Paul in Concert in the Letter to the Romans* (Leiden: Brill, 2003), 307–8, n. 5.

[77] J. Fitzmyer, *Romans: A New Translation with Introduction and Commentary* (New York: Doubleday, 1993), 689.

[78] Campbell, *Christian Identity*,121–39.

[79] On this, see Schaller, "Christus, 'der Diener der Bescheidung'," 268–70.

significance to "the circumcision." It is here that Paul's careful use of terminology makes clear how he views Israel. As servant to the circumcision, Christ confirms God's faithfulness to his people (ὑπὲρ ἀληθείας θεοῦ εἰς τὸ βεβαιῶσαι τὰς ἐπαγγελίας τῶν πατέρων) to show God's truthfulness and to confirm the promises given to the patriarchs. The gentiles (ἔθνη) rejoice with his people (τοῦ λαοῦ αὐτοῦ).

But the gentiles remain ἔθνη, and even in Christ, they are not designated as λαός "people of God." For the church of Jews and gentiles, Paul uses other terms such as σῶμα Χριστοῦ or ἐκκλησία and thus makes it clear that there is an abiding difference between the nations and "his people."[80] People of God or Israel are never used for the church of Jews and gentiles. As Schaller notes, the only possible exception is in the citation of Hos 2:25 in Rom 9:24–26.[81] Although the church of Jews and gentiles shares in these verses the calling of God, this does not mean that we can simply equate the two entities, i.e., the church and Israel-both are called but are not co-extensive since not all those who share in Israel's call also respond to affirm the calling of God in Christ.[82]

In Paul's perspective the blessings that gentiles receive, they receive because Christ became a servant to the circumcision. In and with the blessings to God's people Israel, there is a secondary outcome—gentiles are also blessed but only in association with

---

[80] See Schaller, "Christus, 'der Diener der Bescheidung'," 269–80. Schaller sees this differentiation reflected in Paul's terms in Rom 15, truth, faithfulness in relation to God's people, and mercy towards the gentiles (p. 269). Schaller is quite clear that Paul never uses people of God or Israel as ecclesiological terms (pp. 275–7), (similarly in relation to covenant, see Crüsemann, *Kanon und Sozialgeschichte*, 303–5). In Ephesians both of these terms appear alongside one another, see my article, "Unity and Diversity in the Church: Transformed Identities and the Peace of Christ in Ephesians," *Transformation*, 25 (2008): 15–31; see also Rader, *Church and Racial Hostility*, 247–8, who notes that the church is not only a new creation as suggested by the term, "body of Christ" but also exists in continuity with the redemptive work of God in history which the concept of the people of God emphasizes.

[81] Schaller, "Christus, 'der Diener der Bescheidung'," 275–6, following Bachmann (as in n. 69 above). See also my argument that Paul does not refer first to the gentiles but to northern Israel and only then by analogy to the gentiles: "Divergent Images of Paul and His Mission," in *Reading Israel in Romans: Legitimacy and Plausibility of Divergent Interpretations* (ed. C. Grenholm and D. Patte; Harrisburg: Trinity Press International, 2000), 187–211, esp. 198–200.

[82] See Campbell, *Christian Identity*, 100–101, 130–2.

Israel. But they do not become Israel, they only share the blessings promised to Israel. Thus the priority of Israel, and hence their distinctiveness remains even after the coming of Christ as servant. There is now real potential for joining together in the praise of God, without obliteration of previous identity. Gentiles are now called to share in the Messianic salvation which God's servant to Israel has brought, but gentiles sharing in salvation still remain gentiles just as Israel's identity as people of God likewise abides.

It is this scenario that Paul offers to the Romans as the solution to identity disputes concerning weak and strong. The strong, who have the power, must bear up the weak and thus prevent the destruction of the weak because in Christ they have a common destiny though remaining different. Paul's aim is not to force the differing groups into one unified "church" in Rome. Nor is it his purpose to make all Christ-followers leave their differing places of worship, whether synagogues or house churches, but there must be a recognition of their sharing in salvation through Christ. There is a destiny for both Jew and gentile through God's servant to the circumcised, but a destiny inextricably connected in which the goal is an eschatological salvation for both Jews and gentiles to share in the messianic banquet in a common praise to God. He seeks their reconciliation in Christ. This celebration of the true reconciliation of Jew and gentile is the goal of Rom 15:7–13 and a sign of Paul's vision of the reconciliation of all things in Christ. [83]

It would thus appear that Paul really means to limit the force of ethnic division so as to allow reconciliation of difference in Christ, rather than seeking to diminish ethnic awareness as such. This would indicate that being aware of difference is not the problem but rather allowing this awareness to become a barrier to integration

---

[83] Markus Barth was one of the few scholars who perceived the wider significance of Paul's view of reconciliation between Jews and gentiles in Christ. Especially in his commentary on Ephesians, Barth claimed that only when the church understands her nature as founded on the reconciliation of Jews and gentiles in Christ will she see herself as a place where divisions among peoples are healed, see Rader, *Racial Hostility*, 245. On reconciliation see also R. P. Martin, *Reconciliation: A Study in Paul's Theology* (Philadelphia: Fortress, 1977), 153–4. Most recently, Esler has also noted Paul's concern for reconciliation of subgroups of Judeans and Greeks in Rome, cf. *Conflict and Identity*, 32–33.

and mutual recognition and reconciliation within the body of Christ. Boasting in terms of honor and shame categories is certainly ruled out because this boasting is a boasting in terms of one's fleshly origin, culture and attributes as Jew or Greek, over against barbarian etc., so as to erect barriers between (groups of) Christ-followers.

Conclusion: In Christ—the Locus of Reconciliation

In this essay several understandings of the identity formation of gentiles in Christ according to Paul have been considered. The conclusion arrived at is that Paul can legitimately be described as the architect who labored to construct an identity for his gentile communities. But it must be stressed that though these were new communities without precedent in the ancient world, they did have roots in the Jesus movement and thus via this in Judaism. To describe the Pauline communities as "new creation" has some theological warrant, but we wish to stress that Paul did not have complete freedom to create new identity as he willed. To this extent, he should rather be seen as construing an identity for these rather than being viewed as the originator of a new religion. The origin of Paul's gentile communities was an outcome of the on-going activity of the Jesus-movement, and thus should be viewed as part of that movement reaching out into the gentile world. In this perspective we have been influenced by Holmberg's definition, "Christian identity is the evolving self-understanding of the movement, shaped by a feedback process between its original experience and its evolving history."[84] It was this feedback process that defined and shaped to a great extent even the radical activity resulting in gentiles being accepted as gentiles into the movement. Thus we interpret Holmberg's reference, noted above, to "its original experience" as indicating the connection with, and influence of, the earlier Jesus movement upon Pauline communities. To neglect or ignore this dimension in ascribing identity to gentiles in Christ is therefore a serious flaw.

---

[84] Holmberg, "Understanding the First Hundred Years," 6.

To regard these as an entirely "new creation" is an inadequate description, particularly since Paul tells them to remain as they were when called, thus affirming to some extent their former gentile existence from which all subsequent identity development emerges.

This leads us to view Paul as both construing an identity for gentiles in Christ and as also simultaneously deeply involved in the construction of their particular identity. He shaped the Jesus movement in the gentile world and construed how this process should be guided both in terms of origins and direction. And even in this process, he sought to establish links back to those who were called prior to the coming of Christ, and thus to create meaningful continuity between these and those who as gentiles were not bound by the law, e.g. 1 Corinthians 10. In as much as he did this, he also implicitly recognized a link with those who continued to maintain a Jewish identity in Christ. Thus in this scenario, Paul cannot be represented as being in opposition to the mission to the circumcised led by Peter.

We have sought to demonstrate in this article that the view of identity in Christ as a "third entity" in which previous identities are obliterated is unconvincing. Whilst acknowledging some positive qualities in the view of "in Christ" as an overarching identity we are not fully convinced, however, that this perspective is the best reading of the evidence, in terms of both the ancient and contemporary worlds. "In Christ" identity never exists in isolated form, but is everywhere linked with other identities, whether these are Greek or Roman, American or English.

It also does not seem appropriate to term "in Christ" identity as a Jewish (hybrid) identity because "in Christ" identity in our view, should comprise an overarching identity in as much as it applies equally to Jews and gentiles who follow Christ. However useful a tool the concept of hybrid identity might be in post-colonial cultures, it does not seem an adequate vehicle for the interpretation of Paul's statements about what he regards, rightly or wrongly in his Jewish view of the world, as two distinct entities.

In addition, it must be stressed that the term Israel is not an appropriate identity designation for gentiles in Christ. Paul nowhere in his letters equates gentiles in Christ with Israel. In Gal 6:16 the connecting καί, "and," cannot easily be explained away or ignored. Paul does intend to show his concern for another group not included among the group of Jews and gentiles who abide by the rule that in Christ neither circumcision nor uncircumcision are of paramount importance (Gal 6:15). Paul had the chance to be more explicit concerning Israel in Romans but this letter confirms rather than alters our view of Gal 6:15–16. Only by maintaining that "the called" in the Hosea citation in Rom 9:24 are co-extensive with those in Christ can the church and Israel be equated in this verse. Above all, Paul's description of Christ as "servant of the circumcision" in Rom 15:8 makes it very plain that even here Paul retains an abiding distinction between the role of Christ in relation to Israel and the salvation of gentiles. This failure ever to identify gentiles in Christ with Israel, also makes it less likely that Paul would be willing to ascribe Jewish identity to those gentiles who are in Christ.

Thus Paul's solution to the issue of the formation of gentile identity in Christ, is on the one hand to relate them positively to the narrative of God's purposes for Israel, but on the other hand not to give them an identity as Israel. Though there may, and must have been, tension between being in Christ and being Greek, Roman, or Jewish, there is no absolute incompatibility between them. In fact there could be no possibility of absolute opposition between being in Christ and any other specific identity, in that it is not identities *en toto* that are judged in Christ but only aspects of such. This can be illustrated from Paul's view that whilst gentiles could be related to Israel, they could not become part of Israel. But this was simply because they were gentiles and should remain such, not that Paul intended to condemn Israel. Our conclusion is that in Pauline thought, the one aspect of Jewish behavior that had the potential for alienating from Christ would have been a failure of Jews to recognize gentile Christ-followers as joint heirs with Jewish Christ-followers. But nowhere in Paul do we find a total rejection of Jewish identity as such, any more than we find a rejection of Greek or Roman identity as such.

This confirms our view that respect for difference in Christ was a rule in all the Pauline communities, because reconciliation of all who differ as Jews or gentiles was, according to Paul, the stated reason why Christ became a servant to the circumcised for the glory of Him who is God of all peoples. The reconciliation of difference and not the removal of difference constituted the heart of Paul's gospel. Therefore both gentile and Judean identities can be affirmed in Christ, and with these comes affirmation also of their cultural context. And yet all forms of identity are in this process also simultaneously subject to judgment in and with the gospel, in an ongoing transformation process involving both appropriation and rejection of aspects of the culture, with resultant tensions.

In short, the goal in Paul's theology was that Jews and gentiles in Christ would both join in praise to God, whilst being aware of their continuing difference, thus celebrating a communion enabled in and through Christ. To perceive being in Christ only in terms of an overarching identity, leaves being in Christ somewhat detached from what remains of one's previous identity. If reconciliation in Christ is stressed in such a way that to be in Christ means simultaneously to be involved in the reconciliation of those who are and will remain different, then this would constitute an inherent connection between being in Christ and reconciling different peoples and cultures. The best modern example is how reconciliation has been attempted with some success in South Africa. There could be no suggestion of overcoming the difference there but a great need for reconciling people who are different. Thus Martin is correct in his stress on reconciliation as Paul's chosen term in relating the gospel to gentiles.[85] Gentiles join with Jews to share in salvation in Christ, because through Him, God and human beings, those who are and remain different, have been reconciled.

---

[85] See n. 83 above.

Baptism and the Formation of Identity

Adela Yarbro Collins
Yale University

Introduction

Baptism is an invention of the ancient Jewish prophet we know as John the Baptist.[1] He invented it by adapting and combining elements from the Jewish traditions and practices of his day.[2] One of these elements is the ritual practice of immersion. The book of Leviticus prescribes bathing of the whole body, for example, after a person is healed of a skin disorder.[3] The rabbis understood such passages as mandating a ritual distinct from ordinary washing and used the root טבל, meaning "to immerse," for ritual washing.[4] The situation at Qumran is more complex,[5] but it seems that members of the community practiced a purification ritual involving full immersion.[6] It seems likely then that John was aware of the practice

---

[1] I am happy to contribute this essay to this volume honoring Professor Bengt Holmberg. It was presented at a conference organized by Turid Karlsen Seim, the director of the Norwegian Institute in Rome, on Ritual and Transformation (in Rome from May 8–10, 2008). The Centre for Advanced Study of the Norwegian Academy in Oslo sponsored the conference.

[2] A. Y. Collins, "The Origin of Christian Baptism," *Studia Liturgica* 19 (1989): 28–46; repr. in *Living Water, Sealing Spirit: Readings on Christian Initiation* (ed. M. E. Johnson; Collegeville: Liturgical Press, 1995), 35–57; and in eadem, *Cosmology and Eschatology in Jewish and Christian Apocalypticism* (Leiden: Brill, 1996), 218–38.

[3] Lev 14:9. It is also prescribed for a man cleansed of a discharge (15:13), for a man after an emission of semen (15:16), for the high priest before putting on the holy vestments on the day of atonement (16:4) and after taking off the holy clothing and before putting on his own (16:24), for the one who sets the goat free for Azazel before entering the camp (16:26), for the one who burns outside the camp the remainder of the bull and goat offered as sin offerings before entering the camp (16:28), for the priest who has become unclean before eating of the sacrifices or offerings brought to the sanctuary (22:6). See also Num 19:7–8, where the same procedure is required of the priest who performs the ritual of the red heifer and the one who burns the heifer.

[4] J. Milgrom, *Leviticus 1–16* (New York: Doubleday, 1991), 841–2.

[5] J. D. Lawrence concludes, "it is unclear from the texts of the Scrolls whether all ritual washing involved full immersion, or just certain situations," see *Washing in Water: Trajectories of Ritual Bathing in the Hebrew Bible and Second Temple Literature* (Leiden: Brill, 2006), 142–3.

[6] H. K. Harrington, *The Purity Texts* (London: T&T Clark, 2004), 22–23; R. C. D. Arnold, *The Social Role of Liturgy in the Religion of the Qumran Community* (Leiden: Brill, 2006), 185–6.

of immersion as a repeated ritual for the removal of ritual impurity and perhaps moral impurity as well.[7] He adapted this practice by transforming repeated immersions into a once and for all rite.[8]

An important impetus for John's invention of a new rite was probably his expectation that certain biblical prophecies were about to be fulfilled. Thus biblical prophecy and apocalyptic expectation are two further elements characterizing his innovative practice. His once and for all rite makes sense as a preparation for the divine visitation of the last days, which was expected to involve judgment. In such a context, John may have alluded to Isa 40:3, which describes a voice crying out, calling the people to prepare the way of the Lord in the wilderness.[9] It is noteworthy that the community related to the sectarian Dead Sea Scrolls cited this passage as a prophecy being fulfilled in their communal life.[10]

Another prophetic passage that illuminates John's rite is Ezek 36:22–32.[11] The Lord promises to gather Israel's diaspora, to sprinkle clean water upon them to cleanse them, to give them a new heart, and to put God's spirit within them so that they will be able

---

According to Josephus, the Essenes bathed themselves in cold water, girded with linen wraps, every day before the midday and the evening meals. He calls this bath a "purification" (ἁγνεία), which makes them "pure" (καθαρός) (*B.J.* 2.128–129); for discussion see T. S. Beall, *Josephus' Description of the Essenes Illustrated by the Dead Sea Scrolls* (Cambridge: Cambridge University Press, 1988,) 55–57.

[7] On ritual impurity, see R. de Vaux, *Ancient Israel* (2 vols; New York: McGraw-Hill, 1961), 2.460. On the distinction between ritual and moral purity, see J. Klawans, *Impurity and Sin in Ancient Judaism*, (New York: Oxford University Press, 2000), 1–42. He argues that in "the sectarian literature from Qumran," ritual and moral impurity were not distinguished but constituted a single notion of defilement (ibid., 67–91; quotation from p. 90). On the latter point, see also Arnold, *Social Role*, 160.

[8] L. Hartman, "Baptism," *ABD* 1:583–94, esp. 584. In the book of Acts, John's baptism is consistently spoken of in the singular (1:22; 10:37; 13:24; 18:25; 19:3–4), which suggests that the ritual was not repeated. Josephus also speaks of John's baptism in the singular; see n. 14 below. According to Acts, Apollos, who knew only the baptism of John, was instructed more accurately in the "way of God" by Priscilla and Aquila, but nothing is said about his being baptized in the name of Jesus (18:24–28). Paul, however, baptizes "in the name of the Lord Jesus" those disciples in Ephesus who knew only the baptism of John and had not received the holy spirit (19:1–7). Note, however, that even baptism in the name of Jesus does not always result in the bestowal of the holy spirit (8:16).

[9] In Mark this passage is cited as a prophecy fulfilled by John, who is identified with "a voice crying out in the wilderness" (1:3).

[10] 1QS 8:12–16; 9:17–20; for discussion see A. Y. Collins, *Mark: A Commentary* (Minneapolis: Fortress, 2007), 137–8.

[11] Ibid., 139.

to follow the divine commands.[12] Such a gathering and cleansing, as well as the gift of moral transformation, make sense of John's rite. He presented himself as the agent of God in dispensing as a divine benefaction the gift of forgiveness of sins and in anticipating the bestowal of the divine spirit. The Qumran community alluded to the same prophecy in a description of their expectation of the divine visitation, when God would cleanse human beings of all wickedness with a spirit of holiness and truth that would be shed upon them like purifying waters (1QS 4:18–23). John innovated by enacting the partial fulfillment of this prophecy through his baptismal rite, which can also be understood as a prophetic symbolic action. Josephus (*A.J.* 18.117–118) interpreted John's rite in rational and ethical terms, as a confirmation of a moral transformation that had already taken place.[13] Mark (1:4) interprets it more simply as "a baptism of repentance for the forgiveness of sins."[14]

Mark and Matthew state quite clearly that John baptized Jesus (Mark 1:9; Matt 3:13–16). Luke (3:21–22) implies it, although the agency of John is obscured. John obscures even further the likely historical fact of John baptizing Jesus, but associates John's rite with the revelation of Jesus to Israel (John 1:29–34, especially v. 31). In spite of their predictions that the one coming after John would baptize with holy spirit or with holy spirit and fire (Mark 1:7–8; Matt 3:11; Luke 3:16), the Synoptic Gospels do not portray Jesus as baptizing. Jesus is portrayed as baptizing in the Gospel of John, but this activity seems to express only the role of John as witness to Jesus and the necessity that John decrease so that Jesus may increase (John 3:22–30).

---

[12] Mark separates the cleansing (John's baptism) from the gift of the divine spirit (to be accomplished by Jesus) in 1:8.

[13] That is, they were to practice virtue before being baptized; this practice of virtue is summarized as acting justly toward one another and with piety toward God.

[14] The phrase εἰς ἄφεσιν ἁμαρτιῶν can express either purpose or result.

Baptism and the Formation of a Hybrid Identity

Whether Jesus baptized others or not, we learn from Paul's letters that the rite was well known to his addressees. In the exhortation regarding the divisions within "the assembly of God in Corinth," he asks, "were you baptized into the name of Paul?" (1 Cor 1:2, 13). From this rhetorical question we may infer that they had been baptized "into the name of Jesus" or "into the name of Christ."[15]

Formation of Identity in First Thessalonians

Oddly enough, Paul does not mention baptism in his letter to the Thessalonians.[16] He emphasizes their reception of holy spirit when the gospel was proclaimed to them (1 Thess 1:4; cf. 1:6) and celebrates their turning from idols to God (1:9). An important part of his earlier oral message and of the letter is his exhortation that they conduct themselves in a way worthy of the God who called them into his kingdom and glory (2:12). He expresses the hope that God "himself" may strengthen their hearts so that they will be "blameless in holiness" (3:13).

The transformation of Gentile sinners that Paul advocated is based on worship of the God of Israel and an end to worship of other gods. The "consecration" or "sanctification" of Gentiles also involves their avoidance of sexual immorality (πορνεία). Holiness and honor must characterize their sexual conduct rather than lustful passion, which is typical of "the Gentiles who do not know God" (4:3–5). In summing up his teaching on sexual ethics, he states a principle: "For God did not call us so that we would be unclean, but to holiness," diplomatically including himself in the exhortation of his audience (4:7).[17] He ends the passage with a warning: "It is

---

[15] Cf. Matt 18:20 (gathering "into my name"); 28:19 (baptizing them "into the name of the father and of the son and of the holy spirit"); Acts 8:16 (they had only been baptized "into the name of the lord Jesus"); 19:5 (they were baptized "into the name of the lord Jesus"); Hartman, "Baptism," 586.

[16] I agree with those who argue that Paul did not write 2 Thess; A. Y. Collins, "Christian Messianism and the First Jewish War with Rome," in *Biblical Traditions in Transmission: Essays in Honor of Michael A. Knibb* (ed. C. Hempel and J. M. Lieu; Leiden: Brill, 2006), 333–43.

[17] I take ἐπί here as a marker of purpose or goal and ἐν as a marker of extension toward a goal; see BDAG, s.v. ἐπί, 11; s.v. ἐν, 3.

surely the case that the one who disregards [this teaching] does not disregard a man, but disregards the God who gives his holy spirit to you" (4:8). In the conclusion of the letter as a whole, Paul returns to the theme of holiness: "May the God of peace himself consecrate you completely, and may your spirits and souls and bodies be securely kept intact at the coming of our lord Jesus" (5:23).

A recent Yale dissertation argues, primarily on the basis of Romans, that Paul worked only with two categories of identity, Jew and Gentile. He did not have the notion of a third category, "Christian." His goal in founding communities of Gentiles may be described in terms of new perspectives on the construction of identity provided by the postcolonial theorist Homi Bhaba and the literary critic Mikhail Bakhtin. Paul's letters describe a paradoxical space in which baptized Gentiles become Jews, while at the same time remaining Gentiles. Their situation is similar to the postcolonial category of hybrids. They are neither Jews nor Gentiles, yet both.[18]

Paul's exhortation of the Thessalonians can be understood in these terms. Insofar as they conformed to Paul's expectations, they were no longer Gentiles in the sense that they no longer worshipped the traditional gods of their social context. There may well have been advocates of a sexual morality in that context similar to that recommended by Paul, but his teaching in this regard is clearly based on the stereotype of sexually immoral Gentiles, which Paul appears to have absorbed from his own Jewish upbringing. The same Thessalonians had become Jews in the sense that they had come to know and worship the God of Israel and to live in conformity with what Paul understood as a Jewish, sexually moral manner. They were also Jews in the sense that they had been taught and had accepted Jewish messianic expectations and the proclamation that Jesus, a Jew, is the messiah.[19]

In the rest of this essay, I hope to show that Paul's interpretations

---

[18] J. Garroway, "Neither Jew nor Gentile, but Both: Paul's "Christians" as "Gentile-Jews" (Ph.D. diss., Yale University, 2008).

[19] A. Y. Collins and John J. Collins, *King and Messiah as Son of God: Divine, Human, and Angelic Messianic Figures in Biblical and Related Literature* (Grand Rapids: Eerdmans, 2008), ch. 5.

of baptism, in the letters in which he mentions it, have the same intention, that is, to form his Gentile audiences in such a way that they become Jews without becoming proselytes.

Paul does not say anything explicit about the praxis of baptism in the communities he founded. If the baptism of John involved immersion, as seems likely, that practice probably continued among those who considered Jesus to be the messiah.[20] The actual procedures did not need to be mentioned because both Paul and his audiences knew what they were.[21]

Baptism and Identity in Galatians

In a recent lecture at Yale University, John Scheid argued that, among the Romans, it was only ritual praxis that was obligatory and normative.[22] Many interpretations could be and often were in circulation, but none of these were authoritative. This approach illuminates Paul's letters. The ritual is well known and normative. Interpretations may be invented, each for a particular rhetorical occasion and purpose.

In Galatians, for example, the rhetorical occasion is the turning of "the assemblies in Galatia" to "another gospel" that includes the idea that they ought to be circumcised (Gal 1:2, 6; 5:2). Since Paul had been with them, they had apparently heard that to be children of Abraham and to share in the fulfillment of the promises to Israel, they had to be circumcised, in accordance with the covenant of God with Abraham (Gen 17:1–14). That they had heard something like this may be inferred from Paul's reinterpretation of the usual

---

[20] The *Didache* seems to privilege immersion in flowing water for the baptismal rite, to specify immersion in water taken or diverted from a spring or river as the next best procedure, and standing water in cisterns or other containers as a third option. The text in its final form clearly allows the pouring of water on the head, presumably if there is insufficient water for immersion (7:1–3). For discussion see K. Niederwimmer, *The Didache: A Commentary* (Minneapolis: Fortress, 1998), 125–9.

[21] W. A. Meeks, *The First Urban Christians: The Social World of the Apostle Paul* (New Haven: Yale University Press, 1983), 150.

[22] J. Scheid, "Ritual and the Meaning of Religion" (April 22, 2008). See also idem, "Le sens des rites. L'exemple romain," in *Rites et croyances dans les religions du monde romain: huit exposés suivis de discussions: Vandœuvre-Genève, 21–25 août 2006* (ed. J. Scheid; Genève: Fondation Hardt, 2007), 39–71.

understanding of Abraham as the father of the Jews: he argues instead that it is those who have faith, including Gentiles, who are sons of Abraham. This is so because God had intended all along to justify the Gentiles by faith, just as Abraham's faith was reckoned as righteousness (Gal 3:6–18). Not only are they sons of Abraham, they are also sons of God "through the faithfulness of Christ Jesus" (3:26).[23] How have they become sons of God? By being baptized "into Christ," an event that Paul interprets as "putting on Christ."[24]

As noted already, the standard procedure for baptism in Paul's sphere of activity was immersion. The standard verbal part of the ritual practice was "I baptize you into the name of Jesus" or something similar. Thus Paul's remark that they have been baptized "into Christ" reprises the formula pronounced at the execution of the rite. This brief formula was open to a variety of interpretations,[25] and Paul exploits this characteristic. The context makes clear that the main inference he draws from it and impresses on his audience is that, since Christ is son of God, those baptized "into Christ" are also sons of God. In the context of the rhetorical argument of the letter as a whole, this means that baptized Gentiles do not need to observe the covenant of circumcision made with Abraham or enter into the Sinai covenant brokered by Moses in order to share in the blessings promised to Israel.

A further aspect of the ritual activity may be revealed in the statement "you have put on Christ" or "you have been clothed with Christ." This may indicate that those to be baptized removed their clothes before being immersed. It is unlikely that, at this early date, they put on a special garment after the immersion. In the *Traditio apostolica* attributed to Hippolytus, those baptized put on the same clothing after the immersion that they had been wearing beforehand (*Trad. ap.* 21:3,

---

[23] On the translation, see R. B. Hays, *The Faith of Jesus Christ: The Narrative Substructure of Galatians 3:1–4:11* (2d ed.; Grand Rapids: Eerdmans, 2002), 155–6.

[24] Gal 3:27.

[25] Hartman, "Baptism," 586.

11, 20).[26] This work dates to a period not earlier than the third century.[27]

In any case, by adopting the metaphor "you have put on Christ," Paul plays with a number of ancient cultural aspects of the practice and theme of clothing. In the ancient world, even more than today, clothing signified social status, rank, and degree of wealth or poverty.[28] In an ethical context, one could speak of "taking off" vices and "putting on" virtues.[29] A change of clothing could also indicate a change in customs and nationality.[30] The latter two themes are interesting in light of Paul's project of creating Gentile Jews.

Language about "putting on Christ" may also play with the metaphor of changing clothing as the transition from an earthly to a heavenly existence.[31] In 2 Cor 5:2–4, in speaking about death and the afterlife, Paul shifts from housing metaphors to clothing imagery. The metaphor of "putting on" our heavenly dwelling expresses the idea of "what is mortal" being swallowed up by "life." Similarly, in 1 Cor 15, Paul shifts from bodily imagery and an allusion to the creation of Adam (15:44–49) to clothing metaphors (15:50–54). The shift is made through language about inheriting the kingdom of God and the transformation of those still alive at the coming of Christ (15:50–52).[32] Then Paul affirms that "what is corruptible must put on incorruption and what is mortal must put on immortality." When this happens the prophecy will be fulfilled that "death has been swallowed up into victory" 15:53–54).[33]

From this perspective the metaphor "putting on Christ" suggests that baptism in Gal 3 is, among other things, an anticipation of the baptized being conformed to the image of God's son by sharing in

---

[26] P. F. Bradshaw, M. E. Johnson, and L. E. Phillips, *The Apostolic Tradition: A Commentary* (Minneapolis: Fortress, 2002), 112, 114, 118.

[27] Ibid., 2.

[28] Plato, *Gorg.* 523–524; for discussion see T. Luckritz Marquis, "At Home or Away: Travel and Death in 2 Corinthians 1–9" (Ph.D. diss., Yale University, 2008), 240–41, 266.

[29] N. Dahl, *Studies in Ephesians: Introductory Questions, Text- & Edition-Critical Issues, Interpretation of Texts and Themes* (ed. D. Hellholm, V. Blomqvist, and T. Fornberg; Tübingen: Mohr Siebeck, 2000), 389, 391.

[30] Ibid., 389.

[31] Ibid., 390–91.

[32] Cf. 1 Cor 15:51–52 with 1 Thess 4:13–18.

[33] Cf. Isa 25:8.

his resurrection and attaining a glorified body like his (Rom 8:18–30, esp. v. 29). This inference is supported by the remark immediately following the clothing imagery in 2 Cor 5:5: "the one who has accomplished this very thing for us is God, who has given us the spirit as a guarantee."

Galatians 3:28 is often seen as part of a pre-Pauline baptismal formula.[34] Be that as it may, my interest is in how this verse supports Paul's rhetorical purposes. Paul begins by stating what is his primary concern: that the binary opposition between Jew and Gentile has been mediated by baptism and the new social creation that it entails. He supports this socially disruptive claim with the equally radical claim that the opposition between the enslaved and the free person has also been mediated. Most shocking of all is the claim that the biological distinction between maleness and femaleness has also been mediated or broken down in some way. The second clause of v. 28 explains how all this can be: for you are all one (masculine being or person) in Christ Jesus. The reference to maleness and femaleness may recall the creation of humanity in Gen 1:26–27. Such an allusion makes sense in light of Paul's affirmation later in this letter: "For neither circumcision nor uncircumcision is anything, rather [what is important is] a new creation" (Gal 6:15). This saying may be interpreted in light of Paul's efforts to found communities of Gentiles who became Jews while remaining Gentiles. These communities were a new social creation. At the same time, the breaking down of the distinction between male and female human beings again anticipates the resurrection when, according to the Synoptic Gospels, there will be no marriage because those who rise will be like angels (Mark 12:25; Matt 22:30; Luke 20:35–36).[35]

In Gal 3:29 Paul returns to his main theme in this part of the letter: the Gentiles who have been baptized into Christ are descendants of Abraham and heirs of the promise. In other words, they do not need

---

[34] H. D. Betz, *Galatians: A Commentary on Paul's Letter to the Churches in Galatia* (Minneapolis: Fortress Press, 1979), 181, 184; Meeks, *First Urban Christians*, 88.

[35] Paul's language of incorruptibility and immortality in 1 Cor 15:53–54 implies that procreation is unnecessary for resurrected persons and thus sexual differentiation is irrelevant, if it still exists at all.

to be circumcised or to observe Torah in one of the ways that was normative at the time.

Baptism and Identity in 1 Corinthians

Scholars often assume that the community Paul founded in Corinth included both Jews and Gentiles. An inscription discovered in the ancient city reads ΣΥΝΑΓ ΩΓΗ ΕΒΡΑΙΩΝ,[36] and Corinth is one of only two cities Philo mentions in a description of the Jewish Diaspora (*Legat.* 281).[37] So there was most likely a Jewish community there. Paul says that the only Corinthians he baptized personally were Crispus, Gaius, and Stephanas (1 Cor 1:14–16). Acts 18:8 describes Crispus, with reference to the synagogue in Corinth, as ὁ ἀρχισυνάγωγος. Some commentators assume or infer from this title that he was Jewish.[38] If, however, Tessa Rajak and David Noy are correct that important patrons were honored with this title and it should not be translated "leaders of the synagogue," Crispus may have been a benefactor of the synagogue and not Jewish at all.[39] In his introduction to 1 Corinthians in the revised *Harper Collins Study Bible*, Victor Furnish lists Prisca and Aquila as members of Paul's congregation in Corinth and describes the community as only "predominantly Gentile."[40] Near the end of First Corinthians Paul conveys greetings to his addressees from Aquila and Prisca, who at that time have "an assembly" or "church" meeting in their house in Asia, perhaps Ephesus (1 Cor 16:19).[41] When Paul wrote his letter

---

[36] Meeks, *First Urban Christians*, 48, 213, n. 276.

[37] See ibid., 48, 213, n. 274.

[38] E. Haenchen, *The Acts of the Apostles: A Commentary* (Philadelphia: Westminster: 1971), 535; cf. 407–8. Although Conzelmann does not discuss the identity of Crispus at all, he does provide cross-references to 1 Cor 1:14 and Acts 18:8, so he probably assumed that he was Jewish; *1 Corinthians: A Commentary* (Philadelphia: Fortress, 1975), 36 and n. 43; idem, *Acts of the Apostles: A Commentary* (Philadelphia: Fortress, 1987), 152.

[39] T. Rajak and D. Noy, "*ARCHISYNAGOGOI*: Office, Title and Social Status in the Graeco-Jewish Synagogue," *JRS* 83 (1993): 75–93, esp. 88–89; C. Mount, *Pauline Christianity: Luke–Acts and the Legacy of Paul* (Leiden: Brill, 2002), 131 and n. 126; see also 134–35.

[40] V. P. Furnish, "The First Letter of Paul to the Corinthians," in *The HarperCollins Study Bible: Fully Revised and Updated, New Revised Standard Version* (ed. H. W. Attridge; San Francisco: HarperSanFrancisco with the SBL, 2006), 1932.

[41] Paul himself writes from Ephesus (1 Cor 16:8).

to the Romans, probably from Corinth,[42] Prisca and Aquila were in Rome, and a congregation was meeting in their house (Rom 16:3–5). The association of the couple with Corinth in Acts 18 is unreliable.[43] Finally, some have seen the two parties in the dispute over food sacrificed to idols in 1 Cor 8–10 as identical with "the strong" (οἱ δυνατοί) and "the weak" (οἱ ἀδύνατοι) in Rom 14:1–15:13[44] and have understood "the weak" as including "Jewish Christians."[45] This hypothesis does not fit all the relevant passages.[46] Further, the two groups can be interpreted in other ways.[47] So it may well be the case that Paul's addressees in First Corinthians are exclusively Gentile.

In First Corinthians, Paul's rhetorical purpose is to persuade his addressees to put an end to their factions and to work toward unity.[48] In ch. 6 he rebukes them for bringing charges against insiders[49] in courts administered by outsiders.[50] He begins one of his arguments against such a practice with the principle that even to have accusations against each other is a defeat for them. It would be better to allow oneself to be wronged or defrauded than to do such a thing. This type of argument is common in literature urging concord.[51] From this lofty principle, Paul moves to a threat directed primarily, it would seem, to those who had wronged other members of the community. He declares, "Or do you not know that wrongdoers will not inherit the kingdom of God?" (1 Cor 6:9). He follows this rhetorical question with a list of ten types of wrongdoers. The first five refer to those who commit sexual sins, a list that evokes the

[42] R. Jewett, *Romans: A Commentary* (Minneapolis: Fortress Press, 2007), 18.

[43] Mount, *Pauline Christianity*, 131–39, esp. 133 and n. 138.

[44] For the terms, see 15:1.

[45] Jewett, *Romans*, 835; D. B. Martin, *The Corinthian Body* (New Haven: Yale University Press), 69, 263–4, n. 1.

[46] C. K. Barrett, *A Commentary on the First Epistle to the Corinthians* (New York: Harper & Row, 1968), 194.

[47] Martin, *Corinthian Body*, xv, xviii, 69, 264, n. 2.

[48] M. M. Mitchell has defined 1 Cor as a (single, unified) deliberative letter urging concord; *Paul and the Rhetoric of Reconciliation: An Exegetical Investigation of the Language and Composition of 1 Corinthians* (Louisville: Westminster John Knox, 1991), 65, 297–8.

[49] The "insiders" are dubbed οἱ ἅγιοι and the "outsiders" οἱ ἄδικοι; I take the terms "insiders" and "outsiders" here from Mitchell, *Paul and the Rhetoric*, 116.

[50] 1 Cor 6:1–11; the Greek terms cited in the previous note occur in v. 1.

[51] Mitchell, *Paul and the Rhetoric*, 116–17, n. 315.

ancient Jewish stereotype of "Gentile sinners."[52] After the list he states, "And that is what some of you were; but you have been washed, you have been consecrated, you have been justified through the name of the lord Jesus Christ and through the spirit of our God."[53]

Baptism is not explicitly mentioned here, but the reference to the addressees "being washed" surely refers to the rite. The idea that they were washed, sanctified, and justified "through the name of the lord Jesus Christ" recalls the formula spoken in connection with the immersion.[54] Paul's argument here thus links the activity of the divine spirit with baptism. This activity recalls the prediction attributed to John the Baptist in the Synoptic Gospels that the one who came after him would baptize with holy spirit.[55] Here baptism is interpreted as the washing away of sins, which is linked to consecration and justification. The idea of ritual immersion washing away sins recalls the baptism practiced by John with its goal of the forgiveness of sins.[56] The implication is that the transformation of the baptized is not complete once the ritual has been performed. It is an ongoing process that requires repeated efforts at moral reform and the practice of virtue.

The verb "baptize" itself occurs in the section dealing with the tensions between the faction claiming to have knowledge and thus the freedom to eat meat sacrificed to idols and the faction affirming that such eating is idolatrous.[57] Among the arguments Paul uses to reconcile these two factions is an example from the history of Israel. Just as in Galatians he played with the idea that the Jews are sons of Abraham, here he interprets "Israel" as those who had been baptized into Moses. Being baptized "into Moses" is a prototype of being baptized "into Christ."[58] In claiming that the events happened to the

---

[52] Conzelmann argued that the whole list is typical of Hellenistic Jewish apologetic literature in which catalogues of vice signified "pagan trademarks" (*1 Corinthians*, 100; see also 106).

[53] 1 Cor 6:11. I take the preposition ἐν in both phrases here as instrumental; so, apparently, did Conzelmann (*1 Corinthians*, 103).

[54] See the discussion of 1 Cor 1:13 above.

[55] Mark 1:8; Matt 3:11; Luke 3:16.

[56] Mark 1:4; Luke 3:3; cf. Matt 3:6.

[57] 1 Cor 8–10.

[58] I cannot agree with Mitchell (*Paul and the Rhetoric*, 138, n. 436) that the formula εἰς τὸ Μωυσῆν ἐβαπτίσθησαν signals "party membership" and parallels most directly εἰς τὸ ὄνομα Παύλου ἐβαπτίσθητε in 1 Cor 1:13. It seems more likely that the former is based directly on the formula known both to Paul

generation of the wilderness "as types for us" and that the story was written down as a warning for us,[59] he makes clear once again that the necessary transformation is not complete once baptism has been performed. Rather, we must take care not to become desirous of things that are evil as some, even most, of that generation did.[60] By alluding to the story of the golden calf (Exod 32:1–6) and presumably following an interpretation of it current at the time, Paul makes clear that the evil things they desired and did were idolatry and sexual immorality. According to this interpretation, the wilderness generation committed sins that were typical of Gentiles, according to the Jewish stereotype of Paul's time. He did something similar, as we have seen, in 1 Cor 6 as well as in Galatians. As the passage following the allusion to the wilderness generation shows,[61] Paul's point is that, in spite of their valid knowledge, the faction in favor of eating meat sacrificed to idols should abstain from it instead. He ends this part of the letter with advice that allows the faction claiming knowledge to eat such meat discreetly, but encourages abstinence whenever their freedom may scandalize others.[62]

The last passage in First Corinthians that I would like to discuss is 12:13.[63] As is widely recognized, in this chapter Paul extends "a common political metaphor to the Corinthian situation."[64] Paul uses the metaphor in the way it was typically used in Greek, Roman, and Hellenistic Jewish texts, that is, to combat factionalism.[65] In his application of the metaphor he links the body of Christ to baptism by affirming, "we were all baptized into one body." This affirmation is similar to the argument in Galatians that "you are all one in Christ Jesus."[66] This inference is confirmed by the use

---

and his audience, εἰς Χριστὸν βαπτισθῆναι. The statement about baptism into Moses corresponds to the general situation of his audience (without for the moment alluding to factionalism).

[59] 1 Cor 10:6, 11.

[60] 1 Cor 10:6.

[61] 1 Cor 10:14–22.

[62] 1 Cor 10:23–11:1.

[63] I leave aside Paul's reference to being baptized for the dead in 1 Cor 15:29, since discussion of it would take us too far afield.

[64] Mitchell, *Paul and the Rhetoric*, 160.

[65] Ibid., 161.

[66] Gal 3:28b.

of two of the three antitheses that occur in Galatians: "whether Jews or Greeks, whether slaves or free."[67] Here the contrasts are used somewhat differently. In Galatians Paul's point was that baptized Gentiles are descendants of Abraham and sons of God just as much as Jews of faith are. In this passage, the force of the antitheses is that such differences ought not lead to divisions since their abolition in the resurrection is anticipated by baptism.

As in 1 Cor 6, Paul links baptism and the spirit. Here, however, by saying that their baptism occurred "through *one* spirit," he uses that idea to work against divisions in the community. The unity of the spirit may also make the point that no spiritual gift is more important than the others.

A new element in this interpretation of baptism is the notion that "we have all drunk one spirit." The contrast with the image of "washing" in ch. 6 is striking. "Drinking the spirit" calls to mind Paul's discussion of the wilderness generation in ch. 10: "they all drank the same spiritual drink; for they drank from the spiritual rock that was following them, and the rock was Christ."[68] The context in ch. 10 suggests that the "spiritual drink" in the wilderness is a prototype of the cup of blessing, drunk at the lord's supper, which establishes a fellowship in the blood of Christ.[69] In 1 Cor 12, however, Paul picks up the image of drinking "spiritual drink" again and connects it with baptism. Paul may simply offer a different interpretation of Exod 17:6 in ch. 12. In any case, drinking from the "spiritual rock," which is Christ, can also be a prototype of baptism because Christ can be identified with "the spirit," as Paul does in 2 Cor 3:17.

Baptism and Identity in Romans

As Stanley Stowers has argued persuasively, the encoded audience of Paul's letter to the Romans is Gentiles in "Rome who know something about Jewish scripture and Jesus Christ."[70] The most

---

[67] 1 Cor 12:13.
[68] 1 Cor 10:4.
[69] 1 Cor 10:16.
[70] S. K. Stowers, *A Rereading of Romans: Justice, Jews, and Gentiles* (New Haven: Yale University

obvious purpose of the letter is "to elicit support for Paul's forthcoming mission in Spain."[71] In order to gain this support, however, Paul had to present and explain his gospel to his audience. We can only speculate as to why he had to do so.[72] I find credible the argument that his audience had heard something about his gospel from Paul's opponents and thus he needed to correct distortions of it.[73]

Romans 6 opens with a rhetorical question, "What shall we say then? Let us remain in sin so that grace may abound?" This question "sets up a false inference that could be drawn from the preceding argument."[74] The reply is "Of course not! How can we who have died to sin continue to live in it?" Paul then explains how we have died to sin: "Or do you not know that as many of us as have been baptized into Christ Jesus have been baptized into his death?"[75]

As noted earlier the brief formula recited during the rite of baptism about being baptized "into Christ" was ambiguous, and Paul exploited that ambiguity to craft interpretations of the rite that served his rhetorical purposes. Here his purpose is to argue that his proclamation of justification of the Gentiles apart from the law does not imply that they will continue to be sinful. He does so by introducing the idea that being baptized into Christ signifies being baptized "into his death." In Gal 2:19 he had declared that he himself has been crucified with Christ. Here he affirms that, in the case of all the baptized, the old self (ὁ παλαιὸς ἄνθρωπος) has been crucified with Christ.[76] This old self is equivalent to "the sinful body" (τὸ σῶμα τῆς ἁμαρτίας), which is the self under the dominion of sin and death.[77] The death of this self or body signifies freedom from slavery to sin.[78] Before Paul moves to this elaboration of his interpretation of baptism, however, he seems to interpret

---

Press, 1994), 21–22.

[71] Jewett, *Romans*, 80.

[72] As Jewett does (*Romans*, 88–91).

[73] Garroway, "Neither Jew nor Gentile," 99–103.

[74] Jewett, *Romans*, 394.

[75] Rom 6:3.

[76] Rom 6:6.

[77] Dahl, *Studies in Ephesians*, 396–7.

[78] Rom 6:6.

immersion as being "buried with [Christ]." The resurrection of Christ follows his burial, not directly upon his crucifixion.[79]

With his attention firmly fixed upon life in this world, Paul does not claim that in baptism we rise from the dead, as Christ has risen. Rather, "we walk in newness of life" or "we live a new [kind of earthly] life." Resurrection still belongs to the future: "For if we have grown together with the likeness of his death, we certainly will [also grow together with the likeness] of [his] resurrection."[80] The metaphor of "growing together" or "being planted with" the likeness of his death and resurrection may be related to the image of dying as being sown as a seed, an image that Paul had used in 1 Corinthians 15.

Toward the end of his argument regarding baptism, Paul sums up the example of Christ and applies it to his audience: "For in that he died, he died to sin once and for all; in that he lives, he lives to God. So also consider yourselves to be dead with respect to sin and alive with respect to God in Christ Jesus."[81] Once again the effectiveness of baptism is that it signifies a process that has begun but is not complete.

Conclusion

In the undisputed letters of Paul, he never speaks about baptism as a substitute for circumcision. It makes circumcision unnecessary for baptized Gentiles, but he never says that it is equivalent to circumcision. Further, as we have seen, he does not interpret baptism as signifying that the baptized have risen with Christ. The letter to the Colossians, probably written by an associate of Paul, does both: "In [Christ] also you were circumcised with a circumcision not made by hands with the stripping off of the body of flesh, with the circumcision of Christ. You were buried with him in baptism, in which you were also raised with him through faith in the effective power of God

---

[79] Rom 6:4.

[80] Rom 6:5.

[81] Rom 6:10–11; for the translation of v. 10, cf. E. Käsemann, *Commentary on Romans* (Grand Rapids: Eerdmans, 1980), 160, 170. With him I take the relative pronoun ὅ here as an accusative of object.

who raised him from the dead."[82] And so the creative production of interpretations of the transformative power of baptism continued in the work of Paul's successors. But that is a topic for another day.

---

[82] Col 2:11–12.

The Legal Status of the
Earliest Christian Churches

James D. G. Dunn
University of Durham

Introduction

Enquiry into the earliest spread of Christianity within the Roman Empire is surprisingly often hampered by anachronistic assumptions and by failure to ask appropriate (and necessary) historical questions. The most obvious anachronisms are the casual and unqualified use of terms to describe the participants in this new movement, terms whose historical usage and most characteristic definition only appear at a later date. The fact is that we cannot or should not yet speak of "Christianity," or even "Christian," *without qualification* during the earliest years. So far as we can tell, the term "Christianity" was not invented till the early second century.[1] And even the term "Christian" seems only to have been coming into use in the second half of the first century.[2] So to speak of "Christians" and "Christianity" during Paul's mission, for example, is liable to give a false impression, as though believers in Jesus belonged to and identified themselves as a clearly defined and an already widely recognized distinctive social

---

[1] First used by Ignatius—Ign. *Magn.* 10:1–3; *Rom.* 3:3; *Phil.* 6:1; also *Mart. Pol.* 10:1.

[2] Acts 11:26; 26:28; see also 1 Peter 4:16; Ign. *Eph.* 11:2; *Magn.* 4; *Trall.* 6:1; *Rom.* 3:2; *Pol.* 73; *Mart. Pol.* 3:2; 10:1; 12:1–2; *Did.* 12:4; *Diogn.* 1:1; 2:6, 10; 4:6; 5:1; 6:1–9; Pliny, *Ep.* 10.96. H. J. Cadbury, "Names for Christians and Christianity in Acts," in *Additional Notes to the Commentary* (ed. K. Lake and H. J. Cadbury; vol. 5 of *The Beginnings of Christianity: Part I: The Acts of the Apostles*, ed. F. J. Foakes Jackson and K. Lake; London: Macmillan, 1933), 375–92, makes the important observation: Luke's statement that they were called Christians at Antioch "for the first time [πρώτως]" (11:26) must imply his knowledge of subsequent usage (p. 386). However, it is noticeable that the term appears initially in the usage of those hostile to (or suspicious of) the new movement (Acts 26:28; Tacitus, *Ann.* 15.44.2; Suetonius, *Nero* 16.2). D. G. Horrell, "The Label *Christianos*: 1 Peter 4:16 and the Formation of Christian Identity," *JBL* 126 (2007): 383–91, argues that 1 Peter 4:16 indicates a stage where what was a hostile label, a form of stigma, is coming to be borne with pride by insiders (particularly 376–81). I return to the subject below.

entity. Similarly with the term "church," especially when used with a capital letter, "the Church," or "the primitive Church," as though believers in Messiah Jesus belonged to a clearly defined international organisation, which not only we now may discern with hindsight but which first century contemporaries would have recognized as well, just, in effect, as citizens today will be aware of the local church or cathedral building(s) in their town or city. After all, the term used, ἐκκλησία, still had the more general sense of "assembly," and could describe a variety of gatherings of the time. The fact that Luke, writing most probably in the late decades of the first century, uses names like "the way"[3] or "the sect of the Nazarenes,"[4] is a reminder that the movement which became "Christianity" was only beginning to gain regular and distinctive features.

The problem is compounded when the development of the new movement is set over against "Judaism" as though "Christianity" and "Judaism" were already distinctive religions whose separation was inevitable from the first. Of course, "Judaism" is used by Paul to refer to his way of life and religious practice prior to his conversion (Gal 1:13–14). But what he refers to is probably better described as *Pharisaic* Judaism, a major expression of his ancestral religion, marked by his extraordinary zeal (cf. also Phil 3:5–6), not the whole of what today is better referred to as first century Judaism or "Second Temple Judaism." His conversion was not from (Second Temple) "Judaism" to "Christianity," but from one Jewish sect (αἵρεσις) to another.[5] The problem is obvious: when historical representations of earliest Christianity resort to clear-cut contrasts between Christianity and Judaism, between Jews and Christians, or church and synagogue, then almost certainly a precision of description and identification is being given to relationships which in the event were much less clearly perceived and expressed.

Here however I want to focus on a different weakness in much

---

[3] Acts 9:2; see also 19:9, 23; 22:4; 24:14, 22; cf. 18:25–26; 2 Peter 2:2; possibly reflected in 1 Cor 12:31.

[4] Acts 24:5, 14; 28:22.

[5] Luke uses the term for different Second Temple Jewish sects (cf. Acts 24:5, 14 and 28:22 with 15:5 and 26:5).

historical enquiry into the earliest spread of embryonic Christianity within the Roman Empire. That is the failure to inquire into *the legal status of these earliest assemblies* of believers in Messiah/ Christ Jesus. It is one aspect of the larger issues just alluded to, but an important aspect, since in such a controlled society as the Roman empire within its largest conurbations, the legal status of these assemblies was crucial to their identity and even to their very existence. Which is why it is so surprising that studies of earliest Christianity, not least sociological studies and even those focusing on Rome itself, fail to ask about the legal status of the first such assemblies.[6] There is surely something wrong with any hypothesis regarding "Christian-Jewish" relations within mid-first century Rome which relies on sociological models but neglects to inquire into the social (including legal) realities of the historical context. This brief protest and plea will, I hope, be an appropriate theme for a contribution to the Festschrift of one who has contributed so much and so much of good sense in relation to the sociological study of the NT.[7]

The Legal Status of Roman *Collegia*

Since the pioneering work of Georg Heinrici and Edwin Hatch,[8] it has been increasingly recognized that the closest social parallel

---

[6] E.g. F. Watson, *Paul, Judaism and the Gentiles* (2d ed.; Cambridge: Cambridge University Press, 2007); P. F. Esler, *Conflict and Identity in Romans: The Social Setting of Paul's Letter* (Minneapolis: Fortress, 2003); S. Spence, *The Parting of the Ways: The Roman Church as a Case Study* (Leuven: Peeters, 2004).

[7] I think of course of Bengt's *Sociology and the New Testament: An Appraisal* (Fortress: Minneapolis, 1990), but particularly of his "The Methods of Historical Reconstruction in the Scholarly 'Recovery' of Corinthian Christianity," in E. Adams and D. G. Horrell, *Christianity at Corinth: The Quest for the Pauline Church* (Louisville: Westminster John Knox, 2004), 255–71. His warning against the misuse of sociological models, which "cannot substitute for evidence by filling in gaps in the data" (p. 270), echoes the earlier warning against the "sociological fallacy" by E. A. Judge, "The Social Identity of the First Christians: A Question of Method in Religious History," *JRH* 11 (1980): 201–17; also D. G. Horrell, *The Social Ethos of the Corinthian Correspondence: Interests and Ideology from 1 Corinthians to 1 Clement* (Edinburgh: T&T Clark, 1996), 11–18.

[8] G. Heinrici, "Die christengemeinden Korinths und die religiösen Genossenschaften der Griechen," *ZWT* 19 (1876): 465–526; E. Hatch, *The Organization of the Early Christian Churches* (London: Longmans, 1888).

to the earliest Christian churches were the *collegia*, the voluntary associations or clubs in Roman society. Indeed, the argument of Heinrici and Hatch was that the first Christians imitated the *collegia* in structure and organisation. The information from literary sources on the associations in particular is modest, but the steadily increasing resources of epigraphical data from the later decades of the 19th century and throughout the 20th century have illuminated the historical context with increasing clarity.[9] Already at the beginning of the 20th century Samuel Dill was able to demonstrate how the epigraphical data have opened up to us the world of the great majority of lower-status inhabitants of Roman cities. The point is of crucial importance for the study of Christianity's beginnings, since the literature of the period is so dominated by the ancient perception of history as "the history of kings and queens," or here we should rather say, the history of consuls and emperors, and since the great majority of the first non-Jewish believers in Messiah Jesus were themselves of lower status.

Given the degree of parallel between the associations and the meetings of the first believers in Christ Jesus, the legal status of the associations is of particular interest. Unfortunately the situation is not as clear as would have been most helpful. Technically, associations had to be formally licensed; according to the *Lex Iulia* enacted by Augustus (probably in 7 C.E.) every club must be sanctioned by the senate or emperor.[10] And some would argue on this basis that,

> At least since the time of Augustus, the formation of clubs and associations had been carefully regulated. A *collegium* could apply to the senate for permission, which was granted when a case could be made that some public good would derive from it and no activities damaging to the state were anticipated."[11]

---

[9] Still of immense value is the collection of inscriptional data and its cataloguing by J.-P. Waltzing, *Études historique sur les corporations professionnelles chez les Romains* (4 vols.; Leiden: Peeters, 1895–1900; repr., Hildesheim: George Olms, 1970).

[10] *OCD* 3.352.

[11] U. Schnelle, *Paul: His Life and Theology* (Grand Rapids: Baker Academic, 2005), 154 n. 66, citing M. Öhler, "Römisches Vereinsrecht und christliche Gemeinden," in *Zwischen den Reichen: Neues Testament und römisches Reich* (ed. M. Labahn and J. Zangenberg; Tübingen: Francke,

There is also good evidence of official suspicion of such associations and of bans being imposed on political and occasionally riotous clubs.[12] Often quoted is Trajan's observation to Pliny, in response to the latter's suggestion that an association of firemen might be formed in the province (Bithynia), that "Whatever name we may give for whatever reason to those who come together for a common purpose, political clubs emerge quickly from them" (Pliny, *Ep.* 10.34).

On the other hand, there is little or no evidence that clubs actually had to or did seek official approval and we may rather assume that unlicensed groups were tolerated as long as they did nothing illegal or offensive. The suspicion and infrequent bans directed against overtly political or occasionally riotous clubs do not indicate a negative attitude to associations in general. Philip Harland concludes his discussion of the subject: "Most associations would continue to function openly and undisturbed . . . intervention occurred only when associations were caught up in broader disorderly incidents that were not adequately dealt with locally."[13] For the most part, associations served important aspects of the social, cultural and religious needs of the broad civic community, particularly the middle- and lower-ranking members of society, regularly acting as friendly or welfare societies for their members, including provision of a good burial.[14]

The key point to emerge from this is that while the Roman authorities fully recognized and accepted the social role of the voluntary associations, they nevertheless were instinctively cautious about the possible or even potential dangers of active combinations and social groupings—no doubt much as the British government in late 18th and early 19th centuries took precautions against the potential economic and political ambitions of combinations of

---

2002), 51–71, esp. 61. See also R. Ascough, *Paul's Macedonian Associations: The Social Context of Philippians and 1 Thessalonians* (Tübingen: Mohr Siebeck, 2003), 42–46.

[12] See particularly W. Cotter, "The Collegia and Roman Law: State Restrictions on Voluntary Associations," in *Voluntary Associations in the Graeco-Roman World* (ed. J. S. Kloppenborg and S. G. Wilson; London: Routledge, 1996), 74–89.

[13] P. A. Harland, *Associations, Synagogues, and Congregations: Claiming a Place in Ancient Mediterranean Society* (Minneapolis: Fortress, 2003), 166.

[14] This last point is Harland's main thesis; see his *Associations* particularly pp. 10–14 and chs. 3 and 6.

working men.[15] There is no suggestion that the various churches established by Paul or those in Rome would have had to seek permission from the authorities for their meetings. But the degree of nervousness in the face of harassment displayed in Paul's counsel in Rom 12:14–21, and the strong advice to his audiences that they should keep their heads down and be good citizens respecting the authorities, paying their taxes (13:1–7), and not acting riotously in their assemblies (13:11–14), strongly suggest that Paul was well aware of how vulnerable the little tenement churches were, particularly in the center of the empire itself.[16]

The Legal Status of the Jewish Synagogues

The Jewish Diaspora was extensive in the Roman Empire, Jews being present in substantial numbers in most of the main cities of the empire.[17] It was Roman policy to allow national and ethnic groups to maintain their own religion and customs, and this applied particularly to the Jews. Since Jewish support had been of crucial importance for Julius Caesar in his conflict in Egypt (Josephus, *A.J.* 14.127–139), he and his successors were generally well disposed towards the Jews. In particular, Caesar and Augustus had given Jewish synagogues formal recognition and Caesar expressly exempted Jewish communities from any bans on *collegia*.[18] Josephus makes a point of documenting these decrees and rulings;[19]

---

[15] The Combination Acts of 1799 and 1800 made trade unionism illegal. There were also clauses forbidding employers' combinations, but they never seem to have been enforced.

[16] Livy's account of the suppression of the Bacchanalia in 186 (39.8–19) gives a good indication of the suspicion with which the authorities regarded foreign cults and of the way in which they could gather information; see S. Benko, "Pagan Criticism of Christianity During the First Two Centuries," *ANRW* 2.23:1055–118, esp. 1066–7.

[17] On the spread of Jews throughout the Mediterranean see already J. Juster, *Les Juifs dans l'empire romain: Leur condition juridique, économique et sociale* (2 vols.; Paris: Geunther, 1914), 1:180–209. There were many more Jews living in the diaspora than in the land of Israel itself; see e.g. V. Tcherikover, *Hellenistic Civilization and the Jews* (Philadelphia: Jewish Publication Society of America, 1959) who notes varying estimates (pp. 504–5).

[18] Philo, *Leg.* 156–158; Josephus, *A.J.* 14.215. See further E. M. Smallwood, *The Jews under Roman Rule from Pompey to Diocletian* (Leiden: Brill, 1981), 133–38.

[19] *A.J.* 14.185–267; 16.160–179, including severe warnings to the local authorities in Tralles,

no wonder, since they secured the toleration of and protection for Jewish laws and customs in the empire. These rights included the right of assembly, the right to administer their own finances (including the exceptional permission for the temple tax to be collected and transmitted to Jerusalem), jurisdiction over their own members (including the power to administer corporal punishment, see 2 Cor 11:24), freedom from military service (because of the Jewish requirement to observe the Sabbath), and not least in importance, permission not to participate in the imperial cult.[20]

It is important to underscore the fact that the Jewish συναγωγαί (synagogues) were thus officially regarded as equivalent to, on a par with the *collegia* and θίασοι (religious guilds) of other national and religious groups—the Jewish ethnic association, the devotees of the cult of Kyrios Yahweh, the practitioners of the philosophy taught by Moses. It is also important to note that in most conurbations the Jewish community would have been held in high respect. In particular, Peter Richardson notes that four or five of the synagogues known to us in Rome in the first century had significant names: the Augustesians, the Agrippesians, the Volumnesians, and probably the Herodians.[21] Synagogues could not be named after such powerful individuals (Augustus himself; Marcus Agrippa, Augustus' right-hand man; Herod the Great; Volumnius, probably a tribune of Syria) without their knowledge and permission, which must imply a high degree of status accorded to and social integration achieved by these synagogues.

These συναγωγαί would, of course, have been one of the more homogeneous associations, consisting of Jews as the core members and participants in the synagogue's corporate life. At the same time, however, the typical diaspora synagogue was evidently not an exclusive association, since it welcomed non-Jewish adherents

---

Miletus, Pergamum, Halicarnassus, Sardis and Ephesus (14.241–264).

[20] Full detail in E. Schürer, *The History of the Jewish People in the Age of Jesus Christ: Revised and edited by G. Vermes and F. Millar* (4 vols.; Edinburgh: T&T Clark, 1973–1987), 3.113–23. See further M. Tellbe, *Paul between Synagogue and State: Christians, Jews, and Civic Authorities in 1 Thessalonians, Romans and Philippians* (Stockholm: Almqvist & Wiksell International, 2001), 26–63.

[21] P. Richardson, "Augustan-Era Synagogues in Rome," in *Judaism and Christianity in First-Century Rome* (ed. K. P. Donfried and P. Richardson; Grand Rapids: Eerdmans, 1998), 17–29, esp. 19–28.

and sympathizers (God-fearers) in their gatherings.[22] It was this attractiveness of Jewish beliefs and customs which caused friction in Roman society, since it was it was regarded as insulting to Roman *dignitas* for any Roman to embrace a foreign identity (the national religion of the Judeans).[23] The situation became so serious on several occasions, that government action was taken against the Jewish community in Rome, despite the tradition of special privileges being given to the synagogue congregations. Within the memory of the first generation of Roman Jewish believers in Messiah Jesus Jewish rites had been proscribed by Tiberius (19 C.E.) and Jews expelled from Rome;[24] Cassius Dio also records that (in 41 C.E.) Claudius "ordered them [the Jews], while continuing their traditional mode of life, not to hold meetings" (60.6.6); and the famous record of Suetonius reports a further expulsion of Jews from Rome, probably in 49, since they "constantly made disturbances because of the instigator Chrestus [*impulsore Chresto*]" (*Claud.* 25.4).[25] And we should not forget that the reason why Josephus quoted all the decrees in favor of the Jewish communities in Asia Minor was because of the potential friction between such Diaspora communities and their host cities which occasionally exploded

---

[22] On "God-fearers" see particularly Schürer, *History,* 3.165–8; P. Trebilco, *Jewish Communities in Asia Minor* (Cambridge: Cambridge University Press, 1991), ch. 7; J. M. Lieu, "The Race of the God-fearers," *JTS* 46 (1995): 483–501; I. Levinskaya, *The Book of Acts in its Diaspora Setting* (vol. 5 of *The Book of Acts in Its Ancient Literary Setting*; ed. B. W. Winter; Grand Rapids: Eerdmans, 1996), chs. 4–7, especially the review of the epigraphic evidence in ch. 4; B. Wander, *Gottesfürchtige und Sympathisanten: Studien zum heidnischen Umfeld von Diasporasynagogen* (Tübingen: Mohr Siebeck, 1998).

[23] See e.g. the texts cited by M. Whittaker, *Jews and Christians: Graeco-Roman Views* (Cambridge: Cambridge University Press, 1984), 85–91; L. H. Feldman, *Jew and Gentile in the Ancient World: Attitudes and Interactions from Alexander to Justinian* (Princeton: Princeton University Press, 1993), particularly 298–300, 344–8.

[24] Because "they were converting many of the natives to their ways" (Cassius Dio 57.18.5a; cf. Seneca, *Ep.* 108.22); Tacitus, *Ann.* 2.85.4—"the proscription of Egyptian and Jewish rites"; Suetonius, *Tiberius* 36—"he abolished foreign cults, especially the Egyptian and Jewish rites . . . [and] banished [Jews] from the city."

[25] The two events (41 and 49) are frequently confused, but most likely two separate events are in view. See e.g. A. Momigliano, *Claudius: The Emperor and his Achievement* (Oxford: Clarendon, 1934), 31–37; Smallwood, *Jews,* 210–16; R. Riesner, *Paul's Early Period: Chronology, Mission Strategy, Theology* (Grand Rapids: Eerdmans, 1998), 157–201; Spence, *Parting,* 65–112; S. Cappelletti, *The Jewish Community of Rome from the Second Century BCE to the Third Century CE* (Leiden: Brill, 2006), 69–89.

into serious unrest or riot in cities like Antioch and Alexandria.

The point to emerge here too is that however sound the standing of Jewish synagogues in the Roman empire, however strong their civic approbation, city authorities were so sensitive to potential unrest and so quick to act against associations and religious communities when they became a cause or focus of unrest, that the leaders of such associations and communities had always to be on their guard.

The Legal Status of the First Churches

What then of the standing of the first gatherings of believers in Messiah/Christ Jesus? The most obvious answer is that *they were able to shelter under the authorizations so fully provided for the diaspora Jewish synagogues.* After all, this was a movement which clearly sprang from within Second Temple Judaism and was thoroughly Jewish in character.

Consider first the titles used for the first believers in Messiah/Christ Jesus. They were the "sect of the Nazarenes," and "Nazarenes" was the name by which the Syrian Christians (and the Christians of the eastern empire) became known thereafter;[26] the movement was identified with the Jewish prophet from Nazareth. Similarly "Galileans" persisted as a name,[27] taken up particularly by Julian, who continually links Galileans with Jews;[28] the deep roots of embryonic Christianity in Jesus' Jewish identity and Galilean mission were well enough known. What about the title which was to become most enduring—"Christian"? The inquirer would no doubt have it explained to him that the "Christ" was the Messiah of Jewish expectation; and the opponent would find the fact even more intriguing. More to the point, the fact that Χριστιανοί is a Latinism (the Greek rendering

---

[26] H. H. Schaeder, "Ναζαρηνός, Ναζωραῖος," *TDNT* 4.874–5; see further 875–8.

[27] Thus Epictetus (*Diatr.* 4.7.6): "Therefore, if madness can produce this attitude [of detachment] toward these things [death, loss of family, property], and also habit, as with the Galileans, can no one learn from reason and demonstration that God has made all things in the universe, and the whole universe itself, to be unhindered and complete in itself, and the parts of it to serve the needs of the whole."

[28] Julian, *Contra Galilaeos.*

of *Christiani*) indicates that it was a title initially coined by the Roman authorities rather than a self-designation freely chosen by the first believers themselves. Moreover, as Edwin Judge points out,

> The Greek-speaking synagogues in Rome used the Greek suffix *-esioi* in their names. The suffix *-ianus* constitutes a political comment. . . . It is not used of the followers of a god. It classifies people as partisans of a political or military leader, and is mildly contemptuous.[29]

This strongly suggests that the Roman authorities regarded the participants in this new movement as followers of the person known as "Christ," in some cases making the mistake of thinking that this Christ person was himself active in leading his followers.[30] The important corollary is that the *Christiani* were not perceived as a new cult distinct from the religion of the Jews,[31] but as *a faction within Second Temple Judaism, partisans of the Jew called Christ.*[32]

It should also be noted that Paul's mission almost invariably began in the synagogues of a new city. The point has been repeatedly questioned, particularly in German scholarship, as an expression of an idée fixe that Luke's account of Christianity's beginnings in the book of Acts is consistently unreliable where any theological *Tendenz* is visible.[33] That Paul saw himself as "apostle to the Gentiles" (Rom 11:13) is also seen by many to be sufficient reason to question Luke's account of Paul beginning his mission

---

[29] E. A. Judge, "Judaism and the Rise of Christianity: A Roman Perspective," *TynBul* 45 (1994): 355–68, esp. 363.

[30] This seems to be the case with the famous reference of Suetonius, *Claud.* 25.4, where the assumption seems to be that "Chrestus" was the name of the instigator of the disturbances in Rome.

[31] K. Haacker, "Paul's Life," in *The Cambridge Companion to St Paul* (ed. J. D. G. Dunn; Cambridge: Cambridge University Press, 2003), 19–33, points out that "The very form of the term *Christianoi* does not sound like the name of a new cult worshipping Christ: the appropriate term for such a cultic fellowship would have been *Christastai*" (p. 26).

[32] A. M. Schwemer, "Paulus in Antiochien," *BZ* 42 (1998): 161–80, notes that a recently discovered inscription from the year 20, dealing with the trial against Cn. Calpurnius Piso, charged with the murder of Germanicus, includes the information that the Roman troops in Syria were divided into *Pisoniani* and *Caesariani*, and that this *senatus consultum* was to be prominently displayed on bronze tablets in the most crowded thoroughfare (pp. 171–2).

[33] E.g. W. Schmithals, *Paul and James* (London: SCM, 1965), 60 ("almost impossible to imagine"). The *Tendenz* discerned here would be Luke's concern to "re-Judaize" Paul.

in the synagogue.[34] The possibility apparently does not occur to such scholars that Paul could have seen his mission to *Gentiles* as most effectively carried out, initially at least, in the *synagogue*— that is, directed to winning those God-fearing Gentiles who were already attracted to Judaism but inhibited by the full demands of the law and circumcision from becoming proselytes. When such a well-prepared and already interested Gentile audience was so conveniently to hand, it would be surprising indeed if Paul had not seized the opportunity which the presence of such God-fearing Gentiles in Jewish synagogues gave him; effective alternatives open to him are both obscure and equally unattested in Paul's letters. It is certainly the case, explicitly in Acts and implicitly in Paul's letters, that a breach with the local synagogue(s) regularly followed after some time, though not a breach sought by Paul himself. What would the authorities have made of this? Not, we may infer, that a new cult had been established, a new religion to be identified as distinct from the religion of the Jews. Rather that the local Jewish community was rent by different factions unable to worship together. Insofar as the breach came to their attention, the most likely conclusion they would draw is that there had been a synagogue schism, that a dissenting faction within the Jewish community had set up an alternative meeting/synagogue. Or if the breach was not particularly newsworthy in the reports of the authorities' various agents and informants, they would presumably infer that some new house groups had been set up within the Jewish synagogue community.

The one case where we hear of the authorities being required to take a view of such a breach within the synagogue (or from the synagogue) is in Luke's account of the establishment of the church in Corinth (Acts 18:12–17). This is the occasion when, according to Luke, representatives of the Jewish community in Corinth brought charges against Paul before the Roman proconsul, Gallio,

---

[34] E.g. E. P. Sanders, *Paul, the Law and the Jewish People* (Philadelphia: Fortress, 1983), 179–90; W. A. Meeks, *The First Urban Christians: The Social World of the Apostle Paul* (New Haven: Yale University, 1983), 26; J. L. Martyn, *Galatians* (New York: Doubleday, 1997), 213–16; L. M. White, *From Jesus to Christianity: How Four Generations of Visionaries & Storytellers Created the New Testament and Christian Faith* (San Francisco: HarperOne, 2004), 171–2.

charges which Gallio brusquely dismissed. Luke of course makes much of Gallio's ruling, but rather as Josephus was able to cite historic decrees in favor of diaspora Jewish communities;[35] so the most likely reading of Acts 18 is that Luke was able to draw on an important historical judicial ruling at this point.[36] The relevance and importance of this legal judgment is that Gallio was in effect *ruling on the status of the church/assembly recently established by Paul.*

In is noticeable that the charge brought against Paul is different from the earlier charge of fomenting civil and political unrest in Thessalonica (17:6–7; cf. 16:20–21). Here the complaint is that Paul's mission was "persuading people to worship God contrary to the law" (18:13). The last phrase is ambiguous, probably deliberately so. On the one hand, it would be intended to trigger Roman suspicion of new sects and remind the authorities of various rulings in the past which had been handed down to prevent such sects making inroads into the traditional and civic cults (with consequent disturbance of civic functions and good order).[37] On the other, it would express the synagogue's real complaint: that Jews and God-fearers affiliated to the synagogue were being encouraged to worship without regard to the (Jewish) law (that is, its distinctively Jewish features).[38]

According to Luke, the peremptory ruling which followed was addressed to all the participants as "Jews" (18:14–15).

---

[35] See n. 19 above.

[36] As A. N. Sherwin-White, *Roman Society and Roman Law in the New Testament* (Oxford: Clarendon, 1963) notes: "The narrative in fact agrees very well with the workings of *cognitio extra ordinem*. It is within the competence of the judge to decide whether to accept a novel charge or not. In the middle of the second century there were proconsuls of Asia who were ready to refuse to accept even the generally recognized charges against Christians, and to dismiss them out of hand" (pp. 99–100, 102; see further pp. 99–104).

[37] Cf. K. Lake and H. J. Cadbury, eds., *English Translation and Commentary* (vol 4 of *The Beginnings of Christianity: Part I. The Acts of the Apostles*; ed. F. J. Foakes Jackson and K. Lake; London: Macmillan 1933), 227; Sherwin-White, *Roman Society,* 101–2; B. W. Winter, "Acts and Roman Religion: The Imperial Cult," in *The Book of Acts in its Graeco-Roman Setting* (ed. D. W. Gill and C. Gempf; vol 2 of *The Book of Acts in Its First Century Setting,* ed B. W. Winter; Grand Rapids: Eerdmans, 1994), 93–103.

[38] The imperial edicts recorded by Josephus (n. 19 again) which secured Jewish rights permitted them to live in accordance with their law, so that departure from the law could be counted a breach of the edict. The precedent had been established a century earlier by the local magistrates in Sardis confirming that the resident Jews had the right to decide their own "affairs and controversies with one another" (Josephus, *A.J.* 14.235).

> If it was a crime or wicked fraud, (which) you Jews (bring before me), I would have been justified in accepting your complaint. But if it is questions regarding words and labels and the law which you observe, you must see to it yourselves; I have no intention of acting as judge in these matters.

The importance of this ruling for the earliest churches of Paul's foundation should not be underestimated. For one thing, it refuted the suggestion that believers in Messiah Jesus were in breach of any Roman law, whether in their worship or in their evangelism. And for another, it affirmed that the disputes between the young church and the traditional synagogue were internal to the Jewish community,[39] issues to be determined within their own jurisdiction.[40] The consequences of such a ruling and precedent from such a prominent Roman authority would have been immense.[41] (1) On the legal and political front, the young churches would have been freed at a stroke from the threat of criminal actions against them (for the time being at any rate). They could shelter under the legal protection afforded to synagogues—a vitally important immunity in an empire constantly alert to the possibility that combinations and associations might foster unrest against the state. (2) More broadly, it was equally important that the new groups of disciples should be recognized as part of diaspora Judaism. Nascent Christianity was not yet seen as something distinct from its parent religion; the young churches were still recognized to be both continuous and of a piece with the network of Jewish

---

[39] The reference to "words and labels [περὶ λόγου καὶ ὀνομάτων]" (18:15) may refer to arguments on whether Jesus was indeed "Messiah," but also on whether the new ἐκκλησία could indeed be regarded as part of the Jewish community (just another συναγωγή).

[40] Such Jewish jurisdiction is implicit in Paul's submission to synagogue discipline/punishment in 2 Cor 11:24.

[41] B. W. Winter, *After Paul Left Corinth: The Influence of Secular Ethics and Social Change* (Grand Rapids: Eerdmans, 2001) points out that Corinth modelled itself on Rome (p. 19), so that the influence of a ruling established there would have carried all the more weight; "this brother [Gallio] of Seneca the philosopher was himself a leading jurist, and therefore his ruling was of importance" (p. 279); see also Winter's "Rehabilitating Gallio and his Judgement in Acts 18:14–15," *TynBul* 57 (2006): 291–308. L. V. Rutgers, "Roman Policy toward the Jews: Expulsions from the City of Rome during the First Century C.E.," in *Judaism and Christianity in First-Century Rome* (ed. K. P. Donfried and P. Richardson; Grand Rapids: Eerdmans, 1998), 93–116, notes that Rome had no settled policy on such matters; and legal precedents were important (pp. 94–96).

synagogues scattered round most of the Mediterranean world.

The most obvious deduction to draw from all this is that for the first decade or two of their existence, the churches established by the Gentile mission were seen as part of the local Jewish community, including its penumbra of Gentile God-fearers who linked themselves in some degree with the local synagogue. Even when there was a breach with the traditionalist Jews in a local situation, to the extent that the authorities took note of such a breach, it would most likely have been understood as an internal controversy within the Jewish community. In terms of legal status, *the earliest churches would most likely have been able to shelter* (to the extent that was necessary) *under the license given to and provisions made for the Jewish community to continue observing their own religious customs.*

When Then Were Christians Seen to be Separate from the Jewish Community?

How long was it possible for the earliest churches to shelter under the protection afforded in the empire to Jewish synagogues? Longer, I think, than most historians of earliest Christianity have tended to infer. I have already questioned whether the very title of "Christian" first recorded in Antioch (Acts 11:26) indicates a clear division between church and synagogue.[42] The common inference that the decree of Claudius expelling Jews from Rome in 49 must have resulted in a clear division between tenement church and well established synagogue in Rome is equally open to question. For one thing we do not know how many Jews were expelled.[43] And the assumption that when Jewish believers returned

---

[42] Contrast J. Becker, *Paul: Apostle to the Gentiles* (Louisville: John Knox, 1993): "It is a name that points to the independence of the group . . . an already independent group" (p. 87); and C. K. Barrett, *The Acts of the Apostles* (2 vols.; Edinburgh: T&T Clark, 1994) who is not untypical, but in fact quite anachronistic when he suggests that the coining of the title "Christians" already implied that Christians were "a third race" "clearly distinguishable from Jews" (1.548, 556).

[43] R. E. Brown, in R. E. Brown and J. P. Meier, *Antioch and Rome: New Testament Cradles of Catholic Christianity* (London: Chapman, 1983) suggests only "those Jews who were the most vocal on either side of the Christ issue" (pp. 102, 109); J. Murphy- O'Connor, *Paul: A Critical Life* (Oxford:

to Rome they would have formed different churches from the Gentile churches, and that they (both) would have been distinct from all the Roman synagogues[44] runs counter to the evidence of Romans itself that there were tenement and house groups which included both traditionalist Jews and Gentiles.[45] It certainly cannot be inferred that the traditionally practicing Jewish believers had abandoned their membership of their synagogues and severed their associations with the large and varied Jewish community of Rome.

The account of Paul's coming to Rome in Acts 28 is most unhelpful at this point, since it hardly refers to the churches which we know from Paul's letter to Rome to have been already established in Rome. But at least its account of Paul in continuing discursive relationship with the Jews of Rome (Acts 28:17–31) should not be dismissed out of hand. Almost equally and frustratingly obscure is what may be drawn from Paul's reference to tensions between believers in Rome during his imprisonment there. I refer to Phil

Clarendon, 1996) thinks that the edict of Claudius "concerned only a single synagogue in Rome" (pp. 12, 14); "one or several Roman synagogues" (Riesner, *Paul's Early Life*, 195). It is certainly unlikely that Claudius expelled the whole Jewish community (reckoned at more than 40,000), despite Acts 18:2 ("all Jews").

[44] E.g. U. Schnelle, *The History and Theology of the New Testament Writings* (London: SCM, 1994), the expulsions of 49 "accomplished the final separation between the Christian community and the synagogue" (p. 112); H. Lichtenberger, "Jews and Christians in Rome in the Time of Nero: Josephus and Paul in Rome," *ANRW* 2.26: 2142–76, esp. 2168, 2173; R. Hvalvik, "Jewish Believers and Jewish Influence in the Roman Church until the Early Second Century," in O. Skarsaune and R. Hvalvik, eds., *Jewish Believers in Jesus: The Early Centuries* (Peabody: Hendrickson, 2007), 179–216, esp. 198–99. Spence concludes a lengthy study of "'Christianity' and the Synagogue of Rome": "it is certain that by the time Paul wrote to the Christians in Rome, there existed a social community distinct from the synagogue and consisting of ethnic-Jews and ethnic-Gentiles brought together by faith in Jesus Christ"; his thesis is "that the expulsion [in 49 under Claudius] resulted in either the establishment of a Christian community in Rome distinct from the Jewish community or hastened its development" (*Parting*, 117). But his discussion is flawed by repeated reference to the "church" as a clearly defined entity (e.g. 31–32, 60–61)—he dismisses the significance of the absence of ἐκκλησία from Rom 1:7 too lightly (pp. 281–3); and the appeal to Acts 28 (pp. 10, 114) is undermined by Luke's failure to mention any believers in Rome itself.

[45] Rom 14:1–15:6 envisages mixed congregations—mixed between those following traditional Jewish observation of the laws of clean and unclean (presumably predominantly believing Jews) and those who sat loose to such laws and customs (presumably predominantly believing Gentiles); the fullest recent discussion is by M. Reasoner, *The Strong and the Weak: Romans 14.1–15.13 in Context* (Cambridge: Cambridge University Press, 1999). In the concluding Rom 16 several Jews are among those greeted; Peter Lampe estimates the Jewish component of the Roman Christians in Rom 16 as 15 percent ("The Roman Christians of Romans 16," in K. P. Donfried, ed., *The Romans Debate* [Peabody: Hendrickson, 1991], 216–30, esp. 225), a figure Spence thinks is too low (*Parting*, 277).

1:15–18, assuming, at least for the purposes of this essay that Philippians was written in Rome.[46] Should the "envy and rivalry" referred to there be linked with the tensions of Rom 14 and attributed in part at least to Jewish believers' antipathy to Paul's law-free gospel? If so, we should note that the rivalry is again intra-church, and may have arisen in (large) part at least from the continuing loyalties of the Jewish believers to their synagogue congregations,

In all this it should not be forgotten that for three further centuries a significant proportion of Christians continued to frequent the synagogue on Saturday and to observe the Jewish feasts. We know this from the frequency of exhortations and rulings made by church leaders to dissuade their congregations from so acting.[47] Such continuity of practice must reflect a deeply rooted recognition that Christianity was an offshoot of Judaism, and a continuing desire to maintain the continuum between the two. The situation would have been somewhat like that of the Reformation or even the beginnings of Methodism, when there was as much desire to maintain the continuity of identity as there was recognition that a different structure was unavoidable. The "parting of the ways" between Judaism and Christianity, however divergent from Jewish tradition many/most Pauline founded churches were, did not happen during Paul's life and would have been contrary to his most ardent desires (Rom 9–11).

The most likely occasion for the distinctiveness of the earliest Christians from the wider Jewish community to become clear was the first substantial Roman persecution, under Nero, in 64. The dismal story of Christians being blamed for the great fire of Rome is familiar from the account of Tacitus (*Ann.* 15.44.2–5), written probably during the second decade of the second century:

---

[46] See particularly P. T. O'Brien, *Commentary on Philippians* (Grand Rapids: Eerdmans, 1991), 19–26; Schnelle, *History*, 131–3; also *Paul*, 367–9; M. Bockmuehl, *The Epistle to the Philippians* (London: A & C Black, 1997), 25–32.

[47] I refer to Ignatius, *Magn.* 8–10; Justin, *Dial.* 61; Origen, *Hom. Lev.* 5.8; *Sel. Exod.* 12.46; Chrysostom, *Adv. Jud.* 1; the Council of Laodicea (Canons 16, 29, 37, 38); and *Apos. Con.* 2.61; 5.17; 6.27, 30; 7.23; 8.33, 47; Jerome instances the converted Jew who continues to practise circumcision, to observe the Sabbath, to abstain from (unclean) foods and to keep the Passover (*Epist.* 67.4; 112.15).

> [T]o scotch the rumour [that the fire had taken place to order], Nero substituted as culprits, and punished with the utmost refinements of cruelty a class of men, loathed for their vices, whom the crowd styled Christians [*Christianos*]. . . . First, then, those who confessed were arrested; next, on their disclosures vast numbers [*multitudo ingens*] were convicted, not so much on the count of arson as for hatred of the human race [*odio humani generis*].

What is clearly implied here is that those known as "Christians" were a distinct and recognizable body of people who could be identified and arrested. One can readily envisage that the surge of evangelistic activity referred to in Phil 1:12–18 drew increasing numbers into the movement (Tacitus speaks of "vast numbers") and made the populace at large more aware of the movement. The fact that Tacitus attributes the name "Christians" to the crowd perhaps suggests that the identification was a result of Nero's agents looking for scapegoats and only thus becoming fully aware of "Christians" as a distinct and substantial group. What is quite unclear is whether there was any Jewish involvement in the denunciation of the "Christians," a disowning by the more established Jewish community of the treacherous new movement of Jesus Messiah.[48]

What can be said with more assurance, however, is that Tacitus himself probably did not think of the Christians as clearly distinct from the Jews of Rome. His charge of "hatred of the human race" is a standard charge against the Jews.[49] So it is quite likely that Tacitus at least saw the Christians as a form of Judaism, even though they could be distinguished more precisely as "Christians." This likelihood is strengthened by the later account by the Christian writer Sulpicius Severus of the climax to the siege of Jerusalem, for which Tacitus is possibly the source.[50] This account refers to "the religion [singular]

---

[48] Discussion in Smallwood, *Jews* 218-9.

[49] See details in M. Stern, *Greek and Latin Authors on Jews and Judaism* (3 vols.; Jerusalem: Israel Academy of Sciences and Humanities, 1976–1984), 2.93. As Benko notes: "It cannot be mere coincidence, that the *odium humani generis* with which Tacitus charges the Christians in the Annals 15.44 is nearly the same expression that he uses concerning the Jews in Histories 5.5.1" ("Pagan Criticism of Christianity," 1064).

[50] So argued in Stern, *Greek and Latin Authors,* 2.64–67. The manuscript of Tacitus' *Annals* breaks

of the Jews and Christians." The account continues:

> those religions [plural], though opposed to one another, derive
> from the same founders; the Christians stemmed from the Jews
> [*Christianos ex Judaeis*] and the extirpation of the root would easily
> cause the offspring to perish.

The ambivalence ("religion"/"religions") suggests that Christian
identity emerging in that period was both confused and confusing:
were "Christians" the same as Jews, or a separate religion?
Had Gentile converts become members of a Jewish sect?

Perhaps the distinction between Jew and Christian, the
distinctiveness of Christian from Jew, only became clear after the
Jewish war turned political and social opinion turned against the
Jews generally. At the legal level this turn against Jews was marked
by the institution of the *fiscus Iudaicus*, a poll tax levied on all Jews
after the Jewish war of 66–70. Initially it was levied only on Jews,
that is, ethnic Jews, but apparently not on Gentile proselytes. Under
Domitian, however, the *fiscus Iudaicus* was exacted "with utmost
vigour" (*acerbissime*). That is, according to Suetonius, people who
had previously been exempt from the tax were now compelled to pay
it. Suetonius identifies those affected: "those who without publicly
acknowledging that faith yet lived as Jews, as well as those who
concealed their origin and did not pay the tribute levied upon the
people" (*Dom.* 12.2), that is, judaizing Gentiles and non-religious
Jews.[51] In turn, Nerva countermanded Domitian's unpopular action
by reforming the *fiscus Iudaicus* in 96. His coins proclaim: *Fisci
Iudaici calumnia sublata*, "the malicious accusation with regard to
the Jewish tax has been removed." The point is that Nerva's reform
gave a possibility and impulse to those who wished both to affirm
a Jewish identity and those who wished to deny that they were
Jews. Proselytes and even God-fearers who wished to identify with
Judaism could pay the tax. But those who were unwilling to pay the

---

off in book 16, when his account had reached the year 66, before the outbreak of the Jewish revolt.

[51] Text and fuller details in Stern, *Greek and Latin Authors,* 2.128–30.

tax, even though their religion was very Jewish in character (Gentile Christians), could deny their Jewish roots by claiming exemption from the tax.[52] Perhaps then, ironically, it was an issue of economics and taxation which finally made the legal status of Christians clearly distinct from Jews in the eyes of the Roman authorities.

Conclusion

In conclusion, I should at once admit that much of the above is speculative—inevitably so when our sources are so few and can only give unclear answers to various of the questions we put to them. All I plead is that the fragmentariness of the sources and the unclarity of the answers given should make us alert to the fact that no answer to our questions is firm and definite. This applies particularly to the question of how the first Christians/believers in Messiah Jesus related to the much larger and well established (and respected) Jewish communities of the cities where they resided. Also to the question of how that relationship was perceived by the wider public and the Roman authorities. My own thesis is that the relations were much more extensive and longer enduring, even if only with the margins or minority of the new movement (infant Christianity), than is usually assumed; the fact and status of what is usually referred to as "Jewish Christianity" is an important factor here, whose significance has been too little appreciated. I believe also that the confusion between Jewish and Christian identity among the wider populace and the civic authorities was deeper and longer lasting than is usually recognized. To defend this thesis would take much more than this essay, but here at least I have been able to make a case in relation to the legal status of the earliest Christian churches.

---

[52] See also M. Goodman, "Nerva, the *fiscus Judaicus* and Jewish Identity," *JRS* 79 (1989), 40–44.

Basic Facts About the Synoptic Parables: What They Are and What They Are Not

Birger Gerhardsson
Lund University

Introduction

It happens from time to time that some scholar launches a new thesis about the parables of Jesus, what they are and how they are to be understood. Take, for instance, the thesis that these texts present something which is not supposed to be interpreted or, perhaps, which cannot even be expressed in plain language; they are just to be narrated. A good deal of these fireworks prove to miss the mark widely when they are confronted with the case of history. I shall develop this outrageous statement by recording a series of elementary data about the synoptic parables: what in fact they are and what they are not. I have substantiated these assertions in a number of contributions, partly with the aid of a rather mechanically performed detailed analysis of the relevant texts. For the sake of simplicity, I refer here to these articles in a single footnote.[1] I dedicate this article of homage to the successor of my successor in the New Testament chair at the theological faculty in Lund, Bengt Holmberg (who himself got a successor in 2007).

---

[1] The twenty-four theses in this article are substantiated and motivated above all in the following articles by my hand: "The Narrative Meshalim in the Synoptic Gospels: A Comparison with the Narrative Meshalim in the Old Testament," *NTS* 34 (1988): 339–63; "If We Do Not Cut the Parables out of Their Frames," *NTS* 37 (1991): 321–35, and "Illuminating the Kingdom: Narrative Meshalim in the Synoptic Gospels," in *Jesus and the Oral Gospel Tradition* (ed. H. Wansbrough; Macon: Mercer University Press, 1991), 266–309.

Twenty-Four Facts

The parable material in the synoptic Gospels consists of fifty-five parables in total (five in Mark, twenty-one in Matthew, twenty-nine in Luke). Three of them appear in all three Gospels, another seven (or eight) in Matthew and Luke, and yet another in Mark and Luke. One parable is peculiar to Mark. I do not count the figurative sayings in the Johannine Gospel as parables. I have established the following facts:

1. That all the parables in the Gospels are presented by Jesus; nobody else teaches with the aid of parables.
2. That the parables are not part of the general Jesus tradition but have (together with the logia) been a particular text group and have obviously also been transmitted in isolation from other material. Narrative tradition and sayings tradition are not fused in any of the three synoptic Gospels; they have just been brought together in the composition of the Gospels. No parable is expressed within a narrative tradition (apophthegms are not narratives).
3. That parables and logia are not separated from each other in the Gospels, nor divided up into distinct categories. Apart from a few colloquial statements, all the utterances of Jesus in the Gospels belong to one comprehensive Jewish genre, rendering (παραβολή/משל). We generally make a simple distinction between parables and logia, but we are the ones who make this division; it is not articulated in the texts, though we find it natural and meaningful to do so. In order to do justice to the Hebrew terminology I prefer sometimes to call all the sayings *meshalim* and divide them up into narrative *meshalim* and aphoristic *meshalim*.
4. That the parables—together with the logia—in terms of the form of teaching, thus present Jesus as a *moshel*, a mashalist, a man of pithy sayings and parables.

5. That all the parables are freshly created, none is quoted from literature or narrated as an historical example (as Hellenistic parables could be).
6. That only one of the parables (Luke 16:19–31) is narrated nakedly. All the others are equipped with one or many accompanying statements, which show that they are to be interpreted and commented upon, not simply narrated.
7. That the figurative language in these texts is almost always taken from the world of humans, mostly from their life together. In those parables in which something from nature is mentioned, it does not make up the center alone.[2]
8. That the distance between illustration and what is illustrated is accordingly short, in most cases.
9. That the figurative language in the parables is composite and of different types. It cannot therefore be clarified with a simple, unitary metaphor theory.
10. That the figurative language in the parables is almost without exception traditionally Jewish.
11. That they do not have the form of proclamation. They never appear as an attention-getting placard or as a provocative introduction to a speech (as is the case with most parables in the Hebrew Bible).
12. That they do not present elementary information.
13. That their basic function is indicative. They are intended to clarify, illuminate, mostly also to illustrate.
14. That a number of them (together with their accompanying statements) can have an imperative character as well (they exhort or blame), in addition to their indicative function.
15. That the parables want to call forth σύνεσις (insight) rather than μετάνοια (repentance) or πίστις (faith). Parables challenging to a decision (*Entscheidung*) are few. But every parable wants to make the listeners understand and agree. Note, however, the next point.

---

[2] In the parable of the Sower (Mark 4:3–20; Matt 13:3–23; Luke 8:5–15), nature is in focus, but the narrative starts with the Sower.

16. That the parables in the so-called parable chapter (Mark 4, Matt 13, Luke 8) have a distinct character compared with the other parables; part of that which is said about them cannot be generalized.
17. That they do not directly comment upon some passage from the Hebrew Bible as the rabbinic parables mostly do; the synoptic Jesus does not use his parables for direct exposition of Scripture.
18. That the parables are narrated in a very concise way and strongly stylized to make their point. In contrast to much popular narrating, nothing in the synoptic parables is embroidered. Disregarding a number of word-pairs and parallelistic expressions, hardly one superfluous element, one unnecessary word, has a place in them.
19. That the figures in the parables are all "round characters." Not one of the figures stands out as an individual with idiosyncrasies. The parables give us no base for an individual-psychological interpretation.
20. That the content of the parables is prophetic-messianic wisdom.
21. That their content is more exhortative than evangelistic. Most of them elucidate God's demands upon his people, just a few his grace and gifts—as they are also more parenetic than kerygmatic.
22. That their character nonetheless is haggadic, not halachic.
23. That they do not elucidate the earthly Jesus himself or his mission in Israel. Some of them may, possibly, touch upon him. A number of parables concern, however, the future parousia of the Son of Man for judgment. But not even the parousia is itself the subject of elucidation. In sharp contrast to this, Jesus speaks directly and clearly about himself in numerous logia (e.g. the Son of Man logia).[3]
24. That the dominant theme of the synoptic parables is God's rule/kingdom (ἡ βασιλεία)—using this word as a very wide and vague umbrella term with both present and future references.

---

[3] For the remarkable fact that Jesus speaks so clearly about himself in a great number of the synoptic logia but does not elucidate himself anywhere in the parables, see B. Gerhardsson, "The Earthly Jesus in the Synoptic Parables," in *Christology, Controversy and Community: Festschrift for David R. Catchpole* (ed. D. G. Horrell and C. M. Tuckett; Leiden: Brill, 2000), 49–62.

Concluding Observation

At the end of the so-called parable chapter in Matthew (13:51–52), Jesus makes sure that his disciples have "understood all this" and then says: "Therefore every scribe who has been trained for the kingdom of heaven is like a master of a household who brings out of his treasure what is new and what is old." This logion seems to give disciples who have understood the message of Jesus permission to teach, including coining new sayings, in the spirit and style of Jesus.[4] Yet we do not find in the synoptic Gospels any parable and hardly any didactic logion, in which one of Jesus' disciples speaks in his own name. All *meshalim* (parables and logia) are cited as sayings of Jesus. It is possible, even probable, that some of the synoptic parables are secondary, formulated by some disciple, but such parables seem to be few and it is difficult to distinguish them. The parables of Jesus have certainly been the object of much pondering and discussion on their way from Jesus to the written Gospels, but the "editorial" interferences that have been made in them—clarifications and reformulations as well as new creations—have obviously been minor and discreet. A sign of this is the fact that none of the parables elucidates the earthly Jesus, not such puzzling points as his healings and exorcisms, passion, crucifixion and resurrection. This means that the parables which have been created by disciples keep within the boundaries of the original parables.

As to the aphoristic *meshalim*, the logia, we find that they have not been treated in the same way as the narrative *meshalim*. Certainly hardly any didactic logion is expressed by a disciple in his own name. To that extent the situation is the same with them as with the narrative *meshalim*. But numerous logia say something directly about the earthly Jesus: about his situation and position, his powers and tasks. In fact Jesus often speaks about himself in the logia. And here the most important points in Jesus'

---

[4] For a comprehensive and thorough study about Jesus' exclusive position as the authoritative teacher in the nascent church, see S. Byrskog, *Jesus the Only Teacher: Didactic Authority and Transmission in Ancient Israel, Ancient Judaism and the Matthean Community* (Stockholm: Almqvist & Wiksell International, 1994).

earthly mission are spoken of in plain language: the healings, the exorcisms, the passion, the execution and the resurrection. Early Christianity has not shown the same restrictiveness with the logia as with the parables. On the contrary, Jesus himself may have spoken more directly and boldly in logia than in parables, but hardly so differently as he is said to do in the texts of the Gospels.

I shall not enter further into the question about early Christianity's transmission, interpretation, exposition and other forms of work with the *logia* tradition. My quick comparison with the logia is made here only for underlining what I wanted to draw attention to in this article: how consistently, exclusively, and restrictively early Christianity has handled the narrative *meshalim* of Jesus on their way from Jesus to the written Gospels. What does that reveal? And why did the young church deal so differently with the aphoristic *meshalim* and with the narrative *meshalim*?

"Their Wives Are as Chaste as Virgins, Their Daughters Modest": The Role of Women in Early Christian Apologetics[1]

Judith M. Lieu
Cambridge University

Introduction

In contemporary Christian apologetics and polemics the treatment of women and the roles allowed them have come to occupy a central place, often used as the touchstone of the authenticity and acceptability of religious practice, whether Christian or other. There is no surprise, then, that apologetic concerns also frequently emerge in the discussion of the roles of women in early Christianity. For example, the familiar accounts of the egalitarian character of the early Jesus movement and even of the Pauline communities (Gal 3:28) in supposed contrast to contemporary values, and of the subsequent erosion of genuinely independent roles for women, were driven by particular apologetic needs in the twentieth century. The alternative narratives that have been told, of the women whose autonomous activity can be recovered from non-literary media, in the homes they found in heresy among the Gnostics and Montanists, in charismatic unstructured power among the prophetesses, in the readiness to face a death that made all equal among the martyrs, or in the ultimate denial of their femaleness, in sexual asceticism, these narratives also have served modern apologetic interests. In addition, the "narrative of decline," sometimes inspired by an uncritical mirror-reading of the texts, assumed that subsequent restrictions were the consequence of the apologetic situation in which the

---

[1] It is a pleasure to offer this to Bengt Holmberg in deep appreciation of his contribution to the many academic interests we share and of his personal friendship and hospitality.

early church found itself, according to some perhaps triggered by the disrepute engendered by the inappropriate behaviour of some women (1 Cor 11; 14; 1 Tim 5). Further study has exposed the extent to which both the women in the texts and the modern reader seeking to recover them are entangled by multiple threads of rhetoric and stereotyping which require careful tracing and unravelling.[2]

All this already invites a consideration of the treatment of women in the explicit apologetic writing of the early church as it begins in the second century. Study of early Christian women in this period has tended to concentrate on the Apocryphal Acts of the Apostles and on Martyrdom accounts. However, although the precise definition and delimitation of apologetic is a matter of debate,[3] there can be little disagreement that as an overt exercise in persuasion it adopts explicit rhetorical strategies, and therefore should provide a model for exploring how women are implicated in these. Apologetic purports to address the world outside, although in practice the majority of the early readers of Christian apologetic were "insiders," whether or not this was always actively in the mind of the authors. This double facing, within and towards the outside, makes apologetic particularly adept at negotiating sameness and difference, namely at defining identity. Before long it becomes very evident that the status and behaviour of women was in this respect a cause of considerable concern internally, and treating this as if in a conversation with those outside had its own rhetorical advantages. Thus, to study how women are "used" specifically within apologetic rhetoric is to recognise the importance of the particular literary genre or discourse, its strategies and its goals. The consequence will be to warn against an indiscriminate mining of the various sources in the naive expectation that to do so would yield unmediated historical information about early Christian women.

Although this introduction has focussed on the question of women, it has become a truism to say that in antiquity "men use

---

[2] See M. Y. McDonald, *Early Christian Women and Pagan Opinion: The Power of the Hysterical Woman* (Cambridge: Cambridge University Press, 1996).

[3] See M. Edwards, et al., eds., *Apologetics in the Roman Empire: Pagans, Jews, and Christians* (Oxford: Oxford University Press, 1999).

women to think with"; it is also a commonplace that women are associated with the body and the passions. Hence, it will not be surprising to find that broader issues of sexuality are seldom far distant, nor that the male subject is often the primary focus of interest.

The broader context of early Christian representations is Greek and Roman ideology, where, at least in the literature, the position and behaviour of women were seen as representing the nature and the organisation or ordering of society; women could therefore act as significant markers of Greek-ness, Roman-ness, or barbarian-ness, while rarely, of course, emerging from the shadows and being given a voice of their own.[4] However, there were changes in the discourses of women and of sexuality in the first and second centuries C.E., the age of the apologists, particularly within philosophical writings such as represented by Musonius Rufus and Plutarch. On the one hand these appear to display moves towards a greater symmetry in the treatment of men and women; on the other, self-discipline or *askesis* becomes a major interest with heterosexual, and especially marital, sexual relations replacing the earlier philosophical interest in boys.[5]

Yet if Christian apologists deliberately located themselves within the contemporary Greco-Roman world they were also heirs to the Jewish ethical tradition, as well as, in all probability, to the Jewish apologetic style itself.[6] Although these origins are rarely explicitly acknowledged, the values upheld within this tradition constituted a major theme of Christian apologetic self-representation. Behind both Christian and Jewish ethical apologetic also lies the shared Scriptural tradition, which associates the worship of other gods and sexual immorality with the Gentiles outside and with unfaithfulness to God within; inevitably this association becomes fundamental in various discourses of identity, both in theory and in practice.[7] In

---

[4] See J. M. Lieu, *Christian Identity in the Jewish and Graeco-Roman World* (Oxford: Oxford University Press, 2004), 178–90.

[5] See J. A. Francis, *Subversive Virtue: Asceticism and Authority in the Second-Century Pagan World* (University Park; Pennsylvania State University Press, 1995).

[6] As is often noted, both Aristides' *Apology* and Theophilus of Antioch's *To Autolycus* contain much that would be equally in place within a Jewish writing.

[7] See, for example, C. E. Hayes, *Gentile Impurities and Jewish Identities: Intermarriage and Conversion from Bible to the Talmud* (Oxford: Oxford University Press, 2002).

Hellenistic Jewish writers this particular tradition quickly conforms to a stereotyped pattern: a repeated theme is that other nations are characterised both by idolatry and by sexual immorality, with sexual relations between males high on the list; it is in this that Jewish "difference" lies (*Let. Aris.* 152).[8] For example, in the third Sibylline Oracle the "holy race of God-fearing men" reject idolatry, and "more than any men they are mindful of the purity of marriage, neither do they hold unholy intercourse with boys"; at the same time the implied Gentile (male) audience are urged "to worship the living one and to avoid adultery and indiscriminate intercourse with a male" (*Sib. Or.* 3.595–600, 763–764). The vehement outburst against Rome in the Fifth Sibylline sees only her sexual sins—pederasty again, but also prostitution, incest, and bestiality (*Sib. Or.* 5.166–167, 386–396).

However, although in such tirades the presence of women is both ignored and at the same time implicit, if we look specifically for the role of women, material that is explicitly apologetic is more limited—even though much can be and has been written on the topic of "women" generally in Hellenistic Jewish literature. This is partly a reflection of the problem of defining the genre in Jewish sources; for example, in what follows the treatment of and the interpretation of biblical women by Philo or by Josephus in the *Antiquitates judaicae* will not be analysed, although both authors may have non-Jewish readers/hearers in mind. Moreover, in this period women are used in narrative settings in order to explore the boundaries of the community, and the possibilities and limitations of negotiating relations with "outsiders"—for example in the stories of Esther, Judith, and Aseneth—but these seem to be directed primarily for an internal audience. More ambiguous is the mother of the seven brothers in 4 Maccabees: she acts with "manly" courage and can be identified as "mother of the nation, vindicator of the law and champion of religion," although she is quick to affirm her own adherence to the proper constraints and her submission to her, now dead, husband (4 Macc 15:23–29; 18:6–

---

[8] See J. J. Collins, *Between Athens and Jerusalem: Jewish Identity in the Hellenistic Diaspora* (New York: Crossroad, 1983), 137–75 on the "common ethic."

9); however, the intended audience of this text remains uncertain.

Within the more overtly apologetic writing, the approach and topics present few surprises. For example, even when Josephus implies that Jewish values regarding women and sexuality challenge those of contemporary culture, he evidently sees no need for elaborate defence but expects them to be readily appreciated and admired. When he wants to underline the transparency and coherence of Jewish discourse about God and about daily life, in contrast to the contradictions beloved by other nations, he concludes "and this anybody may hear from our women and domestics themselves" (*C. Ap.* 2.179–181). Women, it is assumed by everyone, cannot be expected to understand the abstruse or esoteric, but that they should acknowledge the absolute priority of "piety" (εὐσέβεια) all would affirm. It is perhaps a reflection of the concerns of the age that Josephus evidently expects that the Jewish laws about marriage should feature prominently in the apologetic self-presentation of Judaism, for he gives them prime place, immediately following his explanation of monotheistic worship and of the centrality of the temple (*C. Ap.* 2.199–203). Although later he includes marital relations among those aspects of Jewish practice that should be most easy, but that some find difficult to sustain (*C. Ap.* 2.234), the examples that he gives would raise few eyebrows: a man can have intercourse only with his wife and this should be used only for the procreation of children; adultery with another man's wife is punishable by death; moreover, women who procure an abortion or expose their children are murderers, for to do so "diminishes the race." The first of these is not biblical, but that reproduction is the only valid reason for sexual intercourse was a common theme in Greek philosophy and much repeated in this period; on the other hand, the anxiety among male authors about abortion, a rare point at which women were in control, is also widespread.[9]

---

[9] On what she terms "procreationism" see K. L. Gaca, *The Making of Fornication: Eros, Ethics and Political Reform in Greek Philosophy and Early Christianity* (Berkeley: University of California Press, 2003), 100–116. On contemporary concern about abortion, see R. Flemming, *Medicine and the Making of Roman Women: Gender, Nature, and Authority from Celsus to Galen* (Oxford: Oxford University Press, 2000), 167–70.

In words—suspiciously according to some—redolent of some New Testament authors he even asserts that the law says that "a woman is inferior to her husband in all things" (*C. Ap.* 2.201).[10]

When subsequently he mocks the Greek gods on the grounds of their lustful behaviour, Josephus does so with an exaggerated hesitancy, appealing to a Jewish disinclination to attack the customs of others—unlike his detractors—and to an interpretation of Exod 22:28 as forbidding the slandering of the gods recognised by others (*C. Ap.* 2.237). Even so, it is the sexual demeanours particularly of Zeus, as king of the gods and putative "Father," that he targets, including his lack of self-restraint towards his wife; but even this Josephus moderates, acknowledging that he is but following the philosophers in such criticisms and in laying the blame on the excesses allowed "the poets" (*C. Ap.* 2.242–254). Thus, even though Josephus assumes that there is something distinctive about such Jewish mores and values, he also assumes that such an account will be admired— and indeed it would be easy to find parallels in Greek and Roman sources with different "others" whose behaviour is despicable.

According to Eusebius' report, in his defence of the Jews (*Hypothetica*) Philo also began the account of the Jewish law with sexual offences, namely those that incurred the death penalty, pederasty, adultery, and rape of a youth, "needless to say of a boy but even also of a girl" (Eusebius, *Praep. ev.* 8.7.1). Philo also emphasises the subjection of wives to their husbands, alongside the control that parents have over their children and generally each person has over their possessions and those under their authority (*Praep. ev.* 8.7.3–4). Moreover, in his account of the Essenes, who here particularly represent the ideals of a holy life, he praises their repudiation of marriage and their notable practice of continence; this leads into a fulsome outburst against the selfishness, seductiveness, and deceitfulness of woman, who in the end enslaves man:

---

[10] See J. M. G. Barclay, *Against Apion* (vol. 10 of *Flavius Josephus Translation and Commentary*; ed. S. Mason; Leiden, Brill, 2007), 284, who accepts the sentence.

[F]or the man who is bound by the charms of a woman, or who by the compulsion of nature is tied in affection for children, is no longer the same person towards others but is entirely changed, having, without being aware of it, become a slave instead of a free man. (*Praep. ev.* 8.11.14–17)

Ironically, it is in Philo's account of the "contemplative" branch of the Essenes, the Therapeutae, that women acquire their own identity to an extent that has received much attention—although it is uncertain whether this treatise also should count as apologetic. According to Philo, these women have joined the sect by an equal act of deliberate decision (προαίρεσις) to that of the male members; they are free self-determining agents, and are praised for this (*Contempl.* 32; 68). In his account of the life of this community the women are for the most part appropriately separated from the men, so only their voices can mingle, but they do finally come together in their banquet, although they are seated separately. These women, however, are mostly "aged virgins" whose commitment to holiness is driven by their love for wisdom and by their indifference to the body (*Contempl.* 68).[11] To drive home the point he is making in this characterisation, Philo places in the middle of this account of the sober celebration of the Therapeutae a denunciation of Greek banquets, and even of the Socratic model Symposium, which, in Xenophon's account, is preoccupied with "common, vulgar love" (i.e. for younger men) which engenders in the soul "the female disease, and renders men effeminate (men-women)" (*Contempl.* 57–60).

Whatever the reality, if any, or the utopian idealism behind his eulogy,[12] for all the rhetoric of difference Philo still exhibits the normative ideas of woman as defined by the body, and of the body as marked by the threat of feminine weakness. Such ideas are familiar throughout the ancient world and have been

---

[11] It might be thought unclear why they should all be aged if indeed they have chosen wisdom as their life-partner. On the Therapeutae see J. E. Taylor, *Jewish Women Philosophers of First Century Alexandria: Philo's Therapeutae Reconsidered* (Oxford: Oxford University Press, 2003).

[12] That they do not represent a historically recoverable reality is argued by T. Engberg-Pedersen, "Philo's De Vita Contemplativa as a Philosopher's Dream," *JSJ* 30 (1999): 40–64.

thoroughly analysed; as apologetic its purpose is not to talk about real females but about how to be a real male. Here the women do indeed serve to demonstrate the superiority of Judaism but not at all because they manifest any revolutionary and egalitarian ideas about the place of women—and it would be hazardous to use them to recover women's religion in diaspora Judaism.

There is little in any of these writers that is surprising within the context of antiquity; each largely represents the aggressive side of apologetics, the demonstration of superiority through sexual mores and through the appropriate control of women according to tacitly agreed common values. There would appear to be no suggestion that they have been forced to mount a defence against attacks on these issues from opponents. This correlates with the apparent fact that among the various slanders laid against the Jews in the ancient world, there were initially none directed at their women or their sexual practices—something that may be surprising given the extent to which such issues were used in the definition of barbarians versus Greeks or of Greeks versus Romans. It is only at the beginning of the second century C.E. that Tacitus described the Jews as adopting separate tables, separate beds, and as abstaining from intercourse with foreign women, while being a people particularly given to debauchery (*Hist.* 5.5.2). There is, however, no evidence that anyone made this charge before him, and equally no sign of any attempt at a defence against it. In addition, anticipating an issue that will shape Christian apologetics, we might have expected more: there is scattered evidence of Gentile women, some of high status, being attracted to Judaism and even of them converting, whatever that might have meant for them.[13] Even though the conversion of the Roman matron, Fulvia, eventually leads to the exclusion of the Jews from Rome under Tiberius, Josephus is content to demonstrate that this is the consequence of the machinations of a scoundrel who was himself a fugitive for transgressing Jewish laws;

---

[13] On this see J. M. Lieu, "The 'Attraction of Women' in/to early Judaism and Christianity: Gender and the Politics of Conversion," in *Neither Jew nor Greek? Constructing Early Christianity* (Edinburgh: T&T Clark, 2002), 83–99.

indeed the accompanying, and much longer, scurrilous account of the deception of a woman convert to Isis is perhaps predicated on the complete acceptability of Fulvia's step (*A.J.* 18.65–84). He describes leading women among the converts at Damascus, as well as the conversion of the women of the royal house of Adiabene, but he sees no need to defend this (*B.J.* 2.559–561; *A.J.* 20.17–35).[14] The evident literary and rhetorical interests at play may advise hesitation in using these accounts as direct historical records, but it is still the case that there is no evidence either of literary attacks against the Jews for such proselytising activities or of any defence of them. The concerns about converts that are voiced, most notably by Juvenal and by Tacitus, are directed towards young men who by converting give up on their *pietas* to parents and country.[15]

Against this background we can turn to the role that women play in early Christian apologetics. Two things prove to be particularly striking: first, there are continuities from the themes of Jewish polemic, alongside new ones; second, in contrast to the Jewish sources, defence is at least as important as aggressive self-presentation. In what follows four interwoven themes will be traced.

Women as the Audience of the Christian Proclamation

Often cited in this connection is the charge made by Celsus in the mid-second century that women were among those whom Christian preachers particularly targeted:

> In private houses also we see wool-workers, cobblers, laundry-workers and the most illiterate and bucolic yokels, who would not dare to say anything at all in front of their elders and more intelligent

---

[14] The conversion of the King Izates proves more contentious but Josephus justifies this by demonstrating God's protection of him.

[15] Juvenal, *Sat.* 14.96–106; Tacitus, *Hist.* 5.5.2. Contrast the account of the charges brought against Pomponia Graecina by her husband for allegiance to an unidentified "foreign superstition" (*Ann.* 13.32).

masters. But when they get hold of children in private and some
stupid women. (Origen, *Cels.* 3.44)

Celsus' polemical rhetoric relies on certain accepted norms which
ensure its effectiveness: first, that women are by definition irrational
and gullible; they are, therefore, hardly good advertisements for
the intellectual credentials of the new religion. The preference
for operating in private rather than engaging in the public arena
confirms this weakness. More importantly, entrapping them in
private households is a violation of the space that belongs to another
(male), and thus undermines the proper ordering of society: it is
a potent symbol of subversion. In Roman thought the control of
women in private is not a private matter. Hence, Celsus goes on
to imply that these "victims" are taught to reject the authority of
their elders and betters. Similarly, in Minucius Felix's *Octavius*,
the Roman opponent, Caecilius, complains that Christians collect
together the most illiterate of society and "credulous women who
give way with the weakness natural to their sex," and immediately
goes on to accuse them of forming a "profane conspiracy" (*Oct.* 8.4).[16]

The apologists do not deny the charge of recruiting women but
they turn such criticism to their advantage. Thus Athenagoras mimics
the categories when he underlines a contrast with the philosophers
who delight in syllogisms, etymologies, and ambiguities: "Among
us you will find ordinary people, artisans, and old women, who
if they are unable to establish by argument the benefit that comes
from their teaching, do demonstrate by deed the benefit from the
exercise of will [προαίρεσις]" (*Leg.* 11.3). Women represent the
accessibility of the Christian message, and its preachers' refusal
to rely on the sophistry often criticised in popular philosophical
teachers; they also represent its practicability—it leads to action,
and women can act. Action, however, is not a second level matter as
compared with reasoning. The word for "will" here is προαίρεσις;
this is the moral purpose or direction of intention which was central
to ethical theory since Aristotle and that in Stoic philosophers

---

[16] However, see pp. 70–71 below for the difficulties in using Caecilius' speech.

such as the first-century Epictetus is the one and only thing that we can control, and that we should control.[17] Athenagoras illustrates this, that when struck or robbed such believers do not retaliate, they give to those who ask and they love their neighbour as themselves. The echoes of the Jesus tradition are evident to modern readers and perhaps to "insiders," but for the implied "pagan" readers the model of the philosopher in action is the message.

Tatian adopts a similar strategy: "You say that we talk rubbish in the company of women, and boys and girls and old ladies"; but he has already pre-empted the charge when he asserted, with some pride,

> With us there is no desire for false glory nor do we employ subtleties of doctrine; … not only the rich practice philosophy but also the poor enjoy the teaching free of charge … We admit everyone who wants to hear, even if they are old women or young boys. (*Orat.* 33.1; 32.1)[18]

Tatian will even describe Christian women as "philosophizing," (φιλοσοφοῦσαι) and he contrasts them with Sappho whom he dismisses as "a wanton girl maddened by love" (33.2). However, Tatian's intention is not to represent such activities as liberating for women or as challenging to society but rather as serving its highest ideals. A little earlier the Stoic thinker Musonius Rufus also asserted the right of women to be taught philosophy: "women have received from the gods the same ability to reason that men have…why is it appropriate for men to seek out and examine how they might live well, that is to practice philosophy, but not women?" The main benefit that he saw coming from this, however, was that it would make them better wives and organisers of their households, chaste and self-controlled (*Disc.* 3).[19]

It would be wrong, therefore, to read the apologists as "ahead of their time," and as representing for women new opportunities afforded

---

[17] E.g. Epictetus, *Diatr.* 2.23.

[18] Young boys (μειράκια) are in classical thought not yet real men.

[19] See B. Levick, "Women, Power, and Philosophy at Rome and Beyond," in *Philosophy and Power in the Graeco-Roman World: Essays in Honour of Miriam Griffin* (ed. G. Clark and T. Rajak; Oxford: Oxford University Press, 2002), 133–55, who stresses the ambiguities and limitations of women's access to philosophy in this period.

by Christianity. They were appealing to debates current within the wider society, in order to define a place for the Christian movement that would be both recognisable and respectable. They were also claiming to contribute actively to such debates; as we shall see, the deeply-rooted associations of philosophy with desire provided material ready for exploitation, and the offer of philosophising to and for women was no guarantee of moral probity.[20] Christian apologists were offering a model-in-practice of how it could be safely pursued.

The Charge of Sexual Promiscuity

The charge of sexual promiscuity may already be a subtext in the pagan accusations that women were the targets of Christian mission "in private"—mission by seduction.[21] This was a well-established polemical *topos*: as noted earlier, Josephus had prefaced his story of what was only a financial deception of Fulvia with that of the contemporary sexual seduction of Paulina, the devotee of Isis. The tradition, particularly implicating "foreign" cults, has a long genealogy and reaches back at least to Livy's influential account of the suppression of the Bacchanalia in 186 B.C.E. (*Hist.* 39.8–22); this, too, involved night time meetings in which both women and men took part, conspiracy, rumours of secret rites, sexual excesses and even murder, effeminate youths, and the threat of the undermining of Rome's military power as well as her social cohesion. While Livy's account is already heavily stylised, it is possible to trace its subsequent literary influence and the fears that it articulates. Contemporary with the apologists, and, as just noted, closer to their self-representation, Lucian's satire *Fugitivi* describes the false philosophers, here Cynics, who abuse attractive boys or pretty women and even seduce the wives of their

---

[20] S. Goldhill, *Foucault's Virginity: Ancient Erotic Fiction and the History of Sexuality* (Cambridge: Cambridge University Press, 1995), 72–78, 94–112, shows how the Hellenistic novels play with this *topos*.

[21] Francis, *Subversive Virtue*, 157, assumes, perhaps too readily, that Celsus has this in mind.

hosts, by promising them that they also might be philosophers.[22]

Already a topic in Livy's account, sexual "mixing" (*mixis*) is a regular theme in the explanations that the apologists themselves give as to the grounds on which the Christians were persecuted—both as a general charge and specifically as involving incest or "Oedipodean intercourse."[23] Justin refers succinctly to "the overturning of lamps, unrestrained mixing and meals of human flesh," while Theophilus of Antioch claims that "the ungodly" say, "That we all hold our women in common, and live in indiscriminate mixing, and even have intercourse with our own sisters, and, most godless and savage of all, that we partake of human flesh" (Justin, *1 Apol.* 26.7; Theophilus, *Autol.* 3.4; cf. Athenagoras *Leg.* 3). These charges raise a number of issues. It has been widely assumed by contemporary scholars that they arose from a misunderstanding of the way that early Christians called one another "brother" and "sister," and of Christian eucharists or "love feasts" (agapes), including the language of eating the body and blood of Christ. This assumption, at least on its own, is probably too naïve and misunderstands the rhetoric involved in such accusations. Josephus reports an elaborate calumny recounted by Apion of the annual fattening, ritual killing, and consumption of a Greek man in the inner chambers of the temple (*C. Ap.* 2.89–102). Philostratus claims that the charges of sorcery against Apollonius of Tyana included that of his killing a young foreigner (*Vit. Apoll.* 7.11, 20). More broadly, it has been shown that charges of cannibalism were more extensive in the Greco-Roman context and that there, as in societies more widely, they articulate deep-rooted anxieties about the threat to the ordering of society.[24]

However, both Josephus and Apollonius respond simply by demonstrating at some length that such an act could hardly leave no evidence or prompt no reports of the victim's disappearance. Yet Christian apologists are slow to make this fairly obvious response, and rarely rely on it alone (Athenagoras, *Leg.* 35.1–3; Tertullian,

---

[22] Lucian, *Fug.* 18; see Francis, *Subversive Virtue*, 64; Goldhill, *Foucault's Virginity*, 94–112.

[23] In Jewish Hellenistic literature "mixing" is used in the rejection of intermarriage.

[24] See A. McGowan, "Eating People: Accusations of Cannibalism against Christians in the Second Century," *JECS* 2 (1994): 413–42.

Apol. 8.6–9; *Nat.* 1.7). Further, the apologists do not generally reply, as they could have done, "you have misunderstood what we do or how we speak." Indeed, of equal importance, it is primarily the apologists themselves who report this charge; moreover, it is not a common theme in accounts of persecution and martyrdom, other than in that at Lyons and Vienne (Eusebius, *Hist. eccl.* 5.1.14). The accusations are not found among pagan detractors, with the sole exception of the "fictional" Caecilius in the *Octavius* of Minucius Felix, who bursts into an extended and vivid account of nocturnal meetings, solemn fasts, and unnatural meals, climaxing in a banquet "with all their children, sisters, mothers, people of every sex and age," where drink inflames "incestuous lust" (*Oct.* 8.4–9.6).

Caroline Bammel has argued that this speech, although "enriched," is fundamentally authentic, and that it goes back to the Roman jurist of the second century, Fronto, to whom Caecilius does appeal (*Oct.* 9.6); she also concludes that Fronto's intervention was a significant impetus towards the persecutions of the period.[25] The issue is made more complex when Tertullian repeats some of the same charges in yet richer detail in order to mock them, but without reference to Fronto; the relationship between the two authors is debated but there is much to suggest that Minucius Felix may be derivative from Tertullian.[26] There is, therefore, a strong possibility that the Christian apologist, Minucius Felix, who is characterised by a "noticeable lack of nervous energy,"[27] has put these vivid details of what had become an apologetic rhetorical topos on the mouth of his opponent in order to expose the self-evident excesses used by the opposition and to refute them. The inescapable echoes in Caecilius' tirade of Livy's account of the Bacchanalia would

---

[25] C. Bammel, "Die erste lateinische Rede gegen die Christen," *ZKG* 104 (1993): 295–311; she points out the many allusions to Livy's account of the Bacchanalian conspiracy. McGowan, "Eating People," 420, also suggests that Fronto helped spread the charges.

[26] See G. W. Clarke, "The Historical Setting of the *Octavius* of Minucius Felix," *JRH* 4 (1967): 268–86. Bammel, "Erste lateinische Rede," argues that Tertullian (*Nat.* 1) was also dependent on Fronto when he dismisses similar atrocities.

[27] Clarke, "Historical Setting," 420. Bammel ("Erste lateinische Rede," 303, 305) herself thinks that Minucius Felix has exaggerated these charges so as to make them laughable, and that he can risk describing them fully precisely because they were no longer credible in his time.

be as effective in such a strategy as on the mouth of Fronto.

Whatever the origin and currency of such charges, in practice, the apologists not only introduce them themselves but they exploit them as a counter-weapon. Theophilus, quoted earlier, continues by protesting that the Greek philosophers Zeno, Diogenes, and Cleanthus themselves advocated cannibalism, while Plato proposed that wives should be held common among all, and that Epicurus recommends intercourse with mothers and sisters (*Autol.* 3.6). Athenagoras asserts that it is not surprising that their opponents invent such stories because they have the same stories about the gods: Zeus had incestuous intercourse with his mother and daughter, and Orpheus was responsible for the Thyestian banquets (*Leg.* 32.5). Aristides simply complains that the Greeks charge the Christians with what they themselves do, intercourse with men, a mother, a sister, a daughter (*Apol.* 17.2 Syr.). Perhaps most revealing is Justin, who is at the same time most restrained about these charges.[28] In his *Second Apology* he asserts that these charges have been made by torturing "our slaves, either children or women"—evidence that traditional associations of the unreliability of the weak remain entrenched (*2 Apol.* 12.4); in his *First Apology*, however, after he has described how Simon Magus was accompanied by Helen who was a former prostitute, he suggests that perhaps it is other groups, like those who follow Simon, Menander, or Marcion, who actually practiced such cannibalism and incest (*1 Apol.* 26). In later Christian anti-heretical polemic, this is indeed precisely what the "orthodox" will claim about their opponents; they will accuse them of seducing women, of being accompanied by disreputable women, of engaging in illicit sex, and even of participating in obscene rites.

Thus, whatever lies behind these charges, and however important they really were in polemic and action against the Christians—a question that it may not be possible to answer—they belong, or they come to belong, to a fixed *topos* of denunciation. The Apologists

---

[28] So rightly, C. Munier, *L'Apologie de Saint Justin Philosophe et Martyr* (Fribourg: Éditions Universitaires Fribourg Suisse, 1994), 44; contrast Bammel, "Erste lateinische Rede," 308, who thinks Justin takes them particularly seriously.

take them up with enthusiasm and they employ them as a gateway to a vigorous counter-polemic. They also mimic them to parade their own virtues: "Thus we are united (mixed) in mind and soul, and have no hesitation about sharing property. Everything is common among us except our wives. We dissolve our partnership at the very point at which other men practice it"—which Tertullian illustrates by the philosophers who shared their wives with their friends (Tertullian, *Apol.* 39.11–13).[29] Throughout this, women are represented as the tools in a male contest in moral superiority, the objects of illicit intercourse, as mothers, sisters, daughters, and so the objects of a discourse in which their own voice plays no part.

Chastity

As has just been illustrated, the direct counter to the charge of sexual promiscuity is the assertion of chastity as a hallmark of the Christians. In the *Apology* of Aristides it appears in its simplest form: "[their wives are as chaste as virgins, their daughters modest, and their men] self-controlled to avoid any illicit intercourse or impurity" (*Apol.* 15.6); the bracketed words, with the unexplained different standards expected of men and women, are found only in the Syriac version but are likely to be original. Here women especially are the measure of the respectability of the community: Tatian mocks the Greeks for believing in the existence of warrior women like the Amazons—probably an example of female courage cited in contemporary discourse[30]—but for slandering those whom he calls "our virgins" (*Orat.* 32.2).[31] "All our women are chaste," he says later, "and our virgins speak of the things to do with God" (33.2); and, again, "aren't you ashamed when you have so many poetesses who are no use at all, and countless prostitutes, as well as good-for-

---

[29] Cf. *Diogn.* 5:6, "They set a common table but not a common bed."

[30] See Musonius Rufus, *Disc.* 4 where the Amazons are cited as evidence that women can be brave: courage makes chastity possible.

[31] M. Whittaker, *Tatian* Oratio ad Graecos *and Fragments* (Oxford: Clarendon Press, 1982), 61, translates, "our gods," a Freudian slip!

nothing men, and yet you disparage the seemliness of our women" (34.2). The frequent repetition of the theme betrays its significance.

Chastity is not only avoidance but can also be a positive force, and this is not restricted to women's behaviour. It is a repeated theme in the *Apologies* that Christians are not even allowed to look on a woman with lust: the tradition of Jesus' teaching on this (e.g. Matt 5:28) has made a deep impression, and is quoted by Justin (*1 Apol.* 15.1, 5), by Athenagoras (*Leg.* 32.1–2) and by Theophilus of Antioch (*Autol.* 3.13). Marriage of a divorced woman, as well as perhaps after the death of a wife, is also forbidden: again the tradition of Jesus' teaching is regularly cited. Justin claims that "we only marry in order to bring up children" (*1 Apol.* 29), and others agree: according to Athenagoras, "each of us thinks of a wife, whom he has married according to the laws we have laid down, only for the purposes of procreation," or, perhaps, "only until children have been born" (*Leg.* 33.1),[32] while for Minucius Felix, "out of a desire for procreation we know only one woman, or none at all" (*Oct.* 31.5). As already noted, this limitation was a well-established theme in the period, claimed for the Jews by Josephus and also a norm in contemporary Stoic thought.[33] It belongs to the contemporary concerns for male self-control and self-mastery against the debilitating threat of pleasure. For Musonius Rufus this does not lead to a negative evaluation of marriage, since marriage and the rearing of children are seen as good for the state—a cause of considerable civic concern in the early Empire. To a limited extent the Apologists might agree with such sentiments—Justin's claim does follow his account of the Christian refusal to expose children (*1 Apol.* 29.1); there is, then, some justification in describing this as an apologetic "appeal to the high moral stature of marriage among Christians."[34] However, Justin's statement that "those who contract a second marriage

---

[32] Given other parallels, a reference to the avoidance of intercourse during pregnancy is less likely.

[33] See above, pp. 60–65; Musonius Rufus, *Disc.* 12: sexual intercourse should only be engaged in within marriage and for the procreation of children; if it is taken for pleasure this is "against the law," even in marriage. See Francis, *Subversive Virtue*, 14

[34] So D. G. Hunter, *Marriage, Celibacy, and Heresy in Ancient Christianity: The Jovinian Controversy* (Oxford: Oxford University Press, 2007), 99.

according to human law are sinners in terms of our teaching" is more confrontational (*1 Apol.* 15.5; cf. Athenagoras, *Leg.* 33.4–6).

Even stronger, as perhaps intended by Athenagoras, is the sense that this is but a concession and is a stage to something yet more decisive. Athenagoras' (?) treatise *De resurrectione* claims that men normally beget children in the hope of some continuity after their own death, a hope that is now met by the Christian conviction (*Res.* 12.2). For Justin the alternative to marriage and to producing children adopted by many is to avoid marriage and to remain completely "controlled": the term used here, ἐγκρατεύομαι, comes to bear a primary sexual connotation in Christian thought, and to denote celibacy. Justin proceeds to illustrate this by the story of a young man who asked for permission to be castrated, although the Roman governor refused consent, and the supplicant had to be content with his own conscience and that of those who were of like mind (*1 Apol.* 29.2–3). Minucius Felix claims that some are embarrassed even by a chaste relationship, and that "many enjoy perpetual virginity of an unviolated body" (*Oct.* 31.5).[35] Although in many ways counter-cultural, such choices could be presented in a positive light and they could resonate with the second century context: Apollonius of Tyana had also decided not to marry or to have sexual intercourse, choosing a more radical stance than was demanded of the ordinary people by his teacher Pythagoras.[36] The Christians "merely" reject the elitism that reserves such achievements for the few.[37]

In the examples discussed so far the subjects are men— Tertullian, again, says that those who choose virginity remain "boys as old men," and do so to be "more secure" (*Apol.* 9.19). That it articulates a masculine anxiety becomes yet more explicit in his claim that, "The Christian is born masculine only for his wife … The Christian, having kept his eyes safe, does not

---

[35] Cf. Tertullian, *Apol.* 9.19, "*virgine continentia.*" Both Tertullian and Minucius Felix, *Oct.* 31, argue that promiscuity might lead to incest because one would not be able to identify one's offspring.

[36] Philostratus, *Vit. Apoll.* 1.13.

[37] See G. S. Gasparro, "Asceticism and Anthropology: *Enkrateia* and 'Double Creation' in Early Christianity," in *Asceticism* (ed. V. Wimbush and R. Valantasis; Oxford: Oxford University Press, 1998), 127–46.

see women; in his mind he is blind in the face of lust" (*Apol.* 46.11–12). This is a competitive rhetoric which addresses other males, and which shares a sense of anxiety in the face of women.

However, the Apologists do not present such chastity as restricted to an exclusively masculine askesis. Justin knows of many sixty- and seventy-year olds, both men and women, who became disciples as children and who have kept themselves undefiled (ἄφθοροι) since then (*1 Apol.* 15.6). More explicitly, Athenagoras claims that there are many men and women among them who grow old unmarried in the hope of a better union with God; they remain "in virginity and in *eunouchia*" (*Leg.* 33.2–3). All this serves an obvious apologetic agenda. Nonetheless, it appears that it was not pure invention, for it is confirmed by the philosopher Galen: he remarked with some amazement on the Christians' restraint:

> For they include not only men but also women who refrain from cohabiting all through their lives; and they also number individuals who in self-discipline and in self-control in matters of food and drink, and in their keen pursuit of justice have attained a pitch not inferior to that of genuine philosophers.[38]

For Galen, true askesis should depend on reason, and his surprise is that Christians achieve the goal while failing generally to demonstrate the control of reason. Rhetorically, these women again are not independent, but serve to underline Christian achievement, and to that extent to shame their male opponents.

For the second century Apologists, such asceticism is rooted not in a rejection of the body but in a concern for it and for its integrity. For this reason their asceticism is practised corporately and not in isolation. This stands in contrast not only to the later fourth century developments but also to Philo's Therapeutae for whom chastity entails physical separation from the rest of society as well as between the male and female members. Alongside his description of monogamy and chastity Athenagoras defends the way they think

---

[38] See R. Walzer, *Galen on Jews and Christians* (London: Oxford University Press, 1949), 15–16.

of each other as family members, sons or daughters, brothers or sisters, fathers or mothers; it is this that inspires their concern that "the bodies of those we think of as kin should remain inviolate and unsullied." Surprisingly, he continues with a description of their practice of kissing: "Again our teaching directs, 'If anyone kisses twice because he enjoyed it … and one must be very scrupulous about the kiss … because if we are mentally agitated by it we are placed outside eternal life'" (*Leg.* 32.5).[39] This may also evoke a philosophical theme but there is perhaps a hint of the sense of the threat of disruption and dissolution that always hung over the tightly knit Christian community even for, or especially for, those on the inside.[40] The rhetoric of chastity could speak as much to the anxieties of the Christian community itself as it did to their detractors outside.

Greco-Roman Promiscuity

Throughout the arguments that have been explored here the promiscuity of contemporary Greek and Roman society has been the consistent counter-point. Here the Christian Apologists were the heirs of their Jewish predecessors, but the Christians wax far more eloquent and at greater length. To some extent this is the real or adopted fervour of the convert who can parade the superiority of their present choices over the grim experiences of the past, still followed by their opponents: according to Justin, Christians are those drawn from every human race who *used* to rejoice in sexual immorality, use magical arts, and worship Dionysius, Apollo and Aphrodite, famed for their sexual activities (Justin, *1 Apol.* 14.2; 25.1); Tatian says that he was converted after he had taken part in the mysteries and tried out the practices conducted "by all" through

---

[39] See R. Penn, "Performing Family: Ritual Kissing and the Construction of Early Christian Kinship," *JECS* 10 (2002): 151–74.

[40] See Goldhill, *Foucault's Virginity,* 85–89, on the kiss in Hellenistic novels as an ironic play on the language of philosophy. P. Brown, "Late Antiquity," in *A History of Private Life from Pagan Rome to Byzantium* (ed. P. Veyne; Cambridge: Harvard University Press, 1987), 235–312, esp. 260, speaks of "solidarity in the face of its own inner tensions . . . the intimate discipline of a tight-knit group," and describes this as the morality of the socially vulnerable.

effeminates and hermaphrodites (*Orat.* 29). For the most part, however, the Apologists assume that no proof of their portrayal is required. Athenagoras rails against those who accuse Christians of the very practices they themselves engage in, and he presents immorality, adultery, and pederasty as the norms of contemporary life (Athenagoras, *Leg.* 34–35). What he, and other Apologists, take for granted is that the Greek stories of the immoral behaviour of the gods and their unashamed retelling in theatre replicate the values of those who revere them: "those who philosophised such things are, by their own doctrines, convicted of godlessness, or of promiscuity and forbidden intercourse" (Theophilus, *Autol.* 3.8); "your legends and tragedies glory in incest, and you read and hear them eagerly; you worship gods who are incestuous, with mother, with daughter, with sister. Understandably then incest is regularly exposed, and always practised among you" (Minucius Felix, *Oct.* 31.3–4).[41]

The point, therefore, is not simply the stories of the immorality of the gods, but the celebration of them in popular entertainment. Theophilus explains that Christians are not allowed to witness "spectacles, lest our eyes and ears are polluted, by participating in the words that are sung there" (*Autol.* 3.15). Tatian, as already noted, dismisses Sappho as a wanton girl, maddened by love, who sang of her own excesses; assuming that she is revered by those he addresses he says "You ought to be ashamed to be shown to be disciples of weak women." He ridicules the artists and sculptors who had portrayed and made statues of a long list of women of dubious reputation, including Praxilla who "said nothing useful in her poems," "Panteuchis when she was pregnant by rape," and Besantis who bore a black child (*Orat.* 33). As a general critique society is being condemned by its cultural choices. Yet the style of argument has specific implications for women: women are defined entirely in sexualised terms, and for this reason alone women should not be objects of the public gaze. It may, of course, be doubted whether many of the putative addressees would have disagreed with the principle.

---

[41] Justin, *1 Apol.* 21, is more cautious, ascribing such stories about Zeus to the demons, because he will need to deal with the apparent similarities with the Christian doctrine of the virgin birth.

Conclusion

Although presented as four separate themes, the presence of women in Christian communities, the charges of promiscuity brought against them, the chastity of men and women, and the licentiousness of Geek gods and of contemporary society, they are in practice tightly interwoven. Together they fashion an important aspect of Christian self-understanding. Within these different apologetic texts there is a surprisingly consistent presentation of women. One aspect of this consistency is not at all surprising for those well-versed in the ancient discourse of women: in the Apologies women are either whores, prostitutes, or else they are excessively chaste; there is no middle ground and no space for women to be defined by anything other than by their sexuality. Women certainly have a stronger profile among the second century Apologists than among their immediate successors but this is no evidence of a brief period of communal recognition.[42]

This also provokes further observations. First, unlike Josephus and Philo, the second century Apologists have little to say about Christian women's submission to their husbands; this contrasts with the regularity of this topos in the later books of the New Testament, and with the common argument that the so-called Household Codes had an apologetic purpose. In contrast to the modern concerns, there is limited interest in family roles; in contrast to the Greco-Roman world there is also no discussion of women's practices or what might be called "women's religion."[43] At the same time, it merits attention that the Apologies provide no information as to whether women held any significant roles within the churches. A century later the pagan philosopher Porphyry would mock the Christians for having "matrons and women as their senate because they were

---

[42] This is not maintained by Tertullian or by Minucius Felix, as many of the quotations from these authors will illustrate, and which tend to stress male practice. It is also not a theme in *Diognetus*. On the other hand, women are involved in the fourth-century transformation of the Christian "philosophical" life into one shaped by asceticism; see Levick, "Women, Power, and Philosophy," 151–3; Hunter, *Marriage*, 74–83.

[43] See R. S. Kraemer, *Her Share of the Blessings: Women's Religions among Pagans, Jews, and Christians in the Greco-Roman World* (Oxford: Oxford University Press, 1992).

predominant in the church."[44] However, given the hints of women's roles that have been found in other texts, the silence of the Apologists should not be taken as negative evidence for the second century. Active leadership is simply not part of their construction of women

Second, female chastity, and indeed the choice for virginity, is presented in socially positive terms. There is something of a contrast here with the *Apocryphal Acts of the Apostles*, which were written about the same date as the Apologies. These also tell of women who choose virginity and celibacy rather than marriage, but it is fully recognised that this presents a defiant challenge and a threat to society; Thecla's response to Paul's ascetic Gospel entails her rejecting her fiancé, and any subsequent suitor, her being rejected by her mother, and her facing a myriad of trials. She makes a deliberate and active choice, which challenges even Paul's conception of the proper order of things. To some extent her choice for chastity renders Thecla marginal, not only in society but also in the church, even in a story which puts her at its centre; although later tradition and feminist readers would say that it also makes her a powerful and authoritative figure. This is a very different construction of asceticism, and of its rationale and its consequences, than the one to be found in the Apologies where ascetic women belong within the community. It does perhaps represent a point of tension that is provoked by the overt address to outsiders.[45]

Thirdly, women also feature significantly in the second- and early third-century Martyr Acts. Although there are a number of significant intersections between the Martyr Acts and the Apologies,[46] the role of women is very different. Like Thecla, many of the women of the martyr accounts are named: Blandina, Perpetua, Biblis, Felicitas, Agathonice; they are vigorous and active, they take

---

[44] Porphyry, frg. 97 in Jerome, *Tract. Isa.* 3.12.

[45] However, Francis, *Subversive Virtue*, 162–79, over-simplifies in his contrast between the radicals (represented by the Apocryphal Acts) and the conservative elements in second-century Christianity.

[46] See J. M. Lieu, "The Audience of Apologetics: The Problem of the Martyr Acts," in *Contextualising Early Christian Martyrdom* (ed. J. Engberg, U. Holmsgaard Eriksen and A. Klostergaard Petersen; Frankfurt am Main: Peter Lang, 2011), 205–23. An earlier form of this paper was given as a companion to that at the Department of the Study of Religion, University of Aarhus, for whose hospitality I am very grateful.

initiatives, and they are given a voice of their own; they are, indeed, explicitly the focus of the gaze both by participants within their own drama and by the readers/ hearers who are offered here a public spectacle. Most significantly, they are women without men. In the Apologies the women who are named are all negative figures, Helen who accompanies Simon Magus, the various Greek goddesses, Sappho, and the other poetesses and subjects of art and sculpture. The contrast is noticeable when we consider the one narrative of martyrdom that does appear in an Apology, the story in Justin's so-called *Second Apology* (*2 Apol.* 2). This is the account of a woman who is converted from a licentious life-style, wishes to separate from her husband because of his excesses but is persuaded by her friends not to do so in the hope that she might convert him. Only when he behaves yet more promiscuously does she finally seek a separation. In retaliation her husband accuses her of being a Christian, but as the result of a legal manoeuvre her trial is postponed.[47] At this point her teacher is accused and it is he, Ptolemaeus, whose trial is described and who is punished by death. Unlike the other Martyr Acts and the Apocryphal Acts, this woman is anonymous—even though subsequent scholarship has claimed to identify her.[48] Unlike the Apocryphal Acts she is hesitant to reject her husband, and the friends who persuade her not to do so are presumably Christians; she only does so when there is no other alternative. Most important, at that point she fades from the story so that her fate is never described, and it is the male teacher, who is named, who dies. She is, it might be said, an entirely suitable woman for an Apology, silent, anonymous, and retiring—much more suitable than would be Thecla or Perpetua, and certainly than Blandina who is of slave status. Despite what was said earlier, it is at this point appropriate to recall 1 Peter 3:1 which urges women to be subject to their own husbands, so that if some are disobedient to the word, they may be won without a word through the manner of life of their wives. The

---

[47] Compare Tertullian, *Apol.* 3.4 where the husband ejects the chaste wife.

[48] She is often identified with the Flora to whom Ptolemaeus, the Valentinian, wrote a letter: so P. Lampe, *From Paul to Valentinus: Christians at Rome in the First Two Centuries* (London: Continuum, 2003), 237–40.

woman of Justin's *Second Apology*, if not of the others, is the heir to this counsel, while also setting a question-mark against its optimism.

The women of the Apologies, as also of these other literary genres, are constrained by rules and expectations that are both driven by and offer a challenge to contemporary values.[49] Here, they serve the literary and rhetorical construction of Christianity as a cohesive way of living within society; they contribute to the developing idea of Christianity as a people—and not simply, despite the language used, as a philosophy. In turn this is an aspect of the widespread use of ethnic categories in the construction of a Christian identity, and of the way in which women figure in such ancient "ethnic" patterns of thinking.[50] As generally in that construction, the strategies adopted by the Apologists include elements both of contrast, of radical difference, but also of continuity, with what it is assumed will be, or should be, recognised as the highest ideals of society. It is easy to see how this serves the distinctively apologetic agenda, within which an apparently conformist stance contains the seeds of a radically subversive programme. This is an agenda that would be no less programmatic for insiders, offering models of behaviour for survival. Moreover, as we have seen, the discourse about women helps to articulate the suppressed anxieties regarding the inherent tensions of tight-knit communities who identified themselves as close kin. Yet the real subjects of this discourse are in each case the men who have to prove their difference, their integrity, their control, and their masculinity. The women of the Apologies have little to tell us about the hopes and achievements of the real women of the early Christian movement.

---

[49] This could be explored by examining the women of the Apocryphal Acts and Martyr Acts in relation, for example, to the Hellenistic novels.

[50] See Lieu, *Christian Identity*.

Pope Benedict's Historical Validation of Jesus' Incarnation

Dieter Mitternacht
Lutheran Theological Seminary, Hong Kong

> Säkulare Sprachen, die das,
> was einmal gemeint war,
> bloß eliminieren, hinterlassen
> Irritationen
> Jürgen Habermas,
> *Glauben und Wissen*

> There is a crack in everything;
> that's how the light gets in.
> Leonard Cohen, *Anthem*

Introduction

Book boxes were carried up into the new residence. Adolph von Harnack glanced at a label, pointed to a book shelf, and said: "theology belongs with belletristic." Harnack was, of course, referring to speculative theology. He himself was a "scientific" theologian, an ardent advocate of relentless historical scrutiny, one who reconstructs the original and the historical characteristics of Christianity. He wouldn't bend to either orthodox or liberal inclinations. His objective was to recover the plain moral teachings of the extraordinary man Jesus.

Just around that same time, Albert Schweitzer put the final strokes to a book on historical Jesus research.[1] With acute precision Schweitzer dismantled the scholarly constructions of from Reimarus

---

[1] A. Schweitzer, *Geschichte der Leben-Jesu-Forschung* (4th ed.; Tübingen: Mohr Siebeck, 1926). The first edition was published in 1906 with the title *Von Reimarus zu Wrede*.

to Wrede, showing how each author's construct resembled a portrait of his own ethical ideals and preferences rather than that of the historical and mysterious figure of Jesus. With a good dose of scholarly sarcasm Schweitzer charged Harnack's historical ambition with the verdict of being a conversion of Jesus' teaching into a gospel for 1899.[2] A case of Harnackian belletristic then?

Together with W. Wrede's and K.L. Schmidt's findings on the tendentious and fragmentary character of the gospel tradition, and following and reinforcing the lead of J. Weiss, who argued that Jesus was an eschatological prophet who saw the kingdom of God as the imminent end of the world, Schweitzer's analysis brought the whole endeavor of historical Jesus research to a halt. Scholars not only had to concur that the liberals' quest for complete and "relevant" portraits of Jesus had to be sacked, but also that Jesus' ideas and actions belonged to a time cloaked in strangeness and mystery.[3]

A new generation of New Testament exegetes lead by Rudolph Bultmann found its way past the cul-de-sac of historical Jesus research by targeting the literary forms of the gospels as mirrors and representations of the emerging faith in the Christ of the church during the second half of the first century instead. The quest for the historical Jesus seemed halted for good, but it returned in two new waves, one that started in the 1950's and one in the 1970's. For the latter wave the Jewishness of Jesus became a central concern.

Timeless Awareness

According to Schweitzer the gospel texts conveyed a dim yet powerful premonition of a mysterious figure, tragic and majestic in one, consumed by the conviction that God's "coming" Messiah would secretly prepare the advent of the messianic kingdom.

---

[2] "In seinem ,Wesen des Christentums' läßt Harnack die zeitgeschichtliche Bedingtheit der Lehre Jesu fast ganz zurücktreten und geht nur auf ein Evangelium aus, mit dem er ohne Schwierigkeiten bis ins Jahr 1899 kommt" (Schweitzer, *Geschichte*, 246).

[3] "In der besonderen Bestimmtheit seiner Vorstellungen und seines Handelns wird er für unsere Zeit immer etwas Fremdes und Rätselhaftes behalten" (ibid., 631).

Exhibiting extraordinary will-power, he pursued his calling even as contradiction stared him right in the face. As hopes of the arriving kingdom of God finally crumbled, his mysterious will-power radiated potently in his last breath on the cross and kindled faith in his resurrection in the hearts of his disciples.

As his live ended in anguish, a powerful flood wave began to flow through history that energized generation after generation and accomplished far more than liberal portraits could have ever achieved.[4] This unknown and nameless figure approaches modern man in the same fashion,

> wie er am Gestade des Sees an jene Männer, die nicht wussten wer er war herantrat. *Er sagt* dasselbe Wort: *Du* aber folge mir nach! und stellt uns vor die Aufgaben, die *er in unserer Zeit* lösen muss. Er gebietet. Und denjenigen, welche ihm gehorchen, Weisen und Unweisen, wird er sich offenbaren in dem, was sie in seiner Gemeinschaft an Frieden, Wirken, Kämpfen und Leiden erleben dürfen, und als ein unaussprechliches Geheimnis werden *sie erfahren, wer er ist.*[5]

With no apparent concern for methodological complications, Schweitzer expected the dissimilar, strange and fragmentary recollection in the gospels to provide an unmitigated premonition of the man from Nazareth. Being touched personally by that 2,000-year-old power wave, Schweitzer turned and went to Africa in order to help the poorest among the poor.

Just about one hundred years later, a new commanding voice lays claim to an unmitigated premonition, this time, however, of the real historical Jesus. Joseph Ratzinger, Benedict XVI, has decided to challenge both academy and church to accept as scientifically valid his construct of the true icon that he has unearthed from underneath the ravel of historical-critical thinking.[6] With a self-

---

[4] Cf. e.g. ibid., 635: "In seiner eschatologischen Welt belassen ist er größer und wirkt, bei aller Fremdartigkeit, elementarer und gewaltiger als der andere [=der Modernisierte]."

[5] Ibid., 642, italics added.

[6] J. Ratzinger (Benedikt XVI). *Jesus von Nazareth: Erster Teil: Von der Taufe im Jordan bis zur Verklärung* (Freiburg im Breisgau: Herder, 2007). The double authorial attribution indicates the author's wish to be heard both as an academic theologian and as a hierarch, both as an academic and as

confidence that matches Schweitzer's, Benedict claims to surpass the quests for the historical Jesus of the 20th century and to accomplish more than just a mirror image of his own ideals.

While the affinities between Schweitzer and Benedict are intriguing, the differences fascinate as well. Whereas Schweitzer's Jesus invigorates the birth of the church in his wilful submission to his own ruin, Benedict's real Jesus enthrals because of his elevated clear-sightedness, always in concordance with his true being and, just like the Jesus of the Gospel of John, always aware ahead of time of what is about to happen. Schweitzer's central concern was to demonstrate how Jesus' *self-image* as Messiah *before* the messianic age was ultimately frustrated, yet lived on in his followers because of his radiant determination. Benedict's concern is to demonstrate how we can know that Jesus *was in fact* God *before* his birth as he asserted that conviction throughout his earthly life.

Schweitzer's premonition stemmed from an encounter with the strange and mysterious to which the texts explicitly testify. Benedict asserts a premonition from the depth dimensions of the earliest texts that may not be noticeable on the surface at first. As subsequent ecclesial elucidation recognizes the truth with ever increasing clarity, what had been there from the beginning is brought to the surface. Since the texts are the outflow of a collective, church-borne awareness through the mystery of the sacrament of an ever-present inner friendship with Jesus, historical validity is confirmed in history. Thus, the unity of Christ and Church is substantiated time and again in the faith that is foundational for everything else.

---

a shepherd, both as professor Ratzinger *and as* Pope Benedict XVI. According to Gottfried W. Locker ("So ändern sich die Zeiten: Das Jesusbuch in reformierter Lesart," in *Ein Weg zu Jesus: Schlüssel zu einem tieferen Verständnis des Papstbuches* [ed. T Söding; Freiburg im Breisgau: Herder, 2007], 53–67, esp. 55), this self-biographical double-assertion anticipates the book's principal flaw: trying to harmonize historical Jesus research with a dogmatic faith in Christ. Just as the book's inner tension is not resolved, the author's ambition to be both lacks conviction: "Nein die Doppelaussage scheint mir keine überzeugende Aussage. Sie suggeriert so etwas wie ein uni-personales Autorenkollektiv, das zu sein ein Papst sich vielleicht wünscht, das es aber weder amtstheologisch noch realkirchenpolitisch gibt ... Joseph Ratzinger ist ... nicht *auch* noch der Papst, sondern *nur* noch – im Sinne von ausschließlich – der Papst" (ibid., 56). Mindful of this, I shall in this article refer to the author as Pope Benedict, Benedict XVI or simply Benedict.

"Das Große am Anfang"

Historical-critical research is doomed to malfunction, Benedict asserts, as long as it subscribes to the unwarranted premise of a collective and largely anonymous evolution of meaning that culminates in the great confessions concerning an incarnated Son of God of whom the earliest layers have nothing to say. The idea that new meaning is added to originally silent sources ("der historisch-kritische Anfangssinn") is unsound even on account of the hermeneutical principal that human words by their own weight ("schon jedes Menschenwort von eigenem Gewicht") always carry a surplus of meaning. No single author can ever intend all that is inherent in the words he is using.

According to Benedict this surplus of meaning is sheltered in the crucial "historical" assurance that the gospel authors produced their texts not as individuals but as integral members of the collective people of God (pp. 18–20). Consequently, the prehistory of the texts and the chronology of the process of interpretation are not stages of truth-evolution but rather of ever increasing clarity of vision. Benedict asserts with great confidence that it is historically more logical that the Great stands at the beginning, "historisch viel logischer, dass das Große am Anfang steht" (p. 21), an assertion which is reminiscent of Stephen Pepper's world hypothesis called *organicism,* according to which an increasing understanding of reality might be compared to a rose bud that breaks open, revealing, as it unfolds, a flower with colors and fragrances, all of which were there from the start.[7]

Thus, Benedict laments deeply that historical Jesus research seems to have succeeded in permeating the collective consciousness of Christianity with the idea that faith in the divinity of Christ is an afterthought. It is not only bad historical research, it is,

> dramatisch für den Glauben, weil sein eigentlicher Bezugspunkt unsicher wird: Die innere Freundschaft mit Jesus, auf die doch alles ankommt, droht ins Leere zu greifen. (p. 11)

---

[7] On the idea of open-ended accounts cf. S. C. Pepper, *World Hypotheses: A Study in Evidence* (Berkeley: University of California Press, 1942), 146.

Consequently, it is natural for Benedict to read the Gospels as reliable testimonies about and of what he calls "the real historical Jesus" ("der historische Jesus im eigentlichen Sinn"). Especially the Gospel according to John, which most scholars would argue has taken a dramatic evolutionary leap towards a "high Christology," actually purports most clearly the solid, unchangeable, historical facts concerning what was there from the beginning. The Fourth Gospel thus represents the culmination of a process of spiritual memorization concerning who Jesus really was as it transcends individual understanding.

> Weil das Erinnern, das die Grundlage des Evangeliums bildet, durch die Einfügung in das Gedächtnis der Kirche gereinigt und vertieft wird, ist darin in der Tat das bloß banale Tatsachengedächtnis überschritten ... Dieses Erinnern ist kein bloß psychologischer oder intellektueller Vorgang, es ist ein pneumatisches Geschehen. Das Erinnern der Kirche ist eben nichts bloß Privates; es überschreitet die Sphäre des eigenen menschlichen Verstehens und Wissens. Es ist ein Geführtwerden durch den heiligen Geist, das uns den Zusammenhang der Schrift, den Zusammenhang von Wort und Wirklichkeit zeigt und uns so in die ganze "Wahrheit" führt. (pp. 273, 276)

Looking at historical reality from this perspective Pope Benedict can confidently claim that Scripture testifies to the real historical Jesus as God's son, himself God. This is articulated in the parables as the mystery of his person and in the Sermon on the Mount as "God's living Torah." Less ambiguous yet consistent with its predecessors, the Gospel according to John unveils Jesus' nature in the great images of water, vine, wine, bread and shepherd, and when Jesus says: "It is I," or "I and the Father are one" he points to the future and prefigures what the council at Nicaea (325 C.E.) will define as *homoousios*.

A Crack in Benedict's Own Construct?

In light of the above, Pope Benedict's strong affirmation of the theological necessity of the historical-critical method (faith rests in the *factum historicum*) comes as a surprise. Of course, he immediately adds a counter affirmation and identifies scientific stringency as the method's principle fault and shortcoming, since it excludes by definition assertions regarding the incarnation. Consistently applied, the historical-critical method therefore obstructs the very *fact* it is set to examine. After all, it is the incarnation that constitutes the *historical* beginning of Christianity.

In line with this, Benedict, on the one hand, praises Rudolph Schnackenburg, as the most respected catholic exegete of the second half of the 20th century, and credits him with "genuinely historical insight" into the fact that the Jesus figure can only be grasped if it is anchored in God. But, he faults Schnackenburg for his agnostic conclusions concerning historical reliability. According to Schnackenburg the nature of the Gospel sources prevents us from constructing a historically reliable picture of Jesus. For Benedict such methodological considerations are inappropriate. No doubt, historical critical research has uncovered,

> eine Fülle von Material und von Einsichten ... durch die uns die Gestalt Jesu in einer Lebendigkeit und Tiefe gegenwärtig werden kann, die wir uns vor wenigen Jahrzehnten noch gar nicht vorzustellen vermochten. (p. 22)

But the method must not be "misused" to examine the reliability of texts or to identify layers of contradictory traditions. Such objectives require other methods and perspectives and should be handed over to proper canonical exegesis (or end-text exegesis) that is based on a "Hermeneutik des Einverständnisses."

Faith thus integrated stipulates that the scripture canon established by the early church is normative for theology *and* history. Scripture in its "final" form is the authentic text, and the church, not the individual author, is the actual subject of scripture. Only thus will theological interpretation of the Bible be able to integrate faith into the interpretive process and uphold historical sincerity ("den Glauben einfordern, aber den historischen Ernst ganz und gar nicht aufgeben").

How historical sincerity corresponds to a sincere use of the historical-critical method remains an open question. Evidently, Benedict does not concern himself with questions of authenticity. There is no historical incentive to investigate *ipsissima verba*, layers of traditions, the composition history of the Bible, or even the diversity of the social history of the Jesus movement. The Bible and especially the Gospels can instead be read "als Einheit und als Ganzheit, die in all ihren historischen Schichtungen doch eine von innen her zusammenhängende Botschaft ausdrückt" (p. 230).

Since the collective ecclesial process of interpretation is of such crucial importance for Benedict, it is surprising that his methodological construct shows a crack at its very core, as he affirms that canonical gospel interpretation is about understanding "den Weg Jesu auf Erden und seine Verkündigung … *nicht* die theologische Verarbeitung im Glauben und Denken der frühen Kirche" (p. 369, italics added). Of course, Benedict's criticism is directed towards form criticism. But if the early Church cannot be trusted as a reliable recipient and interpreter of the *factum historicum*, does not that throw us back to square one and the demand for a stringent historical method? How can the theological and historical reliability of scripture rest in the church as the subject of scripture, a church that purifies the original memory, if the collective theological reflection of that same church poses a danger?

The crack widens as one considers Benedict's assertion concerning the modification of the memory of the earliest testimonies in all four gospels. On the one hand Benedict asserts that the memory needed to be refined before it could become the memory of the church, on the other hand he asserts that the personal memory together with the historical reality constitute the *factum historicum* of the wording (p. 272).

The Historical and the Real Jesus

The basic question, then, is how Benedict's quest for the figure of Jesus, or the face of the Lord, correlates to historical Jesus research. How does the (f)actual historical Jesus compare to Benedict's real historical Jesus? What does he mean when he asserts that the historical critical method leads from within itself to a fundamental trust in the witness of Scripture, canonical exegesis and the authorial triangle that consists of the individual author, the people of God and God?[8]

Benedict claims to build on modern exegesis as he pursues his goal, "den Jesus der Evangelien als den wirklichen Jesus, als den 'historischen Jesus' im eigentlichen Sinn darzustellen" (p. 20).[9] But by merging the attributes "real" (wirklich) and "historical" he actually removes himself from the broad consensus among exegetes that is succinctly expressed by the American Jesuit John P. Meier: "The historical Jesus is not the real Jesus. The real Jesus is not the historical Jesus".[10]

Indeed, Meier seems to assert the irrefutable: compared to Caesar, Cicero or Marcus Aurelius, we really can know basically nothing about Jesus. The sources, including the gospels, are simply too fragmentary. Even if one were to neglect the subjectivity of interpretation and the "softness" of historical science, there still is no way of establishing a "reasonably complete" picture of the real Jesus.[11] We simply cannot know anything about "the real Jesus through historical research, whether we mean his total reality or just a reasonably complete biographical portrait."[12] When scholars refer to the "historical Jesus," they refer to an abstraction and a construction determined by historical science. Each construct is one among several possible interpretations of pieces from a mosaic where most pieces are missing.

---

[8] Cf. Ratzinger, *Jesus von Nazareth*, 16–20.

[9] 20. Benedict seems to use "wirklich" and "wahr" interchangeably, cf. here and p. 143: "der wahre 'historische' Jesus."

[10] J. P. Meier, *A Marginal Jew: Rethinking the Historical Jesus: Volume One: The Roots of the Problem and the Person* (New York: Doubleday, 1991), 21. After almost 20 years since publication, Meier's book still sets the standard for historical Jesus research.

[11] Ibid., 22, see also 23: "With the exception of a relatively few great public figures, the 'real' persons of ancient history—be they Hillel, Shammai or Jesus and Simon Peter—are simply not accessible to us today by historical research and never will be."

[12] Ibid. 24.

Benedict appreciates Meier's description of the limitations of historical-critical research (p. 409) but insists, once again, that the limitations are not definite and that the method points beyond itself to other complimentary methods).[13] The necessary supplements towards which the historical critical method points are, as already mentioned, canonical exegesis and the recognition of divine inspiration through the authorial triad. Benedict confidently asserts that merging the three approaches imparts plausibility to the assertion of the historical reliability of the Gospels.

Precisely how Benedict envisions the feasibility of this merger remains unclear—regrettably, since the claim appears to be at the heart of his concern. But it seems hardly a daring suggestion that Benedict would rather compromise the historical critical method than traditional Christological dogma.[14] For Benedict, so it seems, "real" is not a scientific term in any modern sense of the word, or a reference to the common meaning of factual assertion, but rather an affirmation of the divine, the incarnate, the absolutely true.[15]

---

[13] "[Ü]ber sich hinausweist und eine innere Offenheit auf ergänzende Methoden in sich trägt" (p. 16). Benedict articulated the underlying rationale in his "Regensburger Rede." There he argues for an inner necessity to widen—or rather reinstall—the original concept of reason in order that "Vernunft und Glaube aufs Neue zueinander finden; wenn wir die selbstverfügte Beschränkung der Vernunft auf das im Experiment Falsifizierbare überwinden und der Vernunft ihre ganze Weite wieder öffnen. In diesem Sinne gehört Theologie nicht nur als historische und humanwissenschaftliche Disziplin, sondern als eigentliche Theologie, als Frage nach der Vernunft des Glaubens an die Universität und in ihren weiten Dialog der Wissenschaften hinein. ... Eine Vernunft, die dem Göttlichen gegenüber taub ist und Religion in den Bereich des Subkulturellen abdrängt, ist unfähig zum Dialog der Kulturen." (J. Ratzinger, "Glaube, Vernunft und Universität: Erinnerungen und Reflexionen," n.p. [cited 8 March 2008]. Online: http://epub.uni-regensburg.de/406/). To this Jens Schröter replies: "Die Grundlage bildet eine spezifische Verhältnisbestimmung von Vernunft und Glaube. Nur der Glaube an den einen Gott befreit und 'rationalisiert' wirklich die Welt, heißt es an einer Stelle. 'Rationalität' meint dabei das Einstimmen in das Bekenntnis zu dem Gott, der sich in Jesus zu erkennen gegeben hat. Seit der Aufklärung wird das Verhältnis von Vernunft und Glaube freilich anders bestimmt," see J. Schröter, "Ratzinger und seine Suche nach dem historischen Jesus," *Die Kirche, Evangelische Wochenzeitung* (May 20, 2007).

[14] Benedict's praise (p. 409) for Jacob Neusner's critical review of John P. Meier's book ("Who needs 'The Historical Jesus'? An Essay Review," *BBR* 4 (1994): 113–26) speaks for itself. Cf. also Geza Vermes's comment in *The Times* (May 19, 2007): "we are told that the Pope obeyed the rules of historical criticism. However, he was prepared to abide by those rules only if they confirmed his traditional convictions. Otherwise, he discarded them without further consideration."

[15] Benedict's attempt at unearthing the real Jesus has caused a flood of immediate reactions in the daily press from both scholarly and ecclesial experts. Several books have also been published already (see bibliography). Gerd Lüdemann the most outspoken among the New Testaments scholars calls

Absolute Religious Truth Claims

Benedict's perception of truth is evident from chapter four, where he interacts extensively with Jacob Neusner's *A Rabbi Talks with Jesus.*[16] *The reason why Benedict chose to interact with this popularly written booklet rather than scholarly Jesus books by Jewish scholars such as David Flusser or Geza Vermes,*[17] *becomes immediately apparent. While Flusser and Vermes focus on important aspects of Jesus' Jewishness, Neusner highlights what is crucial for Benedict, namely, the decisive discrepancies that show why, in the end, Judaism and Christendom exclude each other.*

Whereas Flusser had demonstrated that the historical Jesus practiced pharisaic halakha and Vermes that he was basically a Jewish charismatic, Neusner underscores that Jesus, besides being a Jew, time and again violates the Rabbis' interpretation of the Torah and makes his own claims God's claims. Thus, while it is true that Jesus never annulled an iota of the law, it is also true that he added something: himself. But adding to the Torah only God can do. Neusner's inherently logical conclusion is that he must reject Jesus since his claims are unreasonable. In an article in the *Jerusalem Post* ("My Argument with the Pope", May 29, 2007) he summarizes his view of Jesus' Torah-interpretation as follows: "Where Jesus diverges from the revelation by God to Moses at Mount Sinai that is the Torah, he is wrong, and Moses is right."

---

the book "eine peinliche Entgleisung" (*Spiegel Online*, April 26, 2007) and challenges the Pope to treat passages such as Matt 10:18 with the same sincerity as passages that fit into his construct (also Geza Vermes, "Ratzinger and not the Pope" *The Times,* May 19, 2007). Against Lüdemann turns Klaus Berger, accusing him of rational fundamentalism and methodical atheism, welcoming instead Benedict's methodological suggestions as long overdue corrections (*Tagespost*, May 24, 2007). In between the two extremes, we find scholars who emphasize that many of Benedict's assertions only *seem* to be controversial. Had Benedict been up-to-date on historical-critical Jesus research, Michael Wolter laments, he would have known that a great number of scholars today regard many of his assertions as unproblematic, even common ground. The real problem with the Pope's book is his insistence on rising above his own subjectivity ("Wo bleibt der Eigensinn der Evangelien?" *Rheinischer Merkur*, May 24, 2007).

[16] Jacob Neusner, *A Rabbi Talks with Jesus: An Intermillenial Interfaith Exchange* (New York: Doubleday, 1993).

[17] D. Flusser, *Jesus* (2d ed.; Jerusalem: Magnes Press, 1998); G. Vermes, *Jesus the Jew: A Historian's Reading of the Gospels* (London: Collins, 1973).

Thus, since Jesus acknowledges the validity of God's law ("not an iota"), his treatment of the Torah is inherently inconsistent.

Already 1993, Benedict (then still Cardinal Ratzinger) praises Neusner in a blurb on the back page of *A Rabbi Talks with Jesus* for his emphasis on difference, truth claim and his challenging honesty: "The absolute honesty, the precision of analysis, the union of respect for the other party with carefully grounded loyalty to one's own position characterize the book and make it a challenge especially to Christians who will have to ponder the analysis of the contrast between Moses and Jesus."

Of course, Benedict does not welcome Neusner's analysis because he accepts his conclusions, but rather because Neusner provides the analytical blueprint for Benedict's own diametrically opposed assertions.[18] Every time Neusner shows that the texts assert Jesus's unreasonable divine claims, Benedict's convictions are confirmed, namely that the New Testament texts prove the unity of the Son with the Father not only in John's Gospel but also in the other Gospels:

> Der gewaltige Prolog des Johannesevangeliums "Im Anfang war das Wort und das Wort war bei Gott" sagt nichts anderes, als was der Jesus der Bergpredigt und der Jesus der synoptischen Evangelien sagt. Der Jesus des vierten Evangeliums ist ein und derselbe: der wahre "historische" Jesus. ... Nur weil Jesus Gott ist, kann und darf er so mit der Tora umgehen, wie er es tut.[19]

---

[18] It has been pointed out repeatedly that what is really new about this exchange is the fact that a pope actually interacts with a Jew who is critical of the New Testament. See e.g. D. van Biema, "The Pope's Favorite Rabbi," *Time* (May 24, 2007).

[19] Ratzinger (Benedikt XVI). *Jesus von Nazareth*, 143, 148. Cf. C. K. Schönborn, "Der Papst auf der Agora: Über einen Anspruch den allein Gott stellen kann," in *Ein Weg zu Jesus: Schlüssel zu einem tieferen Verständnis des Papstbuches* (ed. T. Söding; Freiburg im Breisgau: Herder, 2007), 43–52, esp. 47–48: "Rabbi Neusner ist wohl deshalb für das Buch von Joseph Ratzinger / Benedikt XVI so wichtig, weil er allen Versuchen, den historischen Jesus vom Christus des Kirchendogmas zu trennen, eine klare Absage erteilt. ... Jesus selber stellt in seinem ganzen Tun und Reden einen Anspruch, der Gott allein zusteht."

A New Shift in Jewish-Christian Religious Dialogue

Underneath the seemingly straightforward exchange between Benedict and Neusner lies their concurrence that the enlightenment heritage of tolerance, as it comes to expression in Lessing's parable *Nathan der Weise,* has to be overcome. Lessing's powerful parable had, of course, taught that the ultimate purpose of any religion is to transcend its own particular expression and point to the overarching, the universal and the inclusive. The lesson to be learned from the parable is that practitioners of religions should consider differences as trivial and peripheral, exclusive assertions of truth or knowledge of God as dispensable, and instead embrace an attitude of tolerance and respect for the other. Neusner puts it bluntly as he asserts that the time has come for "a return to the old disputations, with their intense seriousness about religious truth and their willingness to ask tough questions and engage with the answers" (*Jerusalem Post,* 29 Maj 2007).

Especially since WWII, Jewish-Christian dialogue suffers, as Neusner asserts, from an obsession with looking for the positive in the other, but this is both dishonest and wrong.[20] True dialogue between religions demands instead that each side claims its own truth boldly, articulates differences with precision and then engages in a respectful dispute. Only thus can real dialogue occur. Concerning Pope Benedict Neusner testifies that he is

> so full of respect for the scriptures and for Judaism that this is only a step forward in the Judeo-Christian relationship. ... Both he and I are convinced that knowing what the differences are strengthens the faith of the believers effectively."[21]

---

[20] See J. Neusner, "Einzigartig in 2000 Jahren: Die neue Wende im jüdisch-christlichen Dialog," in *Ein Weg zu Jesus: Schlüssel zu einem tieferen Verständnis des Papstbuches* (ed. T. Söding; Freiburg im Breisgau: Herder, 2007), 71–90, esp. 78–79: "Das wohlmeinende Reden von einer neuartigen Beziehung ist zum einen nicht wirklich aufrichtig, weil jede Seite angestrengt nach irgendetwas Positivem sucht das sie über die andre Seite sagen kann. Sie ist zum anderen, jedenfalls was das Judentum anbelangt, schlicht falsch."

[21] Radio interview, On Point, WBUR Boston, June 19, 2007. Of course, already Rabbi Abraham J. Heshel has argued that "Inter-faith dialogue begins with faith." But Heshel also held that *no* religious community owns the truth and was critical of Jewish isolationism and triumphalism. One

It is therefore high time to lay aside insincere modesty and that false idea of tolerance by which "disputations gave way to the conviction that the two religions say the same thing and the differences between them are dismissed as trivial."[22] Instead, both parties ought to express with precision what separates them and testify to their particular truth, in order to then love, worship and serve the one, common god in peace. For Jews this means accepting that God's Torah is not just one way, "our" way, but *the* way to love and serve the one God.[23]

Similarly unambiguous, Benedict asserts that Jesus not simply "added himself," but in fact created one single people of God, "die Universalisierung des Gottesvolkes kraft deren nun Israel die Weite der Völker der Welt umspannen kann" (p. 132). Neusner clearly seems to have found a soul-mate in the present pope: "Someone once called me the most contentious person he had ever known. Now I have met my match. Pope Benedict XVI is another truth-seeker."[24]

Theology and/or History?

Finally, we must return to the initial query regarding the relationship between theology and history. This is how Neusner characterizes Benedict's Jesus-book in the already mentioned ra-

---

must therefore note the verb "begins" in the quote. One's own faith and religious identity is not the irreducible goal of religious dialogue, but rather the beginning of a burdensome road towards basic understanding and respect for the other's equally valid faith. Rabbi Heshel acted as spokesman for the American-Jewish communities at Vatican II and succeeded (according to "A Conversation with Dr. Abraham Joshua Heschel," December 20, 1972, NBC transcript, 12–13) to persuade Pope Paul VI to erase all references to mission to Jews from the document that would then become known as *Nostra Aetate* (Declaration on the Relation of the Church to Non-Christian Religions).

[22] J. Neusner, "My argument with the Pope," *Jerusalem Post* (Maj 29, 2007).

[23] See Neusner, "Einzigartig in 2000 Jahren, 83: "Ich betone: Mein Ziel ist es Christen zu helfen, bessere Christen zu werden, indem sie zu einer größeren Klarheit über ihren Glauben gelangen; und ebenso ist es mein Ziel, Juden zu helfen, bessere Juden zu werden, weil sie hier – wie ich hoffe – erkennen werden, dass Gottes Tora der Weg (nicht nur unser Weg, sondern *der* Weg) ist, den einen Gott zu lieben und ihm zu dienen, ihm, dem Schöpfer des Himmels und der Erde, der uns gerufen hat, zu dienen und Gottes Namen zu heiligen."

[24] Neusner, "My Argument with the Pope." Cf. also Neusner's somewhat double-edged comment: "Nur ein in Deutschland geborener Papst konnte so mutig die Herausforderung eines theologischen Dialogs mit dem Judentum nach dem Holocaust aufnehmen," see Neusner, "Einzigartig in 2000 Jahren 90.

dio interview (On Point, WBUR Boston, June 19; italics added):

> It's *not* a question of history; it's a question of theology. The pope's description of Jesus is a fully Christian, fully realized, description from all the components of the New Testament. And the argument that we have, is with the argument of the faith of Christianity, which is *not* a distillation of what is historical fact, but which is a fully articulated religious system.

This characterization clearly is not in accord with Benedict's express intent. Benedict and Neusner do not only disagree on who Jesus really was, they also seem to disagree on what science, history and truth is. Neusner distinguishes between history and theology, faith and historical fact in a manner that seems consistent with modernity. Benedict advocates a broadening of the concept of reason and its application where reason and faith come together in a new way, and where the limitations of reason to the empirically falsifiable are overcome.

For Neusner the question of whether the Gospel according to Matthew grants access to knowledge concerning the historical Jesus is at most of subordinate value, for Benedict the historical factuality is absolutely essential, since it contains the anchor and the foundation of truth. For Neusner dialogue between Judaism and Christianity is a dispute between two different religions,[25] for Benedict, Jesus has incorporated within his own person the status of the other and "relinquished" it by fulfilling it at a definite point in history.[26]

It must be emphasized, however, that Benedict recognizes and endorses Judaism as a luxuriant religious cradle for Jesus's piety. By any standard, this is a welcome improvement over polemical distortions and apologetic *ressentiments* that all too often have been

---

[25] Neusner, "Einzigartig in 2000 Jahren, 86: "Das Judentum ist schlicht und ergreifend *eine andere Religion*, nicht nur Nicht-Christentum, es geht nicht um das Judentum als Gegenpol zum Christentum."

[26] See A. Standhartinger, "Der Papst und der Rabbi: Anmerkungen zum christlich-jüdischen Dialog im Jesusbuch Benedikt XVI," in *Ein Weg zu Jesus. Schlüssel zu einem tieferen Verständnis des Papstbuches* (ed. T. Söding; Freiburg im Breisgau: Herder, 2007), 146–157, esp. 150, 151: "An dieser Stelle gerät der Dialog und das Streitgespräch meines Erachtens ins Stocken. Die kanonische Lektüre der Bibel wird einseitig in das Schema Verheißung im Alten, Erfüllung im Neuen Testament gepresst. Daraus entsteht notwendigerweise ein Überbietungsmuster. ... Benedikt XVI geht es um die in Jesus erfüllte Verheißung, um die Überbietung des Mose."

and still are hiding behind the disguise of historical construction. Yet still, the basic tenor of Benedict's description of Israel is that the "real" Israel has been absorbed—since Jesus's entry into the world and history—into God's new big family.[27] Franz Mußner's assertion that Benedict's Jesus-book promotes missionary joyfulness is certainly well taken.[28] Should Neusner's vision of a new shift in religion dialogue come true, we may soon find that we are back to facing high-spirited and dogmatically assertive missionaries on both sides of the supposedly round table who witness—with respect—to each other about their respective religion's exclusive requirements and promises. The purpose of such dialogue, so it seems, is not acknowledgement of commonality but amplification of dissimilarity.

The notion of uncertainty that may disturb the representatives of the "old" school of dialogue as it tries to relate to this new dialogical scenario is paralleled by the exegete's bewilderment

---

[27] See also Benedicts assertion that "[d]ie beiden Sphären – Änderung der Sozialstruktur, Aufbrechen des 'ewigen Israel' in eine neue Gemeinde hinein und der göttliche Anspruch Jesu – sind unmittelbar miteinander verknüpft" (p. 147). It should be noted, however, that Benedict leaves a small door open for the continued autonomous value of "eternal Israel" as he comments on Luk 5:39 ("And no one after drinking old wine desires new wine, but says, 'The old is good'"). This should be taken "ein Wort des Verstehens für diejenigen … die beim alten Wein bleiben wollten" (p. 219). One may assume that this is in conformity with what is written in article II.B.4 of *The Jewish People and Their Sacred Scriptures in the Christian Bible* (Boston: Pauline Books & Media, 2002), where the Papal Bible Commission asserts: "It is because of our common roots and from this eschatological perspective [ref. to Rom 11:24, 26] that the Church acknowledges a special status of "elder brother" for the Jewish people, thereby giving them a unique place among all other religions." The question of the older brother's status is treated by Benedict in his interpretation of the parable of the two brothers (Luk 15:11–32). On the one hand Benedict (*Jesus von Nazareth*) underlines that the father expressly calls the older brother his son. On the other hand he describes the older son as a representative of pious man in general, a piety that is, which views God primarily as law and which is jealous of the younger brother's experience of real freedom: "Sie tragen ihre Freiheit eigentlich doch als Knechtschaft und sind nicht zum wirklichen Sohnsein gereift. Auch sie brauchen noch einen Weg; sie können ihn finden, wenn sie einfach Gott recht geben, sein Fest als ihres annehmen" (p. 252). The fact that these lines are followed by an inclusive pronoun ("So redet mit dem Gleichnis der Vater *uns,* den Daheimgeblieben, zu, damit auch wir uns bekehren und unseres Glaubens froh werden," italics added), affects the impression only marginally, that Israel without Christ is tantamount to subservient piety and lack of the freedom that belongs to a real son. Cf. also *Nostra Aetate,* § 4: "Although the Church is the new People of God, the Jews should not be presented as rejected or accursed by God, as if this followed from the Holy Scriptures. All should see to it, then, that in catechetical work or in the preaching of the Word of God they do not teach anything that does not conform to the truth of the Gospel and the spirit of Christ."

[28] See F. Mußner, "Ein Buch der Beziehungen," in *Ein Weg zu Jesus. Schlüssel zu einem tieferen Verständnis des Papstbuches* (ed. T. Söding; Freiburg im Breisgau: Herder, 2007), 71–90, esp. 97: "Das Buch hilft zur Glaubensfreude. Es ist ein missionarisches Buch."

as he tries to make sense of Benedict's retrospective gospel interpretation. While this writer supports the need of broadening the concept of reason and its application, he finds it difficult to avoid a premonition of being wedged into the old cul-de-sac of apparently dogmatically predetermined analyses.

Benedict's ambition to surmount the limitations of the historical critical method from within the method's own openness does not really leave the starting blocks, even though it is a central concern in the book. The methodological additions of canon exegesis and "historical" theories of inspiration are recognized—even by colleagues who are ready to give the requested advance of sympathy—not as a surmounting of the limitations of the historical critical method, but rather as a clarification by contrast of the limited methodological value of Benedict's suggestions. A broadening of the concept of reason does not necessitate *one* particular interpretation, so that, in the end, Pope Benedict may have to accept that even his Jesus portrait "weit mehr eine Fotografie des Autors und seiner Ideale ist als eine Freilegung einer Ikone."

Constructing the Galilee of Jesus in an Age of Ethnic Identity[1]

Halvor Moxnes
University of Oslo

Introduction

In the present interest in Galilee in the Greco-Roman period two different strands come together. The first is the interest in the history of Galilee within the context of Jewish history.

The other is the interest in Galilee as the place for the historical Jesus. This last interest is based on more than just a question of geographical origin. It is based on idea that Galilee is so to speak the key to understand the specific character of Jesus, his message and acts. Sean Freyne, who has written many of the recent studies of Galilee himself, says that "one occasionally gets the impression that the quest for the historical Jesus is in danger of becoming the quest for the historical Galilee."[2] My focus in this essay is primarily on studies of Galilee that is concerned with the relevance for the understanding of the historical Jesus, although I will try to bring in some of the discussions of the archaeologists and historians of ancient Galilee.[3] My main question is how the present interest in ethnicity to describe identity illustrates what is at stake in the study of Galilee as the place for the Historical Jesus.

---

[1] I am happy to present this essay as a small sign of recognition of Bengt Holmberg's works on the historical Jesus and early Christian identities.

[2] S. Freyne, *Jesus: A Jewish Galilean* (London: T&T Clark, 2004), xi.

[3] I am grateful to Eric M. Meyers and Jonathan L. Reed for helpful comments on an earlier draft of this essay, for making recent studies available to me, and for suggesting further literature. Unfortunately, since the ms was completed in 2008, only literature up to that time could be considered.

Galilee in the History of Jesus Research

The interest in Galilee within the study of Jewish history has exploded with the strong archaeological activity in Galilee over the last 30 years, with new information about the history of Galilee forthcoming every year. This new information has also increased the interest for Galilee in the study of the historical Jesus and early Christianity in general. Sean Freyne's saying about the quest for Jesus as the quest for the historical Galilee contrasts with the situation he described as recently as 25 years ago: "There has been little attempt to examine seriously the Galilean context of Jesus' life, and even less attention has been paid to the kind of Jewish faith and practice one was likely to encounter her."[4]

The lack of interest in Galilee before Freyne wrote his large study was very much due to the state of historical Jesus studies in the so-called Second Quest for the Historical Jesus. Its main interest was in Judaism as a religious system and Jesus' teaching in contrast to that system, and not in specific regions and local diversity. One of the most important books on Jesus in the Second Quest was Günther Bornkamm's *Jesus of Nazareth* (1956/1960) which despite its title says very little on Galilee. And also E. P. Sanders, who importantly changed the perspective of historical Jesus studies to seeing him within his Jewish environment, wrote of *Jesus and Judaism*[5] i.e. in terms of a religious system, where Galilee as a specific area was of little interest.[6] A renewed interest in Galilee came with the Third Quest that moved from a history of religious ideas approach to an integration of religion into social history. This move was part of a larger intellectual paradigm shift in the writing of history, from grand master narratives to an interest in local communities and regions, from ideas to broader cultural contexts.[7]

---

[4] S. Freyne, *Galilee, Jesus and the Gospels* (Dublin: Gill and MacMillan, 1988), 2.

[5] E. P. Sanders, *Jesus and Judaism* (Philadelphia: Fortress, 1985).

[6] In 2002, E. P. Sanders published "Jesus' Galilee," in *Fair Play: Diversity and Conflicts in Early Christianity: Essays in Honour of Heikki Räisänen* (ed. I. Dunderberg, Ch. Tuckett, K. Syreeni; Leiden: Brill, 2002), 3–41, in which he argued that the picture of a Jewish Galilee in the gospels was basically accurate.

[7] H. Moxnes, "The Historical Jesus: From Master Narrative to Cultural Context," *BTB* 28 (1999):

In its interest in Galilee the present stage of Jesus' research is actually raising anew the question that was debated in the 19th century: what was it about the identity of Galilee that could explain Jesus and his message? I have elsewhere pointed out how this question should be seen within a larger social and intellectual context of colonialism and the growing nationalism of the 19th century.[8] The interest in the historical Jesus was also an interest in Jesus as identification figure and a model for European identity. In this context Galilee as the home place of Jesus played an important role, especially as a place for an advanced, "modern" religion compared to the backwards and rigid religion of Jerusalem and Judea. The interest in Galilee today show similarities with the discussion of the 19th century, but the question of identity is discussed in terms of different categories. In the 19th century it was raised as a question of race, whereas in the present stage it is phrased as a question of the *ethnicity* of Galilee. It is ethnic identity that now is in vogue in studies of Galilee, both in the archaeological and historical studies of Galilee within Jewish history, and in studies of Galilee as the place of Jesus.

Changing Taxonomies in Descriptions of Difference and Diversity

In *The Archaeology of Ethnicity* the archaeologist Sian Jones describes the changing taxonomies used to describe human diversity and difference in human and social sciences.[9] Archaeology and history use theories and models especially from anthropology, and therefore archaeologists and historians need to engage in theoretical reflections of their presuppositions: "it is necessary to explore the ways in which the assumptions and concepts used in archaeological

---

135–49.

[8] H. Moxnes, "The Construction of Galilee as a Place for the Historical Jesus," *BTB* 31 (2001): 26–37, 64–77. See now also idem, *Jesus and the Rise of Nationalism: A New Quest for the Nineteenth Century Historical Jesus* (London: I.B. Tauris, 2012).

[9] S. Jones, *The Archaeology of Ethnicity: Constructing Identities in the Past and Present* (London: Routledge, 1997), 40–55.

analysis have been, and continue to be, influenced by discourses of identity in the present."[10] Different definitions of identity used to understand the past reflect our own understandings of "self" and "other." Jones outlines three different historical phases of dominant taxonomies. The 19th century discourse was dominated by race. The second phase, covering a large part of the 20th century was marked by a transition from race to culture. Finally, ethnicity became the dominant concept in the last part of the 20th century.

The early 19th century saw an increased interest in human diversity and in the classification of human groups. The main idea was that "human groups were essentially distinct, primordial entities, characterized by specific physical qualities—a transformation primarily embodied in the concept of 'race'."[11] However, race was understood differently in two major traditions of thought. One was a physical anthropological tradition associated with comparative anatomy; here "racial types" were used to identify mental and cultural characteristics.[12] The other tradition was related to philology and comparative linguistics and saw linguistic characteristics as the most reliable indicator of race.[13] With Darwin and the socio-cultural evolution theory came a different model of classifying human diversity. It was no longer based on a hierarchy of physical types, but on cultural stages within a framework of development and evolution. This model could be used to classify nations that were advanced compared to those who were backwards. Thus, in terms of classifying peoples, the concepts of race, language and culture belonged together within a larger context of nationalism as the dominant paradigm of social thought in the 19th century.[14] The idea that race and nation

---

[10] Ibid., 13.

[11] Ibid., 41.

[12] S. L. Gilman, *The Jew's Body* (New York: Routledge, 1991) traces the history of scientific and popular representations of this tradition applied to Jews.

[13] A significant representative of this tradition is Ernest Renan, both in *Vie de Jésus* (Paris: Michel Lévy frères, libraires éditeurs, 1863), and in many of his philological studies where the characterization of Semitic languages as "dead" languages compared to Indo-European "living" languages was also applied to the racial groups identified with these language families, see H. Moxnes "Renan's Vie de Jésus as Representation of the Orient," in *Jews, Antiquity, and the Nineteenth-century Imagination* (ed. H. Lapin and D. B. Martin; Bethesda: University Press of Maryland, 2003), 85–108, esp. 105–6.

[14] L. Meskell, *Archaeology under Fire: Nationalism, Politics and Heritage in the Eastern*

belonged together became a strong political impetus, and racial classification also played a role in justifying European colonialism.

19th Century: Race and the Non-Jewish Galilean Jesus

The categorization of humanity according to race became a dominant paradigm that influenced all academic disciplines. In *Racializing Jesus* Shawn Kelly has shown how racial ideology influenced biblical studies and their intellectual paradigms in the 19th and well into the 20th century. Kelly traces the influence of German philosophers like Herder, Hegel and Heidegger on biblical scholars and their descriptions of Jesus and Christian origins. Jesus and Paul were described embodying Western values as individuality and authenticity. Jews and Jewish Christians on the other hand were described with characteristics associated with the Orient as in-authenticity and decay.

These paradigms associated with race are reflected in 19th century descriptions of Galilee and Jesus. Scholars like D. F. Strauss and E. Renan agreed that Galilee had inhabitants from various races and that the area represented a "racial mixture."[15] But this observation was used differently by various interpreters. By some German historians, the idea of a Galilee of mixed races was used to distance Jesus from the Jewish people. They argued that racially Jesus was not a Jew, and that this racial difference was more important than Jesus' religious affiliation to Judaism. Renan had a different approach to Jesus and race.[16] He too, started with the observation of the mixed population of Galilee, but distanced Jesus from the very category of race. The term "race" was linked to a debate of the contemporary situation in Europe, and Renan saw Jesus as pre-figuring his ideas of a modern nation not based on race. This does not mean that he abolishes the idea of race altogether, but he appears to use it only for peoples belonging to less developed stages,

---

Mediterranean and Middle East (London: Routledge, 1998), 2–3.

[15] Moxnes, "Galilee," 31–32.

[16] Moxnes, "Renan."

and not for advanced nations. Thus his usage corresponds to the paradigmatic patterns of a contrast between the West and the Orient.[17]

20th Century: From "Race" to "Ethnicity"

The discussion of the race of the Galileans among German scholars in the 19th century belonged to an early stage of the development that in the 20th century led to the Nazi ideology on the "Jewish race." In the period before the World War II, the ideology of a Galilean "Aryan Jesus" was developed by German biblical scholars.[18] After World War II, the racially motivated genocide of six million Jews made a continued use of a race terminology politically impossible. But there were also other reasons why the term race was deemed obsolete. From the beginning of the 20th century there had been a shift from race to an interest in culture. A move away from the idea of culture as a universal process of development to "a plurality of historically conditioned, distinct cultural wholes"[19] made it a useful substitute for race. But the concept culture carried with it many assumptions central to 19th century classifications of human groups. Like race it represented "the world as divided up into discrete, homogenous, integrated cultures (and societies), which were implicitly equated with distinct peoples or 'tribes'."[20]

It was this idea of distinct cultures that was criticized when the concept of ethnicity emerged as a central category to classify peoples after the World War II. Several factors contributed to the emergence of this new concept and the way in which it quickly gained acceptance. One factor was the criticism from within anthropological research that the experience on the ground did not fit the models; for instance that social boundaries did not correspond

---

[17] H. Moxnes, "Jesus som europeer? Jesus-forskningen og Europas problemer i det 19. Århundre," *DTT* 69 (2006): 62–78.

[18] S. Heschel, *The Aryan Jesus: Christian Theologians and the Bible in Nazi Germany* (Princeton: Princeton University Press, 2008).

[19] Jones, *Archaeology*, 46.

[20] Ibid., 48.

with cultural boundaries. On the political level the end of colonialism led to criticism of models that described human groups as "tribes" and "primitive societies." Theories of ethnicity seemed to meet both internal and external criticisms. The focus of study was upon the processes involved in the construction of group boundaries in the context of social interaction. Instead of treating cultural traits like language, material culture, values and beliefs as defining elements of social groups, anthropological studies focused on the *self-definition* of particular ethnic groups in opposition to other groups.[21] But also larger political and social trends played an important role in the increasing interest in ethnicity. Ethnicity became a word that signified minority groups, and it also became a definition of identity in the creation of new nation-states, e.g. in previous colonies, and in Europe, in the break-up of states as in the Balkan, or demands for autonomies within states as in Western Europe.

Ethnicity in Early Christian Studies: From Karl Barth to Fredrik Barth

For most of this period there was little interest among students of the New Testament in categories that described social and group identity. This can be ascribed to general trends in theological studies away from the historical Jesus and Early Christianity to the proclamation of the kerygma. This influence is above all associated with the names of Karl Barth and Rudolf Bultmann. The main interest was in the church more than in society, and when the interest in the historical Jesus received a new start in the 1950s, it focused on Jesus' words and proclamations, not his social context.

So when from the 1980's references in Biblical studies to important works for methods and perspectives shifted from Karl Barth to Fredrik Barth it was a clear sign that something had happened in studies of New Testament and early Christianity. Works by the Norwegian anthropologist became a point of reference first in

---

[21] Ibid., 52.

studies of early Christian groups, later in studies that started to bring ethnicity into focus. The main theoretical shift in the classification of human diversity in the last decades also influenced the study of the historical Jesus in Galilee, and biblical studies in general. There was a shift from fixed categories of "race," "culture," "society," and "tribe" towards a processual analysis of ethnicity as a form of social interaction.[22] This perspective, called "constructionist" or even "instrumentalist," emphasizes the role of social relationships and social agency. This theoretical shift is associated with Fredrik Barth and his introduction to a collection of essays by Norwegian anthropologists in 1969: *Ethnic groups and boundaries.*[23] His starting point was that ethnic groups are not the result of geographical and social isolation, and that ethnicity does not consist in a number of cultural traits. Instead he emphasized the decisions making of social actors, ethnicity as situationally defined and the process of boundary-making. The boundaries, not the content inside, are what constitute ethnicity. Ethnicity is based on establishing difference in opposition to others. Barth sees the central element in ethnicity in the dichotomy between members and outsiders, whereas cultural features play a secondary role and may change. This aspect of Barth's theory has been criticized for reducing ethnicity to economic and political relationships, and neglecting the cultural dimension.[24]

Not all biblical scholars find that Barth's approach is useful for their material, and emphasize that more specific traits are necessary for an analysis of ethnicity in antiquity. These scholars are closer to the "primordial" perspective that places importance on bonds between individuals based on certain "given" factors. Clifford Geertz speaks of "immediate contiguity and kin connection mainly, but beyond them the givenness that stems from being born into a particular religious community, speaking a particular language

---

[22] Ibid., 55.

[23] F. Barth, "Introduction," in *Ethnic Groups and Boundaries* (ed. F. Barth; Oslo: Universitetsforlaget, 1969), 9–38. Barth could draw on his study of ethnic groups in his fieldwork in Afghanistan and Pakistan.

[24] Jones, *Archaeology*, 72–9.

and following particular social practices."[25] This perspective emphasizes the psychological dimension of ethnicity and a "givenness" that transcends alliances and social relationships.

Based on Bourdieu's concept of *habitus* Jones suggests a solution to the lack of a satisfactory theory on the relation between ethnicity and culture in Barth's approach. *Habitus* is made up of durable dispositions towards certain perceptions and practices and thereby it structures new experiences. But this structuring does not happen through a system of rules outside the individual or group; rather, it is dependant upon the human agents themselves by the disposition of *habitus*. In this way Jones is able to integrate some of the continuity in cultural elements that is found in the primordial perspective, but with more flexibility, they are not "givens" in the same way. This results in a definition that includes culture, in what Jones speaks of as "multidimensional ethnicity": "Ethnic groups are culturally ascribed identity groups, which are based on the expression of real or assumed shared culture and common descent (usually through the objectification of cultural, linguistic, religious, historical and/or physical characteristics)."[26]

Moreover, Jones also emphasizes that ethnic identity is not the only form of identity. In analyses of societies "it is necessary to consider the intersection of different kinds of identity—ethnic, class, gender."[27] This is an important caveat against tendencies to focus exclusively on ethnic identities.

Theories of Ethnicity in Early Christian Studies

Theoretical discussions of ethnicity have been central to studies of ancient Israel for a long period,[28] but in studies of the New

---

[25] C. Geertz, "The Integrative Revolution: Primordial Sentiments and Civil Politics in the New States," in *Old Societies and New States* (ed. C. Geertz; New York: Free Press, 1963), 109.

[26] Jones, *Archaeology,* 84.

[27] Ibid., 85–6, quoting T. H. Eriksen, *Us and Them in Modern Societies: Ethnicity and Nationalism in Mauritius, Trinidad, and Beyond* (Oslo: Scandinavian University Press, 1992), 173–9.

[28] See e.g. A. Killebrew, *Biblical Peoples and Ethnicity: An Archaeological Study of Egyptians, Canaanites, Philistines, and Early Israel 1300–1100 B.C.E.* (Atlanta: Society of Biblical Literature,

Testament and early Christianity they have only recently been taken up. In *Why this new Race* Denise K. Buell discusses possible reasons for this delay.[29] Modern understandings of ethnicity and race as fixed categories, especially based on descent, have made scholars think that they could be used to characterize the Jews, but that they were not applicable to early Christians. Buell argues for an understanding of ethnicity and race as both fixed and fluid, i.e. under negotiation and social construction. This fluid understanding she argues, was also found in antiquity. On that basis she suggests that using ethnicity as an analytical category reveals how authors of early Christian texts use ethnicity as a rhetorical strategy for self-definition. Buell's suggestion that ethnicity should be understood as a category that is both fixed and fluid corresponds to Sian Jones attempt to bridge the distinction between the primordial versus the constructionist approach in anthropology. Buell also warns against privileging kinship and descent in definitions of ethnicity over against factors like religion, foodways etc., and holds that it will result in an understanding of ethnicity as fixed. Buell's perspective on ethnicity as both fixed and fluid corresponds to the most recent discussions of Galilean ethnicity as reported in the last part of the essay.

Three other studies deserve mention as examples of how anthropological theories on ethnicity are taken up and developed in analyses of Jewish and Early Christian texts and groups. In *Conflict and Identity in Romans* Philip Esler bases himself on Fredrik Barth's work in outlining a way to study ethnic conflicts in the Mediterranean world. However, he argues for the consideration also of the importance of the primordial dimension of ethnicity. The primordial attachments are characteristic of emic, i.e. insider point of view, and often play a large role for members of ethnic groups. Esler also lists some of the cultural features that make ethnic groups different from other groups: 1) a common name, 2) a myth

---

2005), and A. Faust, *Israel's Ethnogenesis: Settlement, Interaction, Expansion and Resistance* (London: Equinox, 2007).

[29] D. K. Buell, *Why this New Race: Ethnic Reasoning in Early Christianity* (New York: Columbia University Press, 2005), 1–34.

of common ancestry, 3) a shared history or memory, 4) a common culture, e.g. language, customs, 5) a link with a homeland, and 6) a sense of common solidarity. However, Esler follows Barth in that these features are not constitutive of, but can be used to diagnose identity and boundaries.[30]

Dennis Duling combines primordial and constructionist perspectives in developing a theory to study ethnicity in Matthew's Gospel.[31] This combination of perspectives shows that there is great interest in the "given" aspects of ethnicity and also that ancient texts like the Gospels lend themselves to this kind of analysis. Duling has a different organization of his list of features than Esler, the most significant new element is that of family and kinship.

Most recently Markus Cromhaut has developed theories of ethnicity to be used in an analysis of Jesus in a Judean and Galilean context. His book *Jesus and Identity: Reconstructing Judean Ethnicity in Q*[32] has the most sophisticated discussion of ethnic identity theories of all recent books that covers Galilee. Cromhaut combines the ethnic indicators from primordialist theory with Sian Jones' development of *habitus* and contextualizes these perspectives in a Judean setting by help of E. P. Sanders' covenantal nomism.

Galilean Ethnicity at the Time of Jesus

Recent studies of Jesus and Galilee show varying degree of awareness and/or discussion of theories of ethnicity. Issues related to ethnicity may be discussed without referring to such theories, e.g. whether Galilee was a distinct region or not; the identity of the population in terms of descent, diversity of the population and religious behavior or beliefs, as well as socio-economic relations. Sean Freyne who over 30 years has played a central role in the discussion of Galilee has dealt with all of these questions in his many

---

[30] P. F. Esler, *Conflict and Identity in Romans* (Minneapolis: Fortress, 2003), 40–76.

[31] D. Duling, "Ethnicity, Ethnocentrism, and the Matthean *Ethnos*," *BTB* 35 (2005): 125–43.

[32] M. Cromhaut,. *Jesus and Identity: Reconstructing Judean Ethnicity in Q* (Eugene: Wipf & Stock, 2007).

publications,[33] without explicit interaction with theories of ethnicity.

Eric M. Meyers has for many years chaired major excavations in Galilee that have contributed greatly to develop the field of Galilean archaeology and history in the first centuries of the Common Era. His written contributions have integrated literary and material sources, and also engaged in discussion with historical Jesus studies.[34] Meyers set the stage for the discussion of diversity and boundaries for Galilee with a number of important studies on Galilean regionalism.[35] These studies of Meyers appear to have been influential in two directions. Meyers himself and his colleagues and students engaged in the archaeological work and its interpretation have followed up and emphasized the Jewish character of Galilee and the similarity to Judea. In these works "diversity" is applied to variations within Jewish practice and beliefs in both areas. But Meyers' description of the open boundaries of Galilee set in a context of Hellenistic towns also makes it possible to put the emphasis on the interaction and exchange over the boundaries, so that the diversity may be more related to the differing degrees of such interaction.

The most extensive discussion of Jesus in a Galilean context, combining the interpretation of texts archaeological material is found in Jonathan Reed, *Archaeology and the Galilean Jesus.* Reed combines New Testament scholarship with a long experience with archaeology, serving as Director of the Sepphoris Acropolis Excavations in Galilee. In this book he has a chapter on "The Identity of the Galileans: Ethnic and Religious Considerations."[36] He places his discussion within the context of an instrumental, i.e. Barthian, approach to ethnicity. He starts by outlining the contrast to the paradigm of race:

---

[33] See several of the essays in S. Freyne, *Galilee and the Gospels: Collected Essays* (Tübingen: Mohr, 2000).

[34] See most recently E. M. Meyers, "Jesus and His World: Sepphoris and the Quest for the Historical Jesus," in *Saxa Loquentur: Studien zur Archäologie Palästinas/Israels* (ed. C.G. den Hertog, U. Hübner and S. Münger; Münster: Ugarit, 2003),185–97; idem, "The Problem of Gendered Space in Syro-Palestinian Domestic Architecture: The Case of Roman-Period Galilee," in *Early Christian Families in Context.* (ed. D. L. Balch and C. Osiek; Grand Rapids: Eerdmans, 2003), 44–69.

[35] E. M. Meyers, "Galilean Regionalism as a Factor in Historical Reconstruction," *BASOR* 21 (1976): 93–101; idem, "The Cultural Setting of Galilee: The Case of Early Judaism," *ANRW* 19.1:686–701.

[36] J. L. Reed, *Archaeology and the Galilean Jesus* (Harrisburg: Trinity, 2000), 23–61.

> While an earlier generation debated the issue under the shadow
> of Nazi racial theories and scurrilous attempts at an Aryan Jesus,
> the recent discussion's impetus is the recognition of diversity in
> early Judaism and the role of regionalism as a factor in historical
> reconstruction. The present study is indebted to both of these
> recognitions and is much less concerned with the Galileans' racial
> identity in genetic or biological terms, but focuses rather on the
> Galileans' ethnic identity in terms of their socialized patterns of
> behaviour, including religious aspects embedded in this behaviour.
> ... Ethnicity, however, is not simply a matter of genetics, but a
> concept that reflects the symbols and behaviors with which a group
> defines itself and distinguishes itself from others.[37]

With this brief paragraph Reed has outlined the major transition
in construction of identity in a way that is similar to Jones:
from "race" to "ethnicity," and also characteristic elements in
the description of ethnicity according to the constructionist
perspective it refers to "socialized patterns of behaviour," and
"symbols" that a group employs to define itself and to distinguish
itself from others. In addition, he places these general trends
within specific developments in religious and historical studies
of the ancient Middle East: the recognition of diversity in
Judaism and the importance of regionalism. Reed represents a
conscious application of theories of ethnicity on what he from the
archaeological material presents as indicators of "socialized patterns
of behaviour": stone vessels, *miqwaoth,* burials and food practices.

Among the many issues discussed about the identity and character of
Galilee and Galileans in the time of Jesus, I will focus on the discussion
of whether Galileans made up an ethnic group. Two main issues of this
discussion are presented. First, what does the issue of the descent of
the Galileans contribute to this discussion, and secondly, what does
the archaeological material reflecting social behavior contribute?

---

[37] Ibid., 23–24.

Galilean Ethnic Identity: The Question of Descent

Denise Buell argued that privileging the question of kinship and descent represented a way of seeing ethnicity as fixed.[38] Does the discussion of the descent of the Galileans support this claim? In 19th century descriptions of Galilee the mixture of the population of Jews and non-Jews (e.g. Phoenicians, Syrians, Greeks) was a recurring theme, and was expressed by the category "race." The contemporary discussion of the ethnic identity of Galilee is also concerned with the question of a mixed population. It does not use the category race, but discusses the question of the diversity of Galilee in terms of the origin or *descent* of the population.

The start for all discussions of a mixed population in Galilee is the Assyrian conquest in 733–732 B.C.E. and the question of what happened to the original Israelite population.

Richard Horsley revives the hypothesis of A. Alt that after the Assyrian conquest (733–732 B.C.E.) only the elite was deported.[39] The main bulk of the population was allowed to stay behind and probably to continue to run their own affair. Horsley argues that the bulk of the Galileans most likely were descendants of former Israelites with their own distinctive versions of the shared Israelite traditions. With the Hasmonean regime a number of Judeans must have become residents in Galilee, in military garrisons, and as an elite as officers and representatives of the Jerusalem government. Some must have been non-Israelites, culturally or in cultural heritage due to conquests and shifts in rulers. But Horsley reserves the term "Galileans" for the "old" group of inhabitants, the descendants of the ancient Israelites. It is they who define Galilean identity through their use of old traditions, by sticking to the habits of the

---

[38] Buell, *Race,* 9. See W. Sollors, *Beyond Ethnicity: Consent and Descent in American Culture* (New York: Oxford University Press, 1986), 5–6, for a definition of descent relations *in* terms of language of heirs and hereditary qualities.

[39] R. Horsley, *Galilee, History, Politics, People* (Valley Forge: Trinity, 1995), 19–33. In his many studies of Galilee Horsley does not discuss ethnicity theories, but deals with many of the major issues involved: the question of boundaries for Galilee, of the descent of the population, and the question of characteristic beliefs or practices. The most significant aspect of his discussion of Galilee concerns the socio-economic relations in the area.

local villages. Thus, descent is the determining factor in ethnicity.

Horsley's reconstruction has met with much criticism. Here I will present a criticism from the perspective of archaeology advanced by Jonathan Reed. Reed distances himself from previous discussions of Galilean identity that has focused mainly on descent. Descent is a question that cannot be solved by archaeology, although it can provide some indications.[40] Reed draws on results of archaeological excavations, which show almost no finds in Galilee from the period after the Assyrian conquest. Therefore there must have been a de-population also of the lower classes after the Assyrian conquest. There are no traces of Galilean settlements that could support the hypothesis of a continuity of an Israelite village culture. In contrast the archaeological investigations show increase in population in the Hasmonean period of late 2d and 1st centuries B.C.E. Settlements and coins show Hasmoean influence, while gentile sites appear to have been destroyed or left. Reed therefore interprets the increased settlements in Galilee in this period as a result of Hasmonean politics. According to Reed the most likely scenario was that Judeans colonized Galilee and "overwhelmed the few prior inhabitants, who may have been earlier Jewish settlers."[41]

Reed's hypothesis of a non-diverse, Judean/Jewish population in Galilee at the time of Jesus is followed by Mark Chancey and Michael Cromhaut,[42] and appears to have broad support. Defenders of the "mixed population" hypothesis like Burton Mack and others who argue that Galilee was culturally complex have not taken up the recent results by archaeology, and their hypothesis therefore has lost much of its credibility. However, it is raised again from a different angle and with discussion of the archaeological evidence as well as the use of categories of ethnicity by Milton

---

[40] Reed, *Archaeology*, 28–34.

[41] Ibid., 53.

[42] Cromhaut, *Jesus and Identity*, 231–56, does not present any new arguments, but builds primarily on Reed. M. Chancey, *The Myth of a Gentile Galilee* (Cambridge: Cambridge University Press, 2002), does not discuss the issue of ethnicity. He says that the lack of literary material from Galilee in the 1st century C.E. "hinders the detailed application of ethnicity theory" (p. 6). This statement seems to mean that he considers that it is on 1st century material that ethnicity theories shall be applied, not that such theories determine the perspectives of modern scholars.

Moreland.[43] He questions the "fixity" of the ethnic identity, first by challenging the historic reconstruction and second by questioning the meaning of the modern categories. Moreland offers a different type of explanation of the growth in the population of Galilee in the Hasmonean period than the Judean hypothesis held by most archaeologists.[44] He places Galilee within a wider context of the Levant, not primarily in relation to Judea. The entire region of the Southern Levant was under populated until the beginning of the 1st century B.C.E., when growing population created the need for more agrarian settlements. Since there was little in terms of boundaries between Galilee and the Tyrian and Syro-Phoenician territory there was much communication and economic contact in that direction. Thus there was an influx into Galilee starting from the coast, not primarily from Judea, and not part of an expansionist Hasmonean policy. Also the existing indigenous population increased. Moreland presupposes that from the Persian time Galilee had a diverse population, and that a major part of the population in Galilee after the influx in the Hasmonean period were non-Judeans.[45]

Moreland also raises the important question of what it could mean to be Jewish in early Roman Galilee if a large part of the population was non-Judean. He argues that both "Galilee" and "Jewish" are terms that need to be defined before modern historians can make sense of them in the complexities of the Roman period. To say that in the early Roman period "Galilee was Jewish" is of little consequence if it is not explained.[46] If "Jewish" is used as a term to explain Galilean identity Moreland asks what category the term "Jewish" is: "ethnic, geo-political, religious, cultural or serogenetive"?[47] It is difficult for a non-expert in archaeology to evaluate the competing arguments by

---

[43] M. Moreland, "The Inhabitants of Galilee in the Hellenistic and Early Roman Periods," in *Religion, Ethnicity, and Identity in Ancient Galilee* (ed. J. Zangenberg, H. W. Attridge, and D. B. Martin; Tübingen: Mohr Siebeck, 2007), 33–59.

[44] Moreland, "Inhabitants of Galilee," 143–57, bases his projections on a thorough reading of archaeological evidence, tracing material evidence for contact and Syro-Phoenecian influence in Western and Northern Galilee.

[45] Idem, "Inhabitants of Galilee," 133–4.

[46] Ibid., 157–9.

[47] Ibid., 138–9.

Reed, Chancey and Cromhaut for a mainly Judean and by Moreland for a mostly mixed population. But Moreland points to an important question of the meaning of descent for definitions of ethnicity. By many descent is regarded as a secure basis to define Jewish ethnicity as something "fixed," but Moreland points to the fluidity of the category.

Jewish Ethnicity as Patterns of Behavior

Reed holds an understanding of ethnicity as not determined by descent, but by behavior. It is therefore a question of what archaeology can contribute towards a study of behavior. Reed argues that in order to determine a region's ethnicity one should start with how material culture inside domestic space may reflect social behavior.[48] Large scale architecture and language of inscriptions tend to reflect the activity and attitude of the elite and the rulers, and therefore not the population at large. The material from domestic space belongs mainly to four different groups: 1) stone vessels, 2) stepped immersion pools, *miqwaoth*—smaller ones in larger and urban private houses, larger near olive presses, synagogues, 3) burial practices, 4) dietary habits.

The importance of these material finds is that they reflect social use, and that they therefore may provide information for the aspects of ethnicity that Reed has emphasized, following a constructivist perspective: "socialized patterns of behaviour, including religious aspects embedded in this behaviour."[49] Reed speaks of the material mentioned above as "Jewish religious indicators." Reed finds that they signify a pattern of behavior that is also found in Jerusalem and Judea, and that the Galilean population adhered to or adopted (if they were not originally Judean). So whether they were descendants of Judean colonizers or belonged to the (few) prior inhabitants," in terms of ethnicity, the Galileans should be considered Jewish."[50] This general conclusion may be an overstatement. Chancey remarks

---

[48] Reed, *Archaeology*, 44–49.
[49] Ibid., 24.
[50] Ibid., 53.

that even what he calls "unambiguous finds" "allows us only to attest the presence of Jews at a specific site, not to determine that all of the inhabitants of the site were Jews."[51]

A Galilean Jewish Identity?

The results of the discussion by Reed, Chancey and Cromhaut is that the Galileans were Judeans both in terms of their descent and according to a constructivist perspective that sees ethnicity as an expression of "symbols and behaviours with which a group defines itself and distinguishes itself from others."[52] The symbols and behaviors corresponded to those found in Jerusalem and Judea. These aspects of ethnicity take precedence over other markers of identities. Reed also discusses the socio-economic situation in Galilee and finds that Galilean Jews had a different social, economic, and political matrix than the Jews in Judea or in the Diaspora.[53] Reed is to be commended for his recognition of major differences both between Galileans and Judeans, and also among Galileans themselves, but when it comes to what he calls their "common ethnicity" the designation *Jewish* takes precedence.[54] The problem with this conclusion is that even

---

[51] Chancey, *Myth*, 118.

[52] Reed, *Archaeology*, 53.

[53] Ibid., 62–99, 216–18.

[54] In the discussion of the origin of the new settlers in Galilee in the Hasmonean period Reed (*Archaeology*) consciously uses "Judeans" to indicate that they came from Judea (39–43). In some instances and most notable in the conclusion, however, he speaks of Jewish settlers and Jewish Galilee and Jesus as a "Galilean Jew" (216–18). Thus, the geographic origin of the settlers is turned into a terminology with clearly religious connotations. The term "Jews" is a category where the meaning has many modern layers. This makes it important to discuss the significance of the term used of Galilee the 1st century. Several scholars have argued for the use of "Judeans" and "Judeanism" instead of Jews and Judaism when speaking of ethnic identity in the first centuries C.E. The main argument is that Jews and Judaism are more recent categories for a religious group and a religion, and not categories in use in this early period. See Cromhout, *Jesus and Identity*, 2–5; Esler, *Romans*; J. H. Elliott, "Jesus the Israelite was Neither a 'Jew' nor a 'Christian': On Correcting Misleading Nomenclature," *JSHJ* 5 (2007): 119–54; S. Mason, "Jews, Judeans, Judaizing, Judaism: Problems of Categorization in Ancient History," *JSJ* 38 (2007): 457–512. Criticizing this position, A-J. Levine, *The Misunderstood Jew* (New York: Harper One, 2007), 160–6 argues that the term Judean destroys the element of continuity of practice and belief between the ancient period and the contemporary situation that "Jews" and "Judaism" convey.

if one starts by recognizing the complexities of the situation of the Galileans, the conclusion "Jewish" represents a *simplification*, and it also identifies Jewishness primarily by religious indicators.

There seems to be something important at stake by emphasizing "Jewish ethnicity" in such a way that it does not appear as just one aspect of identities, but as a totalizing concept. Chancey illustrates that when he criticizes "scholarly reconstructions that de-emphasize the Jewish character of Jesus' ministry ... by de-Judaizing Galilee distorts Jesus, the Jesus movement, and their Galilean context."[55] Here there is little room for complexity, and it becomes obvious that the defense of a Jewish Galilee is ultimately a defense for a Jewish Jesus. That again appears to be a matter where the historical reconstructions have an almost existentialist relevance. One gets the sense that it is the picture of Jesus as a symbol for modern identities that is at stake in the discussion of a Jewish identity.[56]

The Ethnicity of Galilee and Modern Nationalism

In archaeology and ancient history the term ethnicity functions to establish identities associated with particular groups with whom contemporary groups and nations can identity. The nation state has for a long time been taken for granted as the frame of reference for archaeology.[57] From many young nations we know how archaeological finds play an important part in the project of nation building.[58] Archaeology became part of a large national project of establishing a Jewish presence and links to antiquity in Palestine (from 1948 in Israel). Eric M. Meyers, professor in Judaic Studies at Duke and for many years director of excavations in Galilee, discusses the relations between archaeology and

---

[55] Chancey, *Myth*, 182

[56] See W. Arnal, *The Symbolic Jesus: Historical Scholarship, Judaism and the Construction of Contemporary Identity* (London: Equinox, 2005).

[57] N. A. Silberman, *Between Past and Present: Archaeology, Ideology, and Nationalism in the Modern Middle East* (New York: Doubleday, 1990).

[58] E.g. the finds of several ships from the Viking period in Norway at the end of the 19th century played a role for the politics of establishing Norway as an independent nation in 1905.

nationalism in Israel in an essay with the subtitle: "Making the Past Part of the Present." Meyers writes on the role of archaeology in the early period of Jewish settlements before World War I:

> Archaeology, therefore, played a determinative role in creating a sense of national belonging and identity among the early Jewish settlers; but even more, it inscribed a sense of spatial identity on the land its sponsors sought to inhabit. ... By assuming that the modern Zionist immigrant was ethnically equivalent to the ancient Israelite or Byzantine-period Jew and also that such groups were and remained entitled to a specific piece of territory, the modern "Israeli" archaeologists reveal their essentialist bias and preference for a nationalist ideology.[59]

This emphasis on archaeology as a project of nationalism increased after the establishing of the state of Israel in 1948.[60] But the digging to find new traces of ancient Israeli remains was not the only way to establish a continuity with the past. Another way was to bury traces of many centuries of Arab history in the form of buildings and landscapes, as well as to erase Arab place-names and to re-name them with Jewish names.[61]

The function of archaeology and history to identify past cultural identities that can be used for the purpose of constructing national traditions is not unproblematic.[62] This use of archaeology is "concerned with establishing a legitimate continuity with the past, *not* with understanding historical discontinuities and the evolution of social contradictions."[63] Galilee and Israel/Palestine is a case in point

---

[59] E. M. Meyers, "Archaeology and Nationalism in Israel: Making the Past Part of the Present," in *Zeichen aus Text und Stein: Studien auf dem Weg zu einer Archäologie des Neuen Testaments* (ed. S. Alkier and J. Zangenberg; Tübingen: Francke, 2003), esp. 68.

[60] T. Oestigaard, T. *Political Archaeology and Holy Nationalism: Archaeological Battles over the Bible and Land in Israel and Palestine from 1967–2000* (Gothenburg: Göteborg University, 2007).

[61] M. Benvenisti, *Sacred Landscape: The Buried History of the Holy Land Since 1948* (Berkeley: University of California Press, 2000); Meyers, "Archaeology," 68–69.

[62] A book on archaeology and nationalism in the Eastern Mediterranean and the Middle East is appropriately named *Archaeology under Fire*. The editor Lyn Meskell says that "[a]rchaeological and historical narratives are deeply imbricated with socio-political realities. In this region archaeology matters in very tangible, as well as ideological, ways" (pp. 2–3).

[63] S. B. C. Devalle, *Discourses of Ethnicity: Culture and Protest in Jharkand* (London: Sage

as an example of historical discontinuities and social contradictions. Meyers reflects on this situation in the conclusion to his article on archaeology and nationalism. Today nation-states organize their museums etc. to present the accepted narrative of the past and to enhance the achievements of their own people. But the ethics of contemporary archaeology demands that it pays equal attention to the broadest range of human communities that their material presents. Thus, the ideal of archaeology should be "to facilitate better understanding among different peoples in different nation-states."[64]

Among scholars of the historical Jesus there has been little interest to discuss and reflect over the relations between the past and the present in the use of terminology and categories of identities.[65] Of course the question whether the Galileans in the 1st century C.E. were ethnically Judean/Jewish belongs in a totally different context from the modern one in the state of Israel and the Palestinian territories. Positive responses to that question are mostly not intended as statements about the present political situation.[66] But they will often have political implications. I am not saying that every article or chapter that deals with the ethnicity of Galilee should discuss the ideological and political contexts of historical reconstructions of antiquity. But it surprises me that there seems to be almost no awareness of possible contemporary implications of historic reconstructions of the identity of Jesus and his homeland.

Publications, 2002), 21, my italics.

[64] Meyers, "Archaeology," 77.

[65] But see now the studies in n. 52.

[66] But some studies seem to be so "concerned with establishing a legitimate continuity with the past" that it is difficult to avoid political implications. One recent example is an essay by Mordecai Aviam with 14 maps of distribution of archaeological data from the Galilee, see "Distribution Maps of Archaeological Data from the Galilee: An Attempt to Establish Zones Indicative of Ethnicity and Religious Affiliation," in *Religion, Ethnicity, and Identity in Ancient Galilee* (ed. J. Zangenberg, H. W. Attridge, and D. B. Martin; Tübingen: Mohr Siebeck, 2007), 115-32.

From Ethnicity to Intersectional Identities in Galilee

What has been gained by employing ethnicity in the discussion of the identity of Galilee? In one sense just to enter into the discussion of approaches and perspectives from anthropology and archaeology is necessary for studies of Galilee and of historical Jesus studies, in order to be part of a general academic context and be isolated in a separate niche. Some biblical scholars have not just appropriated theories of ethnicity but have also engaged in adapting these theories to the specific contexts and materials of their fields.[67] But when compared to the perspectives advanced by Fredrik Barth the end result of the focus on ethnicity in recent studies of Galilee has been limited. In contrast to his view that ethnicity does not consist in a number of cultural traits, a focus on stone vessels and *miqwaoth* as "Jewish religious indicators" suggests that they are viewed as cultural traits with fixed meaning, rather than parts of processes engendered by social actors for different and complex purposes.[68] Thus, the underlying concept may be one that determined earlier cultural studies, of ethnic groups as bounded, homogeneous culture-bearing units with continuity over time.[69]

Many studies of Galilee seem to define ethnicity in a very narrow sense with an emphasis on religious identity. Discussions of Galilean ethnicity often conclude with the definition "Jewish." In a context of studies of the historical Jesus the category "Jewish" will easily be understood as an exclusively religious category, so that other aspects of identity play little role.[70] That was the conclusion even in Reed's discussion, although he includes the social, economic, and political matrix in his discussion of Galilean identity. This result suggests that "ethnicity" is too limited a perspective to speak of the identity of Galilee and Galileans, and that it may be too limited

---

[67] See Duling, "Etnicity"; Esler, *Romans*; Cromhaut, *Jesus and Identity*; Mason, "Jews, Judeans."

[68] See the criticism by Moreland, "Inhabitants," and D. E. Oakman, *Jesus and the Peasants* (Eugene: Cascade Books, 2008), 245–79.

[69] Jones, *Archaeology,* 103–4.

[70] Within studies of the historical Jesus and the New Testament it corresponds to a trend of seeing Jesus and the early Christian scriptures in the context of "Judaism" as a religion in contrast to "Christianity," that does not take the broader Greco-Roman context into consideration.

also when it comes to providing a context for the historical Jesus.

Jones suggests that a broader set of categories should be taken into consideration in discussion of social identities. She says that in analyses of societies "it is necessary to consider the intersection of different kinds of identity – ethnic, class, gender."[71] It is this direction the most recent works on Galilee and identity have moved, represented by two major publications where the titles signal new trends. The first book, *Religion, Ethnicity, and Identity in Ancient Galilee*,[72] shows its perspective when it starts by saying "Multiple and complex identities may have been almost the rule, rather than the exception."[73] The title of the other volume, *The Archaeology of Difference: Gender, Ethnicity, Class and the "Other" in Antiquity*, contributes substantial suggestions of how to develop useful models to understand the role *difference* played in the ancient world.[74]

In these studies the question of identities and ethnicities in Galilee (and other regions) is placed in a broader context that takes into consideration both the complexities of the historical region, and the ethical responsibility of scholarship to consider all aspects of human communities equally. These collections of essays are very recent and therefore it will take some time before their perspectives will be reflected in pictures of the historical Jesus. Here I can only suggest a few possibilities. These broader perspectives may imply a break with the specific emphasis on the religious aspects of Galilean identities, which have been so important for the formation of Christianity and rabbinic Judaism. This emphasis on religion has resulted in a focus on relations between Jesus and Jewish leaders, Torah observance, legal and ritual matters etc. that have been of central interest to theologians and scholars of religion. It was this continuity between the past and present that shaped the interest in describing Galilee

---

[71] Jones, *Archaeology,* 85–86.

[72] J. Zangenberg, H. W. Attridge, and D. B. Martin, eds., *Religion, Ethnicity, and Identity in Ancient Galilee* (Tübingen: Mohr Siebeck, 2007).

[73] J. Zangenberg, "A Region in Transition: Introducing Religion, Ethnicity and Identity in Ancient Galilee," in *Religion, Ethnicity, and Identity in Ancient Galilee* (ed. J. Zangenberg, H. W. Attridge, and D. B. Martin; Tübingen: Mohr Siebeck, 2007), 1–10, esp. 2, quoting J. Geiger.

[74] D. R. Edwards and C. T. McCollough, eds., *The Archaeology of Difference: Gender, Ethnicity, Class and the "Other" in Antiquity: Studies in Honor of Eric M. Meyers* (Boston: ASOR, 2007).

in response to present concerns. We might say that both the images of the historical Galilee and the historical Jesus have been shaped, and in one sense limited by modern interests in religion and identity. These most recent publications focus on the intersectionality between gender, ethnicity, class, and between "we" and "other" in a more inclusive way. This also represent a contemporary concern, but it is one that broadens, not narrows, a study of Galilean identities, and one that should be explored in future studies of Jesus and Galilee.[75]

---

[75] I have followed up this suggestion in H. Moxnes, "Identity in Jesus' Galilee – From Ethnicity to Locative Intersectionality," *BibInt* 18 (2010): 390–416.

Johannine Christians—Members of a Renewed Covenant? Jewish/Christian Identity According to the Johannine Letters

Birger Olsson
Lund University

Introduction

Since the end of the second century, the Johannine Letters have been read from a general Christian perspective. Irenaeus (ca. 130–200), bishop of Lyons with good connections eastward in Rome and Asia Minor, interpreted these letters, and the Gospel of John as well, from the perspective of his own time and used them as a tool against the doctrinal dangers that threatened the Christian church.[1] The opponents in the letter became gnostic or docetic false teachers who were attempting to destroy the true Christian faith. From then on this intra-Christian interpretation with a focus on various forms of Christological ideas dominated the reading of the letters both in the church and in the academy.

During the 1970s the situation changed. The discovery of texts near the Dead Sea had provided new reasons and new possibilities for reading the Johannine literature from a Jewish perspective. The new focus on social and economic conditions in society during the 1960s and the discussions in connection with Vatican II raised new questions, among others those concerning the role of traditions and official authority. Attention was more and more directed toward those in the Johannine fellowship who were developing their Christian faith in an advanced way. In a Johannine spirit, these people interpreted the gospel in a new way that those responsible for the Johannine

---

[1] C. E. Hill, *The Johannine Corpus in the Early Church* (Oxford: Oxford University Press, 2006); B. Mutschler, *Das Corpus Johanneum bei Irenäus von Lyon: Studien und Kommentar zum dritten Buch von Adversus haereses* (Tübingen: Mohr Siebeck, 2006).

tradition could not approve of. In this reading, the opponents in the letter became ultra-Johannine Christians who for some reason left the Johannine fellowship.[2] In an ultra-Johannine perspective these opponents took up a central place in the interpretation of the letters.

Some scholars have asked whether these opponents were not actually Jews who no longer wished to confess Jesus as Messiah. Alois Wurm and some others posed this question as early as the beginning of the twentieth century, but they did not convince their contemporary colleagues.[3] Voices in favor of an intra-Jewish perspective have been raised again during the last two decades.[4] In this view, then, the problem in the letters approaches the one we have in the Gospel, the question regarding Jewish faith or lack of faith in Jesus as Messiah, the Son of God, and thus the question whether Jews who believed had eternal life or not (John 20:30–31; 1 John 5:13). I myself have pursued this intra-Jewish perspective in a commentary and only in individual sections of it have I presented an interpretation based on the two other perspectives.[5]

An intra-Jewish perspective on the Johannine letters raises once more the question of the letters' addressees, and whether the Jesus-believing Jews they represent can be described in terms of a renewed covenant. How did these Christians—in the following discussion I refer to them as Johannine Christians—regard themselves? The conspicuous blending of the words "they," "we," and "I" in the letters demonstrates that the author was not thinking only of himself, not

---

[2] See especially R. E. Brown's excellent commentary, *The Epistles of John* (Garden City, New York: Doubleday, 1982), and many commentaries after him.

[3] A. Wurm, *Die Irrlehrer im ersten Johannesbrief* (Freiburg: Herdersche Verlagshandlung, 1903), and the references in H.-J. Klauck, *Die Johannesbriefe* (Darmstadt: Wissenschafliche Buchgesellschaft, 1991), 143–4.

[4] See E. Stegemann, "'Kindlein, hütet euch vor den Götterbildern!'" *TZ* 41 (1985): 284–94; K. Erlemann, "1 Joh und der jüdisch-christliche Trennungsprozess," *TZ* 55 (1999): 285–302; H. Thyen, "Johannesbriefe," *TRE* 17:186–200; D. Rusam, *Die Gemeinschaft der Kinder Gottes* (Stuttgart: Kohlhammer, 1993); T. Griffith, *Keep Yourselves from Idols* (Sheffield: Sheffield Academic Press), 2002; N. Hyldahl, *Om retfærdighed og syndfrihed: En fortolkning af de tre Johannesbreve* (Copenhagen: University of Copenhagen, 2007).

[5] B. Olsson, *Johannesbreven* (Stockholm: EFS-förlaget, 2008). Dr. Richard J. Erickson, Fuller Theological Seminary Northwest, Seattle, is now translating the commentary into English. Wipf and Stock, Eugene, Oregon, will publish the English version. Dr. Erickson has also translated the main text of this article.

even just of the addressees, but rather of a somewhat larger group of Jesus-believing Jews who profess Jesus as Messiah, God's son. The letters can give us some idea about the identity of these Johannine Christians.[6] Did they see themselves as part of God's covenant with Israel, a covenant that God had now renewed by sending his Son into the world as Messiah, visible in Jesus' earthly form, in Jesus' words and deeds from his birth up to and even including his death?[7]

In an article in *Revue biblique* in 1949, Marie-Émile Boismard argues the thesis that the concept of "knowing God" in 1 John takes its content from ideas of a new covenant in Jer 31 and Ezek 36.[8] In the Hebrew Bible to "know God" means to experience God's power and strength and thereby to realize who God is.[9] To "know God" is part of a covenant between God and the people of Israel that requires a special response from the human side: to keep/practice/walk in the commandments (1 Kgs 14:8; Ezek 36:28–29). But the people showed themselves incapable of doing God's will and therefore a new covenant with new conditions became necessary (Jer 31:31–34; Ezek 36:25–26). Boismard points in particular to a pattern in 1 John that gives content to the concept of "knowing God": God is righteous/light/love; human beings must live righteously/walk in the light/love one another, and human beings have fellowship with God/know God/are born of God/are in God and God is in them.[10] The last four descriptions of the Johannine Christian say almost the same

---

[6] The theme of this article is inspired by Bengt Holmberg and his project "Christian identity—The First 100 Years." See B. Holmberg, ed., *Exploring Early Christian Identity* (Tübingen: Mohr Siebeck, 2008).

[7] This investigation should have included the Gospel of John, but I have delimited myself to the letters with the Gospel as a general background material. Raymond Brown refers to ideas about a new covenant when he comments on John 1:14; 6:54, 56; 13:34–5; 14:7–11, 15, 27; 17:5, 26; 19:15; 20:17 and 20:28, see R. E. Brown, *The Gospel of John* (2 vols. Garden City, New York: Doubleday, 1966–1970). See also J. W. Pryor, *John: Evangelist of the Covenant People* (Downers Grove: InterVarsity Press, 1992), and R. M. Chennattu, *Johannine Discipleship as a Covenant Relationship* (Peabody: Hendrickson, 2006).

[8] M.-E. Boismard, "La connaissance dans l'alliance nouvelle, d'après la première lettre de saint Jean," *RB* 56 (1949): 365–91. His interpretation has influenced the notes in *La Bible de Jerusalem* (1956) and *Traduction œcuménique de la Bible* (1972). See also idem, "'Je ferai avec vous une alliance nouvelle,'" *LumVie* 8 (1953): 94–109.

[9] Boismard refers to Exod, e.g. 6:6; 7:5, 17; 29:45–46, to Ezek, e.g. 6:7, 10, 13–14; 7:4, 9, 27 and to Jer, e.g. 4:22; 5:4; 9:2, 5 and 12:15–16.

[10] See 1 John 2:29; 3:5–6; 4:7–8, 11–12, 16; 1:5 –7 and 2:8–10

thing and constitute the foundation for a life in the new covenant.[11] In this renewed fellowship with God the Christians cannot sin.

Thus, according to Boismard, to "know God" in 1 John becomes an experientially based relationship to God and his actions, which in turn requires actions from the human side: to believe and to love. The description in the letter corresponds in detail after detail to the prophecies in Jeremiah and Ezekiel. He mentions especially the use of διάνοια in 5:20, πνεῦμα in 3:24, 4:13, and περιπατεῖν, φυλάσσειν and ποιεῖν with God's commandments as object. Yet there is much more in the letter that we can connect with the thought of a renewed covenant. The question of cleansing from sin gets surprisingly little space in Boismard's presentation, as does the role played by Jesus Christ. He has a general Christian perspective and does not deal with any Jewish material regarding covenant renewals beyond the Johannine letters. Boismard wrote his article before the discoveries at Qumran.

Edward Malatesta's dissertation from 1978, likewise is characterized by a concentration on 1 John and the question of a renewed covenant.[12] In a very text-oriented semantic analysis of the letter from beginning to end, he focuses on the so-called "interiority expressions," i.e., the phrases "to be in" and "to remain in." He provides, however, no evaluative summary of the results. Very seldom does he appeal to parallels from outside the biblical material. Malatesta wants to show how 1 John "uses the interiority expressions as an especially apt manner of describing the interior nature of New Covenant communion." And he arrives at the result that the theology of the letter's author "seems to be based upon the actual fulfillment of the promises of the New Covenant as announced by Jeremiah and

---

[11] The different expressions are used in parallel clauses in 1 John 3:5–6; 4:6–8 and 2 John 11.

[12] E. Malatesta, *Interiority and Covenant* (Rome: Biblical Institute Press, 1978). In a very short survey of research on pp. 22–23 Malatesta refers to H. A. A. Kennedy "The Covenant Conception in the First Epistle of St. John," *ExpTim* 28 (1916–1917): 23–26; Boismard, "La connaissance"; W. Nauck, *Die Tradition und der Charakter des ersten Johannesbriefes* (Tübingen: Mohr Siebeck, 1957); P. Couture, "The Teaching Function in the Church of 1 John (2:20, 27)" (Ph.Diss., Pontifical Gregorian University, 1967) and A. Edanad, "The New-Covenant Perspectives of 1 John: An Exegetical and Theological Study of 1 John and Its Vision of Christian Existence as the Realization of the Eschatological Covenant" (Ph.Diss., Pontifical Gregorian University, 1967).

Ezekiel."[13] Of the eleven texts in the Hebrew Bible that especially promise a new covenant, nine mention the theme of interior renewal.[14] They are connected there with concepts such as heart, spirit, wisdom and observance of the law. In the letter images of a new covenant appear in themes like forgiveness of sin, a new commandment, mutual love and the spirit.

Boismard's and Malatesta's reading of 1 John has been met mostly with skepticism. The most common objection is that there is no explicit reference in the letter to a new covenant.[15] In his review of research on the Johannine letters, Hans-Josef Klauck notes that the elements brought forth by Boismard are indeed found in Jer 31 and Ezek 36, as likewise the immanence-language analyzed by Malatesta, but that there are also obvious differences: the word διαθήκη is missing, the immanence-language goes beyond saying that God dwells among his people, and the reciprocal covenant formula is marked by an indwelling in God. There is a good distance between the statements in the Hebrew Bible and 1 John 4:16: "Einzelthemen wird man mit Gewinn auf dieser Folie lesen können, als einziger Gesamtschlüssel eignert sich das Konzept einer Bundestheologie nicht."[16] As a rule the commentaries on 1 John are also guarded on this point, but Raymond Brown refers frequently to ideas of a new covenant without making it a central theme, as does Ruth Edwards as well in her short presentation of the letters.[17]

---

[13] Malatesta, *Interiority*, 24, 78.

[14] Deut 30:1–10; Jer 24:5 –7; 31:31 –34; 32:37 –41; Ezek 11:14 –21; 16:53 –63; 36:22 –35; 37:21 –28. See also Bar 2:29–35.

[15] See e.g., J. M. Lieu, *The Theology of the Johannine Letters* (Cambridge: Cambridge University Press, 1991), 32: "I shall argue that the absence of explicit covenant language is against Boismard's reading of 1 John." Lieu interprets the expression "to know God" as a covenant relation to God, but adds: "However, 1 John never develops a covenant framework, and instead knowledge of God belongs to a complex of other expressions of religious experience, which have few parallels in Jewish thought" (p. 33).

[16] H.-J. Klauck, *Die Johannesbriefe* (Darmstadt: Wissenschaftliche Buchgesellschaft, 1991), 172. A similar argumentation in J. Painter, *1, 2, and 3 John* (Collegeville: Liturgical Press, 2002), 101–102.

[17] Brown, *Epistles of John*, subject index, "Covenant (New)", R. B. Edwards, *The Johannine Epistles* (Sheffield: Sheffield Academic Press, 1996), 72–73. To know God "harks back to concepts familiar from the Hebrew Bible (Jer. 9:3; 31:34), whereby knowledge of God involves being aware of God's saving actions for people, and of the need to respond with obedience" (p. 73). See also J. Beutler, *Die Johannesbriefe* (Regensburg: Verlag Friedrich Pustet, 2000), 16 –17.

References to a renewed covenant are clearly evidenced in the early Christian church, even though it is only the letter to the Hebrews that directly cites Jer 31:31 –34.[18] In connection with the Last Supper, Paul and Luke reproduce Jesus' words on the blood of the covenant as "the new covenant in my blood" (1 Cor 11:25; Luke 22:20). Ideas of a renewed covenant appear in 2 Cor 3 and can be seen behind the story of the outpouring of the Spirit on Pentecost in Acts 2. Pentecost was celebrated by some Jews as a feast of the covenant's renewal.[19] 1 Pet 1:1–2:10 and John 1:19–4:54 can with advantage be read from a renewed covenant point of view, as can the outpouring of the Spirit in John 20:19 –23.[20] A number of scholarly works on the covenant theme in the New Testament have appeared in recent years, but none of them analyzes Johannine texts.[21]

Therefore, we have no thorough investigation of the images of a new covenant in Johannine texts after Boismard and Malatesta and the literature cited by the latter.[22] The evaluation of an intra-Jewish perspective regarding the interpretation of the Johannine letters and

---

[18] Heb 8:8 –12; 10:16 –17. According to Nestle-Aland's edition there are allusions to Jer 31:31 –34 also in Matt 26:28; Mark 14:24; John 6:45 and Rom 2:15; 11:27.

[19] B. Olsson, "När pingstfestens dag kom förnyades förbundet," in *Så som det har berättats för oss: Om bibel, gudstjänst och tro* (ed. G. Samuelsson and T. Hägerland; Örebro: Libris, 2007), 157–70.

[20] B. Olsson, *Första Petrusbrevet* (Stockholm: EFS-förlaget 1982), 65–67; idem, *Structure and Meaning in the Fourth Gospel: A Text-Linguistic Analysis of John 2:1–11 and 4:1–42* (Lund: Gleerup, 1974), 94–114, 249–56, and S. M. Schneider, "The Raising of the New Temple: John 20:19 –23 and Johannine Ecclesiology," *NTS* 52 (2006): 337–55.

[21] E. Juhl Christiansen, *The Covenant in Judaism and Paul: A Study of Ritual Boundaries as Identity Markers* (Leiden: Brill, 1995); P. J. Gräbe, *Der neue Bund in der frühchristlichen Literatur unter Berücksichtigung der alttestamentlich-jüdischen Voraussetzungen* (Würzburg: Echter Verlag, 2001); S. E. Porter and J. C. R. de Roo, eds., *The Concept of the Covenant in the Second Temple Period* (Atlanta: Society of Biblical Literature, 2003); A. Schenker, *Das Neue am neuen Bund und das Alte am alten: Jer 31 in der hebräischen und griechischen Bibel* (Göttingen: Vandenhoeck & Ruprecht, 2006); T. R. Blanton, *Constructing a New Covenant: Discursive Strategies in the Damascus Document and Second Corinthians* (Tübingen: Mohr Siebeck, 2007), and M. D. Morrison, *Who Needs a New Covenant? Rhetorical Function of the Covenant Motif in the Argument of Hebrews* (Eugene: Pickwick, 2009). Juhl Christiansen analyses the differences and developments with regards to the covenant texts in Jeremiah, Ezekiel, the book of *Jubilees* and the Qumran scrolls. Gräbe has some pages about John 13:34 and 15:4, see *Der neue Bund*, 139–46. See also Pryor, *Covenant People*, 157–80, esp. 160: "While John is aware of and presumes the new covenant of Jeremiah (as 1 John also strongly supports), in his presentation of his Christology and ecclesiology he goes back more readily and consciously to the covenant themes of Exodus and Deuteronomy."

[22] C. Levin, *Die Verheissung des neuen Bundes in ihrem theologiegeschichtlichen Zusammenhang ausgelegt* (Göttingen: Vandenhoeck & Ruprecht, 1985) has no analysis of Johannine material.

new insights into Jewish renewal movements in the period around the turn of the era now justify a new reading of these letters in terms of the self-understanding expressed within them. In what follows, I first treat a development of Shavuot into a feast for renewing the covenant with God and then analyze a series of texts in 1 John that can be related to the frequently adduced texts from Jer 31 and Ezek 36 and parallels. I then proceed to a number of ideas and expressions that from a Jewish perspective are reminiscent of various sorts of covenant texts.

A Renewed Covenant in Jewish Texts

Within priestly circles in the land of Israel during the second century before our era, there developed the idea of an annual renewal of the covenant with God. It was tied to the feast of Weeks, Pentecost, or in Hebrew, *hag shavu'ot* (חַג שָׁבֻעֹת). The word *shavu'ot* means "weeks." The feast was celebrated seven weeks after Passover. By changing a vowel in the word, one gets the meaning "oaths." Reading "feast of Weeks" as "feast of the Oaths" can perhaps partly explain the connection to the covenant.[23]

According to *Jubilees*—remains of fourteen manuscripts of this book were found at Qumran—there is only one covenant between God and his elect, an eternal covenant.[24] Already at the creation, God had separated unto himself a people who would keep the Sabbath. "And they will be my people and I will be their God" (2:19–20).[25] If the covenant is eternal, then there is no need for a new covenant,

---

[23] B. Noack, "The Day of Pentecost in Jubilees, Qumran, and Acts," *ASTI* 1 (1962): 73–85; C. VanderKam, "Shavu'ot," *Encyclopedia of the Dead Sea Scrolls*, 2:871–2, and J. van Ruiten, "The Covenant of Noah in *Jubilees* 6.1–38," in *The Concept of the Covenant in the Second Temple Period* (ed. S. E. Porter and J. C. R. de Roo; Atlanta: Society of Biblical Literature, 2003), 167–90, esp. 185–9.

[24] O. S. Wintermute, "Jubilees," in *The Old Testament Pseudepigrapha, Volume 2: Expansions of the 'Old Testament' and Legends, Wisdom and Philosophical Literature, Prayers, Psalm, and Odes, Fragments of Lost Judeo-Hellenistic Works* (ed. J. H. Charlesworth; New York: Doubleday, 1985), 35–142, esp. 35–51; J. C. VanderKam, *The Book of Jubilees* (Sheffield: Sheffield Academic Press, 2001); van Ruiten, "Covenant of Noah," Abegg, "Covenant of Noah," and Blanton, *New Covenant*, 45–49.

[25] I follow the translation of Wintermute.

although there certainly is need for renewals of the covenant. On the heavenly tablets it is written that the people are to celebrate the feast of Weeks "in order to renew the covenant in all (respects), year by year" (6:17). From time to time the Lord would need to "create for them a holy spirit" and to cleanse them by taking away their sins. The people reply with oaths and promises, with sacrifices and festivals. It thus becomes clear "that they are my sons and I am their father in uprightness and righteousness. And I shall love them" (1:23 –25).

An annual renewal of the covenant during the feast of Weeks seems also to have been the practice at Qumran. Material for such a covenant ceremony, together with regulations for the initiation of new members, is found in 1QS 1:16–3:6.[26] After introductory praise to the God of salvation and truth, the priests recount the momentous deeds that God in his righteousness, grace and mercy has done for Israel. Then the Levites reckon up all of Israel's sins and transgressions. All members confess their sins and God, who is true and righteous, forgives them out of his grace and mercy. Those who belong to God are blessed; those who belong to Belial are condemned. Finally, also condemned is anyone who enters the covenant with "the idols of his heart which he worships," something that is described as a sin that leads to fall, "the stumbling-block of his iniquity."[27] A comment emphasizes that it is God alone who reconciles and cleanses the one who does his will. The renewal of the covenant leads into "the Community of truth" and results in "a holy council, and members of an eternal assembly."[28] Those who belong to this fellowship are characterized by goodness, humility, love, mercy and uprightness toward one another.

The Qumran texts mention "the new covenant" five times, four of them in the *Damascus documents* and once in the commentary on the

---

[26] M. G. Abegg, "The Covenant of the Qumran Sectarians," in *The Concept of the Covenant in the Second Temple Period* (ed. S. E. Porter and J. C. R. de Roo; Atlanta: Society of Biblical Literature, 2003), 81–98, esp. 88–97.

[27] 1QS 2:12. See also 1QH 4:15 and Ezek 14:4, 7.

[28] The translation follows Qimron and Charlesworth, see "Rule of the Community," in *The Dead Sea Scrolls. Hebrew, Aramaic, and Greek Texts with English Translation: Vol 1* (ed. J. H. Charlesworth; Tübingen: Mohr Siebeck, 1994), 1–51.

book of Habakkuk (CD 6:19; 8:21; 19:33; 20:12; and 1QpHab 2:3). It is simplest to interpret "new covenant" as a renewed covenant.[29] The idea of a new covenant comes to expression also through the verb "renew" with covenant as object (1QSb 3:26; 5:5, 21; 1Q34 3:2:6). God's covenant is eternal, but the people of Israel were unable to uphold their part of the agreement and were forced to go into exile. It was not until the first century before our era that the Sinai covenant was renewed "in the land of Damascus" by some who had emigrated "from the land of Judah" when the Teacher of Righteousness interpreted certain portions of the Mosaic law in a new way. These people regarded themselves as the holy remnant of the people of Israel. In the disputes over the true interpretation of God's law, a "new" covenant arose, i.e., a "renewed" covenant. They insisted that their interpretation was the true and correct one. This covenant appears to have then been renewed at every feast of Pentecost in the Qumran community. A particular covenant theology, therefore, with clear-cut regulations, becomes constitutive for the Qumran community's self-understanding and distinguishes it from other Jewish groups.

These ideas of the covenant in *Jubilees* and the Qumran texts have their point of departure at Sinai (Exod 19–24) and build on what is said about this covenant in Exodus and Deuteronomy.[30] Only the concept of a "new covenant" appears to have been taken from Jer 31. One can say that the covenant was renewed already at Sinai, when the people of Israel backslid and began to worship idols (the golden calf). Moses goes before God as intercessor for his people, and at last God responds by describing himself:

---

[29] H. Lichtenberger, "Alter Bund und neuer Bund," *NTS* 41 (1995): 400–414; Gräbe, *Der neue Bund*, 59–61; C. E. Evans, "Covenant in the Qumran Literature," in *The Concept of the Covenant in the Second Temple Period* (ed. S. E. Porter and J. C. R. de Roo; Atlanta: Society of Biblical Literature, 2003), 55–80; Abegg, "Covenant," and Blanton, *New Covenant*, 71–105. These scholars talk about the fellowship at Qumran as "the Community of the New Covenant".

[30] For an analysis of relevant texts, see D. Timmer, "Sinai 'Revisited' Again: Further reflections on the Appropriating of Exodus 19–Numbers 10 in 1QS," *RB* 115 (2008): 481–98. As a summary he says "The group's covenant and cult, improved with respect to the corresponding Sinaitic catergories, identified them as the true Israel while they awaited God's final coming" (p. 481). He focuses on such themes as sin, forgiveness, holiness and divine presence. These categories have been reworked in the special eschatological situation of the Qumran people. Something similar can be said with reference to 1 John with its emphasis of atonement, sinlessness and divine presence.

> The LORD, the LORD, a God merciful and gracious, slow to anger, and abounding in steadfast love and faithfulness, keeping steadfast love[31] for the thousandth generation, forgiving iniquity and transgression and sin,[32] yet by no means clearing[33] the guilty, but visiting the iniquity of the parents upon the children and the children's children, to the third and the fourth generation. (Exod 34:6–7)

There is a significant duality in the divine description here: God forgives and God punishes. In an earlier form this "grace formula" contained a retaliatory rationale with a sharp division between those who love God and keep his commands and those who hate God (Deut 5:9–10; 7:9–10). In later development of this formula (Joel 2:13; Jonah 4:2; Pss 86:15; 103:8; 145:8–9; Neh 9:17) two things happen: (1) The God of retaliation/ vengeance/ wrath/ jealousy disappears more and more, leaving for the most part only the God of love and forgiveness. (2) God's grace and mercy embraces all humanity, not only the people of Israel. Finally we have only the liturgical refrain in Ps 136: "O give thanks to the LORD, for he is good, for his steadfast love endures forever."[34]

Jubilees and the Qumran documents, as we have already mentioned, build upon these covenant texts, but not on Jer 31, if we disregard the term "a new covenant," and certainly not on Ezek 36 either. The prophets Jeremiah and Ezekiel, both of priestly stock, describe in these chapters a renewal of the fellowship with God that has certain correspondences in 1 John.

> The days are surely coming, says the LORD, when I will make a new [καινός] covenant with the house of Israel and the house of

---

[31] The LXX expands "keeping steadfast love" to "who preserves righteousness [δικαιοσύνη] and practices mercy [ἔλεος]". God's righteousness is perceived in his "steadfast love," see H. Spieckermann, "God's Steadfast Love: Towards a New Conception of Old Testament Theology," *Bib* 81 (2000): 305–27, esp. 310–16.

[32] LXX (Exod 34:6): ἀφαιρῶν ἀνομίας καὶ ἀδικίας καὶ ἁμαρτίας.

[33] LXX (Exod 34:7) uses the verb καθαρίζειν.

[34] H. Spieckermann, "'Barmherzig und gnädig ist der Herr …,'" *ZAW* 102 (1990): 1–18, esp. 8–18; J. M. Lieu, "What was from the Beginning: Scripture and Tradition in the Johannine Epistles," *NTS* 39 (1993): 458–77, esp. 461–5.

Judah. … I will put [διδόναι] my law in their inward parts [διάνοια], and I will write it on their hearts; and I will be their God, and they shall be my people. No longer shall they teach [διδάσκειν] one another, or say to each other, 'Know [γινώσκειν) the LORD,' for they shall all [πάντες] know [οἶδα] me, from the least of them to the greatest, says the LORD; for I will forgive ['ίλεως εἶναι] their iniquity [ἀδικίαι], and remember their sin [ἁμαρτίαι] no more. (Jer 31:31–34)

I have inserted into the text several words used in the LXX, since they have corresponding forms in the text of the letter. What is different in comparison with the Qumran texts is the stipulation of the new covenant's scope—it covers all of Israel—and the emphasis on God's law being in the people's heart, giving them thus a direct knowledge of his will.[35] This biblical passage is conspicuous mainly by its absence from Jewish texts in the New Testament era, perhaps because there was a widespread fear of renewal movements.[36] On the other hand, as we mentioned above, it is cited in Heb 8:8–12 (see also 10:16–17), and the concept "new covenant" is used in Luke 22:20, 1 Cor 11:25, and Heb 9:15. See also 2 Cor 3:3–18.

Ezekiel 36 expresses the coming change in a somewhat different way. God says:

I will sprinkle clean water upon you, and you shall be clean [καθαρίζειν] from all your uncleannesses, and from all your idols [εἴδωλα] I will cleanse [καθαρίζειν] you. A new [καινός] heart I will give [διδόναι] you, and a new [καινός] spirit I will put [διδόναι] within you; and I will remove from your body the heart of stone and give you a heart of flesh. I will put my spirit [πνεῦμα] within you [διδόναι ἐν ὑμῖν], and make you follow [πορεύεσθαι] my statutes and be careful to observe my ordinances.

---

[35] See Juhl Christiansen, *Covenant*, 56–58. The new covenant is one that will be established by God in the future, within the framework of history. By a divine act sin will be made impossible, because breaking the law will not be possible in the future. Jeremiah maintains that God's forgiveness is not an effect, but rather the grounds, on which the new covenant rests.

[36] C. Wolff, *Jeremia in Frühjudentum und Urchristentum* (Berlin: Akademie-Verlag, 1976), 116–47; Lichtenberger, "Neuer Bund," 406–10.

> Then you shall live in the land that I gave to your ancestors; and
> you shall be my people, and I will be your God. (Ezek 36:25–28)

With energy, it is claimed that the reason for this act of God is
God himself, God's holy name (Ezek 36:22–23). Jer 31:2–3 refers
to God's grace and God's love. As in other covenant texts, God's
steadfast love is the source and the driving force in the covenant
with Israel.[37] According to Ezek 36:24, God will at this time also
gather his people into the promised land, a concept that shows up in
John 11:51–52 (see also John 4:36 and 10:16), but not in 1 John.[38]

With these ideas in the background, we can read 1 John and
consider "that which was from the beginning." The Hebrew Bible,
according to Judith Lieu, has a place in the forming of 1 John, in
the form of allusions and adaptations of interpretations of the
Hebrew Bible.[39] Texts from the Hebrew Bible in interpreted form
are therefore a part of the thought-world in 1 John. The interpretive
patterns often have parallels in contemporary Jewish exegesis and
sometimes also in gnostic texts. The letter is saturated with the
Hebrew Bible in a way that resembles texts from Qumran, where
direct citations are often lacking. If we take the Gospel and the
letter together, it becomes clear that there was a close engagement
with the Old Testament in the Johannine school. Judith Lieu
demonstrates this with an analysis of the use of Exod 34 in 1 John
1:9–2:2, Gen 4 in 1 John 3:7–9, and Isa 6:9–10 in 1 John 2:11.

We know that some Jews confessed Jesus of Nazareth as the
Messiah, God's son. How did that alter their view of reality? How did
they interpret the coming of the Messiah, God's son, into the world
and his activity in it? What help did they find in the Hebrew Bible and
in their own Jewish perceptions for this interpretive work? Some of

---

[37] Ezekiel takes the renewal a step further than Jeremiah in the direction of individualization.
Personal, inner renewal is in the foreground, Juhl Christiansen, *Covenant*, 59–61.

[38] Olsson, *Structure and Meaning*, 241–8.

[39] To this and to what follows see Lieu, "From the Beginning," 475–77. Mogens Müller talks about
"the hidden context" when he comments on the new covenant in the New Testament, see "The Hidden
Context: Some Observations to the Concept of New Covenant in the New Testament," in *Texts and
Contexts: Biblical Texts in Their Textual and Situational Contexts* (ed. T. Fornberg and D. Hellholm;
Oslo: Scandinavian University Press, 1995), 649–58.

them obviously saw what had happened as a form of renewal of God's covenant with his people.[40] Does this also apply to the Johannine Christians we meet in the Johannine letters? The following passages are worth investigating in the search for an answer to this question.

Central Covenantal Themes
in Interpreted Form in 1 John?

1 John 5:20

In conformity to the rhetorical rules of the day, the letter closes at 5:13 –21 with a kind of summarization, in which the author uses new formulations for ensuring that the message will stick with the hearers, formulations like "sin unto death," "the one who was born of God" (referring to Jesus), "a gift of understanding so that they may know the True one," "the true God and eternal life" (again, referring to Jesus), and "keep yourselves from idols."[41] Three very short paragraphs beginning with "we know"[42] in this closing text take up a few core points in the letter, and as a culmination of this triad, verse 5:20 reads as follows: "And we know that the Son of God has come and has given us understanding so that we may know him who is true; and we are in him who is true, in his Son Jesus Christ. He is the true God and eternal life."[43]

"The Son of God has come." This is the decisively new thing for the Jesus-believing Jews we encounter in the letter. God's son is there in Jesus' character as Messiah, as He who was to come. The full christological description is used also at the end of the verse:

---

[40] See the NT passages mentioned above.

[41] For a further analysis of this important part of the letter as a whole, see my commentary, pp. 250–62.

[42] These three "we know" bring up the many "we know" in the letter, 1 John 2:3, 5, 18; 3:2, 14, 16, 18, 19, 24; 4:6, 13, 16; 5:2, 15. The aim of the letter is that they may know, 5:13.

[43] The clause "so that we may know" has an indicative form of the verb and not a conjunctive one, which is the normal form in clauses introduced by ἵνα. The choice of presence indicative probably underlines that they really know the True One, and that forever.

God's son, Jesus the Messiah.[44] He has given (διδόναι) them a mind (διάνοια) with the result that they know (γινώσκειν) the True One. There is good reason to take these words as a summarizing statement in the letter. The words are a clear reference to Jer 31 and Ezek 36. In Jer 31 God promises to give the people his law within them, in Ezek 36 to give them his spirit in their inward parts.[45] In the LXX "within you" is translated "in your διάνοια"—often in the LXX διάνοια stands in parallel with heart—or "within you." God's law and God's spirit are placed within them. In addition, Ezek 36 speaks of God's giving the people "a new heart" and "a new spirit." The consequence will be that they know God and can accomplish his will.[46] The interiorization of God's law and even the specific choice of words imply that the words in Jer 31 and Ezek 36 concerning a renewed covenant lie behind these closing statements in interpreted form; this shows that what is said is nothing new for the letter's recipients, but something they presumably heard from the beginning. It is something the author takes for granted, not something he has to argue for.

1 John 2:20, 27

"But you have an anoinment from the Holy One, and all of you [πάντες] have knowledge [οἶδα]." These last words are also reminiscent of Jer 31, especially when we lay them alongside what is said regarding the anointing in 2:27, namely, "this anoinment teaches you about all things," "it has taught you," and "you do not need anyone to teach [διδάσκειν] you." With the same emphasis, Jer 31 asserts that the members of the renewed covenant no longer need to give instruction to one another, one brother to another, and to say, "know YHWH." They already have that knowledge within

---

[44] The full notation "Jesus Messiah the Son of God" is used at the beginning, 1:2, in the middle, 3:23, and at the end of the letter, 5:13, 20, and functions as a kind of *inclusio*.

[45] God's gift or gifts form a very central theme in the Gospel of John, see Olsson, *Structure and Meaning*, 177–9, and also in 1 John. See 3:1, 23, 24; 4:13; 5:11, 16, 20.

[46] Jer 31:33 uses the phrase "Know the LORD [יהוה]." The divine name is often circumscribed in Jewish texts as "He", as in 1 John 2:3, or as "the True One" as here. "Jahweh's way" in Jes 40:3 becomes in 1QS 8:13–14 "His way", or in 4QS MS E 1 III, 4 "the way of the truth." The reference to "the True One" prepares the use of the word "idols" in 5:21.

them. Certain formulations echo Jer 31, others are new, not least the notion of anointing.[47] The words "the Holy One" leave it open for both God and Jesus to be the origin and source of this anointing.

The interiorization of God's law and of God himself in a particular individual is expressed in several ways already in Jer 31 and Ezek 36 (God's law, God's spirit, a new heart, a new spirit). 1 John speaks of anointing, seed, spirit and mind (διάνοια), not to mention expressions like to be of God, to be born of God, and the reciprocal "to abide in God and God abides in us." The commentaries frequently discuss whether these words refer to the Spirit or to God's word.[48] Vv. 3:24 and 4:13 refer explicitly to God's spirit. God has given them something of himself (ἐκ τοῦ πνεύματος αὐτοῦ), and in both cases this gives insight, insight "that we abide in Him and He in us," a formulation that in its reciprocal character is reminiscent of a central covenantal formula. There is much that speaks for understanding "anointing" also as primarily referring to the Spirit, the Spirit of truth, as it is presented in John 14–16. Jesus' disciples receive the Spirit/anointing, the Spirit/anointing abides in them, the Spirit/anointing teaches them about everything, and the Spirit/anointing conveys the truth to them. It is thus entirely natural that the author in the following verse insists that they know the truth. It is likely that the addressees received a part of God's spirit when they entered the new fellowship. The spirit of truth—which in Johannine tradition is always coupled with the teaching that comes from Jesus—now gives them access to the truth in the conflict over confessing Jesus as Messiah, son of God. These concepts would then belong to that which was there from the beginning. But here as well the use of Jer 31 and Ezek 36 implies reformulations and reinterpretations that perhaps belong to a later period.

1 John 2:3

"We know Him, if we obey His commandments." To know the God of the covenant and to follow the laws of the covenant are already

---

[47] There are no good parallels in the ancient world to the expression χρῖσμα ἀπὸ τοῦ ἁγίου ἔχειν.

[48] For examples see my commentary, pp. 151–3.

closely tied to the Sinai covenant as it is described in Exodus and Deuteronomy. The connection is there as well in Jer 31 and Ezek 36. To obey God's commandments is a recurrent theme in the letter.[49] Yet there are reasons to distinguish between a common way of speaking of God's commandments in the plural and of God's commandment in the singular. The latter, like the expression "God's word" (1:10; 2:14), stands for the new revelation of God that has come to reality through Jesus Christ, the very foundation for the renewal of the covenant. The double love-command has been reformulated in the Johannine letters and taken on a more precise content: to believe in God's son, Jesus the Messiah, and to love one another (3:23).[50]

The author's manner of explaining the content of the concept of God's commandments (in the plural) in 2:3–11 is worthy of note in regard to the close connection between the idea of a new covenant and Jesus the Messiah, Son of God. It is carried out in three steps:

(1) To obey His commandments is to keep God's word, i.e., to follow the revelation of God that comes through Jesus Christ (2:4–5). Those who do this "know" God and "abide in" God. It corresponds to walking in God's light, mentioned in the preceding section, i.e., to shaping one's life entirely on the basis of the commandment (in the singular) that "we have heard from him and proclaim to you."

(2) To obey His commandments is to live as Jesus lived (2:6–8). This implies a further refining of the idea of keeping God's word/ commandment (in the singular). "Just as Jesus did" is a consistent ethical principle throughout the letter.[51] God's law in the human heart receives its content from Jesus Christ. Likewise the new covenant in the Qumran texts has its foundation in a new interpretation of the law propounded by the Teacher of Righteousness.[52]

(3) To obey His commandments is to love one's brother or sister, i.e.,

---

[49] See 2:3, 4, 17; 3:22, 24; 5:2, 3, and also the passages about doing righteousness and not sin.

[50] For a comprehensive argumentation to distinguish between God's commandments (in the plural) and God's commandment (in the singular) in the Johannine letters, see my commentary, pp. 119–123. So also U. C. von Wahlde, *The Johannine Commandments: 1 Joh and the Struggle for the Johannine Tradition* (New York: Paulist Press, 1990).

[51] See 2:6, 2:29 (?); 3:2, 7; 4:17. To live as Jesus lived is only exemplified in the letters by "to love each other," 3:11–24; 4:7–21, and "to lay down their life for one another," 3:16–17.

[52] Blanton, *New Covenant*, 71–105.

to love those that confess Jesus as Messiah, God's son (2:9–11). This is the third step in the successively precise and concretized content of the idea of keeping God's commandments, presumably conditioned by the specific situation the letter's recipients find themselves in.[53] To know God implies keeping his commandments, which at the end of the day means to love one's fellow believers (4:7–8; 5:2–3).

1 John 1:9

"He who is faithful and just will forgive us our sins and cleanse us from all unrighteousness." The renewed relationship with God rests on God's forgiveness (Jer 31) and on God's cleansing of the people's sin (Ezek 36).[54] The forgiveness and cleansing have their basis in particular characteristics of God, in this case his faithfulness and righteousness. This echoes what is perhaps the most central text of the covenant in the Hebrew Bible, Exod 34:6–7, and the ongoing interpretation of this text in the Hebrew Bible and other contemporary Jewish texts (see above). "The influence of the Exod 34.6 tradition is clear although what we have is not explicit quotation but a developing relationship to the tradition, perhaps liturgically mediated."[55] The similarities have to do not only with the content, but also with certain formulations like the use of the verbs "forgive" and "cleanse" and the paralleling of sin and unrighteousness.

In regard to the background it is a little unexpected that the author uses "faithful and righteous" and not "gracious and merciful," which appear at the beginning of God's self-description at the renewal of the covenant in Exod 34 and which is central in the subsequent development of this theme. We know that the characteristic "righteousness" was included in the LXX's

---

[53] This interpretation is justified by the choice of words and of structural features in 2:3–11 and by parallels with 1:5–2:2. See my commentary, pp. 123–9.

[54] For the strong interrelation between atonement and divine presence in the Sinai covenant and in 1QS, see Timmer, "Sinai Revisited," 492–6.

[55] In this way Lieu summarizes her thorough analysis of 1 John 1:9–2:2 in relation to its background in Exod 34, "From the Beginning," 461–7. She, however, does not mention that these texts have a very central place in the description of the covenant between God and Israel, and she does not give a good explanation to why the author in 1:9 chooses "faithful and righteous" and not, for example, "gracious and merciful."

version of this description of God. God's righteousness is also mentioned often in the Psalms as a parallel to God's grace and God's mercy.[56] The combination of God's righteousness and God's love and faithful acts is especially noticeable in the material regarding the covenant renewal feast at Qumran (see above). If the background to the formulations in 1 John 1:9 is liturgical, then the renewal feast at Qumran should also be taken into consideration.

The theme of God's forgiveness and cleansing from sin is coupled together in 1:7 with Jesus' blood and in 2:12 with Jesus' name.[57] Jesus came to "take away [αἴρειν] sins," according to 3:5, a formulation reminiscent of Exod 34:6 in the LXX, which renders the usual Hebrew word for "forgive" with "take away" (ἀφαιρεῖν). This theme is further developed in the letter with the word ἱλασμός. Jesus is "the atoning sacrifice for our sins" (1 John 2:2); God sent his son "to be the atoning sacrifice for our sins" (4:10).[58] Judith Lieu makes an interesting observation on the use of ἱλασμός in the LXX. It is the only translation for the central word סליחה, "acts of forgiveness" (Dan 9:9; Ps 130:4; Neh 9:17). "The LXX does not use *hilasmos* more regularly for any other Hebrew term … The connection between *hilasmos* and 'pardon' (*slch*) seems to be dominant."[59]

The use of ἱλασμός in 1 John thus does not automatically need to be tied to the Day of Atonement and the sacrificial cultus. Judith Lieu states that,

---

[56] Pss 40:10–11; 51:3 –6; 89:15–16; 103:17; 143:11–12. See also Spieckermann, "Steadfast Love," 311–16.

[57] The passive construction, "your sins are forgiven," should be interpreted as a circumscription of God as agent, and "on account of his name" certainly refers to the name of Jesus, Olsson, *Johannesbreven*, 133, 140–1. In the parallel clause in 2:13 God's forgiveness is replaced by the knowledge of God. Forgiveness takes up the theme in 1:5–2:2 and knowledge of God the theme in 2:3–11.

[58] So according to NRSV. Different translations (propitiation, expiation, atonement, atoning sacrifice, the sacrifice that takes away our sins, the remedy for the defilement of our sins, the means by which our sins are forgiven) show that the meaning of ἱλασμός is still very much discussed.

[59] Lieu, "From the Beginning," 464–5. The unusual plural form סליחות, "forgivenesses," occurs twice in the Hebrew Bible (plus once in the singular) and more than ten times in 1QH, always connected with grace and mercy. Some texts from Qumran seem to be the nearest parallels to 1 John 1:9.

[i]t may be possible that the author combines a number of images, including sacrificial ideas in the earlier reference to the blood of Jesus at 1.7, but his most significant heritage is a liturgical and literary tradition celebrating and re-applying the confession of God made known in Exod 34 – just as forgiveness or pardon belongs to God alone,[60] Jesus now is that forgiveness actualised."[61]

To this I would add that this entire conceptual world is bound to the covenant and the renewal of the covenant in the Hebrew Bible and in other contemporary Jewish texts. The formulations in the letter bear witness to a background in texts about a renewed covenant. Even the choice of God's characteristics, faithfulness and righteousness, are understood best against such a background.

1 John 3:24; 4:13, 15, 16

To be/abide in God is paralleled to knowing God in 2:3–6. This expression is then developed in several verses in the letter into the reciprocal "we abide in God and God abides in us." This use of the verb μένειν ἐν is unique to the Johannine writings. The new covenant relationship between God and the recipients of the letter is expressed in many ways in the letter: have fellowship with, know, be in, abide in, have, be of, be born of, be God's children, etc. Characteristic of the letter likewise are statements such as God's word is in them, God's love is in them, God's sperma is in them, God's son is in them, the anointing is in them, and the truth is in them. It is not a long step beyond that to saying, "God is in them." Jer 31 and Ezek 36 speak of God's gift (the law, the Spirit) within them and in their heart, or, according to the LXX, in their mind and in them.

In contrast to the Gospel, the letter uses the word "abide in" almost solely with reference to the relationship between God and human beings.[62] This use corresponds to the fundamental pattern

---

[60] See Timmer, "Sinai Revisited," 492–3.

[61] Lieu, "From the Beginning," 465.

[62] Sentences like "The Father is in the Son, and the Son is in the Father" are totally missing in the letter, while sentences like "God abides in them, and they abide in God" are not to be found in the Gospel.

of the Sinai covenant in the Hebrew Bible with its two parties, God and the people. It is not a matter of parties of equal status,[63] but it is nonetheless an agreement between two parties with mutual obligations. No one has found a good background for this unique reciprocal immanence formula in 1 John. Some refer to biblical sayings about how God lives among his people in the temple and its worship (2 Chr 6:18; Zech 2:14–15), or about Wisdom's place in the midst of Israel (Sir 24:3, 6; Wis 7:25, 27). Others point to the Pauline formula "in Christ" with its probable association with viewing the congregation as the body of Christ. The question is whether ideas of a renewed covenant would not be a better explanation, i.e., the interiorization of God's law and God's spirit and the frequently recurring reciprocal covenant formulation: "I shall be their God and they shall be my people." The new union with God is expressed in *Jub.* 1:15–25 with words like "they are my children and I am their father," and "I love them." According to Edward Malatesta, who has carried out the most careful analysis of εἶναι ἐν and μένειν ἐν in 1 John, these ancient formulations were interiorized, i.e., God and the divine have entered into particular human persons. 1 John "uses the interiority expressions as an especially apt manner of describing the interior nature of New Covenant communion."[64]

1 John 2:29; 3:9; 4:7; 5:1, 4, 18

To be born of God becomes in 4:7 a parallel to knowing God. The same relation is expressed in two different ways and thereby acquires greater weight in the presentation. The words "be born of Him" appear first in 2:29, utterly unexpectedly. The formulation is assumed to be familiar to the recipients of the letter. The use of "him" to refer to God in a paragraph that otherwise deals with Jesus Christ supports

---

[63] Several scholars refer to the relation between the king and his many vasall kings in ancient vasall treaties as a background. The covenant relations are also compared with the unequal relationships between husband and wife in the ancient society.

[64] Malatesta, *Interiority*, 24. See also pp. 77–79: "The structure of the author's theology thus seems to be based upon the actual fulfillment of the promises of the New Covenant as announced by Jeremiah and Ezekiel," p. 78.

such a claim.[65] Those who love, know God; and those who know God, love (2:3–11). Those who are born of God, love; and those who love, are born of God (5:1–2). "All that is begotten of God" means all who believe and love according to the covenant commandment in 3:23, seen as a special category, as a collective.[66] The description can be understood on the basis of statements about renewal of the covenant in adapted form. The words "be born of Him" also become the means of word-plays in 5:1–2 and 5:18, such that in the latter case, Jesus and the believers are described in the same way. The God of the covenant is one (Deut 6:4), the Father and the Son are one, the Son and the renewed people of God are one, the members in the renewed people of God are one, according to the Johannine writings.

The conceptual world in 1 John gets densely packed as the author nears the letter's end (5:1–5). Here, being born of God is brought into connection with faith. Everything coheres: faith and divine birth; love and divine birth; birth and love for God and for God's children; love for God and keeping God's commandments; victory over the world in the incipient final conflict between God and Satan; and finally, once again, faith. The circle is closed. There is actually nothing new in this paragraph; everything is merely brought together into a coherent whole. If certain parts of this totality have clear connections to covenant thinking, then the rest can also be suspected of having the same connections.

The Sinai covenant made Israel into the children of God, God's sons and daughters (Exod 4:22; Hos 11:1). The covenant renewal, according to quotations from *Jubilees* above, had the same effect. In rabbinic literature the event at Sinai was the day of Israel's birth (*Exod. Rab.* 15:10), the day when God through "living words" gave birth to his son Israel.[67] As sons and daughters of God, they must also live as God's children (Hos 11:1–10; Deut 32:18). These two features characterizing God's children in the Hebrew Bible, the relation to

---

[65] The same can be said about "to have fellowship with Him" and "to know Him."

[66] The use of neuter singular (πᾶν) and not masculine as in 5:1 and 5:18 can be interpreted in this way. See also John 3:6; 6:37, 39; 17:2, 7, 24.

[67] The only passage in the Hebrew Bible and the LXX talking about God begetting (ילד/γεννᾶν) his people is Deut 32:18.

the covenant and the connection to a way of life, show up again in what is said about the renewed covenant in *Jubilees* and in Qumran texts, not least in texts regarding initiation into and renewal of the covenant (1QS 1–4). Divine sonship is a part of the new covenant. The words in 1 John regarding divine birth, reinforced by the mention of God's *sperma* in 3:9, can be understood in terms of their use in contemporary mystery religions or Gnostic and stoic concepts. With reference to what has been said here, to the ethical context of the divine birth, and to the background in ideas of a renewed covenant found in the letter, there is, nonetheless, reason to look first of all to a biblical, Jewish background. Even the idea of a re-birth in 1 Peter 1–2 is embedded in images of the covenant.[68] As for formulations of the divine birth concept, it is significant how covenant ideas have been further adapted and given new forms, something that corresponds to what Judith Lieu says about the use of traditions from the Hebrew Bible in 1 John.[69]

1 John 4:7–21

The close union and fellowship between God and human beings that has now been described has its foundation in God himself. The renewal of the covenant flows entirely from God through Jesus Christ. The letter sums up the new perspective in "God is light" and "God is love." In both cases, these short expressions describe (1) God as revealing himself anew and doing so through Jesus Christ; (2) this revelation as leading to salvation, a new divine life here and now, since what hinders the fellowship between God and human beings, namely sin, is taken away; and (3) a completely new life that carries out God's will as having now become possible. Mutual love becomes something given in and with the renewal of the relationship with God.

In the letters of John this action of God is summed up in the word "love." It replaces most of the positive words that are found in the description of God in Exod 34:6–7 and in later interpretations of this central covenant statement. God's love

---

[68] Olsson, *Första Petrusbrevet*, 37–38, 65–67.

[69] See n. 36.

comes first (4:7–21). God's love is the origin and source of the new thing (the revelation, the forgiveness of sin, the way of life). On this point the letter resembles what is said of the covenant in the Hebrew Bible and of the renewal of the covenant in Jer 31 and Ezek 36 and in other contemporary Jewish writings.[70]

These seven central themes in 1 John can be seen as a coherent whole demonstrating that beneath the various statements in the letter lie conceptions of the covenant between God and the people of Israel and its renewal. The Johannine Christians in these letters view themselves as members of a renewed covenant. This reality has come about through the arrival of God's son and through faith in Jesus as Messiah, the Son of God, and is manifested in the love that is found in him and among them (2:8; 3:16–17, and 4:7–21).

Further Ideas and Formulations with a Covenant Background

To these seven themes we can add a series of formulations in the letter that are most readily explained on the basis of ideas having to do with covenant and covenant renewal.[71] We briefly take them up here in the order in which they appear in the letter.

"Fellowship with him" (1 John 1:6)

In the introduction, the author uses a very broadly inclusive word for the fellowship he is about to discuss in the letter (1:3, 6, 7). The word κοινωνία refers to definite forms of fellowship in the world of that day, but to my knowledge, it does not occur in the contemporary covenant contexts. It includes within it such meanings as participation, unity, fellowship, oneness, and therefore

---

[70] For references and further arguments see Olsson, *Johannesbreven*, 231–4; R. M. Chennattu, *Johannine Discipleship as a Covenant Relationship* (Peabody: Hendrickson, 2006), 182–94.

[71] To these formulations we can add words such as "the elect lady and her children", "the elect sister" in 2 John 1 and 13, the combination of "grace, mercy and peace" in 2 John 3, and the phrase "to walk in the truth" in 2 John 4 and 3 John 3–4. See Olsson, *Johannesbreven*, 21, 48–49, 57, 63, 68–71.

fits well with the covenant fellowship described in the letter. This fellowship includes a fellowship with God, a fellowship with Jesus the Messiah, the Son of God, a fellowship with "us," i.e., with those responsible for the tradition in the Johannine community, and a fellowship with "one another." The use of "Him" referring to God in the phrase "have fellowship with Him," and the formulaic citation "We have fellowship with Him" imply that the formulation is familiar to the recipients of the letter. It is replaced later in 2:3 with "to know Him," which is clearly anchored in a covenant vocabulary. The first major section of the letter (1:5–2:11) is widely inclusive, as is evident in its use of such common concepts as fellowship, light, and darkness. They do not occur again later in the letter.

"Beloved" (1 John 2:7; 3:2, 21; 4:1, 7, 11; 3 John 1, 2, 5, 11)

The word ἀγαπητός is an ordinary Greek word that takes on special content in the Johannine writings. It is used as a vocative six times in 1 John and four times of Gaius in 3 John. The Johannine theme of love colors this word's content and use, and the embedding of "love" and "beloved" in the introductions to the letters of 2 John and 3 John reinforces the connection with Johannine ideas. The phrase "in (the) truth" in these introductions makes it obvious that love belongs with truth in the Johannine letters. Normally, one does not find the word "beloved" in the opening of Greek letters. For that reason it becomes quite conspicuous in 3 John, something reinforced by the clause "whom I love in (the) truth," unexpected in letter introductions.

The word "beloved" is a recurrent description of God's people in the Hebrew Bible (Jer 6:26; Pss 60:7; 127:2). "And I shall love them" become thus the final words in the description of the covenant renewal in *Jub.* 1:23–25. Christians are also called God's beloved (1 Thess 1:4; John 16:27; Rom 1:7). In Exod 19:5, we read that those who enter into covenant with God are to be his treasured possession out of all the peoples. The word for treasured possession, סְגֻלָּה, is rendered in an Aramaic translation as "beloved ones." The people of the covenant are "a people of beloved ones." Even the Johannine "friends" (3 John 15) form a fellowship of beloved people with a special command from Jesus to love each other just as he had loved them (John 13:34; 1 John 3:11; 4:7–21). The word "beloved" in 1 John emphasizes the oneness and solidarity within the Johannine community. The reciprocal, mutual love with God's love as its origin and source is actually a natural consequence of the covenant's renewal.

"A new commandment" (1 John 2:7–8; 2 John 5)

The commandment or message is old, because the letters' recipients heard it from the beginning, i.e., when they came to faith. This is clearly stated both in 1 John 2:7 and in 2 John 5. In 1 John 2:7–8 the author wants to emphasize that the commandment is new, new in a qualitative sense (καινός). What is new about it is obvious in the life style of Jesus and the recipients and forms a part of the new eschatological situation that has become theirs with the coming of God's son (2:8–11; 5:20). The darkness is passing away; the true light is already shining. Even Jesus described the commandment to love one another as "new" (καινός; John 13:34). Many commentators have referred to the use of the word "new" in texts regarding a renewed covenant as a background to this particular usage here. In 1 John this commandment gets its full meaning through the commandment from God in 3:23, to believe and to love. This functions as the "new" law in a renewed covenant.[72] As always, what is new is connected with Jesus and with those who believe in Jesus as Messiah, son of God.

"Love/hate one's brother" (1 John 2:9–11; 3:10, 14–15; 4:20–21)

The word-pair love/hate one's brother recurs several times in the description of the relationship with fellow believers. It is connected with the dualistic pattern in the letter, but the question is whether it does not also have a relationship to covenant texts. Precisely in the context of covenant we hear of loving God or hating God (Exod 20:5–6; Deut 5:9–10; 7:9–10). There are only two alternatives. To love means here primarily to bind oneself to, to be in solidarity with, to serve and to obey. To hate implies the

---

[72] Olsson, *Johannesbreven*, 119–23, 199–200.

reverse. This word-pair is used in other connections as well, and mostly in the sense of prefer/despise (Deut 21:15–17), to love someone more/less than someone else (John 3:19; 12:43; Luke 14:26; Matt 10:37). The choice of the words love/hate one's brother becomes more understandable if we take covenant texts as a background. As in the Qumran texts, the renewal of the covenant divides up God's people/humanity into two parts. Loving and hating describe the relationships to these two categories of human beings.

"Stumbling-block in him/it" (1 John 2:10)

The NRSV translation, "In such a person there is no cause for stumbling," is only one of several alternatives for the Greek text. The word σκάνδαλον usually means "snare," "trap," but is also used in an extended sense of something that leads to a fall, something that causes one to stumble (Lev 19:14; Matt 16:23; 18:7). In John 16:1 the cognate verb means to "fall away from one's faith." Is this sort of σκάνδαλον to be found in the one who loves, or in the light? Who is it who is caused to fall, the person in question here or other persons? There is good reason in both cases to choose the first option.[73] The best parallels are found in texts on the renewal of the covenant: "Create a pure heart and a holy spirit for them. And do not let them be ensnared by their sin henceforth and forever" (*Jub.* 1:21). Anyone at Qumran who wishes to enter the covenant "with the idols of his heart" is condemned. The reason is described as a sin that leads to a fall, "the stumbling block of his iniquity" (1QS 2:11–12).

"Have God/the Father" (1 John 2:23; 2 John 9)

To have God expresses a close fellowship between God and a human being, most likely a covenant relationship. The expression is attested in Johannine writings (1 John 2:23; 5:12: "have the Son"; 2 John 9, and later in the Apostolic Fathers. In *2 Clem.* 2:3 Jews are called "those who seem to have God." At Sinai, Israel became God's treasured possession (Exod 19:5). It implies

---

[73] Olsson, *Johannesbreven*, 117–18, 129, 132.

a mutual relationship: "I shall be your God and you shall be my people" (Lev 26:12).[74] The fundamental rule for the covenant between Yahweh and Israel is this: "You shall have no other gods before/besides me" (Exod 20:3). To have God, then, is associated with other relational words connected with the covenant: to have fellowship with God, to know God, to abide in God, etc.

"Children of God and children of the devil" (1 John 3:10)

The concept of the children of God in 1 John has for several reasons been coupled together with ideas of covenant,[75] but not the paired opposition, God's children—the devil's children. The renewal of the covenant in Qumran however led to a rigid division into two categories. In 1QS 1:16–3:6 those who belong to God are blessed, while those who belong to Belial are condemned. The renewal of the covenant at Qumran had a double effect: it gave the new community an identity and inner coherence, and it distinguished them from other groups.[76] This perspective is evident not least in the dualistic language of Qumran.

"Love one another" (1 John 3:11, 23; 4:7, 11, 12; 2 John 5)

Two themes dominate 1 John: to believe in Jesus the Messiah, the Son of God, and to love one another (3:23). The argumentation for the latter is given the most space. The first summarization of the message, "God is light," issues in the command to love one's brother (1:5–2:11); to keep God's commandments is distilled down in stages to the command to love one's brother (2:3–11); to do righteousness is ultimately paralleled with loving one's brother (2:29–3:10); the message they heard from the beginning is summarized again in 3:11, "that we should love one another"; to love one another becomes part of the renewed covenant's commandment (3:23); "God is love," the second summarization of the message, is used primarily as a motivation for mutual love

---

[74] The covenant is described as a marriage, as "to have a husband" and "to have a wife."

[75] See what has been said above about to be born of God.

[76] Blanton, *New Covenant*, 104–5.

(4:7–11); and finally, the new love for brothers and sisters is woven together with the remaining central concepts of the letter (5:1–5).

Consistently the issue is a love that exists within the Johannine group. In all respects, oneness, unity, concord, and solidarity characterize the new community in the renewed covenant. On this point, there are similarities with the new covenant at Qumran. The love referred to in the letter is not just a general ethical principle, but the love for one's fellow believers is a constitutive part of the renewed covenant. It is in this sense that for the author mutual love is utterly essential to life. God is one. God is love. Thus, those who know God, who are of God, who are born of God, who remain in God, and so on, must likewise be thoroughly drenched in love. Mutual love therefore has its basis in the community of the renewed covenant. Love for fellow believers is thus not simply a general, basic ethical rule, but part of the salvation event in "the last times" that have begun with the coming of God's son.

"His commandment" (1 John 3:23)

I have noted several times already that the occurrence of the central double commandment in the letter—*to believe in Jesus as Messiah, God's son, and to love one another*—has influenced also the letter's organization.[77] The traditional double love-commandment has been interpreted and developed further so that love for God includes believing in God's son, Jesus, the Messiah, and so that love for one's neighbor is specifically intended as love for one's fellow believers. In 1 Peter too, this mutual love is strongly emphasized and embedded in a presentation that builds on images of the covenant at Sinai and its consequences.[78]

"Have eternal life" (1 John 5:13)

The words "life" and "live" belong to the core vocabulary in the

---

[77] The first part is expounded in 4:1–6, the second part in 4:7–21. Both parts are summarized and elaborated in 5:1–12.

[78] Olsson, *Första Petrusbrevet*, 37–8, 62–7.

Johannine documents. In 1 John, they are particularly characterized by their distribution throughout the entire letter, from beginning to end (1:1–2 2:25; 3:14–15; 4:9; 5:11–12, 13, 20). Eternal life stands out as the ultimate goal of God's plan of salvation. It primarily means divine life and it is already here now. Human beings can partake of this life through faith in Jesus as Messiah, God's son, and through a new birth in which God, through Jesus Christ, gives human beings a new life (John 1:12–13; 1 John 3:14–15; 5:12–13, 20). Parallels to the idea of a divine life on earth can be found in contemporary Greek, Gnostic, Platonic and Hermetic texts, but the question is whether even here the closest background is not rather a reworking and continued interpretation of texts from the Hebrew Bible. In Deut 28 and 30:11–20, the covenant is linked with blessings and curses, with life and death. These texts lie behind some of the covenant texts from Qumran, not least 1QS 1–4 regarding the renewal of the covenant. If to this we add the promises of an eternal sojourn in the promised land, a very strong realized eschatology, and perhaps some Greek influence (ideas of immortality), we come very close to the concept of eternal life in the Johannine texts. In every case the concept of eternal life in 1 John is filled with expressions such as knowing God, partaking of God, being born from God, and with various immanence formulas and statements about God's anointing, God's *sperma* and God's spirit in a person. The letter's recipients are to know that they have eternal life (5:13, 20).

"Keep yourselves from idols" (1 John 5:21)

Down through the centuries, probably no statement in the letter has surprised readers as much as this final verse. But from an intra-Jewish perspective and on the basis of a developed tradition of a renewed covenant throughout the letter, these words become perfectly natural in a pastoral letter that places a stern admonition and warning last of all. Be careful that you do not fall away from the God of the covenant, as he has now been revealed through Jesus the Messiah, God's son, and begin to worship other gods. There were risks. Some believers could still fall into sin, and that could well prove that the new eternal life was not as yet a reality here and now. Others might find it difficult to withstand external pressures from both Jewish and Roman authorities. Some members of the community had already returned to their former faith. Jerry Griffith has demonstrated that the author in v. 21 uses a well-established, almost formulaic Jewish polemic attested in contemporary texts. It is used to promote a true Jewish identity and to perpetuate an internal social fellowship.[79] Using a typical Jewish polemic against other Jews may seem surprising, but it occurs in Qumran texts and in other contemporary sources.[80]

Conclusion

It is true that there are no explicit quotations from the Hebrew Bible or explicit references to Jer 31 or Ezek 36 to be found in the Johannine letters. In fact, generally speaking, explicit quotations and clear borrowings from older traditions do not occur at all in these letters. The closest thing to a reference to the Hebrew Bible, the words "not like Cain" in 1 John 3:12, confirms this. At the same time, this verse shows that the letter's author is very familiar with both the Hebrew Bible and later Jewish interpretations of Cain and Abel.[81] Why could not the same thing apply to ideas of a renewed covenant? The individual texts that have been analyzed above do not, each on its own, prove that the author has the concept of a renewed covenant as the basic background for his thinking. But taken together they prove to me that these ideas play a large role in the self-understanding of these Johannine Christians.

If with Judith Lieu we accept "a developing relation to the tradition" in 1 John and acknowledge that ideas of a renewed covenant were common around the beginning of the present era,[82]

---

[79] T. Griffith, *Keep Yourselves from Idols* (Sheffield: Sheffield Academic Press, 2002), 192–212.

[80] For different interpretations and arguments, see Olsson, *Johannesbreven*, 255–6, 262.

[81] "Scripture, or rather a tradition of interpreting Scripture, is part of the thought world which constructs the letter," Lieu, "From the Beginning," 475. See also Olsson, *Johannesbreven*, 201–2.

[82] Lieu, "From the Beginning," 463, 476–7, Chennattu, *Johannine Discipleship*, 182–194, and the references there.

then the conclusion of the foregoing survey is that traditions of a renewed covenant bind together a range of central themes in this letter. Several times I have connected these covenant concepts with what "was there from the beginning," but it is difficult to establish a proper date for this period. There is no consistent reworking of covenant motifs in the letter itself. It obviously forms no part of the letter's rhetoric. There is no argument regarding the question of a renewed covenant. Yet the majority of the presentation is based on ideas that can be related to covenant thinking, not least to Jer 31 and Ezek 36. In this way, the conviction that a renewed covenant has arrived in and with the Messiah's coming contributes to the letter's interpretation. It is not necessary to insist that this covenant theology functions as the "einziger Gesamtschlüssel" for the letter,[83] but it certainly provides the concept that best holds the entire letter together.

On the basis of this presumably early tradition within the Johannine community, we have reason to assume that the Johannine Christians saw themselves as Jews, in fact as *true* Jews.[84] This identity grounded itself in the belief that God's son had come, Jesus, the Messiah. The Johannine Christians had both a Jewish and a Christian identity, if we can put it that way.[85] But at the first, they were like other groups within Judaism who also claimed that they were the true Israel. A parallel with the Qumran community is readily applicable. Once the Johannine Christians could no longer remain part of a Jewish community, they came to be a group unto themselves and saw themselves as united with others, many of non-Jewish origin. Only gradually then, did there develop within the early church an exclusively Christian identity that distinguished between Jews and Christians.

---

[83] Klauck, *Johannnesbriefe*, 172.

[84] The same idea is to be found in Rev 2:9; 3:9; 12:1–17; 21:9–14

[85] Chennattu argues that Johannine discipleship according to the Gospel of John should be regarded as a covenant relationship, see *Johannine Discipleship*, esp. pp. 180–211. "Both first-century Judaism and the Johannine community turned to their common Jewish heritage as they struggled to establish their identity. The covenant motif constituted the central element in that heritage". ... The evangelist takes the OT covenant metaphor, redefines and broadens it, and applies it to the relationship between God and the new covenant community of Jesus' disciples" (p. 210).

Was There a Christian Mission Before the Fourth Century? Problematizing Common Ideas about Early Christianity and the Beginnings of Modern Mission*

Anders Runesson
McMaster University

Introduction

A few of years ago, a Christian Swedish weekly magazine, *Kyrkans Tidning*, published an interview with the Chair of the Jewish community in Stockholm.[1] The topic discussed was a debate that had arisen following a suggested change in regulations, which would prevent fundamentalism and ensure that all programs and activities associated with the synagogue would be firmly based on and communicate democratic and pluralistic values. All activities associated with the synagogue should be evaluated from this perspective. The majority supported the suggested change, but some members had concerns, fearing that the introduction of such a paragraph may result in censorship and suppression of minority views. The background for the suggested change is said to have been several (unrelated) events and conflicts taking place among Jewish communities in Sweden, among which was a debate about an attempted hiring of a teacher for the Jewish School in Stockholm who belonged to the ("Ultra-Orthodox") Chabad movement.

* This study is dedicated to Bengt Holmberg, a much appreciated friend and former teacher. Our common interest in and many discussions of the New Testament and early Christian identity formation—often resulting in quite divergent opinions, which, however, have always been maintained with cheerful attitudes and a deep sense of respect—have been a constant encouragement and source of inspiration. Thank you Bengt!

[1] C. Jaensson Wallander, "Debatt kring stadgar mot fundamentalism," *Kyrkans Tidning* 41 (2007): 10.

In addition to these Swedish events, the Chair of the Jewish Community widens the perspective and refers to international developments in Europe as the reason for the synagogue's suggested change of regulation. Orthodox rabbis, she is quoted as claiming, are moving to Eastern Europe in order to missionize among Jewish communities; they are even sometimes "tangibly taking over synagogues."[2]

This is, of course, a very interesting claim, regardless of the frequency of such purported attempts to influence and change Jewish ways of life. Indeed, the interview highlights the significance of institutional aspects of Jewish life in relation to questions of mission and national and international connections between Jewish communities. As it happens, this is precisely what we see in the ancient material, as we investigate the phenomenon of mission among Jews and (Jewish or non-Jewish) Christ-believers. The present study intends to address questions related to Jewish mission (sometimes referred to in the scholarly literature as "universalism"[3]) and the origins of Christian mission, all firmly set within Greco-Roman society and culture.

While there have certainly been many attempts in history to formulate theologies of mission and define the duties of the Christian in this regard, it is no exaggeration to claim that the post-holocaust era has brought with it for the Western Christian churches radical reassessments of Jewish and Christian relations in light of the role Christian theology played in the horrendous events taking place in Europe during the Second World War. Since Christian theologies of mission more broadly relate to and find inspiration and key texts in the New Testament, the relationship between Christ-believers and other Jews and non-Jews in the

---

[2] "Hon [ordföranden i judiska församlingen] syftar på de ortodoxa rabbiner som flyttar till östra Europa för att missionera bland judiska grupper, sprida sin syn och till och med handgripligen ta över synagogor."

[3] I have discussed elsewhere the use of the terms "universalism" and "particularism" in biblical studies, and believe that these expressions are too vague and therefore misleading: A. Runesson, "Particularistic Judaism and Universalistic Christianity? Some Critical Remarks on Terminology and Theology," *Journal of Greco-Roman Christianity and Judaism* 1 (2000): 120–44. Also published in: *ST* 54 (2000): 55–75. See further below.

ancient world is pushed to the center of the stage. Given that this raises historical questions—and history is a powerful tool in contemporary theological and political narratives—New Testament scholars have engaged these issues in new ways in recent years. The present study is meant as a contribution to this discussion.

We shall proceed as follows. The first part of the essay deals with questions of methodology, definitions, and basic point of departure, since decisions made on such issues will determine much of the outcome of the investigation. We shall then proceed to investigate mission in the ancient world, Greco-Roman and Jewish (including Apostolic-Jewish),[4] on three socio-political levels, all of which are evidenced in ancient sources as structuring society: the private, the semi-public, and the public areas of life. The concluding section will summarize some of the main findings and deal briefly with the contemporary situation in relation to ancient evidence. A main focus throughout the paper, indeed, the force of the argument, is a persistent insistence on the inextricability of the "religious" and the "political," and the consequences of this for our understanding of "mission" in antiquity.

Mapping the Area—Initial Steps

Several important studies on Jewish mission and related topics have been published the last 20 years or so.[5] Two of these, in particular,

---

[4] For this term, see n. 19 below.

[5] L. Feldman, *Jew and Gentile in the Ancient World: Attitudes and Interactions From Alexander to Justinian* (Princeton: Princeton University Press, 1993); M. Goodman, *Mission and Conversion: Proselytizing in the Religious History of the Roman Empire* (Oxford: Clarendon, 1994); J. Carleton Paget, "Jewish Proselytism at the Time of Christian Origins: Chimera or Reality?" *JSNT* 62 (1996): 65–103; S. McKnight, *A Light Among the Gentiles: Jewish Missionary Activity in the Second Temple Period* (Minneapolis: Fortress Press, 1991); J. Ådna and H. Kvalbein, eds., *The Mission of the Early Church to Jews and Gentiles* (Tübingen: Mohr Siebeck, 2000); E. J. Schnabel, *Early Christian Mission* (2 vols.; Downers Grove: Intervarsity Press, 2004). T. L. Donaldson, *Judaism and the Gentiles: Jewish Patterns of Universalism (to 135 CE)* (Waco: Baylor University Press, 2007). For additional studies, especially scholars critical to the theory that Jews missionized non-Jews in the first centuries C.E., see Schnabel, *Early Christian Mission*, 1:93, n. 8. From the Canadian Society of Biblical Studies have come three recent publications with relevance for our topic: T. L. Donaldson, ed., *Religious Rivalries and the Struggle for Success in Caesarea Maritima* (Waterloo: Wilfrid Laurier University Press,

emphasize the importance of defining carefully various phenomena related to our topic, and reserve the term "mission" for a specific activity: evidence of an organized active pursuit to convince non-members to become members of the religion of Judaism.[6] In the comparison with Christianity, Martin Goodman adds the word "universal" and asks (in vain) for non-Christian evidence for a "universal proselytizing mission."[7] Some scholars have even argued that we should abandon the term "mission" completely, due to its theological and anachronistic content.[8]

While careful categorization of the primary sources is crucial to enable meaningful and supportable conclusions based on a wide range of fragmentary comments and hints in the material, many types of definitions bring with them quite serious problems, some of which haunt all investigations into "origins-questions." One of the most basic issues concerns the problem of the level of anachronism inherent in the question itself.

All the questions we ask as historians initially take as point of departure specific and culturally determined ideas about the world, worldviews, religion, terminology etc., which carries within them and perpetuates specific views. The same is true for scholars studying contemporary cultures which are not their own. Once we immerse in the relevant source material, such ideas are relativized, sometimes radically changed, and the question needs to be re-phrased, terminology re-thought. Theories then need to be formulated, the material "translated" in ways that make sense in the modern world. The hermeneutics of these processes are complex and hard to disentangle.

One example may suffice. How much should we let the modern phenomenon, which origins or antique form we seek, control our

---

2000); R. S. Ascough, ed., *Religious Rivalries and the Struggle for Success in Sardis and Smyrna* (Waterloo: Wilfrid Laurier University Press, 2005); L. E. Vaage, ed., *Religious Rivalries in the Early Roman Empire and the Rise of Christianity* (Waterloo: Wilfrid Laurier University Press, 2006).

[6] McKnight, *Light*; Goodman, *Mission and Conversion*.

[7] Goodman, *Mission and Conversion*, 6–7.

[8] L. E. Vaage, "Ancient Religious Rivalries and the Struggle for Success: Christian, Jews, and Others in the Early Roman Empire," in *Religious Rivalries in the Early Roman Empire and the Rise of Christianity* (ed. L. E. Vaage; Waterloo: Wilfrid Laurier University Press, 2006), 3–19, esp. 9–17.

conclusions? In synagogue studies, e.g., it was common for a while among some scholars to take as point of departure 4th or 5th century architectural forms and then conclude that, since these specific forms were not present in the first century, no synagogues existed in the first century. Other scholars would, in response, claim that one has to "de-construct" (not in the Derridaean sense) the 5th century form and then trace specific individual elements back to earlier periods in order to find earlier variants of synagogue architecture. Such a procedure would also enable a reconstruction of developments over time within the same institutional setting.

It is my contention that it is a methodological mistake to define too narrowly a phenomenon and then measure other phenomena against it as either matching or not matching, especially when this is done in a comparison between them over time. Rather, we need to focus on and define a general culture, in our case a general culture of mission, in which diverse but related phenomena occur. When we proceed in this way, I would argue, we shall find that the earliest mission, in its various expressions within the Jesus movement and other Jewish movements, as well as within the Greco-Roman world generally, are intertwined in such a way that "the unique" needs to be understood as variants on a theme. The present study will argue its case within this interpretive frame.

Our comparative material includes (literary, inscriptional and archaeological) evidence relating to Jews (including Apostolic Jews), non-Jewish Christ-followers as well as adherers of other Greco-Roman cults. Since we speak of "religion" and "mission" in specific and culturally determined ways, reflecting our own modern understandings, it is of importance to begin our investigation by challenging the idea that these phenomena were understood in the same way in antiquity. Although quite common a perspective, it is incorrect to state, as Arthur D. Nock does, that "[t]he Jew and the Christian offered religions as we understand religion; the others offered cults."[9]

---

[9] A. D. Nock, *Conversion: The Old and the New in Religion from Alexander the Great to Augustine of Hippo* (Oxford: Clarendon, 1933), 16.

Changing the Facts on the Ground:
The Creation of "Religion" (and "Christianity")

I have argued elsewhere that the formation of Christian identity (and later the emergence of Islam) involved decisive developments that affected modern understandings of what constitutes "religion," and, by implication, have distanced us significantly from the first century Mediterranean world.[10] For our purposes here, the key element is the process by which second century non-Jewish Christ-believers actively divorced what we would call their "religious identity" from what they would call "Judaism," which included a disentanglement of the connections between the ethnos (Jews), their land and law, and their God.[11] This meant, in effect, that the cult of the Jewish ethnos, to which, according to many members of the Jesus movement, non-Jews had been invited as non-Jews, was re-interpreted, or rather re-created, in the likeness of philosophies and Greco-Roman mystery cults, several of which had gone through a similar development in

---

[10] A. Runesson, "Inventing Christian Identity: Paul, Ignatius, and Theodotius I," in *Exploring Early Christian Identity*, (ed. B. Holmberg; Tübingen: Mohr Siebeck, 2008), 59–92. See also S. Mason's persuasive study (although I disagree regarding the translation of *Ioudaioi*): "Jews, Judaeans, Judaizing, Judaism: Problems of Categorization in Ancient History," *JSJ* 38 (2007): 457–512. P. F. Esler, *Conflict and Identity in Romans: The Social Setting of Paul's Letter* (Minneapolis: Fortress, 2003), 73, writes: "[P]urely religious affiliation allegedly discovered in the ancient world may be an anachronistic illusion. … Religion as we understand it did not exist in the ancient world." See also P. Fredriksen, "Mandatory Retirement: Ideas in the Study of Christian Origins whose Time Has Come to Go," *SR* 35 (2007): 231–46.

[11] Ignatius would be the earliest example of this development. On the relationship between these aspects of ethnos, land, law, and god generally in the Greco-Roman world, see Mason, "Categorization." The connection between these aspects within Judaism has led several scholars to argue for the translation of *Ioudaioi* as "Judeans" rather than "Jews"; see, e.g., Esler, *Conflict and Identity*, 40–76, especially 68–74; Mason, "Categorization," J. M. G. Barclay, "Constructing Judean Identity after 70 C.E.: A Study of Josephus's *Against Apion*," in *Identity & Interaction in the Ancient Mediterranean: Jews, Christians and Others* (ed. Z. A. Crook and P. A. Harland; Sheffield: Phoenix Press, 2007), 99–112, esp. 110–112, and n. 20. J. Kloppenborg, "Judaeans or Judaean Christians in James?" in *Identity & Interaction in the Ancient Mediterranean: Jews, Christians and Others* (ed. Z. A. Crook and P. A. Harland; Sheffield: Phoenix Press, 2007), 113–35, writes (p. 113, n. 2): "Throughout this paper I use the rather awkward locution 'Judean' and 'Judeans' rather than 'Jewish' and 'Jews' in order to underscore the fact that in the first century C.E., the term Ἰουδαῖος is still primarily a marker of geographical origin or domicile (like Kitian, Phrygian, Lydian, etc.), rather than a designation of the beliefs held by such persons." While I do not agree with this translation on the basis of current self-definition among Jews, I understand the emphasis on these aspects of Judaism as a valid and very important point necessary to avoid anachronisms in the analysis of the first century.

earlier periods. This was a step unforeseen by Paul, who maintained—and in Rom 9–11 emphasized—the ethnic boundaries and the central position of the Jewish people in (and even outside) the new movement.

Similar (but not identical) developments, in which an ethnic component was original but became relativized, can be seen in several of the Mysteries, e.g., the Egyptian mysteries of Isis and Osiris, the Greek Eleusinian mysteries, and the Persian Mithras cult. Their membership was open and, like other mysteries, basically egalitarian (with the exception of the Mithras cult, in which no women participated). People with different ethnic identities could participate in various such mysteries, without neglecting their cultic obligations in other (social and political) contexts.

For Judaism, there was the possibility for non-Jews of conversion as well as adhering more loosely to the God of Israel (the so-called God-fearers) within a synagogue community context. This, however, did not mean that the ethnic, and therefore national components were compromised or lost.[12] Rather, converting to Judaism implied taking upon oneself all aspects that belonged to a people, including the law. Conversion meant a merging into another ethnos.[13] Even for those who did not convert (and thus did not undergo circumcision if male), the Jewish people was at the centre of the worship of the God of Israel; such individuals remained in their original ethnic self-identity, an identity which allowed them to worship this god just as well as other gods (just like people could be members of multiple mysteries and associations without compromising loyalty to anyone of them.)

In brief, as Steve Mason notes, what we call "religion," was, in antiquity, integral to at least six areas of life: ethnos, cult, philosophy, familial traditions/domestic worship, voluntary association

---

[12] Cf. S. J. D. Cohen, *The Beginnings of Jewishness: Boundaries, Varieties, Uncertainties* (Berkeley: University of California Press, 1999), 137; also quoted by Barclay, "Constructing," 110, n. 16.

[13] That this was not unproblematic in antiquity is clear from discussions in, e.g., rabbinic literature. Some authorities maintained that certain laws should not be followed by proselytes (because they were not ethnically Jews), whereas other rabbis argued that a proselyte was like a Jew in every respect, and that all laws and rituals should apply equally to them as to any other Jew. Some rabbis rejected the idea of accepting proselytes at all (*b. Yebam.* 47b, 24b), while others embraced converts (*b. Ber.* 57b; *b. Ned.* 32a; *b. Šabb.* 31a). Several texts mention mission (*m. 'Abot* 1:12; *b. Pesah.* 87b; *Gen. R.* 39:14; *Gen. R.* 84:4; *Gen. R.* 90:6, cf. 91:5; *Eccl. R.* 8:10).

(*collegia*/θίασοι), and astrology and magic.[14] Since Jews and Christ-believers, whether Jewish or not, lived in this cultural setting, we need to ask the question about mission in relation to each of these areas. Although Jews surely were unique enough to be recognized as a specific group (as we know from Greco-Roman writings), as Hans-Josef Klauck says, "[a]n outsider could have the impression that Jewish groups were like cultic associations that came from the East and venerated a highest god, and the same is true of the Christian communities in the Graeco-Roman cities."[15]

The wider contextual frame for our inquiry thus forces us to abandon our modern category of "religion"—and the idea of a mission of a "religion"—and ask for comparative material related especially to ethnos,[16] national and domestic cults, associations and mystery cults, and philosophy.[17] Activities related to these phenomena were played out on basically three levels of society: the public, the private, and the in-between semi-public sphere where associations existed.[18]

This means that we have to analyze the evidence for "mission" from a variety of perspectives that are triggered by these social levels, including political and national aspects and motivations. None of these levels can be said to communicate more authentic expressions of what we would call "religiosity" than another.

In the following, we shall ask what the inappropriateness of the category of "religion" for the first-century situation means for our understanding of "mission" and the nature of such phenomena. Since the Jesus movement, Apostolic Judaism,[19] was "religionized" into "Christianity" in late antiquity, we shall, consequently, have to abandon several conceptions related to "Christianity" too, in order to

---

[14] Mason, "Categorization," 482–88. See also P. A. Harland, *Associations, Synagogues and Congregations: Claiming a Place in the Ancient Mediterranean Society* (Minneapolis: Fortress Press, 2003), 61.

15 H-J. Klauck, *The Religious Context of Early Christianity: A Guide to Graeco-Roman Religions* (Minneapolis: Fortress, 2000), 54.

[16] Cf. Fredriksen, "Mandatory," 232: "gods run in the blood; cult is an ethnic designation/ethnicity is a cultic designation."

[17] Of these categories, Mason has suggested that philosophy comes closest to what we refer to as "religion" today; see "Categorization," 486. We shall return to this below.

[18] See, e.g., Klauck, *Context*, part 1.

[19] For the terminology, see Runesson, "Inventing Christian Identity," 72–74.

reconstruct first-century scenarios. Goodman is certainly correct when saying that the history of scholarship often reveals an unconscious "Christianization of the study of ancient religions."[20] However, it is equally important to note that ancient cults and varieties of Judaism, including Apostolic Judaism, have been religionized. Here we have, then, two major pitfalls threatening to turn our investigation into a gazing at our own reflection at the bottom of the well: the religionizing of "Christianity" and the Christianization of the Roman Empire.

Space does not allow for all of the aspects concerned to be dealt with; we shall, however, discuss some of the key features that will highlight the distinctive nature of the first-century situation in relation to later developments.

Pre-Christian Mission Beyond "Religion"

Defining "Mission"

The term "mission" has, as so many other terms used in scholarship, recently been called into question as anachronistic and basically theological in nature.[21] I would still use "mission" in the sense of *the intent and/or strategies used to influence others, passively or actively, to change their views and/or their behavior.* With such a lowest common denominator definition, it is fairly easy to show that missionary activities took place among Greco-Roman groups as well as among various Jewish groups, including Apostolic Jews. We need, therefore, to develop a more nuanced lens, so that the evidence can be categorized into meaningful groups of material; such groups of material can then be used for comparative analysis.

I have argued elsewhere for at least three basic categories, which are wide enough not to impose anachronistic or culturally isolating limits on the sources, which would make it difficult to compare various aspects as well as trace developments and influences between

---

[20] Goodman, *Mission and Conversion*, 3.

[21] See e.g., Vaage, *Religious Rivalries*, esp. the editor's contribution "Struggle for Success."

different groups of people.[22] I shall include some examples from Judaism, to clarify what is meant; we shall return later to discuss Greco-Roman traditions.

Proselytizing Mission
- Refers to attempts by members of one group to convince non-members to join their group. (Examples include Eleazar the Galilean, who, contrary to Ananias, insisted on the circumcision of the King of Adiabene; Josephus, *A.J.* 20.34–48. We find also, in this category, the forced circumcision practiced by some of the Hasmonean rulers as they annexed conquered areas.)

Ethno-Ethic[23] Mission
- Refers to attempts by members of one group to influence the behavior and/or worship of non-members, without asking them to join the group. (Examples would include the thought pattern revealed in the book of Jonah; it seems, also, that Ananias and another anonymous Jew mentioned by Josephus may have engaged in such mission: *A.J.* 20.34–48.[24])

Inward Mission
Refers to attempts by a member of a group to influence the behavior and/or worship of other members of the larger group to which they all belong. (Examples of this type of mission are legion, both in the Hebrew Bible, the New Testament, and throughout Jewish and Christian history.)[25]

Each of these types of mission can be divided into two basic categories: active or passive. The former would involve active

---

[22] Runesson, "Particularistic Judaism."

[23] I have modified this term somewhat from my original proposal "Ethic-Religious mission."

[24] It is not entirely clear whether Ananias promoted a proselytizing mission in general, and just made an exception strictly for the king, for political reasons. With regard to Izates' mother, Helena, it is implied in the story that she had become a full convert to Judaism; see discussion in Donaldson, *Judaism and the Gentiles*, 334–5.

[25] Cf. Goodman, *Mission and Conversion*, 5: "On a social scale broader than that of the household, Jews, Christians, and pagans from time to time, alike took it for granted that *within* societies religious deviants had to be brought into line, if necessary by force, to avert the hostility of the divine and disaster for all."

outreach to the targeted individuals or groups, but does not have to be planned and executed by a larger group; individuals could also be active in this regard, without explicit institutional or other authority or financial support behind them. Passive mission refers to a pattern of though expecting others to change their behavior and/ or cultic status as a consequence of the individual missionary's, or group's, way of life and other activities. For example, some Jews expected that non-Jews would join them on their own accord when the time was right and God would reinvent the world.[26]

A brief summary of these definitions of mission form may look as follows:

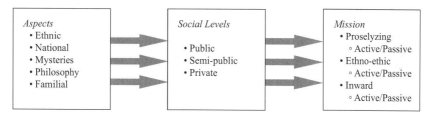

Figure 1. Parameters and Analytical Lenses

Outlining Parameters and a Mode of Procedure

If we now bring together what we have said in the two previous sections, we may outline a methodological strategy for tackling questions of "mission" in antiquity, and thereby also the origins of later Christian mission. I would like to emphasize four points in this regard.

---

[26] We find such expectations in the book of Isaiah, but also with the historical Jesus, partly in the Gospel of Matthew and in the Gospel of John.

1. What we call "religion" was, in antiquity, played out on three
    social levels:
    a. Public level (civic/state/empire concerns).
    b. Semi-Public level/Association level (voluntary groups/cults
       and their concerns).
    c. Private level (domestic, familial concerns).

2. On these levels, respectively, various aspects of what we call
    "religiosity" were triggered. For example:
    a. Civic, national, ethnic, colonial aspects were triggered on the
       public level.
    b. Aspects of individual salvation and/or morality, sometimes
       ethnic aspects, were triggered on the semi-public level.
    c. Aspects of daily life activities and how they are intertwined
       with various forms of the divine, familial and ancestral
       protection and well-being, were triggered on the private level.

3. Each level and the aspects it triggers need to be dealt with in
    terms of various forms of "mission and expansion."

4. As we analyze mission, understood as either proselytizing,
    ethno-ethic, or inward, we need to keep separate,
    a. intentions on the part of the group or individual as stated in
       our sources onthe one hand, and
    b. actual practices and techniques applied by these people on
       the other. (Techniques and strategies used can be identical
       between different groups while at the same time the
       intentions and goals of respective group may be different;
       still, the use of similar strategies may tell us something about
       the cultural mindset of both groups and how they thought
       they would win new members.)

In the following, we shall deal first with the role of the house as
an "underground" facilitator for the spreading of cults. Much focus
in the study of mission has been put on semi-public and public
levels of society; the private sphere had, however, an important
role to play precisely when cults spread, as a channel for change

that was often resisted on the public level. We shall then continue with evidence related to the semi-public and public levels and see how mission is played out there. Needless to say, there are no sharp boundaries between these three spheres of ancient life; seen as concentric circles, with the core circle being the private level, the shift between circles as they expand beyond each other would be a grey muddled area.[27] Still, the ancients did distinguish between them in word and deed,[28] and the movements that can be discerned between them, both between the private and the semi-public, and between the semi-public and the public, are of key importance to our quest for understanding ancient mission and expansion.

The Private Sphere: The Role of the House in Spreading a Cult

The private sphere triggered a range of cultic acts associated with the well-being and protection of the family (which could range between the nuclear family to others involved in the household, e.g., slaves); household gods and house altars were involved for all but the Jews—and those non-Jews (God-fearers and Christ-fearers[29]) who interpreted their allegiance to the God of Israel in exclusive terms. Daily rituals around, e.g., meals, as well as life cycle rituals for individuals involved in the household were in focus.

At first glance, it seems inappropriate to speak about forms of mission in this setting, since the focus is on individual family units and their interests in securing the benevolence of the gods with regard to their own safety and wellbeing. One could certainly speak of inward mission within the family unit to ensure correct sacrifices and behavior, but this would be of little interest here. For

---

[27] For example, rituals and cultic acts related to death permeated all three levels of society.

[28] Cf. J. Scheid, who notes the legal aspects: "Religions in Contact," in *Religions of the Ancient World: A Guide* (ed. S. I. Johnston; Cambridge: Harvard University Press, 2004), 112–26, esp. 113.

[29] The term refers to non-Jewish adherers to Jewish communities following the pattern advised by Paul. They were like God-fearers, but theologically with full membership "in Christ." See Runesson, "Inventing Christian Identity," 73.

our purposes, taking seriously the nature of cultic acts as intimately and inextricably intertwined with political and other matters of importance to state and society, it is more significant to point at what happens between the levels in terms of the aim at controlling or influencing people's cultic acts. There are two directions of influence that should be noted: 1) actors on the public scene wanting to control private cultic rituals on the one hand, and 2) private individuals who feel a need to expand, or allow the expansion of, their own worship beyond the immediate context of their household.

In the first case, the will to influence moving in the direction from the public to the private, the reason for action is simply to protect state and society by ensuring that pollution following an incorrectly performed sacrifice in the domestic sphere should never happen. Plato, e.g., wants to rule that sacrifices in the private sphere be forbidden. If someone feels he or she wants to sacrifice, such sacrifices must be brought to and performed by experts: the priestly personnel at public temples.[30] Since the aim here is to protect shared space and communal life (the state), the type of mission should be defined as inward: political boundaries are, just as much as any group boundaries, what defines the aim and the (suggested) actions taken. Whether effective or not, such inward mission, policing if you like, aimed at controlling cultic behavior was most likely present from time to time in Greco-Roman society empire-wide.[31] "Polytheism" was not the same as "tolerance" or "religious freedom" as we understand these terms today.

In the second case the movement is in the opposite direction: the will to influence other's cultic behavior (mission) begins within the private household and expands beyond it into the (semi-) public sphere. Two examples are especially instructive here. The establishment of the Egyptian cult of Sarapis on Delos in the third century B.C.E.,[32] and the modification and opening up of a private

---

[30] Plato, *Leg.* 10.909d–910d. Note the suggested death penalty for impiously performed sacrifices in the private realm.

[31] Such "policing" of cultic behavior also extended into the semi-public level of society, i.e., associations. See further below.

[32] *IG* XII/7 506; *IG* XI/4 1299; plan of the remains of Sarapeion A: P. Bruneau and J. Ducat, *Guide*

cult of Agdistis to people beyond the household in Philadelphia, Asia Minor (first century B.C.E.).[33] Both of these examples have been treated at some length by others; our interest here is to note the movement itself from the private to semi-public spheres of society.

In the case of the Sarapis cult on Delos, we find some important elements that may be generalizable. An individual, a priest from Egypt named Apollonius, brings a cultic statue of Sarapis with him to Delos and sets it up in his rented (private) house. Later on, his grandson, Apollonius the Younger, had a dream in which the god commanded him to construct a temple for him. There was an increase of adherents to the cult preceding this move; Klauck suggests these were immigrant Egyptians.[34] There is no reference, however, specifically to the ethnic identity of the new adherents. The temple is met with local resistance, legal proceedings follow, but the grandson is vindicated; the temple, which has been excavated (Sarapeion A[35]), stands.

We have no explicit evidence of missionizing efforts of any of these men, but we know that this cult, foreign to Delos, grew. Michael White notes that, as a result of the establishment of Sarapeion A, "Egyptian cults grew in popularity, with three different temples and a position of prominence in that region of the island known as the 'terrace of the foreign gods'"[36] If the Apollonius family recruited worshippers in an Egyptian immigrant setting, these efforts would have to be defined as inward mission with the ethnic component carrying the explanatory force.

The crucial event for understanding what happened, however, is the building of the temple.[37] This act may be seen, in and of itself, as propagating the "effectiveness" of this god to others, using culturally

---

de Délos (3d ed.; Paris: Boccard, 1983), no. 91, fig. 71. Cf. Sarapeion C: ibid. no. 100 (fig. 82).

[33] *SIG* 3/985 = *LSAM* 20. Cf. Knock, *Conversion*, 216–217; Klauck, *Context*, 64–68; L. M. White, *The Social Origins of Christian Architecture: Volume I: Building God's House in the Roman World: Architectural Adaptation Among Pagans, Jews, and Christians* (Valley Forge: Trinity Press International, 1990), 45.

[34] Klauck, *Context*, 64.

[35] Bruneau and Ducat, *Guide de Délos*, no. 91.

[36] White, *Social Origins*, 33.

[37] Cf. the documentation on papyri of a certain Sarapis worshipper, Zoilos, who, in 257 B.C.E., was told in a dream to erect a temple for the divinity in a city in Asia Minor (Goodman, *Mission and Conversion*, 28).

attuned strategies of establishing a presence in public space in a setting that is not ethnically connected to the god in question. Doing so would reduce the space on the sacred island dedicated to other gods. Such a move can hardly be understood without assuming, at least to some degree, that the Sarapis worshippers aimed at expanding even beyond their own ethnically defined members; they must have thought of the power of their god to extend beyond their own people, a wish on the part of the god to be present in and control other parts of the world in addition to Egypt (and travelling Egyptians). Proselytizing mission, in other words.[38]

Important to note here, however, is that we find no political authority behind this expansion; the expansion is not the initiative of a nation. Still, the spread of the cult through the building of the temple was met with local resistance. Such resistance may well have been grounded in fears that the balance would be disturbed; local gods were pushed back and had their power sphere threatened. This would make for unhappy gods, and unhappy gods would make for unhappy humans.[39] Somehow, however, perhaps through the proven power of Sarapis, this cult was accepted and added to others, even achieving prominence with additional temples built.[40] As this process continued, the ethnic identity of the members of the cult was weakened and eventually understood as unimportant, even though the Egyptian origin of the cult was never concealed or forgotten.

In the case of the development of a private cult of the goddess Agdistis in the household of a certain Dionysius in Philadelphia we see yet another example of how household cult could expand beyond the original parameters of the house.[41] In this inscription, we see what Klauck calls a "modernising" of the cult leading to the reduction of the prominence of the goddess and the inclusion of a "larger Graeco-Hellenistic pantheon with visible altars and

---

[38] Again, proselytizing mission is not necessarily defined as exclusive in nature; joining one such group does not have to exclude membership in other associations or cults. The term proselytizing only indicates, positively, the aim and result of including new members in one's own group.

[39] Cf. Fredriksen, "Mandatory," 232.

[40] Sarapeion B (*GD*, no. 96) and Sarapeion C (*GD*, no. 100).

[41] *SIG* 3/985 = *LSAM* 20.

images."[42] With this follows rules related to medical ethics, which emphasizes the position and importance of the family. At the same time, the household opens up to others who would like to join worship in this manner. These new worshippers were, according to Klauck, probably drawn from neighboring and related households. Whether these new members were won via close household networks or not, we see here the establishment of a voluntary association of a cultic nature.[43] We may safely assume that this expansion of the private cultic activities to include a larger group of likeminded people was the result of some sort of spreading of the word among neighbors and beyond. This means proselytizing mission on a semi-public level, although most likely not systematized or on a larger scale. The ethical component of the modified cult probably had some attraction, and those involved most likely would have wanted to spread these ideals.

These and other examples indicate that "private" in antiquity did not mean what we understand by "private" today. In antiquity, cult in the private sphere would have an impact on society at large, and so could not be isolated or left without some control. In modern day Europe and North America, the rhetoric of "private" in terms of religion is used to de-politicize religion, effectively separating different spheres of society, compartmentalizing society, and thereby neutralizing "religion" and "religious rites" as unimportant for the protection of the state.[44] This has implications for how mission is understood.

In sum, in terms of *intentions* we may conclude that people involved in public affairs could argue for a (corrective) inward mission directed to the private sphere in order to protect state and society. The *strategy* was to argue for the issuing of laws that could be used when enforcing compliance with state demands. What the authorities would call law and order, those who were targeted would call persecution. From an analytical point of view, we may note the

---

[42] Klauck, *Context*, 68.

[43] For a categorization of associations, see Harland, *Associations,* 28–53, esp. 44–52.

[44] This in turn has often resulted in a lack of sensitivity on the part of the authorities in various nations in relation to the worldview(s) of religious groups, some of which have never accepted such compartmentalization of private and communal life. This is not, however, the place to expand further on this issue.

close connection between mission, law and persecution. We shall return to this when discussing developments in the public sphere.

The *intensions* of the Apollonius family on Delos and Dionysius' household in Philadelphia in Asia Minor were to promote the cult of specific deities, without insisting on exclusiveness. There are no signs indicating that any of them aimed at transforming society via the cult, although the moral code in the Philadelphia case combined with expansion beyond the household comes close to such an aim. The *strategy* for expansion of the Sarapis cult was to claim a place in public space by building a temple to the god; in the Philadelphia case we see modifications to the cult as well as architectural rearrangements within the house to accommodate worship in a temple like setting.

For Judaism, worship was collective, and whatever took place in the household would be within an inner-Jewish frame of reference. We have no direct evidence of mission on this level, since we do not have early evidence of private houses being renovated into association buildings.[45] However, the very construction of cultic buildings such as synagogues would have been perceived as claiming space and recognition, in brief, promoting the god, in society. The main difference between such Jewish construction and Greco-Roman expansion is the ethnic aspect, which was maintained within Jewish communities. We shall return to this in the following section, which shall deal with the semi-public level. We shall also suspend treatment of Christ-believers to that section.

---

[45] While White has previously argued that the Ostia and the Delos synagogues were examples of such renovations of private houses for synagogue use, these conclusions were incorrect as has been shown in several studies of these buildings by Anders Runesson, Donald Binder, and Monika Trümper. These buildings, which are our oldest remains of Diaspora synagogues, were constructed for (semi-) public use from the beginning. The earliest evidence of renovations of private space is the Stobi inscription from the late second century. See A. Runesson, D. D. Binder and B. Olsson, *The Ancient Synagogue From its Origins to 200 C.E.: A Source Book* (Leiden: Brill, 2008), nos. 179, 102, 187.

The Dynamic Space In-Between:
Associations and Mysteries

As is well known, various forms of associations (*collegia*/θίασοι)—
"smaller than the city ... yet larger than the family"[46]—flourished in
first century Greco-Roman society.[47] Such groups began to develop
around the time after Alexander the Great, then representing a
new phenomenon in the ancient world. Although all associations
included cult of some sort, we shall here be dealing with those who
established their membership around a specific cult, and whose
identity was "expressed in terms of devotion to the deity or deities"[48]

While the traditional perspective has been that associations came
into being as a result of a feeling of alienation among ordinary
people in relation to larger political and administrative structures as
empires were established, this "origins-explanation" can no longer
be maintained without modification.[49] Instead, associations often
reflected a sense of belonging within ancient society and the structures
of the *polis*; they took part in a system of benefaction integral to Greco-
Roman society.[50] Membership was primarily drawn from non-elite
strata, but we find dependency on civic and imperial elites, mainly
as benefactors, sometimes as leaders.[51] There seems to have been
at least some sort of relationship between specific cults in different
places around the Mediterranean, creating a sense of connectedness
beyond the local cultic community to which the individual belonged.[52]

This does not mean that cultic associations were unproblematic from
the perspective of the state. As Goodman notes, the worship in some
associations of foreign gods could be seen as not integral to a stable

---

[46] Klauck, *Context*, 42.

[47] The most comprehensive and recent study and categorization of associations is found in Harland, *Associations*; see especially 28–53.

[48] Ibid., 44.

[49] The traditional view may be represented by Klauck, *Context*, 43–44.

[50] See Harland, *Associations*, 89–112: "The inscriptional evidence from Asia provides a concrete illustration of the continuing importance of the polis and its structures as a locus of identity, cooperation, and competition from members of many associations and guilds, reflecting various social strata of society. These groups were often participants in civic vitality, not symptoms of decline" (p. 112).

[51] Ibid., 52.

[52] Cf. Goodman, *Mission and Conversion*, 27–28.

society and, in fact, as constituting a "positive threat."[53] How, then, were such cults spread, and what was the purpose of spreading them?

We have already addressed the issue of introducing foreign cults and the movement from the private to the semi-public level of society. The question of mission in the present section relates to why and how associations on the semi-public level of society developed strategies to influence others and establish, maintain, and expand their membership. There is some literary evidence of initiates of Greco-Roman cultic associations who, as they travelled, expanded the influence of their god(s) by establishing associations in new places.[54] It is quite clear also from archaeological evidence that new cults spread and were established all over the Roman Empire.[55]

Understanding the expansion of cults within social context may direct our attention to the system of benefaction, and how associations competed to establish themselves through winning the favorable attitude of wealthy benefactors. Other strategies for claiming a place included establishing and embellishing separate association buildings, perform public processions, and, as Roger Beck words it, set in motion spectacle, with the aim of promoting the deity.[56] Beck continues: "cults of this type may not have proselytized systematically, but they certainly proclaimed systematically."[57]

---

[53] Ibid., 17. Cf. Harland, *Associations*, 161–173.

[54] One example is Livy's (famous) description in his Roman history of the rapid spread of a Bacchic association among men and women, coming to Rome from Etruria (39.8–19). Even some elite individuals from "noble families" became members (39.13). Livy, who presents the initiates as immoral criminals committing all sorts of horrible crimes, tries to explain the spread of the cult by referring to the attractions of wine and feasting (39.8). The cult was eventually forbidden in Rome and Italy, and all Bacchic shrines were destroyed, exempting only those where there was an ancient altar or sacred image. Those who needed to gather to perform the rites had to secure permission from both the praetor and the senate (39.18). Note also the conversion story in Apuleius' novel *Metamorphoses*, and the Isiac procession in 11.7–11.

[55] See examples discussed by R. S. Ascough, "'A Place to Stand, A Place to Grow': Architectural and Epigraphic Evidence for Expansion in Greco-Roman Associations," in *Religious Rivalries in the Early Roman Empire and the Rise of Christianity* (ed. L. E. Vaage; Waterloo: Wilfrid Laurier University Press, 2006), 78–98, and R. Beck, "On Becoming a Mithraist: New Evidence for the Propagation of the Mysteries," in *Religious Rivalries in the Early Roman Empire and the Rise of Christianity* (ed. L. E. Vaage; Waterloo: Wilfrid Laurier University Press, 2006), 175–94.

[56] Beck (ibid., 176), notes that similar events of miracles etc. were ascribed to Christianity in ancient sources; many scholars interpret this as a major source of Christianity's success in its mission.

[57] Ibid., 176.

While we should be aware that proclaiming divinities in these ways was not done exclusively in order to secure and extend membership, such aims must surely be included, not least from a social perspective (economic realities are, after all, also realities, and associations were dependent upon them too). In other words, when we try to answer the question of why certain cults proclaimed their gods in these ways, we may note several intentions that all come together, for the worshippers, in the will to secure protection and safety for oneself and the group's members by expanding the influence of a specific god. Proclaiming the effectiveness of a god was in and of itself an act of piety, and proselytizing mission was the understood (side?)effect of such strategies.

Not all cults would follow a similar pattern, Mithraism being the most obvious exception. While Mithraism certainly expanded and spread over the empire, it was not by such explicit means as those described above. Rather, spread of the cult was achieved by "commendation of friend to friend, by co-option among likeminded adult males in delimited social contexts; also that, in all likelihood, recruitment among kin and via patron-freedman relationship played a significant part."[58] Though the strategy is different, it would be, as I see it, a distortion of the picture of what happened not to call this proselytizing mission. In the analysis, the *intention* needs to be treated separately from the *strategies* used. Also, we need to note that proselytizing mission need not entertain exclusivist claims; membership in one cult would not necessarily exclude membership in another.

The intentions of those who spread Greco-Roman cults may not have been to penetrate into the public sphere of society and change the religio-political status quo on a state level. Yet, we know that some of these foreign gods reached into the public sphere. The last important ones to achieve such success in Rome were Isis and Sarapis, who became public deities in the first century c.e.[59] In

---

[58] Ibid., 193. Beck refers to Rodney Stark's very similar description of both modern recruitment to new religious movements and his theory of the rise of Christianity.

[59] Cf. Scheid, "Religions in Contact," 121.

the case of Sarapis, we thus have evidence of a cult who had the ability to successfully move both between private and semi-public contexts (the Delos example discussed above), and then between the semi-public and public spheres of society. We shall return to this below since one (transformed) offshoot of an Apostolic-Jewish group managed not only to attain public status, but also to do it with exclusive claims to preserving a stable society.[60]

A word on philosophy before turning to Judaism. Goodman discusses important aspects of philosophy and mission, although he tends to define away the conclusions that would seem to follow from his description.[61] Philosophers spread their ideas to others and wanted universal enlightenment; they wanted to change the lives and attitudes of others. Some of them formed or belonged to philosophical schools (e.g., Pythagoreans and Epicureans); others did not seem to form collectivities into which new members could be included (e.g., Stoics, Cynics). An effect of their activities could, for those who listened, be a radical break with the past, a conversion experience, resulting in life-long adherence to the philosophical school in question.[62]

Although no uniform pattern emerges, it seems to me that in order to describe what went on, the word mission need to be applied. As with the cults discussed above, no ethnic component is involved in terms of entrance requirement. Goodman talks about educational mission, as he defines it, and rejects the term proselytizing mission. It would seem more appropriate, as I see it, to allow for both terms in order to cover the spectrum.[63]

In any case, we find in Greco-Roman society not only a multitude of cults and philosophies, but also that members of, or adherers to, these groups tried to convince others to join them in one way

---

[60] Cf. Goodman, *Mission and Conversion*, 18.

[61] Ibid., 32–37.

[62] As described by third century C.E. historian Diogenes Laertius (*Vitae* 4.3.16–17).

[63] The question is whether one would need to be able to point to a group and membership in order to use the term "proselytizing." Cf. the modern New Age movement, which is rather hard to define and displays various forms. Yet, individuals may act as missionaries who want everyone to adhere to specific sets of beliefs and behaviors without requiring group membership. Since the aim is to have people leave their old worldviews and attain new ones, it seems logical to speak of proselytism.

or another, either in a community or by changing their ways of life as a consequence of believing in the missionized teachings. Movements spread from the private sphere into the semi-public, as well as between cults and philosophies in the semi-public sphere. While philosophies may entertain and missionize exclusive claims, cults were not exclusive in terms of demands on members.

Where does Jewish mission fit in this overall picture? Answering this question, we need to note, firstly, that Judaism was a state cult with Jerusalem as its center. The temple tax reminds us that this state cult was to be adhered to by everyone belonging to the ethnos, wherever they lived in the world. In the Diaspora, Jewish communities were understood as associations, however, and this presents us with a scenario worthy of note. Mission, as we shall see, could take place on both levels with an interesting link between them.

There can be no question that non-Jews converted to Judaism, both by free will and as a consequence of the use of force. We also know of a group of non-Jewish individuals, commonly referred to as "sympathizers" or "God-fearers," who were more loosely connected to Judaism within Diaspora synagogue contexts. Although we have important material dating back to around, and even before, the Babylonian exile, conclusive evidence (literary and epigraphic) begins to emerge in the first century B.C.E. and extends into the Talmudic period. In terms of attitudes to mission, the nature of the sources reveals positive remarks (by Jews), negative reactions (by non-Jews and Jews), and neutral mention of "proselytes."[64] The material is similar to what we have seen with regard to Greco-Roman mission in the semi-public sphere: we have clear evidence of movement between cults and philosophies. The question is, then, how that movement came about.

---

[64] For source material and brief discussions of it, see L. Feldman and M. Reinhold, *Jewish Life and Thought Among Greeks and Romans* (Philadelphia: Fortress, 1996), 123–135 (conversion) and 137–145 ("sympathizers"/"God-fearers"). For inscriptions, see M. H. Williams, *The Jews Among the Greeks and Romans: A Diaspora Source Book* (London: Duckworth, 1998), 169–179 (includes inscriptions). See also M. Stern, ed., *Greek and Latin Authors on Jews and Judaism: Edited with Introductions, Translations and Commentary* (3 vols.: Jerusalem: Israel Academy of Sciences and Humanities, 1974–1984).

I would suggest the following line of argument on the semi-public level. The Jews of the Diaspora were well integrated in Roman society at this time (around the first century B.C.E. and C.E.), and archaeological and epigraphic evidence indicate that Jews took part in society in much the same way as non-Jews.[65] This means that they constructed their association buildings ("synagogues") adapting to local architectural styles,[66] and they took part in the same system of benefaction as everybody else. This system implies competition among associations in securing funding for building projects. When Jews in Ostia introduced a gift to the synagogue with the words *Pro salute august[orum*[67]*]* (for the health of the emperor[s]), they claimed a place in Roman society, proclaiming the God of Israel as relevant to that society.[68] Displaying the name of benefactors, who could be Jewish or non-Jewish, would not only honor the benefactor but also make a public statement that the Jewish community *and its God* has been found important in the eyes of influential citizens.[69] This would create attention (and attraction) in and of itself. In addition, the "cultic" building itself functioned "rhetorically" in much the same way, making a statement to all who lived in the city.

Although we do not hear of public processions in the case of the Jews, we have access to literature intended for non-Jewish readers, like Josephus' *Contra Apionem* (as well as *Antiquitates judaicae*), which elevated Judaism as superior to non-Jewish ways of life and proclaimed the God of Israel as powerful for non-members, able to give protection and happiness to anyone who would worship him. The God of Israel is in control of world history, and converts will be rewarded.[70] As Mason states, "[w]hether Judaism was a missionary

---

[65] This is one of the main arguments of Harland, *Associations*.

[66] For discussion and bibliography for synagogues before 200 C.E., see Runesson, Binder, and Olsson, *Ancient Synagogue*.

[67] For the plural reading, *augustorum* (AUGG), see *JIWE* 1, no. 13; A. Runesson, "The Synagogue at Ancient Ostia: The Building and its History from the First to the Fifth Century," in *The Synagogue of Ancient Ostia and the Jews of Rome: Interdisciplinary Studies* (ed. B. Olsson, D. Mitternacht, and O. Brandt; Stockholm: Paul Åström, 2001), 29–99, esp. 86, n. 322.

[68] Note also that sacrifices for the emperor were made in the Jerusalem temple.

[69] An interesting example is the Julia Severa inscription: see Runesson, Binder and Olsson, *Ancient Synagogue*, no. 103.

[70] So S. Mason, "The *Contra Apionem* in Social and Literary Context: An Invitation to Judean

religion or not, Josephus tried to be a Judean missionary in Rome."[71]

Seen together, archaeological, epigraphic, and literary sources indicate that Jews interacted with non-Jews in ways that would have signaled to non-Jews that joining this group and worshiping the God of Israel was encouraged and would bring benefits to the person who became a member. We are looking in the wrong direction when we understand proselytizing mission to be limited to modern methods of conversion in contemporary Christian contexts. Within the ancient context, we find that Jews used techniques that would make sense to their neighbors in terms of encouragement to join their communities.

Thus, many Jewish communities and also individuals seem to have been intentionally proselytizing in the first century C.E.: this is indeed the most likely explanation for the many proselytes we hear of in the sources, as well as the God-fearer phenomenon itself.[72] As to the latter, the following may be said. If cults and philosophies attracted adherers and members, then it is likely that the use of the same or similar techniques of proclamation would attract both new full members to Judaism and people who would expect and take for granted a non-exclusive membership. Since full conversion demanded exclusive membership and rejection of other gods and one's native tradition, indeed it was perceived as joining another ethnos, its laws and its way of life, including support for Jerusalem,[73] those who would take for granted non-exclusive adherence to various cults and associations would continue to do so within a synagogue context. Such individuals were not turned away by Jewish communities.

Philosophy," in *Josephus' Contra Apionem: Studies in its Character and Context with a Latin Concordance to the Portion Missing in Greek* (ed. L. Feldman and J. R. Levinson; Leiden: Brill, 1996), 187–228; for the argument regarding *A.J.*, see esp. 147–148. Mason concludes regarding *C. Ap.* that "both the form and content of the tract, not to mention the creative energy it reflects, are best understood if Josephus was here continuing his effort to further interest in Judean culture—including a recommendation of conversion" (p. 159). An important aspect here is Mason's analysis of the genre of *C. Ap.* which he concludes should be identified as *logos protreptikos*, a genre used by later Christian apologists with the purpose to "draw people away from traditional philosophy and into Christian groups that now understood themselves as philosophies" (p. 171). Earlier, P. Bilde had also identified *C. Ap.* as an example of missionary literature, see *Flavius Josephus Between Jerusalem and Rome* (Sheffield: JSOT, 1988), 120.

[71] Mason, "Social and Literary Contex," 173.

[72] Cf. Josephus, *C. Ap.* 2.282–284.

[73] Cf. Tacitus, *Hist.* 5.5.1–2.

Rather, as a sign of acculturation, they were incorporated loosely and this eventually gave rise to the idea that various subsets of laws, minimal requirements, should apply to them as non-Jews.[74]

The phenomenon of God-fearers is thus a result of Jewish insistence, contrary to, e.g., Egyptian Isis worshippers, on the ethnic—and therefore public and national—aspect of their identity, in a semi-public Greco-Roman context. As we see in some instances, such status could even be missionized (the Adiabene case), reminding us of much earlier traditions in the Book of Jonah that would demand compliance with Jewish ethno-ethic standards without conversion to the Jewish people. We note, therefore, that Jewish mission could also be of the ethno-ethic type, not only proselytizing.

The exclusive membership was unique, although vaguely related to philosophies, rather than cults (it seems Josephus alluded to this relationship when presenting Judaism to non-Jews). Combined, however, with the ethnic aspect (and the laws that came with it), this evoked strong negative feelings among some Greco-Roman authors. The following quote from Tacitus (*Hist.* 5.5.1–2) regarding non-Jews who convert to Judaism is revealing (emphasis added):

> [T]he other customs of the Jews are base and abominable, and owe their persistence to the depravity. For the worst rascals among other peoples, *renouncing their ancestral religions*, always kept sending tribute and *contributing to Jerusalem*, thereby increasing the wealth of the Jews; ... Those who are converted to their ways follow the same practise, [of cutting themselves off from other peoples] and the earliest lesson they receive is to *despise the gods, to disown their country*, and to regard their parents, children, and brothers as of little account.[75]

For our purposes it is of interest to note that, within synagogues in the Greco-Roman world, Jewish communities could engage in

---

[74] Cf. different rabbinic traditions regarding Adam (*Gen. R.* 16:6; *Deut. R.* 2:25; *Num. R.* 14:12) and Noah (*b. Sanh.* 56a–b; *Gen. R.* 34:8; *Deut. R.* 1:21) as well as special regulations for non-Jews once the Messiah has come (*Gen. R.* 98:9). Adam, Noah, Abraham and Jacob are all mentioned as receivers of a different number of laws in *Exod. R.* 30:9. See also Acts 15:20.

[75] Trans. Moore, LCL.

mission, both proselytizing and ethno-ethic, that placed the God of one of the defeated nations at the center of their worldview, with loyalty directed to its capital, Jerusalem, and to Jewish law.[76] With this in mind, it is reasonable to assume that the God-fearers won would far outnumber the proselytes.[77]

Behind missionary attitudes and practices lay convictions that the God of Israel was the God of the whole world, and that this God controlled, ultimately, world history. The Hebrew Bible abounds in statements to this effect, especially in Psalms, but also in some of the prophets. Worshipping such a God would make sense also to people who were not Jews. Since the ethnic aspect is connected to the land and to the public sphere, and has implications for Apostolic-Jewish mission, we shall return to this in the next section. Suffice it to note that whereas we have seen movement between the private and semi-public sphere as we discussed Greco-Roman cults, here we find tensions with political overtones arising from the interrelationship between the semi-public and public spheres. Such tension is, in fact, accentuated in Apostolic-Jewish mission.

While we do not find general evidence of Jewish mission indicating movement from the private sphere to the semi-public in the first century, Apostolic-Jewish mission, although focused on the semi-public arena, was also connected in certain respects to the private sphere. It is clear from Paul's letters that Christ-believers could gather in homes, just as we have seen that some Greco-Roman cults did.[78] To what extent these homes were remodeled[79] in the earliest period is impossible to say, although we have one example, perhaps the earliest, from Capernaum of a private house in which one of the rooms was transformed into a cultic room,or association

---

[76] Cf. Seneca, *Superst.*, quoted by Augustine, *Civ.* 6.11: "The vanquished have given laws to their victors" (Trans. Gummere, LCL).

[77] The fact that the exclusivity of philosophies would be reserved mostly for the elite, and non-exclusivity of the cults and associations would be embraced by the greater number of the population, supports such a conclusion.

[78] See e.g., 1 Cor 16:9; Phlm 2; Rom 16:5; all discussed by Paul Trebilco in his contribution to the SNTS seminar "History and Theology of Mission in the New Testament: Global Challenges and Opportunities"; Lund 2008.

[79] Cf. above the changes made to the house of Dionysius in Philadelphia.

room.[80] Apostolic Jews as well as Christ-fearers were also found in synagogues as subgroups, a fact which both makes sociological sense and is confirmed by Acts.[81] In terms of Apostolic Judaism, it is safe to say that it spread via a network of synagogues and with the "subversive" help of private houses.

This is both similar to and different from the spread of Greco-Roman cults. The similarity lies in the use of the private house as a "platform" for introducing new cultic elements. The difference is, of course, that Apostolic Jews and non-Jews were closely related to synagogues and had a network in place that could be used, whereas new Greco-Roman cults that were introduced via the private sphere had to construct buildings themselves and create community networks in the semi-public sphere.[82] This process had already been achieved, to a large degree, by Jewish communities before the arrival of Apostolic Judaism in the first century.[83] The spread of Apostolic Judaism is, therefore, intimately intertwined with the social networks established by other Jews, as well as earlier and other Jewish missionary activities among non-Jews, which had created active interest in Judaism.

In brief, the techniques used by apostolic Jews, as far as they were new, were embedded in the matrix created by Jews before and around them. Most of this early mission must be defined as inward mission, since it was carried out within a network of synagogues and directed to the audiences there, including God-fearers who were worshippers of the God of Israel already.[84]

---

[80] See A. Runesson, "Architecture, Conflict, and Identity Formation: Jews and Christians in Capernaum From the 1th to the 6th Century," in *Religion, Ethnicity, and Identity in Ancient Galilee: A Region in Transition.* (ed. J. Zangenberg, H. W. Attridge, and D. B. Martin; Tübingen: Mohr Siebeck, 2007), 231–57. Although this house may indicate a broader pattern, it should be noted that in this case we are dealing with a specific site remembered as related to an apostle (and Jesus); it soon developed into a pilgrimage site.

[81] Cf. here, e.g., the work of M. D. Nanos with regard to Rome: *The Mystery of Romans: The Jewish Context of Paul's Letter* (Minneapolis: Fortress, 1996) and Galatia: *The Irony of Galatians: Paul's Letter in First-Century Context* (Minneapolis: Fortress, 2002).

[82] Cf. the case of the introduction of Sarapis cult on Delos, as discussed above, and the spread of the Bacchanalia in Italy in the second century B.C.E. as recounted by Livy in his Roman history (39.8–19).

[83] Cf. Acts 15:21.

[84] Cf. the work of R. Stark here, *The Rise of Christianity: How the Obscure, Marginal Jesus Movement Became the Dominant Religious Force in the Western World in a Few Centuries* (San Francisco; Harper Collins, 1997). A. Reinhartz's critical discussion of Stark's theory is important:

In fact, reading Acts, Paul's letters and the Johannine letters, for example, there is very little evidence of a proselytizing mission that extends beyond Judaism and the synagogue context. Even such an obvious example of proselytizing mission as Paul's Areopagus speech (Acts 17:16–20) needs to be seen in this context:

> While Paul was waiting for them in Athens, he was deeply distressed to see that the city was full of idols. So he argued *in the synagogue* with the Jews and the devout persons [ἐν τῇ συναγωγῇ τοῖς Ἰουδαίοις καὶ τοῖς σεβομένοις], and also *in the marketplace* [ἐν τῇ ἀγορᾷ] every day with those who happened to be there. Also some Epicurean and Stoic philosophers debated with him. Some said, "What does this babbler want to say?" Others said, "He seems to be a proclaimer of foreign divinities." (This was because he was telling the good news about Jesus and the resurrection.) So *they took him and brought him to the Areopagus* and asked him, "May we know what this new teaching is that you are presenting? It sounds rather strange to us, so we would like to know what it means."

It is telling that Paul is said to be upset about non-Jewish cult in Athens, and that his *first* reaction is to go to the synagogue and debate this with *the Jews and "the devout,"* the latter likely referring to God-fearers. Since he is also said to have gone to the marketplace, the agora, the author likely assumed his readers to understand that what Paul would be arguing about in the synagogue context would be the necessity of preparing non-Jews for the eschaton by instructing them to reject their gods and turn exclusively to the God of Israel. Proselytizing mission, then, necessitated inward mission. As the speech that then follows at the Areopagus indicates, eschatological concerns provided Paul with his incentive for proclaiming the effectiveness and importance of his God. It should be noted, however, that while Paul is said to have spoken informally to people in the agora, the programmatic proselytizing speech in the public space of the Areopagus comes, in the narrative, as the result

---

"Rodney Stark and 'the Mission to the Jews,'" in *Religious Rivalries in the Early Roman Empire and the Rise of Christianity* (ed. L. E. Vaage; Waterloo: Wilfrid Laurier University Press, 2006), 197–212.

of Paul having been brought there by non-Jews: he is not presented as going there on his own initiative. The primary context of mission remains the synagogue, even when non-Jews are concerned.

While the social reality and techniques used by apostolic Jews are to be seen within the larger context of other missionary activities in the Greco-Roman world, the Apostolic-Jewish intention, ideology and aim were different in some key respects. This is related to the public sphere and imperialism, to which we now therefore turn.

Claiming the World: Colonialism as Theo-Political Pattern for Proselytizing Mission

Up till now we have dealt with the private and semi-public spheres of Greco-Roman society, also noting how they are interconnected both with each other and with the public sphere. Many foreign gods, originally having entered Roman society via private cult, were eventually incorporated in Roman public religion. The intention behind distinguishing between these levels of society in the analysis is not to argue for isolation between them, but to allow for new insights to emerge as we focus on each level at a time.

In this section, I would like to put the emphasis on mission seen from a public perspective, highlighting both movements emanating from the state going outward, as well as movements coming from semi-public associations directed inward toward the heart of the empire. The central interpretive key used in the discussion is—and should be—a steady focus on the undisputable fact of the inextricability of what we call "religion" and political realities in the ancient world. This means, among other things, that whatever is done against the gods is done against the state, and vice-versa; what the state does involves the gods of the state. Let us begin with the latter.

Conquest and Mission

The victories of the Roman Empire, the very building of the empire, was an achievement resulting from collaboration between a people and their gods. Reinforcing Roman rule over other peoples also meant the expansion of the rule of Roman gods; Rome "ruled by Jupiter's will."[85] This did not, however, mean that the gods of the conquered peoples were always rejected. Rather, Roman piety could materialize in the ritual of *evocatio deorum*, asking gods of besieged cities to leave the cities before the conquerors dealt the fatal blow, which would lay walls and buildings in ruins.[86] The gods could then be taken to Rome, and be made, one way or another, to serve Roman interests. The point I would like to make is, quite simply, that conquest and empire building was in and of itself a form of mission, indeed, we could say a modified proselytizing mission. The boundaries of the "group" were the same as the political boundaries, and the incorporation of people from outside the empire into the empire meant the expansion of the realm and power of the Roman gods.[87] In this way, order is upheld and empire sustained. Since the Romans were said to seek world dominance, this is indeed, to use Goodman's terminology, a form of "universal" proselytizing mission. Interestingly, the only form of Greco-Roman cults that Goodman would consider to identify as a "proselytising religion" was "the imperial cult, the worship of the emperors."[88] Implied in this mission was the adoption of "a specific frame of

---

[85] W. Carter, *Matthew and the Margins: A Socio-Political and Religious Reading* (London: T&T Clark, 2000), 110; see also 39–40.

[86] See J. Kloppenborg, "*Evocatio Deorum* and the Date of Mark," *JBL* 124 (2005): 419–50.

[87] This perspective is often (anachronistically) overlooked in studies on mission, which mostly proceed from a post-enlightenment perspective on "religion." However, although quite different in nature from Roman imperialism, the same basic theological logic applies to, e.g., the Thirty Years' War (1618–1648) in Europe and the rhetoric behind protestant, not least Swedish, expansion. This is so despite the fact that we can discern factors other than "religious" creating and sustaining the conflicts. (Being a Swede, at that time, was equivalent to being a Lutheran Christian according to the internal theological logic of the state church system.)

[88] Goodman, *Mission and Conversion*, 30–32. "In some ways, then, the imperial cult in the early Roman empire was a fine example of a proselytising religion, if … it is justified to treat the varied forms of emperor worship found in different areas of the empire as disparate manifestations of a single cult" (p. 31).

mind—namely, loyalty to the Roman state."[89] In the context of the present discussion, such a conclusion follows naturally from a wider imperial perspective and makes (ancient) sense. In sum, then, we have here a universal proselytizing mission, claiming the world as the possession of specific gods, with the center located in Rome.

With this identified as the wider context, we see the importance of including violence and military conquest in our discussion of mission: such aspects are, indeed, inherent to the phenomenon of mission itself when we consider it as it played out in the public sphere of ancient societies. Directing our attention to Jews and Judaism, such a claim is confirmed. Contrary to Scott McKnight's statement that "force" is not "worthy of consideration in a study on missionary activity," violence is very much part of the problem.[90]

Especially instructive is the policy of forced conversion under John Hyrcanus (135–104 B.C.E.), Aristobulus I (104 B.C.E.), and Alexander Jannaeus (104–78 B.C.E.). After having conquered Idumaean territory in his third military campaign, Hyrcanus forced the Idumaeans to undergo circumcision and keep Jewish law, since the area was now considered to be Jewish.[91] After him, Aristobulus I conquered the Ituraeans and likewise forced these people, if they wanted to remain in the land (now defined as Judea), to undergo circumcision and follow Jewish law.[92] Finally, Josephus tells us that Alexander Jannaeus destroyed Pella because of their refusal to follow the "national customs of the Jews," thereby implying a policy similar to Hyrcanus' and Aristobulus I's.[93]

Noting, as we did earlier, the connection between land, law, god and people, Salo Baron's comments on these episodes are interesting. If

[89] Ibid., 31.

[90] McKnight, *Light,* 77. McKnight refers to the forced conversions under the Hasmoneans, but he also mentions Jdt 14:10, and Esth 8:17 under his heading "force" (p. 68).

[91] Josephus, *A.J.* 13.257–258; cf. 15.254. Strabo also mentions the conversion of the Idumaeans (*Geogr.* 16.2.34), as does Ptolemy the Historian, *Hist. Herod.*, quoted in Ammonius, *Adfin.*, 243; the latter of the two authors explicitly mentions force as the method of conversion. Hyrcanus' destruction of the Samaritan temple on Gerizim should be seen in this context too (Josephus, *A.J.* 13.254–256).

[92] Josephus, *A.J.* 13.318–319. Timagenes, as quoted by Josephus (*A.J.* 13.319), confirms the conversions but does not mention force.

[93] *A.J.* 13.397.

the areas conquered were regarded as, historically, part of the Jewish nation, the motive behind the forced conversions may have been to prevent the profanation of the land through worship of other deities.[94] Seen from a wider perspective, it simply made political sense to protect the land and honor the god by enforcing divine law in annexed territories. As with Roman conquests, force is part of such mission, although specifics of Jewish law and history formed the unique aspects of the process in the Hasmonean case. Contrary to Roman imperialism, however, the Hasmonean conquest was restricted to what was understood to be Jewish territory historically; we find no "universal" mission in this specific case, as we do with the Romans.

In fact, it is interesting to note that despite repeated claims in the Hebrew Bible that the God of Israel is the God of the whole world, and thus that the nations, ultimately, are dependent on Israel's God,[95] we hear of no military campaigns intended to ensure such dominion. Israel is even told that it should missionize to the non-Jews (clearly expressed in Pss. 9:12; 96:3, 105:1),[96] and we see similar attitudes in Deutero- and Trito-Isaiah.[97] In Isa 66:18–24 we have an explicit description of how active proselytizing mission to nations other then Israel is to be carried out in an eschatological future. Other traditions are less clear and may refer to active ethno-ethic mission (cf. the Book of Jonah as a model for this pattern of thought).

There is a tendency in the sources to link theo-political ideas about the God of Israel being the God of all nations, an eschatological future when this conviction shall materialize as experienced reality when all peoples shall worship in Jerusalem,

---

[94] S. W. Baron, *A Social and Religious History of the Jews: Vol. 1: To the Beginning of the Christian Era* (New York: Columbia University Press, 1952), 167. G. Alon, *Jews, Judaism, and the Classical World: Studies in Jewish History in the Times of the Second Temple and Talmud* (Jerusalem: Magness Press, 1977), 187, argues that the notion of the uncleanness of non-Jewish territory was of pre-Hasmonean origin, and that impurity in this regard was related to worship of other gods.

[95] See, e.g., Pss 9:12; 18:50; 22:8; 46:11; 47:9; 48:11; 57:10; 67:2–3; 82:8; 87:4–6; 96:3, 5; 98:2, 4; 105:1; 108:4; 110:6; 113:4; 117:1; 126:1–2; 145:12.

[96] A. A. Anderson, *The Book of Psalms* (2 vols.; Grand Rapids: Eerdmans, 1972), 1:105–6 and 2:681, 726, dates all three Psalms in the postexilic period, but suggests that Ps 96 may contain older parts, and that Deutero-Isaiah may be dependent on its "universalism."

[97] The following passages are relevant: Isa 45:9ff, 22–23; 49:6–7, 22–23; 52:10; 61:5–6. Note also mission aspect in Isa 54:4–5; 56:1–8.

and a final divine judgment which will make this possible. The scenario also involves the restoration of Israel. Although eschatology and mission are not always connected (cf. the Qumran community), the two often go hand in hand. When they do, and when eschatological realities are felt to be near at hand, political dimensions are triggered and strategies developed to realize them.

We shall now turn to Apostolic Judaism, to illustrate this point.

Restoration and Counter-Colonialism: The Margin Strikes Back

Space will not allow detailed presentation of the evidence regarding mission and the historical Jesus. It seems to me, however, that the current consensus that Jesus was concerned only with the Jewish people and not the non-Jews is correct. The Kingdom of God, the undisputed centre of Jesus' preaching, healing and exorcisms, fits within a restoration-theological frame in which the goal is a reunited Kingdom of Israel. It seems equally clear, however, that Jesus expected the restoration of Israel to lead to a renewed world, and thus that the nations, indirectly, would be affected.[98] Jesus' inward mission may thus have had wider or global intentions, implicitly, but this is difficult to prove. Many of Jesus' followers, on the other hand, were quite explicit in this regard, in terms of intentions and aims. A revealing summary of such aims is put in Jesus' mouth in Acts 1:6–8:

> So when they had come together, they asked him, "Lord, is this the time when you will *restore the kingdom to Israel* [ἀποκαθιστάνεις τὴν βασιλείαν τῷ Ἰσραήλ]?" He replied, "It is not for you to know the times or periods that the Father has set by his own authority. But you will receive power [δύναμις] when the Holy Spirit has come upon you; and you will be my witnesses in Jerusalem, in all Judea and Samaria, and *to the ends of the earth* [ἕως ἐσχάτου τῆς γῆς]."

For the author, the restoration of Israel is intimately connected to the reinvention of the world, and the latter must precede the former, it

---

[98] Metaphors like "light of the world" and "salt of the earth" (Matt 5) demand interpretations concerned with global realities, but do not imply active proselytizing mission.

seems. For the latter to happen, active mission is necessary, and the entire world is the task. The politics here are clear: the God of Israel is, through the voice of Jesus, claiming the world as his dominion. What was envisioned in Psalms is said to be about to be realized in a world dominated by other gods, the gods of the Roman Empire. The claim made is within the same theo-political empire-logic as the Romans lived by, with the difference that Apostolic Jews will work for the exclusive rule of one God alone. More importantly, the strategy of expansion is to use non-military means to achieve a political goal. As we see when the story of Acts unfolds, this means a focus on the semi-public sphere for the spread of the cult, primarily within synagogues, but with the aim of reaching beyond and into Rome itself.

What we see, then, is a mirror image of empire, but reversed in terms of the strategy used to reach the goal. The intention and aim is the same, the strategy different. Acts is a description of how to "attack" the gods of Rome with the expectation of taking over the empire, i.e., the world. If Rome's gods fall, then Rome will fall and be replaced by Jerusalem, which will, finally, be realizing theo-politically its true nature as the center of the world.

The same colonial pattern is found in Matthew's Gospel.[99] While Jesus before his death is quoted as prohibiting expansion outside Judea (Matt 10:5–6), and thereby reflecting more of the same concerns as the Hasmoneans,[100] the power and authority to rule the world is achieved as a result of the cross and the empty tomb (Matt 28:18–20):

> And Jesus came and said to them, *"All authority in heaven and on earth* [πᾶσα ἐξουσία ἐν οὐρανῷ καὶ ἐπὶ τῆς γῆς] has been given to me. Go therefore and make disciples of *all nations* [πάντα τὰ ἔθνη] baptizing them in the name of the Father and of the Son and of the Holy Spirit, and teaching them to *obey everything that I have commanded you.* And remember, I am with you always, to the end of the age [ἕως τῆς συντελείας τοῦ αἰῶνος]."

---

[99] Cf. J. Riches, "Matthew's Missionary Strategy in Colonial Perspective," in *The Gospel of Matthew in its Roman Imperial Context* (ed. J. Riches and D. C. Sim; London: T & T Clark, 2005), 128–42; see esp. the sections on "Political Claims" (pp. 137–39) and "Territorial Expansion" (pp. 140–41).

[100] Though without military force as part of the strategy; see further below.

Read within the cultural context of the first century Mediterranean world, far from the Sunday school flannel boards, the intense theo-political force of this text is unmistakable. Nothing less than the entire world, i.e., what was at the time ultimately in the hands of Roman gods, is claimed.[101] All nations shall be conquered for the God of Israel, but without military means or violence. Again, the aim is a mirror image of the empire and its will to dominate. The strategy is, however, different: the take-over of the public realm in Greco-Roman society via a war waged on the gods, beginning, socially, in the semi-public sphere. In the end, all nations shall obey what Jesus' has taught his own people, which is, according to the Matthean narrative, the Jewish law.[102] The last point deserves attention. If Jewish law shall be observed by all nations, this implies conversion to Judaism, including circumcision for men,[103] and a giving up of non-Jewish culture. This, it seems to me, is indeed the culmination of the message of Matthew. The story begins with a group of non-Jews from the East, the magi, recognizing that the legitimacy of the Jewish king extends beyond the Jewish people to include themselves (Matt 2:1–12); then we hear of a centurion (from the West, one might add), who recognizes and need the power of the Jewish Messiah (Matt 8:5–13). We also meet a Canaanite woman (the historical enemies of the Jews[104]), who, rightly in the eyes of Jesus, identifies her place in relation to the Jewish people and their Messiah as a dog eating crumbs falling from its master's table (Matt 15:21–28). This is set within the frame

---

[101] A realization of the offer Jesus had rejected from the devil in Matt 4:8–9: Πάλιν παραλαμβάνει αὐ τὸν ὁ διάβολος εἰς ὄρος ὑψηλὸν λίαν καὶ δείκνυσιν αὐτῷ πάσας τὰς βασιλείας τοῦ κόσμου καὶ τὴν δόξαν αὐτῶν καὶ εἶπεν αὐτῷ· ταῦτά σοι πάντα δώσω, ἐὰν πεσὼν προσκυνήσῃς μοι. The internal logic of the offer is that the devil controls these territories, which were under Rome's dominion; the implication is clearly that Matthew identifies Rome's gods with the devil. Fighting off the devil, then, implies fighting the Roman Empire in order to liberate the world from the devil's rule (via Roman gods). Cf. Carter, *Matthew and the Margins*, 110–11.

[102] See, e.g., Matt 5:17–6:24, 7:21; 19:17; 22:36–40; 23:23.

[103] Several scholars have read this text as demanding conversion and circumcision, i.e., proselyte status, of converts to this apostolic Jewish group. See especially D. Sim, *The Gospel of Matthew and Christian Judaism: The History and Social Setting of the Matthean Community* (Edinburgh: T&T Clark, 1998), 247–55.

[104] See W. D. Davies and D. C. Allison, *A Critical and Exegetical Commentary on the Gospel According to Matthew* (3 vols.; T&T Clark: London, 1991), 2:547.

of a negative general portrayal of non-Jews in Matthew, non-Jews representing everything that good Jews should not be or do.[105]

In other words, Matthew presents us with a generally negative picture of the non-Jewish world, in which the only exceptions to the rule are individuals representing eastern and western wisdom and power, as well as the historical enemies of Israel—and all are subordinating themselves to the Jewish Messiah. The centripetal force of the eschaton begins with Jesus during his lifetime, but when all authority on earth has been achieved after his death and resurrection, when sin and its political consequences are eliminated (cf. Matt 1:21), the world shall obey the law of the God of Israel.

Further support for this reading is found in Matthew's version of the Gadarene demoniacs (Matt 8:28–34). This story tells us how non-Jewish culture is erased as Jesus enters non-Jewish cities and their surrounding areas. The demoniacs live among ritually unclean tombs and the demons are eventually sent into ritually unclean swine, which are drowned in the water.[106] Since Jesus explicitly forbids mission among non-Jews in 10:5–6, it is probable that the demoniacs' identity is narratively to be understood as Jewish.[107] The two Jews in a non-Jewish area live in a ritually unclean environment, including issues of food and sacrificial animals. As Jesus approaches this non-Jewish area—in the holy land[108]—the Jews living there are freed from impurities: the tombs, the swine, and the demons are associated with a place that needs to be liberated.

The non-Jewish majority ("the city") reacts negatively as their culture (their concern was with the swine rather than the disappearance of the demons) is being erased in the "sea" (θάλασσα), into which the swine disappeared, and they consequently ask Jesus to leave their area.[109] Demons and pigs go together, and

---

[105] Cf. e.g., Matt 5:47; 6:7. See also D. Sim, *Christian Judaism*.

[106] Note also that swine were common sacrificial animals in non-Jewish cults.

[107] And more specifically as Matt 10:6 states, they would be what the author considers to be "the lost sheep of the house of Israel."

[108] Gadara was located in the Decapolis, but would have been part of Matthew's "biblical land"/the holy land; cf. U. Luz, *Matthew 8–20* (Minneapolis: Fortress, 2001), 23–24.

[109] Cf. Mark's very different version of this story (5:1–20).

the defiled land is cleansed as Jesus approaches it as "the Son of God." The story is concerned, in this case, with Matthew's holy land and its status, but in 28:19–20 the disciples are told to conquer the entire world with Jewish law in much the same way.

For Matthew, further, Jerusalem is the holy city and thus the center of the world;[110] the world, in turn, is just about to find out that this has been the reality all the time. Since the Roman Empire in fact works with the devil to achieve world dominance (see n. 101 above), God's judgment and rule will mean liberation for all.

Matthew's perspective is quite close to the Christ-believing Pharisaic Jews in Acts 15:5 in terms of circumcision of non-Jews. Indeed, as I have argued elsewhere, Mattheans were most likely Christ-believing Pharisees breaking away from the larger Pharisaic community.[111] This would explain both Matt 23:2–3 and the critique of Pharisaic mission (23:15).

A final example of Apostolic Jewish mission is found in Paul. In the interest of space we shall only note that Paul's view of the way Jewish proselytizing mission should be carried out differed significantly from Matthew's. For him, non-Jews must remain non-Jews, and thus the renewed world would consist of both categories, all worshipping the God of Israel. A unity in diversity, with Israel at the center as the cultivated olive tree from whose rich root non-Jewish individuals "in Christ" are fed (Rom 11:17–24). Still, Paul's aim was the same: via semi-public networks to "attack" Greco-Roman gods and ultimately replace Rome with Jerusalem as the world's center.[112] The "imitation" of empire is also evidenced in his determination to visit—and missionize—Spain, representing the western end of the earth and the empire.[113]

---

[110] Jerusalem was regarded as holy by Matthew both before and after Jesus' death; see Matt 4:5; 27:53. In Matt 5:35 it is stated that the earth is Israel's God's footstool and that Jerusalem is "the city of the Great King." It is hard to imagine a more explicit statement of where the world's center is—and by implication, where it is not.

[111] A. Runesson, "Re-Thinking Early Jewish–Christian Relations: Matthean Community History as Pharisaic Intragroup Conflict," *JBL* 127 (2008): 95–132.

[112] For the Jewish people as a center in Paul's theology, see Rom 9–11; the central position of Jerusalem is evidenced in, e.g., the Jerusalem collection, 2 Cor 8–9; Rom 15:25–28.

[113] Rom 15:28.

In conclusion, Apostolic-Jewish mission was formed after Roman imperialism, but reversed the strategy to achieve world dominion. Eventually—and oddly—this strategy actually worked, and this cult on the semi-public level was chosen by later Roman rulers who made it into exclusive state religion for the protection and preservation of society.[114] By then, however, "Christianity" had developed far beyond Apostolic Judaism in many significant aspects, and mission was now Christian mission, not Jewish mission.

Conclusion: From Jerusalem to Rome—A One Way Ticket

Was there, then, a Christian mission before the fourth century? In the end, the answer to this question is to some degree a matter of definition. There is good reason to make a distinction between Apostolic-Jewish and Christian mission and place the origins of the latter no earlier than the second century; it's full development on all levels of society, however, comes only in the fourth century. How should we explain this development?

I have argued in this study that Jesus and the earliest Jesus movement were involved in eschatologically motivated variants of Jewish mission, working with strategies and within an ideological matrix familiar to other Jews. Jewish mission, then, was carried out in the first century, not only by Apostolic Jews, but also by others within Judaism. In addition to the specific source material, which is best explained by this theory, including an individual missionary as Josephus,[115] this perspective is confirmed on a more general level by Greco-Roman material. A key aspect of our approach has been to methodologically isolate three social levels of ancient societies, the private, semi-public and public levels, and read the evidence for mission in each of these contexts respectively. While we see examples of movement between the private and semi-public sphere,

---

[114] Cf. Goodman, *Mission and Conversion*, 18.
[115] So Steve Mason, as discussed above.

the competition is played out mostly on the semi-public level. From there, cults could also penetrate into the public sphere, which, eventually, was precisely what happened with Christianity, as it became a "religion."

I have described the development of Christian identity in this regard elsewhere and shall not repeat that discussion here.[116] Key aspects were the "re-categorization" of Christ-belief as an association with a nature similar to that of other cultic associations or philosophies,[117] excluding altogether ethnic identity as a criterion for membership. This development is found in Ignatius, but spread from then on quite rapidly, most likely since other eastern cults had already travelled the same route and the pattern was familiar to people.

This did not mean the disappearance of Apostolic Judaism and its missionary activities. While Justin Martyr accepted Apostolic-Jewish forms of beliefs and practices, he expressed concerns about their mission, which he states must cease.[118] Apostolic Jews may have continued to emphasize the connection between people, land, law, and God, as did other Jews, but the crucial step for Christ-belief to gain access to the Roman public sphere had already been taken at the very moment non-Jewish adherers in the second century divorced Christ-belief from its ethnic dimension. In the fourth century, the exclusive nature of this form of non-Jewish Christianity proved to be a politically powerful tool, even to the point where it could be brought in as state religion. The journey from Jerusalem to Rome had succeeded, but in ways neither Paul or Luke, nor Matthew could have imagined. Instead of a return ticket with a triumphal procession in Jerusalem in sight, developments along the way turned out to be of a one-way nature.

As Theodosius I begins his persecution of Greco-Roman cults by the end of the fourth century, aiming at protecting and preserving the empire in collaboration with the God of Israel (interpreted non-ethnically as the Christian God), we come full circle, so to speak.

---

[116] Runesson, "Inventing Christian Identity."

[117] For the relationship between mystery cults and philosophy in this regard, see e.g., G. Bornkamm, "μυστήριον," *TDNT* 4:808–10.

[118] Justin Martyr, *Dial.* 47.

We have seen this form of mission and its theo-political logic before in the public sphere, both in Rome and with the Hasmoneans. Christian mission on this level eventually results in the issuing of laws restricting Jews in their communal life and, after centuries, the eradication of the last of the Greco-Roman cults.[119] While Rome in the first century ruled by Jupiter's will, they now ruled by the will of the Christian God, with much the same ingredients involved: military power, coercion, issuing of restricting laws. The force of the mission was, compared to earlier periods, enhanced by the exclusive nature of the religion, with destruction of *all* other temples and cults.[120] Most of this mission is to be defined as inward mission, played out where Rome had already secured political power.

Christian mission carried out after this point in the semi-public and private sphere, although equally exclusive in its claims, was often but not always in agreement with the public mission; conflicts and inner-Christian persecution was the result. There is no need or space here to reiterate the history of Europe that followed, other than to mention the conflicts and wars that developed in the footsteps of the reformation, and the refugee problem that was created (many of whom came to North America), as well as the role of Christian mission in Western colonialism in general—and its force in the later countering of colonial strategies as we see in the development of Liberation Theology. What really stands out throughout history is the close connection between mission and violence in various forms as we enter the public sphere. It seems inevitable, regardless of the type of cult.

Today most Christians (and others) think of mission as divorced from politics, as a religious phenomenon, some would say an offer of a gift, taking place in the private sphere of society. As with contemporary Jewish mission, most forms of such mission is to be defined as inward mission, attempts to reinvent, or "defend," what one believes to be true forms of worship. While Jewish proselytizing

---

[119] For the latter process, see E. Sauer, *The Archaeology of Religious Hatred in the Roman and Early Medieval World* (Stroud: Tempus, 2003). Laws relating to Jews are conveniently collected in A. Linder, *The Jews in Roman Imperial Legislation: Edited with Introductions, Translations, and Commentary* (Detroit: Wayne State University Press, 1987).

[120] Sauer, *Archaeology*.

mission is debated regarding the first century, all agree that it existed in late antiquity but disappeared sometime after the Talmudic period. Today, as we noted in the introduction, inward mission is common, although the events described in the article quoted are more rare perhaps.[121] It is interesting to note that this type of inward mission, attempts to "take over synagogues," comes close to much of what we see in the New Testament. We should perhaps also note that some Jews, although they are few, would argue for proselytizing mission today.[122] Others, also few, would actively engage in ethno-ethic mission of the seven Noahide commandments.[123]

Most discourses on contemporary Christian mission within the churches emphasize missionary outreach as a key task for Christians, not seldom claiming it to be inextricably linked with Christian identity.[124] Further, the basic assumption behind almost all theologies of mission is a de-ethnocized replacement-theological paradigm. Lately, however, intensified since the 1960s, an inner-Christian debate has surfaced as to how "mission" is to be defined.[125] The background for this discussion touches upon

---

[121] See n. 1.

[122] See, e.g., L. J. Epstein, "Why the Jewish People Should Welcome Converts," *Judaism* 43 (1994): 302–12.

[123] Although few would actively missionize Noahide commandments, many feel an obligation to supply information about this form of worship if asked by non-Jews. See e.g., J. D. Bleich, "Teaching Torah to Non-Jews," *Tradition: A Journal of Orthodox Jewish Thought* 2:18 (1980), 192–211. An example of former Christians who converted to Noahide "religion" is a group called Emmanuel, in Athens Tennessee. This group was founded in 1990 by a former Baptist pastor, J. David Davies. He is seen by some as the *de facto* leader of Noahides worldwide. On the development of the doctrine of Noahide commandments, including discussion of its reception in Christianity, see the standard work of K. Müller, *Tora für die Völker: Die Noachidischen Gebote und Ansätze zu ihrer Rezeption im Christentum* (Berlin: Institute Kirche und Judentum, 1994).

[124] Cf., e.g., *Ad Gentes*, ch. 24, §23: "Although every disciple of Christ, as far in him lies, has the duty of spreading the Faith, (1) Christ the Lord always calls whomever He will from among the number of His disciples, to be with Him and to be sent by Him to preach to the nations (cf. Mark 3:13)." See also ch. 6, §35: "the whole Church is missionary, and the work of evangelization is a basic duty of the People of God."

[125] This is true also of Sweden, where the world's largest Lutheran church has its home. See, e.g., the work of Biörn Fjärstedt, then director of The Church of Sweden Mission, later bishop of Gotland, *Missionen skiftar ansikte: Missionsteologi i tiden* (Stockholm: Verbum, 1991), a book that generated debate involving both scholars (e.g., Bengt Holmberg) and laypeople. For a recent discussion of mission, including New Testament perspectives, see D. Bosch, *Transforming Mission: Paradigm Shifts in Theology of Mission* (Maryknoll: Orbis Books, 1991).

the relationship between Western colonialism/imperialism and the spread of Christianity along with Western culture as well as the church's involvement in local culture and attempts in many places in non-Western countries in the wake of Vatican II (1962–1965) to realize visions of inculturation and emphasize the necessity of localized understandings of Christian faith and life. In our age of globalization on many levels, when cultures and religious traditions meet on a more frequent basis than ever before, such discussions are by no means destined to fade, but rather to escalate.

In conclusion, then, Christian mission as we understand it today evolved fully with the creation of the category of "religion" in late antiquity. The inherent tensions and the pattern of empire distinguishable already in the first century, in the New Testament, present a theological challenge to the modern postcolonial world. This task, which lies ahead of us, is interdisciplinary in nature and ought to involve not only theologians but also exegetes of the New Testament and the Hebrew Bible, as well as scholars of early Judaism and Patristics.

Statues and Identity: Dion of Prusa's (Dio Chrysostomos) Rhodian Discourse (*Or.* 31) and the New Testament

Karl Olav Sandnes
MF Norwegian School of Theology, Oslo

Introduction

Present-day visitors to the remaining sites from the ancient world, and even more to museums housing the treasures of the Greco-Roman world, are impressed by the many statues. They are revealing as to their beauty and style. Tourists admire them as pieces of art, which they indeed are. But they are also indices to the social world of their time. They are monuments of the distribution of power between individuals and society, a visualization of the power-game. The statues lend information on both past and contemporary communal life. *Oratio* 31, the far longest of Dio's extant speeches, is a window into many aspects of the world in which Christianity took its roots. A reading of this text is, therefore, by itself of relevance to New Testament studies, especially to how the culture of honor and shame formed the identity of the people of antiquity, Christians included. This means that the topic of this article is linked up with two of Bengt Holmberg's most important scholarly contributions, namely on the distribution of power[1] and sociology in New Testament studies.[2]

---

[1] B. Holmberg, *Paul and Power* (Philadelphia: Fortress, 1980).

[2] Idem, *Sociology and the New Testament* (Minneapolis: Fortress, 1990).

The Rhodian Discourse: The Situation

The speech purports to have been delivered in public to "men of Rhodes" (1–4). Dio says that they probably expect him to speak of some private matter, and will be surprised to find him addressing an issue of general interest which concerns the city: "the situation of which I speak is very bad indeed" (2).[3] He speaks thus because he considers himself a friend of Rhodes, and therefore able to address them in a frank way. The preface has the ring of a real speech. Taken as a whole, however, *Or.* 31 appears embellished and expanded on later. As pointed out by Christopher P. Jones, there is no reason to doubt that Dio gave a speech at Rhodes during one of his visits on the island.[4]

The issue addressed in this speech is the statues of Rhodes.[5] This island was noted for its high numbers of statues. *Oratio* 31.146 says that the inhabitants rejoice in the multitude of their statues, which, at the time of Pliny the Elder still (*etiamnum*) amounted to the number of three thousands (*Nat.* 34.36),[6] thus competing with Athens, Olympia and Delphi. Pliny says that Mummius after having conquered Achaia filled *urbem* (Rome) with statues; in doing so he initiated a Roman custom of bringing Greek art to Rome. The Latin *etiamnum* assumes that the number of statues at Rhodes had somewhat decreased.

In addressing the question of the statues and a practice spreading, namely that of switching inscriptions, so that the statues are being re-used, Dio enters a topic raised very much by the time in which he was living: the edge between past and present. The presentation of the speech (below) will make clear the following: the statues represent the venerable heritage of the Rhodians, but in the present Roman honoraries visiting the place call for signs of honor to be

---

[3] If not given otherwise, citations are from the LCL.

[4] C. P. Jones, *The Roman World of Dio Chrysostom* (Cambridge: Harvard University Press, 1978), 26.

[5] Dio uses various terms for statues, but the recurrent term is ἀνδριάς; see H-J Klauck, and B. Bälber, *Dion von Prusa: Olympische Rede oder über die erste Erkenntnis Gottes, eingeleitet, übersetzt und interpretiert von Hans-Josef Klauck, mit einem archäologischen Beitrag von Balbina Bäbler* (Darmstadt: Wissenschaftliche Buchgesellschaft, 2000), 207–8.

[6] Pliny, *Nat.* 36.23 and 34 mentions an Asinius Pollio who collected works of art in his Roman public library; some of his works of art were collected from Rhodes.

conferred upon them. Rhodians, as well as other Hellenistic cities sought a way out of this dilemma by reusing ancient monuments, and thus saving the expense of making new ones.

The situation addressed in this speech is interwoven into Dio's argument; situation and argument are not easily separated. At some places in his speech, Dio is interrupted by exclamations from his Rhodian audience, be they real or imaginative. These interruptions are revealing as to the situation which called for his speech. In *Or.* 31.105, the audience states the situation briefly and concisely: "but we simply must [ἀνάγκη] honour the commanders who rule over us, one and all." The honor conferred (τιμᾶν) to Roman rulers is here the raising of statues; in this speech τιμή and cognates appears more or less synonymous with the erection of statues.[7] The Greek ἀνάγκη expresses that the Rhodians found themselves in a situation leaving them without any choice. The power of the Romans as a key factor in the practice of switching statues is also found in the interruption mentioned in *Or.* 43. The Rhodians present an apology for their embracing of this practice. They do not touch statues raised in honor of Romans; the practice is limited to those raised for Macedonians and Spartans.

The Argument

Dio has been told that the practice of switching statues started with statues that were broken or had fallen from their pedestals. These were not always recognizable and therefore easily recycled. The next step was statues which were not damaged, but where the inscriptions were missing. This, then, paved the way for re-using well-preserved statues, but nonetheless of old age (*Or.* 31.141–142). Dio takes this description to be true, and it captures a development which, in his view, will grow worse, and finally bring a breakdown of Greek identity and morality, to which honoring benefactors is crucial. He forms some

---

[7] This is the case in, for example, *Or.* 37.29. See also Chr. Habicht, *Altertümer von Pergamon VIII 3. Die Inschriften des Asklepieions* (Berlin: de Gruyter, 2000), 79, n.1.

images by which his forceful rhetoric summarizes his argument. An adequate description of the Rhodian practice,[8] is, according to Dio, to say that they treat their statues as though they were houses. A house is due to changes, simply because the inhabitants change over time. When the former owner does not stay in the house any longer, it becomes the house of someone else, and when he or she passes away it will be inherited or bought by another owner. House and owner is an ever-changing combination (*Or.* 31.115). The Rhodians treat their statues in much the same way. The statues can be seen as actors (ὑποκριταί) making different characters and roles at different times: "so likewise your statues assume different roles at different times and stand almost as if they were acting a part" (*Or.* 31.155). The same statue can be a Greek, but at another time a Roman, and perhaps later on a Macedonian or a Persian. Sometimes the clothing, foot-gear and the style betray this fraud, says Dio. He therefore, ironically, suggests that the statues should be made of clay instead. This would save the Rhodians a lot of expense (*Or.* 31.9, 100),[9] and it would be in accordance with how they treat the honors conferred upon their benefactors. As things are now, the Rhodian statues are less permanent than figures of wax; they are like cheap dolls, which parents buy for their children (31.152–153). The dolls referred to were made of clay, and therefore easily broken. Such is the situation to which Dio addresses himself. The speech is rather repetitious, but the following is an attempt to summarize the main arguments.

The Challenge of Peaceful Times

We have seen that Roman power rules the situation, which this speech is addressing. To Dio the presence of Roman rule is a kind of Janus-face. Roman rule has ceased endless wars and finally brought

---

[8] A similar practice is attested in *Or.* 37.40. This speech is often attributed to Dio, due to the parallel ideas expressed, but it is most probably written by Favorinus; cf. Cicero *Att.* 6.1 on the statue of Africanus in Rome. Philo relates such an incident in Alexandria when the inhabitants urgently needed to pay honour to Caligula. They refurbished an old statue (*Legat.* 134–135). Philo considers this an outrageous act of flattery. For further examples see H. Blanck, *Wiederverwendung alter Statuen als Ehrendenkmähler bei Griechen und Römern* (Rome: L' Erma di Bretschneider, 1969).

[9] Jones, *Roman World*, 28.

peace upon the world and upon Rhodes. His audience now lives in times of peace and relaxation (ἐν εἰρήνῃ καὶ ῥαθυμίᾳ) (*Or.* 31.165). According to *Or.* 31.104, the Rhodians live at a time of peace. Their ancestors did not enjoy this, although "they too would have preferred to keep out of danger [μὴ κινδυνεύειν]," and find security. This brings to mind Paul's text in 1 Thess 5:3: "'There is peace and security [εἰρήνη καὶ ἀσφάλεια]."[10] All this echoes Pax Romana[11] and imperial propaganda.[12] Dio is by no means anti-Roman, but he finds Roman rule a challenge for upholding morality and Greek identity, to which the statues are an important index. Peaceful times bring prosperity; in its wake follow temptations, described as αἰσχύνη and ἀταξία. Thus, Roman rule might bring enslavement to base instincts (*Or.* 31.125). To Dio this is not only a concern to uphold morality, but also to preserve Greek identity. The Rhodians have, due to the peaceful times, acquired richness beyond any other Greek polis (*Or.* 31.100–107). They are privileged beyond their ancestors as well. The latter were poor, but they were not unprincipled (πονηροί) as Dio holds his contemporary Rhodians to be (*Or.* 31.115). Their practice makes them meaner than the Romans themselves. Roman emperors have removed statues and brought them to Rome to embellish their own city (*Or.* 31.151). For the purpose of his rhetoric, Dio is here not critical of the Roman greed, as is Josephus.[13] Dio says that the Romans put the statues up in the most sacred places of Rome (forum), and they did not remove the name from the statues. In this way the Greek statues were, ironically, better off in Rome than among the Rhodians, simply because they were taken care of by the Romans.

---

[10] Translations of biblical texts are from the NRSV. The quotation marks put here by the NRSV edition are fully justified; Paul is here quoting imperial propaganda. See M. Tellbe, *Paul Between Synagogue and State: Christians, Jews, and Civic Authorities in 1 Thessalonians, Romans, and Philippians* (Stockholm: Almqvist & Wiksell International, 2001), 123-26.

[11] Well summarized in Velleius Paterculus, *Hist. Rom.* 2.89.

[12] Cf. Acts 24:2; Tacitus, *Agr.* 30–31, Livy, 34.7.1 (*pax et tranquilitas publicae*), Plutarch, *Mor.* 408b–c. See G. Gilbert, "Roman Propaganda and Christian Identity in the World-View of Luke-Acts," in *Contextualizing Acts. Lukan Narrative and Greco-Roman Discourse* (ed. T. Penner and C. Vander Stichele; Atlanta: Scholars Press, 2003), 233–56.

[13] According to Josephus, the greed of Roman officials contributed considerably to the war with Rome (e.g. *B.J.* 2.272–283), although statues are not involved here.

An Act of Impiety

The benefaction system serves a mutual interest; the beneficiaries are cared for in various ways, and they pay honor to their benefactors.[14] Dio considers it a sacred obligation to show respect and gratitude to those who have contributed to the common good. Benefactors are to be honored next to the gods (*Or.* 31.6, 37). There is a distinction between ἀσέβεια, wrongs committed against the gods, and ἀδικήματα committed against human beings, says Dio. But he goes on to blur that distinction, in order to finally give it more or less up (*Or.* 31.12–15). In the first place, offences committed against the dead are generally seen as acts of impiety, and this principle applies to the matter of the statues (*Or.* 31.15, 80). Secondly, benefactors are compared to the parents who conferred "the first and greatest benefactions." Those who wrong (ἐξαμαρτάνοντες) the parents are held guilty of impiety (ἀσέβεια) (*Or.* 31.15).[15] Thirdly, benefactors are heroes to be considered semi-divine, and their "divinity" is increasing as time passes (*Or.* 31.57–58, 80, 95–98). Again Dio imagines a Rhodian counter-argument, namely that their practice is restricted to very old statues with no inscriptions on them (*Or.* 31.90–94). He reverts their attention to the fact that statues with no inscription are often those of persons with a special fame. For instance, statues of the gods are left unnamed, and this is also often the case with heroes, says Dio. The Rhodians run the risk of giving a Heracles statue to a "so-and-so," since they lack knowledge and a sense of antiquity. It is as though one would accept nefarious actions on old tombs, but not on newer ones. That lapse of time brings about ignorance is no excuse to introduce the practice of the Rhodians. Thanks to their virtuous life, benefactors are friends of God; in fact, they are

---

[14] P. Veyne, *Bread and Circuses: Historical and Political Pluralism* (London: Penguin Books, 1992), 11–13, 117–31; G. W. Peterman, *Paul's Gift from Philippi: Conventions of Gift-Exchange and Christian Giving* (Cambridge: Cambridge University Press, 1997), 51–88.

[15] This brings to mind Philo's presentation of the commandment to honour the parents (*Decal.* 106–120; *Spec.* 2.224–241). The parents stand "on the borderline between mortal and immortal." They partake in the nature of both man and God: "Parents are … to their children what God is to the world" (*Spec.* 2.225). This is due to their capacity of begetting, but Philo also emphasizes that they pass on virtues to their children. Dishonour and punishment is to come upon those who do not pay their parents due respect, as with benefactors (εὐεργέται) (*Spec.* 2.234).

the nearest of kin to the gods (εἰσὶν ἔγγιστα αὐτῶν) (*Or.* 31.57).

Finally, many of the statues are found within the precincts of the sanctuaries (ἐν τοῖς ἱεροῖς); some physically stand even very close to the statues or images of the gods themselves. The statues share the sanctity of the gods. Custom forbids wronging those who take their refuge (ἀσυλία) in the temples, says Dio (*Or.* 31.87–89 cf. 44.2). The Rhodians are wronging their benefactors at the very place, which offers protection even to wrongdoers. It is sacrilege (ἱερόσυλος) to touch anything in the temples. Moreover, the statues are rightly seen as votive offerings to the gods; a fact demonstrated by the inscriptions they bear (*Or.* 31.89):

> So-and-so set up a statue of himself (or his father, or of his son) as dedicate to a god (whatever god it might be). Hence if one removes the name of the person so honoured from any of the other dedications and inscribes the name of a different person, are we to say that the person now in question is alone not guilty of impiety?[16]

This is clearly a rhetorical question Dio answers affirmatively.

Is Honor Limited by Time?

The power of the Romans has brought a new time upon the world and upon Rhodes, and the Rhodians are now willingly shifting their statues. According to Dio, they are exchanging benefactions for power (31.43–44). The statues erected in former times honored benefactors, but now these statues are recycled to honor political power (δι᾽ ἰσχύν): "For all know how much more permanent a benefaction is than power, for there is no strength which time does not destroy, but it destroys no benefaction" (*Or.* 31.43–44). Dio holds against the Rhodians that they are robbing their good men of their honor, stealing what rightly belongs to them (*Or.* 31.65).

---

[16] Klauck, and Bälber, *Dion von Prusa*, 208 comments on Dio's argument here: "Die Götterbilder wiederum tragen normalerweise keine Namensaufschrift (31,91). Dennoch gewinnt das Standbild eines Menschen (ἀνδριάς), wenn es, was häufig vorkam, in einem Heiligtum aufgestellt war, den Charakter eines Weihegeschenks (ἀνάθημα), das zu beschädigen – etwa durch Entfernen der Inschrift – ein Frevel ware" (31, 87–89 vgl. 44,2)."

Property for which a price is paid is to remain with the owner, says Dio (*Or.* 31.59). Benefactors have paid their price of virtue, very often a costly one—far beyond the price for erecting a statue. He imagines some Rhodian saying that the former benefactors have held their honors for a long time; they have, so to say, received their due honor. To this Dio responds: "For it will not be possible for you to prove that those men have been honoured for a longer time by the city than the city has been the recipient of their benefactions" (78). Dio denies that time brings the honor to fade since the Rhodians are still beneficiaries of the actions honored. By turning their back to the past, they appear as immoral since they continue to enjoy what the past brought upon them. Furthermore, this is insulting their benefactors and dishonoring them (*Or.* 31.27–29, 82).

In *Or.* 31.84–85, Dio turns nasty in his argument. The practice now embraced by the Rhodians is comparable to the act of *damnatio memoriae*, the practice of erasing the public memory of a person, declaring him an enemy of the state. Such measurements were not taken very often. Roman history gives some examples, the most prominent from the perspective of Dio himself being Sejanus (Dio Cassius *Roman Hist.* 58.10–12, cf. Suetonius, *Tib.* 65) and Domitian.[17] As for Domitian, Suetonius says that the Senate used ladders to bring down the images of the emperor, and that they passed a decree that his inscriptions should be "erased and all record of him [*omnem memoriam*] obliterated" (*Dom.* 23).

A Breakdown in Morality?

The issue of benefactions is indeed a question of virtues; virtue received as εὐεργεσία and virtue conferred as τιμή. The practice of recycling signs of honour is, therefore, undermining both law and custom (*Or.* 31.58). The Rhodians are violating the very morality on which their present situation is based: "Would you, then, be willing to give back the favours in return for which you voted those honoured men their statues?" (*Or.* 31.160). Benefactions rendered

---

[17] Other examples given in Blanck, *Wiederverwendung*, 17–18, 23, 98, 109–13.

to the ancestors are—like the ancestors themselves—a succession (διαδοχή) from which one cannot withdraw without wronging oneself (31.62–64). Honor conferred on benefactors becomes—due to the Rhodian practice—merely signs of flattery (*Or.* 31.37, 87, 108–110, 112–113). In acting thus they deprive their signs of honor of all confidence.[18] They are, in fact, putting at risk their relationship to the Romans as well; they are not that stupid and ignorant, says Dio (31.111). Furthermore, they do not want to rule people who are acting like slaves. When honor is deprived of confidence, Rhodes finds itself unable to find benefactors willing to put their property at risk for the well-being of the community. Like salesmen who will not do business with people whose measures are dishonest, so the benefactors will cease doing good to Rhodes (*Or.* 31.38). The system of mutual obligations is thus ruined by having become suspect (*Or.* 31.24–25). The depriving of the honors bestowed by a city is equal to making the punishment it inflicts on criminals ineffectual. Dio draws a picture of a society where disorder, ingratitude, envy and meanness rule; all this follows in the wake of neglecting the benefactors of old.

Public Property?

Dio imagines his audience saying that the statues belong to the city, not to the individual (*Or.* 31.47); a lengthy discussion of this is found in 31.47–57. The fact that the statues are set up on public ground does, according to Dio, not make them public property; this would in general rule out the principle of ownership. The ships in the harbor are found on public ground, but are still private property. Furthermore, the statues are not to be removed since they are set up according to decrees officially recorded. It is considered a serious crime to change official decrees from their tablets, and Dio asks if it is less serious to "erase" the decree, which caused a statue to be erected (*Or.* 31.86). He takes the Artemis temple of Ephesus as an example or illustration: ὡς τύπῳ (*Or.* 31.56).[19] People depositing

---

[18] In his speech, *Lept.* (see later), Demosthenes speaks of the ἀπιστία of Athens in a similar situation (e.g. 36–38, 44, 83, 167).

[19] There are variant readings here in some mss, but M.M Mitchell, *Paul and the Rhetoric of*

money there, that is, on state property, do not expect the temple or the city to seize their money (cf. *Or.* 31.65). The Ephesians "would sooner, I imagine, strip off the adornment of the goddess than touch this money" (*Or.* 31.55). The Rhodians who are much better off financially than this city of Asia Minor, do not live up to the Ephesian standard.

The Greek Heritage

Athens epitomized the Greek heritage and culture. When Leptines (see below) suggested a law to withdraw all rights of public immunity awarded from the city, Athens confirmed its glorious past by resisting this proposal. According to Dio, Athens has now declined and betrayed the history and culture of classical Greece (*Or.* 31.117, 121). He, therefore, contrasts Rhodes with Athens; Rhodes is now "the last true heir of Hellenism."[20] The richness of Rhodes put them in a special situation, and gives them a responsibility to perpetuate Greek identity, to which honoring benefactors is so important (*Or.* 31.146–151, 157). In *Or.* 31.160, Dio gives a depressive picture of what has become of the greatness of Greece; in short "stones" and "ruins." In *Or.* 31.162 he presents the greatness of this legacy, to which Rhodes is the only heir: leadership, administration of the city, distinguishing between honor and dishonor, deliberating in council and making judgments, sacrificing to the gods, festivals. Being sensible to the difference between honor and dishonor thus becomes a mark of Greekness (*Or.* 31.159). In short, Dio says: "It is that you ought to be all the more jealous about your city and to be indifferent to nothing that takes place there" (*Or.* 31.164). The rhetorical power of this argument, albeit exaggerated,[21] is strong indeed. The question of the statues is a matter of preserving Greek identity.

Nonetheless, Dio acknowledges both the need and the right to

Reconciliation: An Exegetical Investigation of the Language and Composition of 1 Corinthians. Louisville (Westminster John Knox Press, 1991), 148, rightly makes reference to 1 Cor 10:1–13 where the same noun is found in a text of deliberative rhetoric.

[20] Jones, *Roman World*, 30. For the polemic against Athens, see also H. von Arnim, *Leben und Werke des Dio von Prusa* (Berlin: Weidmannsche Buchhandlung, 1898), 220–21.

[21] Jones, *Roman World*, 29–32.

honor Roman officials. He suggests more modest ways of doing this, ways that do not compromise the whole system and deprive it of its confidence. In *Or.* 31.107–110 he says that the spirit with which honor is given is the more important. This spirit can be shown in terms of gifts of friendship, lavish entertainments, dining in the city hall, and receiving the people's acclamation. This brings Dio to mention the Olympian crown of olive leaves, "preferred to life itself" by many. The worthiness of this crown depends entirely on the fact that it is not given carelessly and not received for naught.

Dion of Prusa's *Rhodian Speech* is itself a kind of recycling practice. Once in his speech he mentions the law of Leptines, proposed at the time of Demosthenes at Athens (*Or.* 31.128):

> to the effect that all should be deprived of the privileges of exemption from public duties who had received it from the people, with the exception of Harmodius and Aristogeiton, and that for the future it should be no longer permissible to grant to any this gift.

This proposal is known from Demosthenes' speech *Adversus Leptinem*, which Dio's speech emulates.[22] Dio Chrysostom, and the essence of his argument reiterates Demosthenes' forceful attack on Leptines.

What Does This Bring to New Testament Studies?

The question from which we proceed is rather: what use can New Testament exegesis make of the Rhodian speech? Generally speaking, the Orations of Dion of Prusa have played a role in New Testament exegesis for a long time. An outstanding example is the collection of alleged parallels listed by Gerard Mussies.[23] This is definitely a place

---

[22] On the rhetoric of emulation see K. O. Sandnes, "Imitatio Homeri? An Appraisal of Dennis R. MacDonald's 'Mimesis Criticism,'" *JBL* 124 (2005): 715–32, esp. 722–8.

[23] G. Mussies, *Dio Chrysostom and the New Testament: Parallels Collected* (Leiden: Brill, 1972). For the sake of curiosity, A. F. Hallam's, *Concurrences between Dio Chrysostom's First Discourse and the New Testament* (Capitalist Press, 1985), is to be mentioned. Hallam argues that Dio Chrysostom was the final editor of the New Testament; a thesis based on the statistics of concurrent terms, phrases

to start such studies, but the parallels are taken randomly. Hellenistic studies on New Testament texts draw heavily on Dio's works; he is a recurrent figure particularly in studies interacting with Paul and Greco-Roman philosophy and philosophers or sophists.[24] Dio's speeches provide a background against which it is instructive to read Paul's letters. Nonetheless, due to the topic of this speech it lends itself to any study of the ancient benefaction system and the way New Testament texts reflects or negotiates this system of honor.[25] The present article summarizes this and points out some related issues.

Bruce Winter and Benefactions in New Testament Texts

Oratio 31 is like an index to stock terminology on benefactions and benefactors. The following gives some examples; to most terms mentioned here the cognates are included as well: ἀνὴρ ἀγαθός (good man), εὐεργεσία (the act of doing good), τιμή (honor or statue), προεδρία (front seat/seat of dignity), ἐπιγραφή (inscription), πόλις (city), σωτηρία (benefit), εὔνοια (goodwill) κοινός (common), ὑπέρ (for the sake of),[26] στέφανος (crown), ἀρετή (virtue), εἰκών (image or statue), ἀνδριάς (statue).[27] Bruce Winter has rightly pointed out that this vocabulary has found its way into many New Testament texts. He makes a strong case that admonitions to do good, found in texts such as Rom 13:3–4 and 1 Pet 2:14–15, are to be interpreted within the framework of the ancient benefaction system. These injunctions correspond to common ways of referring to the performing of public benefactions.[28] Winter claims that these

---

and ideas.

[24] See e.g. A. J. Malherbe, *Paul and the Popular Philosophers* (Minneapolis: Fortress Press, 1989), and B. W. Winter, *Philo and Paul among the Sophists* (Grand Rapids: Eerdmans, 2002). Both draw heavily upon Dio Chrysostom.

[25] The relevance of this for New Testament studies has been demonstrated by works drawing on insights from cultural anthropology; see e.g. B. J. Malina, *The New Testament World: Insights from Cultural Anthropology* (Atlanta: John Knox Press, 1981); J. J. Pilch and B. J. Malina, *Biblical Social Values and Their Meaning: A Handbook* (Peabody: Hendrickson, 1993), 7–9, 95–104, 110–14, 133–6.

[26] This preposition introduces the beneficiaries, be it the city or people or the like (*Or.* 31.61–62); in 31.75 it denotes dying for the city; *i.e.* in order to save the city.

[27] These terms correspond very much with what is found in F. W. Danker, *Benefactor: Epigraphic Study of a Graeco-Roman and New Testament Semantic Field* (St. Louis: Clayton, 1982).

[28] See B. W. Winter, "The Public Honouring of Christian Benefactors Rom 13.3–4 and 1 Peter

admonitions urged Christians to do benefactions to the city, and that some Christians, in fact, acted as public benefactors. From this claim, Winter draws two obvious conclusions. The common picture of the early Christians living secluded lives, more or less isolated from the public, in an attempt to escape public attention, proves false. Furthermore, some Christians must have been of very considerable means, holding significant positions in society, in terms both of status and wealth; in short, some of them were public benefactors. The number of Christians from the social and political elite was thus sufficient to put its marks upon New Testament paraenesis.

I have elsewhere critically examined this view in detail.[29] Here it suffices to say that Winter's construction of elite-Christians, in my view, depends too much on the appearance of benefaction terminology per se. He has beyond doubt proved that knowledge of this social practice is assumed in the Pauline epistles as well as in First Peter. But their use of benefactor terminology does not necessarily imply that the whole system is in place. As for First Peter, I have argued that the moral of celebrated citizens is applied to the believers generally, due to the fact that they are described as nobilities, as a chosen royal people (1 Peter 2:9). This nobility of the addressees is ascribed to them, and this aspect of their identity would place them among those from whom ancient society expected public benefactions. On the other hand, their alienation, depicted throughout 1 Peter, would place them among people from whom public benefactions were not expected. From this dual identity, develops a confusion of the roles vis-à-vis the benefaction system. Benefaction terminology thus enters the epistle by way of a transformation of values.[30]

2.14–15," *JSNT* 34 (1988): 87–103, and idem, *Seek the Welfare of the City: Christians as Benefactors and Citizens* (Grand Rapids: Eerdmans, 1994), 11–60.

[29] K. O. Sandnes, "Revised Conventions in Early Christian Paraenesis—'Working Good' in 1 Peter as an Example," in *Early Christian Paraenesis in Context* (ed. J. Starr and T. Engberg-Pedersen; Berlin: de Gruyter, 2004), 373–403.

[30] Sandnes, "Revised Conventions," 392–5, 399–400.

Halvor Moxnes's Intrepretation of Dio

Halvor Moxnes has taken the orations of Dio Chrysostom as a point of departure for presenting the "honor culture" which Paul addresses in Rom 12.[31] Moxnes presents "the dilemmas and the conflicts within the honor-beneficence system … His [i.e. Dio's] criticism of those who seek honor is contrasted with his vision of the ideal Hellenistic city and of the relations between its citizens."[32] Moxnes states that Dio's concern was to eliminate the dissension caused by the competition inherent in the benefaction system. Dio instead emphasizes the "inner freedom" that it was possible to maintain under Roman rule (*Or*. 44.12; 48.9). Moxnes argues that "Dio's criticism of the quest for honor is actually aimed at the political system itself, which worked through an interlocking arrangement of benefices and public honors and offices."[33] Dio develops the ideal of a quiet life,[34] where friendship and goodwill prevail in the city (*Or*. 66), somewhat similar to the quietism that underlies New Testament household codes: "Dio here sets up an alternative to the external expression of honor consisting in statues, portraits, seats of honor, etc."[35] Dio's critical engagement with the benefaction system gives an analogy to the way Paul modifies his discourse about honor in Rom 12.

From the perspective of *Or.* 31, Moxnes has overstated Dio's criticism of the system of benefactions. This particular speech demonstrates a fundamental approval of the system. Dio does not do away with the whole system; on the contrary, the statues on Rhodes bear witness to the past benefactors who created Rhodes' greatness. The practice of labeling the statues with new names was to him a betrayal of the city's past. Their proud heritage was intimately connected with the system of public services. In the light of *Or.* 31, it seems overstated to say that Dio offers an alternative vision of life in

---

[31] H. Moxnes, "The Quest for Honor and the Unity of the Community in Romans 12 and in the Orations of Dio Chrysostom," in *Early Christian Paraenesis in Context* (ed. J. Starr and T. Engberg-Pedersen; Berlin: de Gruyter, 2004), 203–30.

[32] Moxnes, "Quest for Honor," 204–5.

[33] Moxnes, "Quest for Honor," 208.

[34] Cf. 1 Thess 4:11–12 and the admonitions of the Pastoral Epistles.

[35] Moxnes, "Quest for Honor," 210.

the city. This is not to deny that Dio voices a philosophical criticism of public and outward honors in other places. In *Or.* 67 he speaks about the philosopher who disregards popular opinion, and who instead seeks to realize the Delphic proverb "know thyself": "Then he will bid farewell to honours [τιμάς] and dishonours and to words of censure and of praise uttered by foolish persons ... Instead, what is called popular opinion he will regard as no better than a shadow" (*Or.* 67.3).

But in *Or.* 31 things look somewhat different from this philosophical critique of the "honor culture." Here Dio does not want the Rhodians to betray their heritage and Greek identity to please the Romans. The present rule of the Romans sets an agenda where friendship, goodwill and the philosophical life were ways to cope with Roman power, but Dio firmly holds that this should not be combined with a lax attitude towards the monuments of the past. The statues epitomize the benefaction system. By necessity, therefore, the erection of statues implies acceptance of the benefits brought to the city through the system of benefactions. *Or.* 31, therefore, adds a perspective neglected in Moxnes's contribution.

No doubt, Dio thus shows a complex attitude to the honor culture of his time. This is the case even when he calls for what Moxnes labels an alternative, found in Dio's urge for ὁμόνοια, friendship and goodwill. His appeal for concord was aimed at keeping Roman intervention at the lowest possible level, but this is not to be contrasted with the position of local nobilities, upheld very much by the system of benefaction. As demonstrated by Giovanni Salmeri, Dio's plead for concord, in fact, was a guarantee for the continued power of the nobilities of the ancient Greek cities: "ὁμόνοια and εὐταξία certainly were close to the heart of the lord and master in Rome, but they were even closer to the hearts of the provincial notables."[36]

Not even his *Or.* 44 where Dio renounces on the signs of honors his fellow citizens of Prusa want to confer upon him, attests Moxnes's view that Dio is really holding an alternative option (*Or.* 44.2):

---

[36] G. Salmeri, "Dio, Rome, and the Civic Life of Asia Minor," in *Dio Chrysostom. Politics, Letters, and Philosophy* (ed. S. Swain; Oxford: Oxford University Press, 2000), 53–92, esp. 79–80, 75–8.

> For it is quite sufficient for a reasonable human being to be loved by
> his own fellow citizens, and why should the man who has that love
> need statues too or proclamations or seats of honour. Nay, not even if
> it be a portrait statue of beaten gold set up in the most distinguished
> shrines. For one word spoken out of goodwill and friendship
> is worth all the gold and crowns and everything else deemed
> splendid that men possess; so take my advice and act accordingly.

This philosophical statement certainly points towards a critique of
outward signs of honor. However, the following paragraphs of this
Prusa-speech confuse the picture. Dio now (3–5) recalls the honors
bestowed upon members of his family; his mother—somewhat
unusual—was honored with both a statue and a shrine. *Oratio* 44.5
brings together this glorious past with the present, due to the fact
that there still are benefactors in Prusa; he no doubt includes himself
among them: "there is no reason to abandon hope so long as the
city continues to bear noble, patriotic men [ἀγαθοὺς καὶ φιλοτίμους
ἄνδρας]." This statement perpetuates the system of benefaction
and the bestowing of honors, and thus reveals that Dio's attitude
was ambivalent. He looked beyond outward signs of honor without
abandoning the glorious past epitomized in statues and other signs
of honor.[37] Hans von Arnim has suggested that the complex picture
left by Dio's writings on the issue of benefactions and honor,
demonstrated in the contrast between *Or.* 31 and 66, is caused by
a development in his position: "Kann ein grösserer Gegensatz zu
den Grundgedanken der rhodischen Rede gedacht werden? Dieser
Gegensatz beruht auf der persönlichen Entwicklung Dios."[38] In *Or.*
66 Dio is critical of those who seek the honor of the crowd. He
even calls striving for crowns, front seats and public proclamations

---

[37] Plutarch's attitude to statues in *Praec. ger. rei. publ.* (*Mor.* 798A–825F) seems to be more
consistently philosophically based. He considers this practice as racing for glory; φιλαρχία and
φιλοτιμία are negatively coined (*Mor.* 798e–f; 799a, 802d–e; 806c; 813c; 816a–b; 819e–820f). In
Dio's *Or.* 31.21 (cf. 31.87) φιλοτιμεῖσθαι is used in a positive sense, thus demonstrating, in this speech,
a different perspective than Plutarch's. Plutarch takes famous persons of the past as his examples.
Cato, for instance, refused to have a statue made of himself, saying "I prefer to have people ask why
there is no statue of me rather than why there is one" (*Mor.* 820b), thus, ironically enough, indicating
how deep the system of outward honor had penetrated the mind even of its ancient critics.

[38] Von Arnim, *Leben und Werke*, 212–13 (quotation on p. 213).

a malady (*Or.* 66.1–2). A blatant example of the contrast between *Or.* 31 and 66 is what he says about the crowns conferred upon the athletes. While in *Or.* 31.21 he praises the athletes' striving for the crown an example to be imitated,[39] in *Or.* 66.5 he speaks ironically of the "leaves" they are seeking.[40] I am reluctant to smooth out the contrasts found in Dio's writings by reference to his own development.

The Benefaction—an Established Custom or "Law"

In his speech Περὶ νόμου (*Or.* 75), Dio Chrysostom praises the law for the "rewards which it has established for their benefactors, having devised crowns and public proclamations and seats of honour" (*Or.* 75.7). To each good man (ἕκαστος τῶν ἀγαθῶν) the law declares that they be publically acclaimed as such.[41] Dio does not consider this to be a separate law. The law about public acclamation of benefactors is nothing more than an appendix to laws which render thanks for kindnesses in general; father to son, that is, private kindnesses (*Or.* 75.6), thus bringing to mind Philo who brings together benefactions and the commandment about honoring the parents (see above). In other words, it is the law, which requires justice to happen. The law requires that thanks be rendered in proportion to what one has received. The Rhodian speech addresses the benefaction system from this perspective (*Or.* 31.118, 135–142). This explains why neglecting the obligation to honor the benefactors by Dio is seen in terms of transgression, (παράβασις) (*Or.* 31.12, 64, 76 cf. 75.2, 5). In *Or.* 31.64, παραβαίνω is used synonymously with ἁμαρτάνω. Παραβαίνω and cognates are in the New Testament used with special reference to violating a law (Matt 15:2; Rom 2:23; 4:15; 5:14; Gal 3:19; 1 Tim 2:14).[42] In his discussion Dio speaks

---

[39] Thus also in *Or.* 75.7–8.

[40] This is not the only instance where Dio holds contrasting views. In *Or.* 53 he praises Homer, while he in his Trojan Discourse (*Or.* 11) says that Homer was a deceiver, presenting a story full of lies. He turned the events upside-down. People have become so accustomed with his lies that they trust them.

[41] Dio says that this acclamation happens in three words. He does not mention what the words are, but suggestions have been made for ἀνὴρ ἀγαθός ἐστι; see B. W. Winter, *Seek the Welfare of the City: Christians as Benefactors and Citizens* (Grand Rapids: Eerdmans, 1994), 31, and the Loeb-edition of Dio Chrysostomos, Vol. V, p. 247 n. 2.

[42] See J. Schneider, "παραβαίνω," *TDNT* 5:736–42.

about the violation of this law in ways, which bring to mind some particular New Testament passages. The following presents a reading made plausible by the perspective of the Rhodian speech.

Abolishing the Law

Dio speaks of the Rhodian malpractice in terms of annulling the law: ὅλον τὸ πρᾶγμα καταλῦσαι (*Or.* 31.24), which can be rendered "doing away with the whole system."[43] It is worth looking at this phrase. Dio uses a verb having both a concrete and a metaphorical meaning here. In *Or.* 31.22 and 63, καταλῦσαι refers to taking down a statue or demolishing a public building given by a benefactor, by rendering it bereft of any honor. *Oratio* 31.86 draws on the image of the benefaction system as a law for the polis. If anyone chisels out only one word (ῥῆμα) from an official tablet, he will be put to death. Similarly with a person "erasing one jot of any law [κεραίαν νόμου τινός], or one syllable of a decree." Rhetorically he then asks if erasing the inscription on a statue is a less serious crime. What does Dio have in mind here? In a Jewish Greek-speaking context (see below), it is easier to imagine the precise meaning of κεραία. Dio uses this term synonymously with γράμματα, ψήφισμα, and συλλαβή. The comparison, made by Dio, with removing a part of a sculpture indicates the meaning of κεραία. It probably refers to a stroke of a letter.[44] This finds corroboration in Plutarch's *Mor.* 1100a where it says that Epicurus quarreled with his teachers περὶ συλλαβῶν καὶ κεραιῶν (according to LCL "syllables and serifs"). This is opposed to the true wisdom of the philosopher, thus suggesting that κεραία here is the simplest form of letters taught children at the very beginning of their instruction,[45] here metaphorically for "a minor detail." This text assumes contempt for the basic instruction given by encyclical teachers;[46] κεραία thus indicates

---

[43] Cf. *Or.* 31.14, 86.

[44] LSJ s.v. has "apex of a letter."

[45] R. Cribiore, *Writing, Teachers, and Students in Graeco-Roman Egypt* (Atlanta: Scholars Press, 1996), 31, 140–41.

[46] See K. O. Sandnes, *The Challenge of Homer: School, Pagan Poets, and Early Christianity* (London: T&T Clark 2009).

insignificance. Philo (*Flacc.* 131) mentions Lampo who perverted justice by tampering with the documents, even changing κεραία. This leaves us with κεραία as a word for written insignificance, a stroke, decoration,[47] accents or breathings in an inscription.

The phrase "abolishing the law" and the κεραία of the law brings to mind Matt 5:17–18:

> Do not think that I have come to abolish the law [καταλῦσαι τὸν νόμον] or the prophets; I have come not to abolish [καταλῦσαι] but to fulfill. For truly I tell you, until heaven and earth pass away, not one letter, not one stroke of a letter [ἰῶτα ἓν ἢ μία κεραία], will pass from the law until it is accomplished.

Matthew's Gospel has precisely the same dual meaning in its use of καταλῦσαι as does Dio. The verb refers to the opposite of building construction, that of tearing down (Matt 24:2; 26:61; 27:40), and in the text quoted above this vocabulary is used forcefully in a figurative way. The exact meaning of the terminology in Matt 5:18 is somewhat uncertain, but it clearly refers to smallness or insignificance. The mentioning of ἰῶτα works within both a Hebrew and Greek speaking context;[48] κεραία is different; the word does not appear in the LXX. Luke 16:17 has only τοῦ νόμου μίαν κεραίαν, thus rendering Jesus' logion in a wider setting.

Blotting out the Name

The thought behind Dio's argument is, of course, that the switching of statues implies to render void decrees made by the city: what is written (γράμματα or ἐπιγραφή) is blotted out (*Or.* 31.9, 20–21, 29, 53, 61, 71, 124). These texts demonstrate that the decree led to the inscribing of a name: "Hence, if one removes the name of the person so honoured from any of the other dedications, and inscribes the name of a different

---

[47] See Cribiore, *Writing, Teachers, and Students*, 115, speaking about "small strokes decorating the top and bottom of verticals."

[48] See J. Nolland, *The Gospel of Matthew: A Commentary on the Greek Text* (Grand Rapids: Eerdmans, 2005), 220.

person [τὸ ὄνομα ἄλλον ἐπιγράψῃ]" (31.89). Dio therefore considers the Rhodian practice tantamount to that of blotting out a name.

He compares this malpractice to an Athenian law, namely that of erasing the name (τὸ ὄνομα ἐξαλείφεται) of a citizen condemned to death (31.84–85). Thus the city declares that a person is no longer a πολίτης, but has become an alien (ἀλλότριος), thus bringing to mind the practice of *damnatio memoriae*. The verb ἐξαλείφειν is used repeatedly in *Or.* 31 to describe the practice Dio attacks, and it refers to the erasing of decrees, inscriptions and names.[49] This Athenian law about the blotting out of a name combines the motif of judgment, citizenship, and alienation. This brings to mind Rev 3:5: "I will not blot your name out of the book of life, I will confess your name before my Father and before his angels," a recurrent motif in the book of Revelation.[50] Revelation 3:5 evolves around the same basic motifs as found in Dio's Rhodian speech; judgment, citizenship and alienation. The blotting out of the name is usually, and most relevant indeed, seen in the light of Exod 32:32 where Moses asks God to be blotted out of the book which God has written, and in the tradition which followed in the wake of this text.[51] But the idea of a heavenly register of citizens finds a relevant parallel also in the Athenian practice mentioned by Dio.

An example of the Athenian practice is given by Xenophon in *Hell.* 2.3.50–56 where Critias is said to strike (ἐξαλείφειν) the name of Theramenos off the register of citizens; he thus became a person outside the register (ἔξω τοῦ καταλόγου). This allowed the council to condemn him to death. As an outsider vis-à-vis the catalogue he was, in fact, liable to death. Theramenos was compelled to drink the hemlock. This makes a relevant analogy to "the book of life" in Rev 3:5. Having one's name erased from this book means death.[52] Dio

---

[49] See K. Koolmeister, T. Tallmeister, and J. F. Kindstrand, *An Index to Dio Chrysostomus* (Stockholm: Almqvist & Wiksell International, 1981), s.v.

[50] See Rev 13:8; 17:8; 20:12, 15; 21:27.

[51] D. E. Aune, *Revelation 1–5* (Dallas: Word, 1997), 223–5; C. E. Hemer, *The Letters to the Seven Churches of Asia in their Local Setting* (Sheffield: JSOT Press, 1981), 148–9. Relevant texts are e.g. Ps 69:29; Dan 12:1; *Jub.* 30:20–23; *1 En.* 47:3; 104:1; 108:1; Phil 4:3, Luke 10:20.

[52] Cf. Rev 20:15.

does not explicitly say that the Rhodians are condemning their past benefactors to death, but this element is implicitly at work in his rhetoric. The motif of blotting out the name in biblical texts, particularly in Revelation, assumes a practice, which Dio here gives us access to.

Jesus—Worse than the Rhodians

The very heart of Dio's argument in this speech is that benefactions demand honor rendered in a visible way. Without outward signs of honor, μαρτυρία or σύμβολα, the mutuality involved in the system falls apart.[53] Olympian athletes will certainly withdraw from the competition if they know that their name will be removed from the statue of the winner, and taken by someone else's name (*Or.* 31.21–22). The malpractice of the Rhodians will leave the city destitute of benefactors. Jesus of the Gospels is critical of the attitude Dio urges. The way Jesus addresses piety in Matt 6:1–6, 16–18 marks a contrast between outward and inward honor, and the expectations of mutuality involved in acts of benefactions which, in fact, strike against the core of Dio's argument. The forceful rhetoric of Jesus is seen in Matt 6:16 where he says that the hypocrites disfigure (ἀ φανίζειν) their face with an aim to be seen (ὅπως φανῶσιν τοῖς ἀνθρώποις); obviously a word-play. But Dio's text adds to this rhetoric, since ἀφανίζειν is a recurrent verb in *Or.* 31 for removing a name from a statue. Reading Jesus' words in the light of this, implies that the hypocrites pretend to remove their name and memory, with an eye to be observed. A similar critique is echoed in Matt 23:5–7 as well. The setting of the text is obviously Jewish, not that of a Greek city like Rhodes; nevertheless the mentioning of seats of honor corresponds with the sign of honor Dio recommends the Rhodians to render in the future (*Or.* 31.16, 29, 108, 110). I imagine Dio, for

---

[53] For reciprocity as a basic principle within the system of benefactions, see G. W. Peterman, *Paul's Gift from Philippi: Conventions of Gift-Exchange and Christian Giving* (Cambridge: Cambridge University Press, 1997), 1–9, 51–89.

the sake of my argument here, raising his voice, claiming that Jesus is about to ὅλον τὸ πρᾶγμα καταλῦσαι.

Summary

Dion of Prusa's *Rhodian Speech* lends itself to a presentation of the benefaction system in the ancient world. Dio vehemently opposes what he considers a Rhodian malpractice, namely that of switching statues or the inscriptions and names engraved on them. In this way, then, outward symbols of honor were recycled. This practice served two ends; the Romans did get their signs of honor, and the Rhodians saved expenses. But Dio holds against the Rhodians that they are betraying their past. The speech is an index to the system of benefactions, and sheds light on numerous New Testament texts and the motifs of "abolishing the law" and "blotting out of a name" from the register of citizens.

In the speech in question, Dio argues from the conviction that statues are signs of Greek identity. We are here reminded of Josephus' report about the disorder that erupted at Caesarea Maritima shortly before the war (*B.J.* 2.266–270). It began as a dispute over the identity of the city. The Jews made reference to its Jewish founder, Herod the Great. The Greek citizens, however, pointed to the style of the city which to them clearly betrayed its Greekness: "Herod would never have erected the statues and temples [ἀνδριάντας καὶ ναούς] which he placed there had he destined it for Jews" (*B.J.* 2.266).[54] Somehow the Christians seem to have perpetuated this critical stance of the Jews towards statues. It is, therefore, possibly not by chance that it is held against the Christians, according to Minucius Felix (*Oct.* 10.2), that they had "no publicly known images [*nulla nota simulacra*]." *Simulacrum* is a visual presentation, an image, often used synonymously with *statua*.[55] Christian hesitance against statues may well be due both to their marginalized position in the

---

[54] Cf. Tacitus, *Hist.* 5.5.
[55] See *OLD*, s.v.

ancient world, and to Biblical restrictions on images. This article has argued that this hesitance cannot be isolated from the values expressed by the raising of statues, the benefaction system. For true, the Christians did not abandon this. It was interwoven into the very fabric of social life, as can be seen in for example the sponsors of Paul's mission and churches. But the New Testament has preserved a value-critical perspective worth noting, and this appears more clearly when read against the background of Dio's *Rhodian Speech*.

Ephesus and Power: Early Christian Textual Prototypes of Authority in a Local Perspective

Mikael Tellbe
Örebro School of Theology

Introduction

No one working with issues relating to the distribution of power and the exercise of authority in the early Christian movement can neglect the important doctoral work of Bengt Holmberg, *Paul and Power: The Structure of Authority in the Primitive Church as Reflected in the Pauline Epistles* (1978). Holmberg's study was a pioneering work in at least two ways. First, in terms of methodology it was one of the first New Testament studies that made significant use of sociological models in the task of analyzing ancient texts. Holmberg elaborated on Max Weber's theories concerning "charismatic authority" and the "routinization of charisma" in examining the nature and development of authority structures in the primitive church. Above all, Holmberg paid attention to the dialectic process between theology and social structure. The nature of authority is in itself a social phenomenon, not a theological interpretation of social phenomena. Holmberg's warning of "the fallacy of idealism" in New Testament studies has today become almost classic. With this concept Holmberg wants to put up a flag of warning against "the view that the determining factors of the historical process are ideas and nothing else, and that all developments, conflicts and influences are at bottom developments of, and conflicts and influences between ideas."[1] Historical phenomena cannot not only be explained by

---

[1] B. Holmberg, *Paul and Power: The Structure of Authority in the Primitive Church as Reflected in the Pauline Epistles* (Lund: CWK Gleerup, 1978), 205.

underlying theological structures; there is always a continuous dialectic between ideas and social structures. For example, Paul's theology of charisma probably did have an effect on the Corinthian church, "but not before it had been formulated and certainly not in any simple, straightforward fashion as if ideas could act directly on social structures".[2]

Secondly, Holmberg's study was pioneering not only in terms of methodology but also in terms of its result, since it provided a new way of looking at old issues of authority and legitimacy. According to Holmberg, all authority in the primitive church should be considered as ultimately flowing from the same source, viz., Jesus Christ the founder. Legitimacy is a question of claiming a close relation to Christ, what Holmberg calls "the proximity of the sacred."[3] Temporal, geographical and personal proximity to the sacred origin endows a person with an exalted status as compared to persons who are otherwise like him. However, it is not sufficient to have known Jesus Christ personally (or being one of the first converts in place): "The crucial form of proximity to the sacred is that of being in close contact with the sacred ratio, the divine Word."[4]

At the local church level, Holmberg discerns a functional differentiation that within a short time became institutionalized, i.e., developed into offices. This differentiation was raised largely by itself, influenced by pneumatic and social differences within the

---

[2] Ibid., 206. In general, a majority of scholars have endorsed Holmberg's position on this point. Others have warned for the risks of anachronism, determinism and reductionism in applying modern models to ancient texts. E.g., E. A. Judge, "The Social Identity of the First Christians: A Question of Method in Religious History," *JRH* 11 (1980): 201–17, argues that an intrinsic commensurability between ancient and modern societies cannot be demonstrated. In dialogue with Holmberg, Judge warns against "the sociological fallacy," i.e., to use modern social theories as though they can be "safely transposed across the centuries without verification" (p. 210). In *Sociology and the New Testament: An Appraisal* (Minneapolis: Fortress, 1990), Holmberg responds to Judge and others: "We should not be overwhelmed by models, thinking that they must be right and our data wrong, because they don't fit the model. Nor should we presuppose that our data set is so unique or outside ordinary human experience that human, i.e., at bottom social, patterns of meaning can't contribute anything to its understanding" (p. 15). See also the counter critique of Judge's position in P. F. Esler, *Community and Gospel in Luke-Acts: The Social and Political Motivations of Lucan Theology* (Cambridge: Cambridge University Press, 1987), 13–15.

[3] Holmberg, *Paul and Power*, 198.

[4] Ibid., 198.

local congregation but without much organization on the part of Paul. Holmberg provides three ways of looking at the nature of authority in the primitive church: charismatic authority, institutionalized authority, and dialectical authority.[5] Charismatic authority is the predominant type, based mainly as it is on the endowment of divine and extraordinary gifts:

> The most powerful manifestation of charisma is to have received the commission to preach the Gospel from the Lord himself or to mediate divine revelation direct from the Spirit, or to expound the Holy Scriptures and transmit the Jesus-tradition.[6]

However, Holmberg points out that the church must also be characterized as an institutional charismatic movement, especially since it exhibits elements of traditional and rational-legal authority. Holmberg draws the conclusion that the process of institutionalization was both "open" as it may proceed in many directions but also "controlled" by a corporate tradition which guided the emerging functional differentiation and its institutionalization. Even after one generation's institutionalization the tradition was relatively "open" and variable, especially in regard to new conditions and problems. As Holmberg points out: "Different apostles and missionaries within the same tradition may go different ways in the continuous process of institutionalization."[7] Finally, Holmberg observes a dialectic operating at different levels. First of all, it is a dialectic between ideas and social structures, between theology and social needs. Moreover, there is a dialectic between the responsibility of all and the charge of specific leaders, between the institutionalized apostolic authority and local authority, and between "ideal interests" of the members of the charismatic group, the "routinization" of their motives and the systematic needs of the movement.

Holmberg demonstrates that the institutionalization of authority in the Pauline region was not a late development but was well on its

---

[5] Ibid., 198–204.
[6] Ibid., 198–9. Cf. ibid., 136–61.
[7] Ibid., 186. Cf. pp. 162–95.

way in the middle of the fifties. The process of institutionalization
in the primitive church should thus not be regarded as a fixed or
predetermined process, although we must acknowledge that
as time passed by the institutionalization of church life would
be increasingly guided by corporate tradition and, accordingly,
progressively less free to develop in a variety of directions.[8] It is
thus the corporative tradition and the struggle to preserve and guard
this tradition that guides the emerging functional differentiation
and its institutionalization in the primitive church. The overall
process in which legitimation operate in the formation, expansion,
solidification and transformation of the symbolic structure is
described by Holmberg as "cumulative institutionalization," aptly
divided into primary institutionalization (the process that already
begun in the group around Jesus) and secondary institutionalization
(the process that continues in the community of Christ-believers in
a system of doctrine, cult and organization).[9]

In the following, I will elaborate on this secondary stage of
institutionalization in a local perspective, namely the claim of
legitimacy and the development of authority structures in the
early Christian texts that we could locate to the geographical area
of western Asia Minor and the city of Ephesus by the end of the
first century and the beginning of the second century C.E. No other
ancient city can be connected with so many early Christian texts as
Ephesus: 1–2 Timothy, Rev 2 and Ignatius' letter *To the Ephesians*
are explicitly addressed to Christ-believers in Ephesus. In addition,
Acts 19–20 gives Luke's version of the early Christian mission in
Ephesus. A majority of scholars also locate the Johannine Letters to
this city, and later on, Paul's Letter to the Ephesians was obviously
connected to the city.[10] All of the early Christian texts that could be
connected to Ephesus display one interesting feature in common,
namely that they contain demarcations against people or groups that
for some reason or the other are labeled "deviants" and are excluded

---

[8] Ibid., 200.
[9] Ibid., 178–80.
[10] Following 𝔓⁴⁶ א* B* etc., and taking the phrase ἐν Ἐφέσῳ (Eph 1:1) as a later addendum.

or marked off from the ingroup of Christ-believers.[11] In 1–2 Timothy there is a group of Jewish-Christian gnosis-teachers promoting an ascetic lifestyle that are marked off (1 Tim 4:1–3; 6:20; 2 Tim 2:18), in Rev 2 there is a group called "Nicolaitans" that is accused of practicing idolatry and fornication, and in Ignatius' letter *To the Ephesians* we meet a group with probably a docetic teaching (Ign. *Eph.* 6:2; 7:2; 8:1–2; 9:1–2). First John mentions a group of Jewish (?) secessionists who deny that "Jesus is Christ/Messiah" (1 Joh 2:18–27; 4:1–6). This image of a diverse movement with several fractions is confirmed by Luke's story of the early Christian mission in Ephesus, and in particular by Paul's prophetical *ex eventu*-address to the Ephesian elders in Miletos (Acts 20:29–30).

Apparently, the authors of the texts that could be located to the Ephesus area at the end the end of the first century c.e. and the beginning of the second century c.e. were involved in an intense struggle for legitimacy, i.e., the right to claim authority for the "sacred tradition." However, they do so in different ways. In analyzing these issues, I will pay particular attention to how the different authors define issues of authority and legitimacy of their respective tradition and where they place the locus of authority. I will begin with briefly outlining how the authors try to establish contact with and define the proximity to the "sacred tradition." This attempt to claim closeness to "the divine Word" is not only crucial for the authority and identity that the author claims for himself,

---

[11] Despite the amount of texts connected to this geographical area, there has been a notable lacuna in New Testament research concerning the history of early Christian believers in Ephesus. However, the last decade or so of New Testament studies demonstrates a new interest in the early Christian movement in Ephesus. Since 1995, seven major studies have been published that deal with the Christian movement in Ephesus in the first and second century; see W. Thiessen, *Christen in Ephesus: Die historische und theologische Situation in vorpaulinischer und paulinischer Zeit und zur Zeit der Apostelgeschichte und der Pastoralbriefe* (Tübingen: Francke, 1995); M. Günther, *Die Frühgeschichte des Christentums in Ephesus* (Frankfurt am Main: Peter Lang, 1995); R. Strelan, *Paul, Artemis and the Jews in Ephesus* (Berlin: de Gruyter, 1996); M. Fieger, *Im Schatten der Artemis: Glaube und Ungehorsam in Ephesus* (Bern: Peter Lang, 1998); P. Trebilco, *The Early Christians in Ephesus from Paul to Ignatius* (Tübingen: Mohr Siebeck, 2004); S. Witetschek, *Ephesische Enthüllungen 1: Frühe Christen in einer antiken Großstadt: Zugleich ein Beitrag zur Frage nach den Kontexten der Johannesapokalypse* (Leuven: Peeters, 2008), and M. Tellbe, *Christ-Believers in Ephesus: A Textual Analysis of Early Christian Identity Formation in a Local Perspective* (Tübingen: Mohr Siebeck, 2009).

but also for the legitimacy the author receives in the believing communities and, in turn, for the process of the formation of social identity and the prototypical believer. As we will see, the claim of authority and legitimacy and the shaping of the prototypical leader belong together.[12] For the sake of convenience—but certainly with the risk of generalization—the prototypes formed by each author respectively will be artificially categorized as the prototype of *the Pastor* (1–2 Timothy), the prototype of *the Prophet* (Revelation) and the prototype of *the Presbyter* (1–3 John).[13]

---

[12] In the following, I will use categories borrowed from social identity theories. Stressing the interaction between personal and social identity, the social theorist John Turner argues that a person's self-concept tend to vary in particular group situations, notably by movement along a continuum from pronounced personal identity at one end to pronounced social identity at the other. The central idea is that of "self-categorization," referring to the operation of the categorization process as the cognitive basis of group behaviour. "Self-categorization" means that people define themselves in terms of membership in particular shared social categories, see J. C. Turner, et. al., *Rediscovering the Social Group: A Self-Categorization Theory* (Oxford: Blackwell, 1987), 42–43, 46–47, 49. Cf. P. F. Esler, *Conflict and Identity in Romans: The Social Setting of Paul's Letter* (Minneapolis: Fortress, 2003), 25. In any such categorization process, people tend to exaggerate the differences between categories (accentuation or intergroup difference) and simultaneously minimize the differences within categories (assimilation or intragroup similarity); see D. G. Horrell, "'Becoming Christian': Solidifying Christian Identity and Content," in *Handbook of Early Christianity: Social Sciences Approaches* (ed. A. J. Blasi, J. Duhaime and P.-A. Durcotte; Oxford: Altamina, 2002), 309–35, esp. 312. Cf. H. Tajfel, *Human Groups and Social Categories: Studies in Social Psychology* (Cambridge: Cambridge University Press, 1981). As an image of depersonalization, when a person stops being preoccupied by personal agendas and becomes concerned with the interests of the group, Turner draws attention to the development of the idea of prototypicality, the prototypical group member (Turner et al., *Rediscovering*, 46–47, 79–80). Social identity theory and self-categorization theory see the self, the group and the prototypical group member as cognitive categories. This idea develops from the practical behaviour of actual group members, in particular its most prominent members, e.g., the leader(s) of the group, cf. S. A. Haslam and M. J. Platow, "Your Wish is Our Command: The Role of Shared Social Identity in Translating a Leader's Vision into Followers' Action," in *Social Identity Processes in Organisations* (ed. M. A. Hogg and D. J. Terry; New York: Psychology, 2001), 213–39. Inside the group, members who act like the prototypical group member will be more appreciated, get a higher status and have more influence on the other members.

[13] For a more elaborated analysis of the following sections, see Tellbe, *Christ-Believers*.

Prototypes of Authority

The Prototype of the Pastor

In 1–2 Timothy the authority of the Jesus-tradition goes back to Paul's encounter with the risen Christ on the road to Damascus: Paul's legitimacy is derived from the greater authority of Jesus. The rhetorical function of 1 Tim 1:12–20 in the beginning of the letter-argument is not only to legitimize Paul's ministry as an apostle of Jesus Christ, but also to legitimize Timothy as Paul's representative in Ephesus; from the very start of the argument of 1 Timothy, the author wants to stress that the task given to Timothy to encounter the deviant group of teachers in the community ultimately rests upon Paul's own encounter with the risen Christ. This has been made clear in accordance with prophecies previously made concerning Timothy (1:18), highlighting and legitimizing the close relationship between Paul and his appointed successor in the community.[14] The same point is picked up in the beginning of 2 Timothy (1:8–14): Jesus Christ has been revealed to Paul and he has entrusted him with the true gospel and by the work of the Spirit this tradition has also been entrusted to Timothy. He is therefore urged to be a good guardian of the tradition handed over to him by the apostle (1:14). As Paul's "true child in the faith" and his appointed agent in Ephesus, Timothy shares Paul's authority and legitimacy. Timothy is thus given a position of authority over the believing community that includes the responsibility to keep the "sacred tradition" pure (1 Tim 1:3–4; 4:6–16), to order the life relationships of the community (5:1–16), and to appoint, exercise discipline and mete out justice in the case of elders (5:17–22). Hence, structures of authority and legitimacy are created that ultimately rest on Paul's own call to be an apostle and teacher of Christ (1 Tim 1:1; 2:7; 2 Tim 1:1, 11).

Since Paul himself is not present, the true Jesus-tradition entrusted to him, and in turn to Timothy, should be guarded and passed on

---

[14] L. Oberlinner and A. Vögtle, *Anpassung oder Widerspruch? Von der apostolichen zur nachapostolischen Kirche* (Freiburg: Herder, 1992), 51–52.

carefully. In order to safeguard this tradition, the author argues for structures of authority and leadership that rest upon personal relationships and confidence: Jesus—Paul—"many witnesses"—Timothy—"faithful men"—the believing community: "And the things *you* have heard from *me* through *many witnesses*, these entrust to *faithful men*, who will be able to teach *others* also" (2 Tim 2:2; italics mine). Although we may not find a formal or institutionalized chain of succession argued here,[15] the verb παρατίθημι suggests some kind of successional idea built into the authority structures of 1–2 Timothy.[16] Emphasis is given to the necessity of properly transmitting the authoritative Jesus-tradition, the "sound teaching", and to the authority of the tradition that is linked to the authority of carefully selected and authoritative local teachers.

Hence, in order to protect the true tradition, the author creates certain "Sicherungselemente,"[17] particularly manifested in the central role given to the teacher (διδάσκαλος)[18] and the explicit hierarchical leadership structures of 1 Tim 3:1–13 and 5:17–20, evolving around the roles of the ἐπίσκοπος, πρεσβύτεροι/πρεσβυτήριον and διάκονοι respectively. These structures are closely interconnected to the patriarchal and hierarchical structures of the ancient family, in particular as the model ἐπίσκοπος should be a married man "who manages his own household well" (1 Tim 3:4). Accordingly, the family becomes the standard notion of the community of God, significantly being labeled "God's household" (1 Tim 3:15; cf. 2 Tim 2:20–21), an image primarily stressing the idea of orderliness.

---

[15] *Contra* Oberlinner and Vögtle, *Anpassung*, 67–68.

[16] The verb παρατίθεμαι is picked up from 1 Tim 1:18, where Paul "entrusts" Timothy to carry on the mission he himself has been entrusted by Jesus Christ. In 1–2 Timothy, the idea of παραθήκη occurs three times (1 Tim 6:20; 2 Tim 1:12, 14), all occasions stressing the idea of guarding the true tradition that has been entrusted to Paul and Timothy.

[17] E. Schlarb, *Die Gesunde Lehre: Häresie und Wahrheit im Spiegel der Pastoralbriefe* (Marburg: N. G. Elwert, 1990), 360.

[18] 1–2 Timothy display a particular high frequency of terms belonging to the διδασκ–word group διδασκαλία, διδαχή, διδάσκαλος, διδάσκω, διδακτικός): the term διδασκαλία is used eleven times (1 Tim 1:10; 4:1, 6, 13, 16; 5:17; 6:1, 3; 2 Tim 3:10, 16; 4:3; διδασκαλία occurs altogether fifteen times in the Pastorals, over against six in the whole of the rest of the NT). The term διδάσκαλος occurs three times (1 Tim 2:7; 2 Tim 1:11; 4:3), διδάσκω four times (1 Tim 2:12; 4:11; 6:2; 2 Tim 2:2), διδακτικός two times (1 Tim 3:2; 2 Tim 2:24), and διδαχή once (2 Tim 4:2).

Thus, we find that 1–2 Timothy exhibit a clear degree of cumulative institutionalization and routinization with regard to leadership structures. The Pastoral Letters articulate a stage in the primitive church when the contours of organization are becoming more pronounced; here "we see the beginning of co-ordination of the organization and ministry of the congregations."[19] Paul the apostle is no longer present to exercise leadership and supervision and the locus of authority is found in the representative ministry of Timothy and in a local leadership preserving the authoritative teaching of the apostle from deviant teachings and stabilizing the life of the community.

The Prototype of the Prophet

In the book of Revelation the locus of authority is spelled out in clearly divine terms, having its origin in God and the risen Jesus Christ. The authority of John the Prophet is founded on a "revelation of Jesus Christ" which God gave to him (Rev 1:1) and on the commission to prophetic ministry received by the risen Jesus Christ on Patmos (1:1–2, 9–20). John makes clear from the start that his prophecy is divinely inspired; he speaks the word of God on a direct calling of God and Jesus Christ (1:11, 19). The story is not his own; it is "the revelation of Jesus Christ". In fact, his words are not his own, he is a witness and prophet of the word of God (1:3; 22:7, 10, 18–19).[20] Marking the *inclusio* of John's revelations, the book closes with Jesus himself reappearing in order to give the final authority and legitimation of John's visions (22:12–16). In this inclusion we also find a promise of blessing for those who read it (1:3; 22:7), underlining the significance of the text at hand. In 22:18–19, John reinforces his blessings by adding a threat: Whoever would add or subtract

---

[19] I. H. Marshall, *A Critical and Exegetical Commentary on the Pastoral Epistles* (Edinburgh: T&T Clark, 1999), 171. Cf. also J. P. Meier, "*Presbyteros* in the Pastoral Epistles," *CBQ* 35 (1973): 323–45, esp. 345.

[20] G. Carey, *Elusive Apocalypse: Reading Authority in the Revelation of John* (Macon: Mercer University Press, 1999), points out that the concept of witness in Revelation plays a crucial role in legitimating John and his message: "Like the 'faithful and true witness' Jesus, John's words are 'faithful and true'. So John is identified not only with the saints of the highest status, his discourse assumes the authority of Christ" (p. 122).

from the message should expect damnation. Furthermore, the Jesus-tradition is validated by the prophet's heavenly journeys, where the prophet receives visions of God on his throne and of the slaughtered but victorious Lamb. What John sees and hears is important, absolutely fundamental for his claims of authority. Here we find a tradition of authority that draws from Jewish apocalypticism, where the apocalyptic literature typically built the locus of authority and legitimacy on heavenly journeys with prophetic-charismatic visions and utterances. Thus, from a rhetorical perspective, apocalyptic is especially effective for building ethos and establishing authority.[21]

The emphasis on prophetic tradition is strong in Revelation: John is given the title "prophet" and he writes "prophecy" (1:3; 10:7, 10–11; 11:6, 18; 19:10; 22:7–10, 18–19), divinely inspired by the Spirit (1:10; 4:2; 17:3; 21:10). Thus, as a prophet, John speaks the words of the Jesus Christ (2:1, 8, 12, 18; 3:1, 7, 14), being commissioned to "write what you have seen, what is, and what is to take place after this" (1:19; cf. 1:11; 10:8–11; 21:5). Revelation contains two call-narratives, one in 1:9–20 and the second in 10:8–11:2, the second functioning as a resumption of the first call. The function of these narratives is to legitimize John as a receiver and transmitter of revelatory visions. The locus of authority of John's prophetic activities does not rest in John himself, not even the office given to him, but in God the Father and the risen Christ. The readers should pay careful attention to this and read his prophetic scroll as a sacred writing with divine authority (explicitly expressed in the *inclusio* of

---

[21] Cf. Carey, *Elusive Apocalypse*, 77–92, esp. 92: "Through dreams, dialogues with heavenly figures, tours of heavenly regions, and lessons about primeval history or the fundamental elements of the cosmos, visionaries demonstrate their exclusive knowledge." L. Carlsson *Round Trips To Heaven: Otherworldly Travelers in Early Judaism and Christianity* (Lund: Department of History and Anthropology of Religions, Lund University, 2004), 22–29, argues that heavenly travels were essential in communicating the identity and legitimacy of the seer: "The heavenly travellers had, unlike the others, received the ability to have direct contact with God. This ability made up the *primary* consequence of their new identity" (p. 24). Legitimacy often came only from the inner circle of followers: "The Tradition Groups who transmitted narratives of heavenly journeys were often made up of marginalized people within Judaism and Christianity, while other groups/directions within both religions were sceptical. This is reflected in the heavenly journey texts that, in several cases, have a polemicizing characteristic. The legitimacy which a group gave to the heavenly travellers was built upon views which had arisen because of the special religious and social context in which it lived" (pp. 26–27).

1:3 and 22:18). Thus, in presenting himself as a prophet, John seeks legitimation and wants to secure "the absolute and unconditional acceptance of the divine authority of his apocalyptic message."[22]

The book of Revelation is a book of conflicts. However, it is not only a matter of conflicts between the believing group and the wider society; there are also traces of ingroup conflicts. John the Prophet confronts other local, rivaling prophetic groups or circles that were active in the churches of Asia Minor (e.g., the false apostles of the Nicolaitans, the group of "who hold on to the teachings of Balaam" and the prophetess Jezebel), persons and groups who are labeled "false" (2:2) and propagate "the deep things of Satan" (2:24). In dealing with these issues, there is a remarkable silence concerning structures of leadership and authority in Revelation. We meet the more general group of "saints and apostles and prophets" (18:20), where faithful believers are described generally as "saints and prophets" (16:6; cf. 11:18; 18:24). On the whole, the terminology used of positions of leadership and offices is veiled in apocalyptic and symbolic language. Instead of explicitly addressing the local church leader(s), the author ambiguously addresses "the angel of the church."[23] Even the frequently used title "elder" (πρεσβύτερος) is veiled in spiritual and symbolic language, not referring to local, earthly leadership positions but to heavenly beings in front of the throne of God.[24] The title "apostle" (ἀπόστολος) is used of itinerant "deviant" prophets or teachers in the letter to the church in Ephesus ("who call themselves apostles," 2:2), indicating that these were not resident leaders. Otherwise, the title is used in a more general way (18:20), or in reference to the twelve apostles (21:14). Thus, there is a remarkable silence concerning local leadership structures

---

[22] D. E. Aune, "The Prophetic Circle of John the Patmos and the Exegesis of Revelation 22.16," *JSNT* 37 (1989): 103–16. I find it likely that John addressed a specific circle of prophets (referred to in 22:9, 16), who served as transmitters and teachers in the distribution and presentation of Revelation to the seven churches. For detailed arguments in favour of this view, see Aune, "Prophetic Circle."

[23] Since ἄγγελος refers to heavenly beings on all other occurrences in Revelation, the ambiguous title "the angel of the church" (ὁ ἄγγελος τῆς ἐκκλησίας, 2:1 and *passim*) most likely refers to an angelic being (representing the church before the heavenly council). For a good discussion of this expression, see D. E. Aune, *Revelation 1–5* (Dallas: Word Books, 1997), 108–12.

[24] See Rev 4:4, 10; 5:5, 6, 8, 11, 14; 11:16; 14:3; 19:4.

in Revelation; in fact, the prophets are the only "officials" in the believing communities addressed in Revelation. Of course, this does not imply that John was not familiar with such forms of leadership structures; on the other hand, if he would have been familiar to them, it seems even more noteworthy that he does not address these leaders.

The Prototype of the Presbyter

First John has a clear polemical thrust, being written in response to a group of people who have left the ingroup of believers because of their specific understanding of the identity of Jesus Christ (2:19–23; 4:1–6; 5:1–5). However, no hint is given in the letter of a community structure that speaks of leaders or offices in superior position who are appointed to guard the tradition and the believing community from deviant teaching. According to 1 John 1:1–4, the author is a witness (not an "apostle") who belongs to a group of collective witnesses ("we"). The purpose of 1 John is not to distinguish this group from other Christ-believers, but rather to include the readers ("you") in the group of witnesses and, accordingly, with the Father and the Son; "that you may have fellowship with us—and our fellowship is with the father and with his Son, Jesus Christ" (1:3). The author does not seek authority as an individual; together with his readers he belongs to a group that saw themselves as standing in continuity with the first witnesses and maintaining the continuity and unity of the tradition rooted in that witness. Together they will form a community that bears witness of the tradition of Jesus Christ. The author appeals to no other grounds of external authority to buttress his position. The authority is rooted not in appointed offices or in inherited roles but in a group of witnesses and, as such, it is potentially available to every member of the community.[25]

---

[25] J. Lieu, *The Theology of the Johannine Epistles* (Cambridge: Cambridge University Press, 1991), 24–26. Although the author of 1 John regularly addresses the recipients as τεκνία (e.g., 1 John 2:1, 12, 28), παιδία (2:14, 18) or ἀγαπητοί (1 John 2:7; 3:2, 21; 4:1, 7, 11; 3 John 1, 2 , 5, 11), he associates himself with the community as one of its member (2:28; 4:7). This is particularly highlighted by the author's inclusive use of "we" throughout the letters (e.g., 1 John 4:12–16), referring to the whole community (together with the author). The author claims little of himself that cannot be said of the community (cf. 1:3 with 1:5; 1:2 with 4:12; 1:3 with 1:6, and so on). As pointed out by Lieu (*Theology*, 25), the author's "individual identity becomes absorbed in that of the community as a whole and of

It is thus this community, not the author himself nor specific persons or offices, which is the primary locus of authority. The locus of authority is placed in the presence of the Spirit, "the Spirit of truth" (4:6), in the community of the believers: "But you have an anointing from the Holy One, and you all know (the truth)" (2:20). The Spirit, given to all believers, will not only lead them to the truth but will also give legitimacy and guarantee the true Jesus-tradition: "And as for you, the anointing which you received from him abides in you, and you have no need for anyone to teach you" (2:27). The "anointing" (χρῖσμα) dwells within the believers, indicating that the expression has primarily to do with the indwelling of the Spirit in the community of believers. Nonetheless, since the Spirit guarantees the truth and the central content of this truth concerns true knowledge and understanding of Jesus as Χριστός (2:20–22), the χρῖσμα does not only refer to the presence of the Spirit in the community but also to the received word, teaching or tradition. The main point of the author's argument is that because of the presence of this "anointing" in the believing community there is no need of a teacher. As a matter of fact, no leadership title of any kind is mentioned in 1 John. Instead, the locus of authority is first of all located in the "true" Jesus-tradition as proclaimed and transmitted by its first witnesses (1 John 1:1–4) and received by the believing community (1:5; 2:7, 24; 3:11; 5:20; 2 Joh 5). Accordingly, the locus of authority in 1 John is ultimately collective: since the Spirit is given to everybody, it is located in the whole believing community.

The author of 2–3 John refers to himself as an "the elder" (ὁ πρεσβύτερος, 2 John 1; 3 John 1), without further defining its meaning. However, the title πρεσβύτερος seems not to be used here with the same technical meaning as in the Pastorals (or in Ignatius), where authority is specifically connected with appointment of an office.[26] Even if the title indicates a position of authority over the

---

each member."

[26] R. A. Campbell, *The Elders: Seniority within Earliest Christianity* (Edinburgh: T&T Clark, 1994), 207, calls the use of πρεσβύτερος in singular in 2–3 John "the most puzzling use of πρεσβύτερος in the New Testament." While I basically agree with Lieu (*Theology*, 92) that "there is nothing in the title 'Elder' or in the letters to align their author with a particular 'non-institutional', and even less

recipients in the letters (and could potentially even refer to the role of an overseer), the appointed or official meaning of the title is clearly played down; it seems rather to refer to a person that exercises authority by virtue of his role as a venerated old man and bearer of the Jesus-tradition and, as such, he has a position of authority.[27] However, as the dispute about authority with Diotrephes in 3 John demonstrates, he does not seem to have been the prime leader of the local community (at least not of that community). Diotrephes, "who loves to be first among them" (3 John 9), was certainly a leader in prominent position who refused to welcome iterant "brothers" and excluded disobedient members (v. 10). In fact, Diotrephes may even have viewed himself as the appropriate ἐπίσκοπος of the community in question. Hence, this controversy seems to correspond to the fundamental struggle "between Spirit and office, church order and the independent charismatic life."[28] If this reconstruction of the situation is correct, it is even more interesting to pay attention to that even though the conflict between the presbyter and Diotrephes seems to have been a conflict concerning authority and office—Diotrephes claiming sovereign authority over against the presbyter who refrained to stress the positions and offices— the presbyter avoids addressing the conflict with Diotrephes by referring to certain titles or positions. This follows the demarcations made in 1 John, where we observed a clear tendency to play down certain offices in favour of the crucial role of the community.

Furthermore, although the presbyter has a sense of his own authority, the primary locus of authority is not derived from his own position but from the true Jesus-tradition (as defined by the author) and the believing community as the bearer of this tradition (1 John 1:1–4; 2 John 1–2, 5, 9; 3 John 3–4, 12). As to the rest,

---

charismatic, style of ministry," the author of 3 John does not seem to use title with clear reference to a certain office.

[27] There are clear indications among second century authors that πρεσβύτερος was a term that did not identify men who had a particular office but men of high standing in the early church (e.g., Papias [*apud* Eusebius, *Hist. eccl.* 3.39.4], Irenaeus, *Haer.* 1.27; 4.26–27; 5.33; Clement of Alexandria, *Ecl.* 11.1; 27.1, 4). See also G. Bornkamm, "πρεσβύτερος κτλ.," *TDNT* 6.51–83.

[28] G. Strecker, *The Johannine Letters: A Commentary on 1, 2, and 3 John* (Minneapolis: Fortress, 1996), 261.

there is a remarkable lack of hierarchical structures in the Johannine Letters. It is rather the "horizontal" and family relations that are highlighted: the author addresses repeatedly the believing group as a whole (e.g., 1 John 1:1–5) and the recipients are addressed as "children," "beloved" or "brothers" (e.g. 2:1, 7, 12, 14, 18, 28; 3:7, 13, 18; 3 John 2). In the phrase "children of God" (1 John 3:1–2) or in the specifically familiar expression "the chosen lady and her children" (2 John 1), the idea of "horizontal" and "vertical" identity is combined: having been reborn into the family of God, the true believers now live together in a community of family relations.

Conclusion

The three text-corpuses examined all belong to the second (or third) generation of believers, seeking contact with and establishment of the "sacred tradition." We found specific "tradition-bearers" in all texts, but they are not the same and the way of claiming the authority and legitimacy of the true Jesus–tradition differs. Whereas the author of 1–2 Timothy locates the locus of authority in the Pauline tradition and its transmission by authorized and appointed leaders and teachers, the author of Revelation seems not only deliberately to neglect the Pauline tradition but also to play down certain leadership structures. Instead of locating the locus of authority in apostolicity, tradition and the role of the teachers and "sound teaching," John the Prophet locates the authority in divine encounters and in the commission to speak directly the word of God and of the risen Christ to the community. In the book of Revelation, the role of prophets and revelations are emphasized at the expense of the role of the teachers and the transmission of the tradition by certain offices. In stressing the role of the prophet and direct inspired speech and visions, John the Prophet wants to establish an alternative way to ensure and protect the "sacred tradition" than the ongoing "routinization of the charismata" in certain offices and leadership structures that was most likely prevalent in most of the Christ-believing communities in western Asia Minor.

In contrast to this, the authority and legitimacy of the true Jesus-tradition in the Johannine Letters is neither built on apostolic callings nor on prophetic ascensions, but on the presence and indwelling of the Spirit in the community of the believers. John the Presbyter plays down the use of certain titles and offices, even explicitly stressing that the believing communities are not in need of teachers (since they all share the Spirit). Accordingly, the presbyter communicates a more "relational", or even "mystical" (particularly expressed with the μένειν–terminology), understanding of authority and legitimacy; the locus of authority is not derived from a particular leader or office, but from the community as a whole functioning as the "tradition-bearer" under the "anointing" (Spirit/ tradition) and as the members and witnesses who "abide in God".

Prototypes of Authority in Competition

So far we have paid attention to local rivalries and conflicts over the authority and to the right to define and control the Jesus-tradition in the texts that could be located to Ephesus. The prototypes of the Pastor, the Prophet and the Presbyter are all shaped in polemic with other concurrent and "deviating" prototypes of the ideal Christ-believer. However, there are reasons to suspect that the authors of our texts did not only write in response to prototypes, which were explicitly described as deviating, but that they were also engaged in some kind of interaction with or response to other current prototypes of early Christian belief in Ephesus. Could the authors of 1–2 Timothy, Revelation and 1–3 John have written in response or even in competition to each other? The issue at stake concerned the right to define and control the Jesus-tradition, and our texts demonstrate a remarkable diversity on definitions and arguments about authority and legitimacy. Similarly, Ignatius' letter *To the Ephesians* (ca. 110 C.E.) may not only be read as a letter in response to docetic teaching, but also in response to, or in dialogue with, other possible contemporaneous prototypes of early Christian belief in Ephesus and western Asia Minor. Let us elaborate further on this thesis.

The Presbyter in Response to the Pastor

Several scholars have pointed out that the Pauline and the Johannine traditions stand quite close to each other in terms of Christology, anthropology, pneumatology, eschatology and ethics. However, as far as structures of authority and legitimacy are concerned, there are some significant differences. The author of 1–3 John seems to avoid the idea of a tradition based on certain offices explicitly, and particularly the role of teachers as those who safeguard the true Jesus-tradition. Whereas the author of 1–2 Timothy stresses the role of recognized and authorized teachers, John the Presbyter writes his first letter without any mention of a specific leader, and even explicitly denies the role of teachers. According to 1 John, the locus of authority does not reside in the specific office of the teacher but in the community of believers as a whole. This emphasis should not only be taken as a direct response to the suggested role of teachers among the secessionists, but as a general reflection of the author's understanding of church ministry and of the role of the community of believers. Although John the Presbyter acknowledges some leadership structures (mainly the presbytery in 2–3 John), he also seems to deliberately pass over hierarchical community structures and to place the locus of authority in the "tradition" and the community (e.g., 1 John 1:1–4, and the dealing with Diotrephes in 3 John). By and large, this suggests that the Johannine Letters were written in critical response to other contemporary ideas concerning authority and legitimacy, such as those expressed in 1–2 Timothy.

The Prophet in Response to the Pastor

Turning to the Book of Revelation, which was most likely written towards the end of the first century, we may assume that John the Prophet was not only familiar with the influence of the Pauline tradition in western Minor Asia, nor with the institutionalization of the Pauline churches. He probably also wrote in response to the situation among the congregations, which he addressed. There are several reasons that speak in favor of this proposal. First, we have already paid attention to the apparent silence concerning local leadership structures in Revelation; in fact, the prophets are the only "officials" in the churches addressed in Revelation. This does not imply that John was not familiar with other forms of leadership structures. If he was indeed familiar with them, it seems even more remarkable that he did not address these leaders. It is also worth noting that John the Prophet speaks of the twelve apostles without including Paul or even mentioning that Paul also had been called as an apostle. He seems to neglect the Pauline tradition completely. Was the author of Revelation not familiar with this tradition? Or, as Walter Bauer suggests, the Pauline tradition was no longer present in this geographical area.[29] Considering the impact of Paul in other early Christian texts from the same period and later (e.g., Ignatius and Polycarp), it seems quite unlikely that Paul would have been completely forgotten in western Asia Minor. It is more likely that John the Prophet deliberately made no use of his knowledge of Paul.

My suggestion is that John's silence on the Pauline tradition and on certain church offices belong together; John the Prophet deliberately plays down this tradition in order to seek acceptance for an alternative form of authority founded on divine visions and prophetic utterances. Adela Yarbro Collins appropriately points out that John "was perhaps in competition with them (bishops, elders or deacons in any of the communities)."[30] In particular, John the Prophet neglects the office of the teacher otherwise so prevalent in 1–2 Timothy, and John does not build his authority as a prophet on received tradition but on revealed knowledge. The proclamation of the "word of God" in Revelation (e.g., 1:2; 19:9) is not built on the tradition conveyed by appointed teachers, but on prophetic utterances and apocalyptic visions mediated by inspired prophets. Thus, we find certain tensions between the more "routinized" understanding of the charisma in 1–2 Timothy and the more "inspirational" understanding in Revelation. This development can also be discerned in other parts

---

[29] W. Bauer, *Orthodoxy and Heresy in Earliest Christianity* (London: SCM, 1972), 83–84.

[30] A. Yarbro Collins, *Crisis and Catharsis: The Power of the Apocalypse* (Philadelphia: Fortress, 1984), 137.

of the New Testament. These tensions are not easily harmonized but they can best be explained as arising from a deliberate response by the prophet to defend the communities of believers, not only from false prophets/teachers, but also from community structures, which he did not consider to be divinely inspired.[31]

Secondly, John himself takes the role of the prophet. In the Hebrew Bible, the role of a prophet is frequently that of a seer or oracle engaged in radical critique of the present order and practices, which he often declares to be oppressive or unjust, and he envisions a new world of a better order and justice. The successful prophet proclaims a transformation of the old order and a vision of the new. If we apply this to the author of Revelation, we may find implications of the vision of a new heaven and a new earth, as well as of his critique of existing political and social order, for the structures of the community of believers. There is some evidence from other prophetic and apocalyptic writings that eschatological symbols were employed in order to undermine power structures and to articulate a critique of "institutionalizing" tendencies in ancient Judaism as well as in the early Christian movement. For example, the *Ascension of Isaiah*, a Christian apocalypse roughly contemporary with Revelation (most likely dating from the early decades of the second century C.E.), could be read as an explicit reply to other prophetic schools and to the institutionalization of church offices.[32] Elaborating on the

---

[31] According to G. Theissen, *A Theory of Primitive Christian Religion* (London: SCM, 1999), John's vision of the ideal community was given in order to challenge a more "institutionalized" understanding of the church: "[John the Prophet] completely ignores the offices in the church which already existed at that time ... His ideal community is egalitarian and charismatic internally, but externally he insists on a clear separation from this world" (p. 245).

[32] In *Ascen. Isa.* 3:21–31, the seer criticizes people "who love offices," predicting "many wicked elders and shepherds" (3:24) in the communities of believers, people who will act as false prophets, making "ineffective the prophecy of the prophets who were before me, and my visions also. ... in order that they may speak what bursts out of their hearts" (3:31). The seer reacts against a corrupt church in the hands of leaders who have ambitions for power, positions and certain offices; "there will be much respect of persons in those days, and lovers of the glory of this world" (3:25). The text lashes out against clerical officialdom, warning that "among the shepherds and the elders there will be great hatred towards one another" (3:29). The primary complaint against the office-holding elders is that "they will make ineffective the prophecy of the prophets" (3:31), and will not pay attention to visions. In contrast to the low estimation of the elders, the *Martyrdom and Ascencion of Isaiah* praises the ministry of "a circle of prophets" consisting of some forty prophets who had come together to exchange prophesies and mediate the principal prophet's ("Isaiah's") ecstatic visions to the people.

rhetorical and social setting of the author of the *Ascension of Isaiah*, Robert Hall argues that this writing stems from an early Christian prophetic school, which was at war with other similar early prophetic schools.[33] Hall proposes that the *Ascension of Isaiah,* by its stress of the descent and ascent of the Beloved, and by its belief in the possibility of heavenly ascents to see God (*Asc. Isa.* 6:1–17; 3:13–4:22), fought a battle against other prophetic schools, and even went beyond them by stressing the experience of heavenly trips to see God. Referring to the refutation of false elders, shepherds and prophets in *Asc. Isa.* 3:21–31 and recognizing that both works come from a similar milieu (Syria), Hall also argues that the *Ascension* opposes just the sort of prophetic episcopacy represented by Ignatius.[34]

This social setting addressed by the *Ascension of Isaiah* has some interesting parallels to that of 1–2 Timothy, where we, in addition to the critique of false elders and prophets, also find the regular presence of charismatic gifts and prophetic utterances in the community (mentioned in connection with office and leadership, 1 Tim 1:18; 4:14; 2 Tim. 1:6) and belief in the descent of a heavenly visitor (e.g., 1 Tim 2:4–5; 3:16). Like the author of the *Ascension*, John the Prophet not only plays down structures of hierarchical leadership in favor of the charismatic office of the prophet, but he also bases divine revelation, not primarily on the descent of Jesus, but on heavenly trips to see God (the ascent of the prophet). The *Ascension of Isaiah* seems to have been written in response to the ongoing routinization of charisma in the communities of believers in Syria or Palestine. In a similar vein, John the Prophet seems to have been engaged in a critical response to the continuous institutionalization of the Pauline churches in western Asia Minor.

---

[33] R. G. Hall, "The Ascension of Isaiah: Community Situation, Date, and Place in Early Christianity," *JBL* 109 (1990): 289–306, esp. 306.

[34] Ibid., 305–6.

The Bishop in Response to the Prophet

In turning to Ignatius the Bishop, we find a textual prototype that seems to be an extension and development of the prototype of the Pastor (1–2 Tim), in particular concerning structures of authority, legitimacy and leadership. Ignatius similarly stresses that the locus of authority lies in the ministry of the teacher, albeit "there is then only one teacher" (Ign. *Eph.* 15:1; cf. *Magn.* 9:1–2). Above all, the locus of authority and legitimacy is placed particularly in the office of the bishop and the presbytery, the guarantees of the authenticity and reliability of the true Jesus-tradition. Ignatius could thus be taken as evidence that the Pauline tradition in Ephesus continued well into the second century (cf. Ign. *Eph.* 12:2). However, there are some indications that Ignatius was also familiar with other Christ-believers in Ephesus. Ignatius had apparently a broad focus, as he writes "to the church, worthy of all felicitation, which is at Ephesus in Asia" (inscr.). He probably addressed "all" Christ-believers in Ephesus with the intention of uniting them under one bishop (cf. Ign. *Eph.* 5:2; 11:2). Even so, Ignatius seems to be aware of people who were not part of the community over which Bishop Onesimus presided, i.e., of some who were not "within the sanctuary" and who did "not join in the common assembly". These people are warned, "not to oppose the Bishop" (Ign. *Eph.* 5:2–3). The exhortation to come together in obedience and unity under the bishop and the presbytery is repeated in Ign. *Eph.* 13:1: "Seek, then, to come together more frequently . . . for when you come together frequently the powers of Satan are destroyed" (cf. also 20:2). The implication is that some people did not meet with the bishop or did not acknowledge his office.

Considering that Ignatius commends the Ephesians for their "good order in God, for you all live according to truth, and no heresy dwells among you" (Ign. *Eph.* 6:2; cf. 9:1), it seems that it was not primarily for doctrinal reasons that some "opposed the Bishop." Who then, were those who did "oppose the Bishop"? They were probably not found among those who were influenced by the prototype of the Pastor (1–2 Timothy), but among those who argued for other kinds of authority structures, e.g., those who were influenced by the prophetic-apocalyptic tradition of John the Prophet. As we previously observed, Revelation seems to play down the kind of leadership structures found in 1–2 Timothy in favor of the charismatic leadership of the prophets. We have no definite evidence that Ignatius knew the book of Revelation, but since he wrote about a decade later to some of the same communities (Ephesus, Philadelphia and Smyrna), it is likely that Ignatius would have been aware of the ideas articulated by the prophet. In addition to the two groups traditionally recognized as opponents in Ignatius' letters, docetists and judaizers, Ignatius also seems to have faced opposition from a third group, *viz.*, prophetic Christ-believers who resisted current attempts to impose episcopal order, and who accused Ignatius of false prophecy. Ignatius counters by insisting that the idea of the mono-episcopacy is not his own but "the Spirit preaching" (Ign. *Phld.* 7:1–2). He seems to be aware of that some of his addressees valued charismatic gifts, particularly the gift of prophecy, and he therefore wanted to articulate that he also had the inspiration of the Spirit. According to Christine Trevett, "Ignatius' prophecy had been tested and found wanting, for he was dealing with a group which knew all about prophecy."[35] In response, Ignatius is careful to point out that the threefold structure of bishop—presbyters—deacons is established by Jesus Christ, "in security according to his own will by his Holy Spirit" (Ign. *Phld.* inscr.). Apparently, Ignatius wants to stress that the divine power is operative in the threefold ministry of bishop, presbyters and deacons.

Following this proposal, we previously noticed that Robert Hall suggests that Ignatius opposed just the sort of prophetic group that produced the *Ascension of Isaiah*.[36] Like the prophetic groups in the *Ascension of Isaiah*, Ignatius' ideal community order reflects and represents the heavenly order and establishes the intimate connection between the heavenly and the earthly church, particularly as bishops, presbyters and deacons typify God, Christ and the apostles.[37] The prophetic school of the *Ascension of Isaiah*

---

[35] C. Trevett, "The Other Letters to the Churches in Asia: Apocalypse and Ignatius of Antioch," *JSNT* 37 (1989): 117–35, esp. 129.

[36] Hall, "Ascension of Isaiah," 304–6.

[37] E.g., Ign. *Eph.* 5:1–2; *Smyr.* 8–9; *Trall.* 2:2; 3:1; *Magn.* 6:1; 13:2.

combated false shepherds and elders who claimed authority from God and sought positions of power (*Asc. Isa.* 3:21–31). With this parallel in mind, it seems likely that Ignatius responded to a similar critique of the mono-episcopacy from a prophetic group, which maintained that the ongoing routinization of the charisma in the offices of the bishop and the presbytery demonstrated a lack of prophetic inspiration and a corruption of the church. Such a group may have been inspired by the activities of John the Prophet.

Thus, Ignatius the Bishop wants to show that he himself is familiar with prophecy and he anticipates that his readers would recognize the prophetic language he uses. Ignatius seems anxious to be acknowledged as a prophet, wanting to hold together the idea of monarchical episcopacy and prophetic ministry. The most likely setting is that in Ephesus he confronted a prophetic group of people, who did not acknowledge mono-episcopacy, and who caused tensions between prophetic-apocalyptic activities and episcopal structures, i.e., between prophetic and priestly ministry. Thus, although Ignatius may not have written in immediate response to John the Prophet, there is a great deal to suggest that he wrote in response to a kind of early Christian prophetic tradition similar to the one we meet in Revelation.

Concluding Remarks

At the end of the first century and the beginning of the second century C.E., there were several textual traditions and prototypes of authority and legitimacy that could be located to the geographical area of Ephesus. On the one hand, we have those prototypes argued in the "canonical" texts that survived from this area (1–2 Timothy, Revelation and 1–3 John) and, on the other hand, we have the prototypes advocated by those being labeled "deviant" by the authors of these texts. By the turn of the first century C.E. there was apparently explicit rivalry and struggle concerning the right to claim the authoritative Jesus-tradition and to spell out the legitimate identity of the true Christ-believer. I have argued that there are three

distinct ways of claiming authority and legitimacy of the Jesus-
tradition in the "canonical" texts: 1–2 Timothy (the Pastor) stress
the role of the hierarchical structures of leadership, particularly the
role of appointed teachers, Revelation (the Prophet) gives emphasis
to the role of prophetic ministry and prophets, while the Johannine
Letters (the Presbyter) stress the corporate role of the believing
community. The texts in focus give evidence of that there were no
uniform authority structures in the communities of the early Christ-
believers in Ephesus. As we have observed, there are certain internal
tensions between the ways our authors attempted to connect to the
"sacred tradition" and argued for an authoritative tradition. These
diverse prototypes of authority were all argued, in Bengt Holmberg's
terms, with "the proximity of the sacred" as the critical focal point.
In doing so, the Pastor stresses the importance of protecting the
tradition, the Prophet accentuates the need of visionary experience
and the Presbyter emphasizes the role of the community of the
Spirit. Since the texts addressed readers in Ephesus and were kept
and circulated early on in this geographical area, I find it likely that
the authors did not only articulate their convictions in response to
deviating groups and prototypes but also in response to each other.

The authors in question are thus all involved in the continuous
process of institutionalization in the early Christian communities
in western Asia Minor.[38] As Holmberg points out in his study, the
process of institutionalization was an "open" process. Even within
a limited geographical area such as the city region of Ephesus, this
process apparently did not lead to uniform results. Furthermore,
we must be careful not to think of this process as only a process
moving from charismatic authority to the institutionalization of
charismatic authority into certain offices and leadership structures,
e.g., as those we see in the Pastoral Letters. It was not simply a
matter of tensions between "charismatic" and "institutionalized"
structures or that some of the structures argued were more or

---

[38] Cf. D. E. Aune, "The Social Matrix of the Apocalypse of John," *BR* 26 (1981): 16–32: "If a
continuum of simple to complex polity were constructed, the Apocalypse and the Johannine Letters
should be placed at the lower end of the scale, the Pastorals and Ignatian corpus at the upper end and
the remaining [New Testament documents] documents scattered at various points in between" (p. 23).

less charismatic or institutionalized than the other. In fact, by stressing the role of the Spirit in the process of transmission of the tradition all of our texts give evidence of a "charismatic" understanding of the Jesus-tradition. However, they differ in the way they understand the role of the Spirit in issues relating to authority and legitimacy. While the Pastor connects the Spirit to the appointment of offices and the protection of the tradition, the Prophet stresses the connection between Spirit and prophecy, and the Presbyter the relation between Spirit and community.[39]

Holmberg concludes in his study that the institutionalization of authority in the Pauline region was not a late development but was well on its way in the middle of the fifties. My comparison between the Pastor, on the one hand, and the Presbyter and the Prophet, on the other, suggests that the "cumulative process of institutionalization" of leadership structures as those we may find in 1–2 Timothy is not necessarily a very late first century or early second century phenomenon, as commonly suggested. In fact, our analysis give some support of the thesis that both the Presbyter and the Prophet presume and respond to an "institutionalized" or "routinized" understanding of community and leadership structures as those we find in 1–2 Timothy. Accordingly, the different prototypes should not necessarily be seen as a development from charismatic authority to routinization of authority along a chronological scale but as different terminals of poles. As Holmberg points out, "the rather non-charismatic character of charismatic authority in Pauline churches should warn us from being too quick to postulate a theory of development that holds that every church must pass from a chaotic, 'charismatic' state

---

[39] For example, the Pastor, the Prophet and the Presbyter connect the role of the Spirit to the transmission and protection of the true Jesus-tradition (1 Tim 4:1; Rev 19:10; 1 John 4:1–3, 6; 5:6–8), and all of them presume the crucial role of the Spirit in their respective claim of authority. However, in spelling out the specific task of the Spirit we may discern different emphases: the Pastor connects the role of the Spirit to the authority of church offices, in particular the office of the teacher (1 Tim 4:14; 5:17–22; 2 Tim 1:6–14), the Prophet connects the role of the Spirit to divine utterances, prophetic visions and the office of the Prophet (Rev 1:4; 2:7, 11, 17, 29; 3:6, 13, 22; 14:13; 19:10; 22:17), whereas the Presbyter connects the role of the Spirit to the authority of the community (1 John 2:20–21, 27).

to an ordered, non-charismatic one."[40] In the texts that circulated in Ephesus by the end of the first century and the beginning of the second century, we find this most clearly expressed in the locus of authority argued by the author of 1–2 Timothy (the Pastor) and the author of the Johannine Letters (the Presbyter), a tension between office based authority structures and community based authority structures. Hence, we must allow for more fluid models.

In his ground-breaking study, Holmberg presented three ways of looking at the nature of authority in the primitive church: charismatic authority, institutionalized authority, and dialectical authority. Interestingly, we could find examples of all this in a limited geographical area like that of the city of Ephesus. In particular, we find a kind of dialectical authority in Ignatius' Letters. Addressing the citywide community of Christ-believers in the early second century, Ignatius seems clearly aware of other opinions concerning the monepiscopacy and he writes with the intention of bringing different traditions and groups in Ephesus together under the single monepiscopacy of Onesimus. Although Ignatius is a noticeable example of institutionalized authority, he clearly advocates the need of charismatic authority. From Ignatius' attempt to bring the tradition of the Pastor, the Prophet and the Presbyter together under the authority of *one* bishop, we may conclude that the institutionalization of the life of the Christian communities was increasingly guided by corporate traditions and authority structures. Accordingly, it became progressively less free to develop in a variety of directions.[41]

---

[40] Holmberg, *Paul and Power*, 161.

[41] With this article, I would like to thank Bengt Holmberg for the invitation to participate in the Early Christian Identity-project at Lund University 2003–2006. In particular, I would like to express my gratitude for his friendship and supervision of this rewarding project, throughout marked by Bengt's scholarly enthusiasm, judicious insights and great devotion. Being such a scholar, he is an example for us all.

The Letter to the Romans and Paul's Plural Identity: A Dialogical Self in Dialogue with Judaism and Christianity[1]

Gerd Theissen
University of Heidelberg

Introduction

Paul is said to be the second founder of Christianity. There is no doubt that he demarcated Christianity both from Judaism and from paganism, giving Christianity a proper theological and collective identity.[2] Even if he was not the only one in Early Christianity to take this step in establishing a new religion, he is certainly the best known. Paul defined Christian identity vis-à-vis Judaism in general theological antitheses, opposing Christ and Moses, works and faith, law and promise as well as God and idols. And he continued the traditional Jewish strict demarcation from the idolatry and morality of the pagan world. At the same time, he defined Christianity as an open community for both Jews and Gentiles, for free people and slaves, for men and women. This created congregations with an internal plurality of groups with different religious and cultural backgrounds. We may say that theologically he stressed Christianity's differences to Jews and

---

[1] This article is based on a main paper given at the European SBL Meeting at Vienna 25 July 2007. I dedicate the article to Bengt Holmberg, one of the pioneers of a socio-historical interpretation of Paul's mission and theology. My thanks go to Eric Weidner and Rosemary Selle for improving my English text.

[2] The term "collective identity" does not refer to a collective reality that is independent of human individuals, but to an imagined community. Many individuals share the same concept of themselves as members of a group. Cf. B. R. Anderson, *Imagined Communities* (London: Verso, 1983). For a discussion of the concept of personal and collective identity cf. J. Straub, "Identität," in *Handbuch der Kulturwissenschaften: Vol. 1: Grundlagen und Schlüsselbegriffe* (ed. F. Jaeger and B. Liebsch; Stuttgart: Metzler, 2004), 277–303.

Gentiles, while socially he underlined its universal openness for all.[3]

As far as we can see, this demarcation from Judaism and his universalistic tendencies were Paul's reaction to an attempt by Jewish Christian missionaries to (re-)integrate the new Christian congregations into Judaism by demanding circumcision and the observance of food laws as the two basic identity markers of Judaism.

Paul's first attempt to refuse such a reintegration was the epistle to the Galatians, a very polemical letter denouncing the acceptance of some requirements of the law as backsliding into paganism. His polemics in Galatians was specific and seemed to be limited to ritual norms—though a much deeper basic conflict is already looming in the background. His second attempt in the letter to the Romans was much more balanced and without crude polemic, but at the same time the conflict seems to be deeper. In this letter he criticises the law not only as a basis of ritual requirements, but as a general failure in ethical and soteriological terms. Paul is dealing with three soteriological theses here:[4]

In Rom 1–3:20 he opposes the idea that fulfilling the law is a way to salvation. He disputes the soteriological concept of *salvation by works* or *justification by the law*. His antithesis is: nobody is able to fulfil the law. All people are sinners.

In chapters 3:20–8:38 he develops the following thesis: since nobody is able to fulfil the law, faith is the only way to salvation. Here, Paul represents a soteriological concept of *salvation by faith* in spite of sinful deeds.

In chs. 9–11 he surpasses this thesis by a predestinarian view: even before human beings come into existence and are able to do anything good or bad, God has already elected or rejected them. From this Paul develops a third soteriological concept: *Salvation by election* or predestination independent of all human deeds.

To sum up, Paul is dealing with three soteriological concepts: salvation by works, by faith and by election. There is no doubt that

---

[3] Both tendencies combined are the best missionary strategy up to our days: a visible profile in theology and a social openness for all people.

[4] I take the idea of three soteriologies in the letter to the Romans from H. Räisänen, "Römer 9–11: Analyse eines geistigen Ringens," *ANRW* 25.4: 2891–929.

Paul is discussing these in a dialogue with Jews and Judaism. His concept of Judaism is certainly influenced by his Jewish identity and by his experience with Jews and Judaism. But what kind of Judaism does he have in mind? Is this Judaism uniform, particular or pluralistic?

Starting with the first possibility, Paul's general antithesis of Jewish works of law and Christian faith suggests that he had a uniform Judaism in mind. In the letter to the Romans he explicitly speaks of Jews only (juxtaposed to Greeks) without distinguishing different currents within Judaism. E. P. Sanders defined the religious structure of the uniform Judaism which Paul had in mind as "covenantal nomism."[5] Such a covenantal nomism does indeed combine elements of the three soteriological concepts we encounter in the letter to the Romans:

- Covenantal nomism presupposes *salvation by election* because God's election precedes his commandments; nobody enters the covenant without being elected.
- Covenantal nomism also comprises *salvation by faith* because Israel trusts in God to be merciful if Israel does not live up to his demands.
- Covenantal nomism does not at all exclude *salvation by works* insofar as works are necessary for staying within the covenant.

We may further ask: Does Paul still share this basic structure of Judaism of covenantal nomism? Does he only oppose Jewish exclusivism excluding Gentiles from salvation (J. G. D. Dunn)?[6] If that were the case there would not be a break with the basic structure of his Jewish faith. Or does the basic structure of Paul's Christian faith differ from covenantal nomism, replacing it by a new structure,

---

[5] E. P. Sanders, *Paul and Palestinian Judaism: A Comparison of Patterns of Religion* (London: SCM, 1977).

[6] J. D. G. Dunn, "The Justice of God: A Renewed Perspective on Justification by Faith," *JTS* 43 (1992): 1–22; idem, "Yet once more—'The Works of the Law,'" *JSNT* 46 (1992): 99–117.

e.g. participationist eschatology (E. P. Sanders)[7]? If that were the case Paul would indeed break with the structure of the Jewish religion. And we may further ask whether he represents Judaism in a fair or in a distorted way.

Let us now consider the second possibility, namely, that Paul had a particular Judaism in mind when he wrote his letters to the Galatians and to the Romans. In Phil 3:5 he admits to being a Pharisee and to being motivated by *zeal*. In Gal 1:14 he describes himself as a Jew who surpassed all his contemporaries regarding this *zeal*. He is quite aware that not all Jews are like him and therefore his Jewish faith was not representative for all Jews. Nevertheless, he attributes this zeal to Israel as a whole when he writes in Rom 10:2–3: "I testify that they have a *zeal* for God; but it is not enlightened. For, being ignorant of the righteousness that comes from God, and seeking to establish their own, they have not submitted to God's righteousness." Here, Paul seems to generalise the attitude of zeal, the characteristic feature of his personal Jewish piety, as if it were a feature of Judaism as a whole. However, it may be that he was so deeply embedded and absorbed in his particular Judaism that he could not even imagine other forms of Judaism.[8]

In this paper I want to develop the third possibility, namely, that Paul is dealing with a pluralistic Judaism and that he was living a pluralistic Jewish identity—comprising in himself the personalities of a Diaspora Jew, a Pharisaic Jew, a zealous Jew and, last but not least, a Christian Jew. My main thesis is: Paul had a pluralistic Judaism in mind when he wrote the letter to the Romans—and he himself was a pluralistic Jew who was familiar with different currents of Judaism, all of them leaving traces in his thoughts. Paul was a dialogical self with many persons.[9] But I want to combine

---

[7] Sanders, *Paul and Palestinian Judaism*.

[8] There is no doubt that Pharisaism was Paul's home within Judaism. Those who take Pharisaism to be the dominant current in Judaism locate Paul therefore in the midst of mainstream Judaism. Cf. the very instructive article by J. Frey, "Das Judentum des Paulus," in *Paulus Leben – Umwelt – Werk – Briefe* (ed. O. Wischmeyer; Tübingen: UTB, 2006), 5–43. But we must be aware that not all Pharisees shared the ideal of "zeal." As a zealous Jewish fundamentalist Paul certainly did not represent mainstream Judaism.

[9] Cf. H. H. M. Hermans and H. J. G. Kempen, *The Dialogical Self: Meaning and Movement* (San

this third possibility with the two other approaches. The line of my arguments will now be sketched out and then developed in depth.

Firstly, covenantal nomism does not cover all variants of Judaism. I prefer to characterise the whole of Judaism as an "ethical monotheism," covenantal nomism being the main current but not the only one. Judaism also comprises ethical legalism and predestinarian faith.

Secondly, through his biography Paul was familiar with different currents of contemporary Judaism. He started his life in the Diaspora and moved to Palestine, where he probably encountered different Jewish groups before he made his choice. Successively, he tried to live different forms of Judaism.

Thirdly, his acquaintance with different forms of Judaism explains why he is dealing with three contradictory soteriological concepts in the letter to the Romans: salvation by works, salvation by faith and salvation by election. Not only successively but simultaneously he lived in different Jewish traditions.

Fourthly, the historical situation and context of the letter explains this discussion with a pluralistic Judaism. It is not a modern anachronism to attribute a plural identity or a "dialogical self" to Paul. There are analogies in Paul's time. Paul himself is aware of pluralism being a part of his personality. But the situation of writing the letter to the Romans also explains this pluralism.

Ethical Monotheism

Although I think that the structure of covenantal nomism covers a large part of Judaism, I prefer to label Judaism as an "ethical monotheism."[10] This term encompasses a theist and an ethical

---

Diego: Academic Press, 1993); J. A. Belzen, "Culture, Religion and 'the Dialogical Self': Roots and Character of a Secular Cultural Psychology of Religion," *Archiv für Religionspsychologie und Seelenführung* 25 (2003): 7–24.

[10] According to B. Lang, "Israels Religionsgeschichte aus ethnologischer Sicht," *Anthropos* 101 (2006): 99–109, Israel's faith is an "ethical monotheism." This label represents an old tradition in biblical studies going back to the interpretation of biblical prophecy by liberal theologians in the 19th century.

element, with the theist element taking precedence. God's action always takes precedence over human re-action; the ethical element comes in second place. There are several advantages of the term "ethical monotheism" as opposed to "covenantal nomism."[11]

Firstly, the term "monotheism" includes all that Jews regarded as characteristic of their religion and is a better term for distinguishing it from Christianity, whose christological monotheism with its cultic worship of a second being beside God certainly called pure Jewish monotheism into question (L. Hurtado).[12]

Secondly, the monotheistic God is not simply the God who elects Israel but also the creator God of all people. One of the problems Paul is dealing with is the tension between the universal creator God and the particularity of Israel as well as between the universal God and his particular covenant.[13] This problem within Judaism was answered in emerging Christianity.

Thirdly, ethical norms comprise law, prophecy and wisdom. The term "covenantal nomism" only highlights the law (νόμος), but neglects wisdom and prophecy. It is true that the law is more than just ethics: the law comprises ritual norms. But the equal status of ritual norms and ethics in Judaism is no obstacle to emphasising the ethical implication of Judaism. On the contrary, Judaism interprets ethical action as worship, as action undertaken in the presence of God. This gives such action high status. The concept "ethical monotheism" therefore comprises the ritual aspect of Judaism, too.

Fourthly, the adjective "ethical" gives positive connotations to the often devalued "justification by works" or "salvation by deeds." Ethical action is relevant for salvation in Judaism. Ethics has an enhanced status. Jewish texts which underline the relevance of

---

[11] Covenantal nomism and monotheism form the basic axioms of Judaism, but there are also two basic tensions of Judaism indicated in two basic axioms: (1) the tension between theocentricity and anthropocentricity; (2) the tension between universalism and particularism, see G. Theissen, *The Religion of the Earliest Churches: Creating a Symbolic World* (Minneapolis: Fortress, 1999), 212–17.

[12] L. W. Hurtado, *One God, One Lord: Early Christian Devotion and Ancient Jewish Monotheism* (Philadelphia: Fortress, 1988); idem, *Lord Jesus Christ: Devotion to Jesus in Earliest Christianity* (Grand Rapids: Eerdmans, 2003).

[13] D. Boyarin, *A Radical Jew: Paul and the Politics of Identity* (Berkeley: University of California Press, 1994).

works for salvation are also texts which offer an opportunity to non-Jews. They do not belong to God's chosen people, but they perform good deeds. We need not redefine Judaism as a crypto-Protestant religion of grace in order to give it a fair treatment!

Ethical monotheism always contains a mixed causal attribution of salvation. There are three patterns of attribution:[14]

The first and most widespread pattern of attribution is *synergism* (that is characteristic for *covenantal nomism*). Salvation is created by a combination of God's election for entering the covenant and the consecutive obedience of human beings for staying in the covenant. Salvation is causally attributed to both God and humans. This is how Josephus characterises the Pharisees: "these ascribe all [προσάπτουσι πάντα] to fate and to God, and yet allow, that to act what is right, or the contrary, is principally in the power of men, although fate does cooperate in every action" (*B.J.* 2.162, cf. *A.J.* 13.172).

The second pattern of attribution is *belief in predestination*. Particularly among elitist groups in Judaism such as the Essenes we find the conviction that God elects for the purpose of obedience to the law. Thereby, God predestines for salvation. Salvation is created exclusively by God, i.e. it is primarily attributed to God. Josephus attributes this predestinarian conviction to the Essenes (*A.J.* 13.172).

The third pattern of attribution is *legalism (or salvation by works)*. Some groups on the margins of Judaism (like proselytes and God-fearers) believe that the human being enters the covenant by taking on God's commandments. Gentiles and Jews are subject to the same judgement according to their works. Ethical behaviour is thus relevant to salvation. Salvation is attributed primarily to the

---

[14] For applying attribution theory to the analysis of religion see B. Spilka, P. Shaver, and L. A. Kilpatrick, "A General Attribution Theory for the Psychology of Religion," *JSSR* 24 (1985): 1–20; B. Spilka, R. W. Hood, B. Hundsberger, and R. Gorsuch, *The Psychology of Religion: An Empirical Approach* (3d ed.; New York: Guilford Press, 2003).

human being (cf. *Second Enoch*,[15] *Apocalypse of Zephaniah*[16]). Josephus associates such a pattern of attribution with the Sadducees.

Paul was a Pharisee. In the (Pharisaic?) *Psalms of Solomon*[17] we find a synergistic pattern of attribution. Israel's election by God is irreversible: "For you did choose the seed of Abraham before all the nations, and did set thy name upon us, O Lord; and this shall be for ever" (*Pss. Sol.* 9:9). But earlier in the same psalm we find the words: "Our works are subject to our own choice and power, to do right and wrong in the works of our hands" (*Pss. Sol.* 9:4). Paul the Pharisee puts it like this: "I worked harder than any of them—though it was not I, but the grace of God that is with me" (1 Cor 15:10). His own work and the grace of God are juxtaposed.

These two factors, the theist and the ethical factor, may be emphasised within different strands of Judaism in different ways. According to Josephus, the Essenes stress the theist factor, the Sadducees the ethical factor. The predominant covenantal nomism prefers a moderate synergism and is represented by the Pharisees in Palestine. In spite of its different currents Judaism forms a unity, but a unity with variegated patterns of attribution with regard to salvation. At the margins of Judaism, there are other patterns than just the moderate synergism of covenantal nomism—but all of them are within the framework of an "ethical monotheism." And it is significant that in this respect there is no difference between Judaism and Christianity. In the Gospel of Matthew the ethical factor is stronger, in Paul's

---

[15] See R. J. Bauckham, "Apocalypses," in *Justification and Variegated Nomism: Vol 2: The Complexities of Second Temple Judaism* (ed. D. A. Carson, P. T. O'Brien, and M. A. Seifrid; Tübingen: Mohr Siebeck, 2001), 135–87, esp.151–6: *Second Enoch* is a testimony of "legalistic work-righteousness." C. Böttrich underlines the universalistic tendency of this text, see Böttrich, *Das slavische Henochbuch* (Gütersloh: Gütersloher Verlagshaus, 1995); idem, *Weltweisheit – Menschheitsethik – Urkult: Studien zum slavischen Henochbuch* (Tübingen: Mohr Siebeck, 1992).

[16] Bauckham, "Apocalypses," 156–60. In the *Apocalypse of Zephaniah* the righteous are included in the people of God by their righteousness.

[17] The *Psalms of Solomon* may be interpreted as representing a "covenantal nomism" with regard to Israel, but at the same time they represent a "legalism" with regard to the righteous within Israel. Cf. D. Falk, "Psalms and Prayers," in *Justification and Variegated Nomism: Vol.1: The Complexities of Second Temple Judaism* (ed. D. A. Carson, P. T. O'Brien and M. A. Seifrid; Tübingen: Mohr Siebeck, 2001), 35–56, esp. 35–51: Law is not the "means of gaining the status of righteousness." "Law is everywhere assumed, however, in the group-distinctiveness that pervades these psalms: 'we' are a law-keeping group and 'they' are a law-breaking group."

letters the theist factor is. Both factors, the human and the divine, are always present. It is not the soteriological pattern of attribution that makes the difference between Judaism and Christianity, but the transformation of ethical into christological monotheism.

Paul's Biography

If Judaism was pluralistic, this does not necessarily mean that Paul shared a pluralistic attitude. On the contrary, people with zeal, like Paul, reject pluralism. His persecution of a deviating minority in Judaism shows that he did not tolerate pluralism. It is possible that he was deeply embedded and absorbed in one current of Judaism without any empathy in other Jewish currents and without any understanding of other forms of Jewish piety. But the few dates of his biography suggest that he knew different forms of Judaism from experience and that all of them left their traces in his thoughts and life.[18] His persecution of the Christians is no counter-argument because he could not maintain his role as persecutor. He was converted from his former Jewish piety to a new Jewish-Christian piety. It is true that he affirms with regard to his Jewish past: "This one thing I do: forgetting what lies behind and straining forward to what lies ahead" (Phil 3:13). But this affirmation in a polemical situation must be balanced with the claim that God had set him apart before he was born (Gal 1:15). His life in Judaism had already been part of his life as God's messenger. He is aware of a continuity in his life in spite of his conversion. And there is no doubt that he also stresses the continuity between Judaism and Christianity and very often refers to Jewish traditions in a positive way.

Paul started his life in the Diaspora, where he must have been familiar with Jewish Diaspora mentality. There are many ideas

---

[18] On Paul's youth and development, see M. Hengel (in collaboration with Deines), "Der vorchristliche Paulus," in *Paulus und das antike Judentum* (ed. M. Hengel and U. Heckel; Tübingen: Mohr Siebeck, 1991), 177–293; K. Haacker, "Der Werdegang des Apostels Paulus: Biographische Daten und ihre theologische Relevanz," *ANRW* 26.2: 815–938; idem, *Paulus: Der Werdegang eines Apostels* (Stuttgart: Kath. Bibelwerk, 1997).

in his letters which can best be explained with a socialisation in a non-Jewish environment, above all his Greek language, traces of rhetorical traditions and some philosophical ideas such as the opposition of nature and law (Rom 2:12–16), the concept of the ἔσω ἄνθρωπος or inner nature (2 Cor 4:16; Rom 7:22), the popular concept of consciousness and liberty (1 Cor 10:29), and the topos of the unfree will (Gal 5:17; Rom 7:15, 23). He came from a family which must have cultivated its Jewish heritage because he is proud of being a Hebrew born of Hebrews (Phil 3:5). This includes knowledge of the Hebrew or the Aramaic language.

Paul moved to Palestine in order to study the law. As a "Hebrew" he had no linguistic problems with living and studying in Palestine. Moving to Palestine probably brought about a change in his religious attitudes. His statement in Phil 3 about being a Pharisee is often interpreted as referring to a pharisaic family and a pharisaic family tradition. But this is unlikely. We have no testimony of Pharisees in the Diaspora. And in Phil 3:4–5 Paul himself lists six personal characteristics, three of them referring to his origin and family. He is circumcised, he is a member of one of the tribes of Israel and he is a Hebrew born of Hebrews. These three characteristic features are ascribed to Paul; he did not achieve them by his decisions and deeds. But then there is a change in the list. The next three items are all introduced with the Greek κατά. They belong together. The list starts with κατὰ νόμον "as to the law", followed by κατὰ ζῆλος "as to zeal" and κατὰ δικαιοσύνην "as to righteousness." All of these characteristics are the result of his deeds. The standard expression κατὰ νόμον is generally opposed to κατὰ φύσιν in antiquity—an opposition Paul is familiar with according to Rom 2:12–16. If Paul is a Pharisee, being a Pharisee κατὰ νόμον cannot be his family heritage. Being a Pharisee is a result of his decision in the same way that his *zeal* and his *righteousness* are not inherited attitudes. Therefore, we may conclude that it was probably in Palestine that Paul first became a Pharisee. There had already been a development in his pre-Christian life. Possibly, his conversion to Christian faith was not his first religious transformation. So we notice at least three stages in his life: the beginnings as a Diaspora Jew, becoming a Pharisee (probably in Palestine), and conversion to Christian faith. Paul was familiar with at least three Jewish mentalities: the mentality of a Diaspora Jew, of a Palestine Pharisee and of a Jewish Christian.

But we may even distinguish more stages of his development. I assume that he did not only know the average Pharisaism, but also special currents within Pharisaism. In the biographical note in Gal 1:14 he says: "I advanced in Judaism beyond many among my people of the same age, for I was far more zealous for the traditions of my ancestors." The reference group in this comparison "the people of the same age" is not all Jews, but only those Jews who loved and studied the traditions of their ancestors, i.e. the Pharisees. Saying that he "advanced" beyond many of them suggests that he experienced at least two phases in his Pharisaic education. The verb προκόπτω, "to make progress," is a technical term (Epictetus, *Diatr.* 1.4). This προκόπτη may refer to joining the group of the Pharisees. But Paul himself characterises this progress as increase in *zeal*. We know that the ideal of zeal was especially marked and widespread in the "fourth philosophy" of Judas of Galilee. According to Josephus, this was a breakaway group from the Pharisees which was prepared to use coercion even against other Jews (*A.J.* 18:23–25). Judas of Galilee stood for an activist synergy: only if human beings work for their own liberty will God support them: "They also said that God would not otherwise be assisting to them, than upon their joining with one another in such councils as might be successful, and for their own advantage; and this especially if they would set about great exploits, and not grow weary in executing the same" (*A.J.* 18:5). The ideal of the Zealot is formulated here: active commitment to the law is the precondition for help from God. I assume that Paul became a Pharisee after his arrival in Palestine—but that within Pharisaism he joined some groups characterised by the ideal of *zeal*. This need not mean that he joined the groups that exercised violent resistance against the Romans. A general ideal of *zeal* was current among many Jews. Even politically moderate

Jews admired Pinehas because he killed Simri the apostate.[19]

To sum up, we may say that Paul was probably acquainted with different Jewish mentalities and different patterns of thought. His conversion to Christianity was the last step in a series of changes. At least we can assume a change between his Judaism in the Diaspora and in Palestine—and probably a further development from a general Pharisaism to a Pharisaic group cultivating *zeal.* In the end, he became a messianic Jew believing in Jesus Christ. He was not bound to only one form of Judaism. He was familiar with a pluralistic Judaism.

Three Soteriological Patterns in the Letter to the Romans

Romans is Paul's final reckoning with his relationship to Judaism and his former Jewish faith. Paul is not necessarily dealing with a uniform Judaism. On the contrary, he had personally experienced different forms of Judaism. Therefore, it is significant that he discusses in the letter to the Romans three types of soteriology which contradict each other. He deals with the three basic possibilities of "ethical monotheism" as distinguished above: salvation by work, by faith and by election. The three soteriological patterns may contain traces of his staggered religious biography. But I should underline that the order in which he treats the types of soteriology is logical in itself. In the first part of the letter Paul rejects *salvation by the law* (Rom 1:18–3:20). He shows the impossibility of *legalism.* Justification by works and salvation by the law is only theoretically conceivable for Jews and Gentiles (Rom 2:6–16). In reality it is impossible since everyone sins. To sin means both breaking the law *and* being proud of the law. This is why Paul can criticise the boasting of the law by a teacher of the law so sharply (2:17–24). Boasting is in

---

[19] L. H. Feldman, "The Portrayal of Pinehas by Philo, Pseudo-Philo and Josephus," *JQR* 92 (2002): 315–45. In Acts 23:12–22 we hear of an attempt by fanatic Jews to kill Paul, because he is an apostate. These Jews imitate Pinehas and share the ideal of zeal. But Paul's nephew betrays the plot to Paul and saves him. His action shows that Paul's family has contact to fanatic Jews. We may assume that Paul himself belonged to such zealotic circles. Their zeal means above all aggression against other Jews, not primarily against the Romans.

this case also a nomistic sin—breaking the law *plus* pretending to fulfil it *plus* being proud of the law as a guide to true life. In summary, the first part shows that all human beings, Jews as well as Gentiles, would be lost if there were no other form of soteriology. This becomes apparent in Rom 1:16–17 and 3:21–29.

The concept of *salvation by faith* in the second part of the letter (Rom 3:21–8:31) is an answer to the general doom of humanity. In these chapters Paul is modifying *covenantal nomism*. Entering the "covenant" with Abraham works by faith in justification alone (Rom 4), not by birth but by new birth (Rom 6:1–9). Entering the covenant is followed by ethical obedience which is only possible by means of inner transformation corresponding to a transformation of the whole world (Rom 6–8). Once again, sin also involves a wrong nomistic attitude: the sinful person is deceived by the law. It does not keep people in obedience (as in covenantal nomism) but leads them astray into disobedience (Rom 7:11). In these general statements on the law Paul reflects his personal experience as persecutor.[20] Motivated and deceived by the law, he once persecuted the Christians. This was a wrong way—it was not only wrong because he transgressed the law but on the contrary because he was motivated by zeal to fulfil it. The Spirit had to transform him into a new being and replace the law. He had to be transformed through the crucified and resurrected Christ. Thus, the law of the Spirit and of life must liberate the human being from the law of sin and death (Rom 8:2). But what about the non-Christian Jews, who live by the law and who do not believe in Jesus Christ? They would be lost if there were not a third kind of soteriology.

In the third part of the letter Paul develops the concept of *salvation by election*, his third type of soteriology (Rom 9–11). While justification is for those who have already acted sinfully, election is for those who do not even exist yet (Rom 9:11–12). This is why God can save people independently of their actions and their faith, even if they are enemies of the Gospel (Rom 11:28). Action on their part is excluded not only because it is sinful but also because it is in principle impossible. Therefore Paul says: no human being can bring anyone

---

[20] See R. Jewett, *Romans: A Commentary* (Minneapolis: Fortress, 2007), 440–73.

down from heaven or up from hell for the purpose of salvation (cf. Rom 10:6–7). In these chapters of Romans, God is so powerful and sovereign that he can even save his enemies, who do not believe. The salvation of all of Israel is presented in analogy with Paul's own conversion. Christ appeared to him, an enemy of the gospel, and won him for himself. In a similar way, at the approaching end of time Christ will appear to the Jews and win them for himself despite their hostility. All will be saved, just as Paul himself was saved. [21]

There is no doubt that the sequence of the three types of soteriology in the letter to the Romans is logical in itself. The deficiencies of one soteriological pattern lead to the next. But basically they contradict one another. If people are saved by works, faith in Jesus Christ's work of salvation is not necessary. If faith alone can save, those who do not believe have no chance of being saved. If election is the only basis of salvation before all works, this salvation is independent of faith and non-faith. Paul is full of contradictions, as H. Räisänen has shown.[22]

I think some of the contradictions can be explained by the fact that these three types of soteriology are in dialogue with the main currents of a pluralistic Judaism. In his letter Paul is reproducing tensions within Judaism. It is mostly in the first and the third part of his letter that we can recognise particular Jewish mentalities and groups.

When Paul rejects the idea of *salvation by works or justification by the law* in the first part (Rom 1:18–3:20), he does not construct a distorted Judaism which never existed. He is discussing an attitude which actually existed and can be located mostly in the Diaspora. The text is transparent for this "Sitz im Leben" of Jewish ethical legalism. Paul indeed leads our imagination to the Diaspora in these first chapters. He speaks of Jewish monotheism in contrast to pagan polytheism. He recognises that monotheism is one option among wise Gentiles but that they do not worship the one and only God (Rom 1:18–25).[23] Similarly, Josephus criticises Gentile philosophers.

---

[21] O. Hofius, "Das Evangelium und Israel: Erwägungen zu Römer 9–11," *ZTK* 83 (1986): 297–324, esp. 320: "Israel kommt auf die gleiche Weise zum Glauben wie Paulus selbst!"

[22] H. Räisänen, *Paul and the Law* (2nd ed.; Tübingen: Mohr Siebeck, 1987).

[23] The following topics refer to Gentiles as imagined environment in Rom 1:18–3:20: the *theologia naturalis* (1:18–20), polytheism (1:23–25), a hint to the cult of the emperors (1:23): the polemic against

Some of them knew the one and only God but they did not dare to oppose the polytheistic way of worship like Moses did (Josephus, *C. Ap.* 2:169). Furthermore, Paul underlines the moral consciousness of all people, both of Gentiles and Jews, and he criticises Jewish teachers who do not live up to their own teaching. He is afraid that such teachers will denigrate the image of Jews among Gentiles (Rom 2:12–24). There is no doubt that in Rom 1:18–3:20 Paul has Diaspora Judaism in mind and that he is arguing against an ethical legalism which was at home in this Diaspora. There, ethical action according to the law indeed had a high status through comparison and competition with non-Jews. In his apology of Judaism, Josephus presents it self-confidently as a religion of the law for Gentile readers.[24] Moses is a law-giver. Those who keep the law will be rewarded with life after death (Josephus, *C. Ap.* 2.182). It is therefore not a distortion of Judaism to call it a religion of the law. That is exactly what it considers itself to be, presenting itself for Gentiles as an ethical religion based on Mosaic law, and exceeding other religions in its humaneness (Josephus, *C. Ap.* 2.157–219). Here, Josephus does exactly what Paul calls "boasting". He is proud of the Jewish laws and feels superior to the Gentiles. We often find texts from the Diaspora expressing such an ethical legalism. I am thinking of the *Apocalypse of Zephaniah* and *Second Enoch* in particular. The aspect of election is not emphasised in Josephus' presentation for outsiders. Hence, one could counter that this is indeed intended merely for outsiders, adapting to the categories of the social environment. But to this we may respond that a group exists within its presentations of itself, and especially within the idealised presentations. Some Jews wanted to match the description they gave of themselves here. In competition with other non-Jewish groups they sought to be an

---

homosexuality (1:26–27), the *lex naturalis* of the Gentiles (2:12–16), a Jewish teacher provoking anti-Jewish feelings among Gentiles (2:17–24), the invisible circumcision that is also ascribed to Gentiles (2:25–29).

[24] Cf. P. Spilsbury, "Josephus," in *Justification and Variegated Nomism: Vol. 1: The Complexities of Second Temple Judaism* (ed. D. A. Carson, P. T. O'Brien, and M. A. Seifrid; Tübingen: Mohr Siebeck, 2001), 241–60. He speaks of a "patronal nomism": "people enjoy gratitude in the practice of their lives for the divine benefaction which is God's law" (p. 259).

ethical religion of the law and they were proud of what they were. In ethical consensus with their environment, they wanted to exceed and "over-fulfil" ethical norms according to the law. Paul rebuffs this mentality sharply. In his view Jews cannot surpass Gentiles with good works. All are sinners. Nobody can be saved by works.

Let us now look at the third type of soteriology, *salvation by election,* developed by Paul in Rom 9–11. Here, we may find the imagined "Sitz im Leben" of his thoughts as well. While the first three chapters in the letter to the Romans guide our imagination to the Diaspora, to Jews living among idolatrous Gentiles, in chs. 9–11 our imagination is led to Jews in Palestine living in a Jewish environment. Paul starts in ch. 9 by listing the privileges of Israel: the adoption, the glory, the covenants, the giving of the law, the worship and the promises, but above all the Messiah according to the flesh. Most of the privileges do not have a particular location—except the Messiah according to the flesh. His living place was Palestine. And indeed, Paul mentions Zion twice in the following chapters— both times referring to the Messiah. He localises the stone that will make people stumble in Zion (Rom 9:33 = Isa 28:16). The stone is the Messiah. And he announces a messianic salvation starting from Zion: "Out of Zion will come the Deliverer" (Rom 11:26 = Isa 59:20–21a). The Messiah will come from Jerusalem. In these three chapters Paul enters into an internal dialogue within Judaism. Ten times he uses the signification "Israel",[25] which he has never used before in the letter to the Romans, while he uses the signification "Jews" only twice (9:24; 10:12), even though it is preferred in the letter before (nine times). Israel is a self-designation of Jews, "Jews" is the designation which other people give to Jews. There can be no doubt that we are listening to an internal Jewish dialogue. According to Rom 10:2 the whole of Israel is motivated by zeal. Indeed it was in Palestine that Paul was grasped by zeal and that he persecuted Christians. The ideal of "zeal" includes a competition between various Jewish groups and pressure on other groups among the people. The statements about Israel imply a deep split between different

---

[25] Rom 9:6, 27 (twice), 31; 10:19, 21; 11:2, 7, 25, 26.

groups having Abraham as their ancestor: between the successors of Isaac and Ishmael, of Jacob and Esau, of the children of promise and the children of the flesh. When Paul refers back to Elijah, he relates to the Christians as a minority in Judaism that is comparable to the seven thousand Israelites who refused to worship Baal.

When Paul attributes zeal to all Israelites, he generalises his Jewish attitude of zeal in his pre-Christian days. Paul was indeed shaped by Palestinian Judaism that was zealously observing the law. He himself speaks of how "zeal" (ζῆλος) motivated him to persecute the Christian community (Gal 1:13–14; Phil 3:6). But now he confronts the synergetic activism of the ζῆλος ideal with faith in election and predestination that excludes all human activities. And he redefines "zeal" in a new manner. Representatives of the true *zeal* are not Jewish groups but Gentiles if they convert to Christianity. They may trigger the conversion of the unbelieving Jews. Therefore, he interprets his ministry for the Gentiles as a ministry "in order to make my own people jealous" (παραζηλόω, "making jealous," shares the root with ζῆλος) (Rom 11:11, 14). If Jews become Christians in this way it is not their own achievement, it is like "life from the dead" (Rom 11:15). Only God can resurrect the dead.

If Paul had an ethical Judaism in the Diaspora in mind in the first part of the letter, a Judaism competing with Gentiles, he has a zealous Judaism in Palestine in mind in the Israel part of this letter, Jewish groups competing with one another. He opposes the attitude of ethical legalism with the thesis that all human beings are sinners, and he opposes the Palestinian religiosity of zeal with the thesis that salvation is due to God alone, who has already elected people before their birth. It is not as clear-cut what kind of Judaism Paul has in mind in the central part of the letter (in chs. 4–8). But we may assume that he is dealing with mainstream Judaism, a moderate Pharisaic synergism of God's grace and human works, substituting this synergism by his paradox "synergism" of God's grace and human faith, which is not synergism in the strict sense because faith is not the condition to receive grace, but the way (or *modus*) grace works in human beings.

We may conclude: the letter to the Romans is the document of

Paul's dialogue with different strands in Judaism. But Paul does write his letter to a Christian congregation. He must be convinced that his dialogue with Judaism will be helpful in this dialogue with the Christian congregation at Rome. The basic problem of the Roman Christians was indeed their relationship with Judaism. A few years before (49 C.E.) conflicts between the adherents of Christ and other Jews had caused the banishment of Jewish Christians from Rome by a decree of the Emperor Claudius. Since then Gentile Christians had dominated in the new Christian congregation at Rome, the Jewish Christians who stayed there becoming a minority. Many of the so-called "weak" must belong to this Jewish Christian minority; they refused to eat meat or drink wine in order to reduce conflicts with other Jews by avoiding all contamination with pagan cult. Many of the "strong" belonged to the Gentile Christians. There was rivalry between the groups. Paul must have anticipated that the Roman congregation feared his arrival in Rome would increase these tensions, since he was an exponent of a liberal Gentile Christianity. Therefore he underlines that he will not endanger peace between these groups. When dealing with a pluralistic Judaism his thoughts are aimed at a pluralistic Christianity in Rome.

In the first part of his letter (Rom 1:18–3:20) Paul demonstrates that all are equal in respect to a negative status. All are sinners. Jews have no advantage in comparison with Gentiles even if they are proud of the Law and of circumcision. Gentiles also have a natural law and their hearts can be circumcised. All boasting by Jews is therefore an illusion (Rom 2:17–24). Paul radicalises a Jewish ethical legalism in order to establish a fundamental equality of all human beings, of Greeks and Jews. If they are judged according to their deeds nobody is superior. Paul is targeting above all a Jewish feeling of superiority.

In the third part of the letter to the Romans (9:1–11:36) Paul demonstrates a different equality. He does not struggle with a claim of being superior by moral activity, but by God's predestinarian activity. Such a predestinarian faith excludes moral superiority: Before people are born or have done anything good or bad they are loved or hated (Rom 9:11–13). But Paul radicalises this sovereignty of God: God is also free to revise his decision. God says to those who have not been beloved that they are beloved (Hos 2:25 = Rom 9:25). Because God is able to revise his election nobody should be proud. Boasting is excluded: "But if some of the branches were broken off, and you, a wild olive shoot, were grafted in their place to share the rich root of the olive tree, do not boast over the branches. If you do boast, remember that it is not you that support the root, but the root that supports you" (Rom 11:17–18). In Rom 9–11 Paul radicalises a Jewish predestinarian faith in order to establish a fundamental equality of all human beings, of Gentiles and Jews. Gentiles have been disobedient, but are now obedient. Jews are now disobedient, but God has the sovereignty to save them. Both groups are equal: "For God has imprisoned all in disobedience so that he may be merciful to all" (Rom 11:32). Here, Paul is targeting above all a Gentile Christian feeling of superiority.

Paul deals in his letter to the Romans with a plural Jewish identity and this gives him the sensitivity to deal also with a Christian plurality. He offers to the different groups in the Roman congregation a new collective identity based on faith in Christ, and he refuses all boasting based on an alleged superiority of human moral activity or based on the superiority of God's predestinarian activity.[26]

To sum up: the three soteriological concepts in the letter to the Romans, salvation by works, by faith and by election, are developed in dialogue with different strands in Judaism. The impossibility of salvation by works is an answer to the ethical legalism found in the Diaspora. The exclusive salvation by faith is an answer to the synergism of covenantal nomism, the attitude of mainstream Judaism. Salvation by election opposes the ideal of zealous competition especially in Palestinian Judaism. Through his biography Paul was acquainted with these three forms of Judaism. He represents a plural Jewish identity. His dialogue with this Jewish plurality is at the same time a dialogue with a plurality of Christian groups in Rome. And

---

[26] I agree with P. F. Esler, *Conflict and Identity in Romans: The Social Setting of Paul's Letter* (Minneapolis: Fortress, 2003).

his dialogue with these groups is formed by an internal dialogue with his own past. In the letter a "dialogical self" of Paul is speaking.

The Historical Plausibility of Pluralistic Thinking and Plural Identity

When developing these ideas on a plural Jewish identity of Paul in dialogue with a pluralistic Judaism I wondered again and again whether my results were anachronistic. Paul seems to be too modern a person. Pluralism is a modern situation. Personalities with a plural identity are much more at home in our society than in antiquity. Therefore we must ask: is it historically plausible that Paul did not only experience several stages diachronically in his development but that he was a person with a plural identity in a synchronic sense?

Paul is not the only one with such a plural identity. Josephus, too, is familiar with different forms of Judaism through his biography. In his vita he writes: "At about the age of sixteen I determined to gain personal experience of the several sects into which our nation is divided. These, as I have frequently mentioned, are three in number— the first that of the Pharisees, the second that of the Sadducees, and the third that of the Essenes. I thought that after a thorough investigation, I should be in a position to select the best" (Josephus, *Vita* 10). His writing shows that he indeed has a good understanding of the different currents of Judaism. He calls himself a Pharisee, but is able to describe this group very unfavourably.[27] He charges the fourth philosophy (with pharisaic origin) with being responsible for the Jewish war. But the last speech of Eleazar at Masada bears witness to an admiration of the defender of Masada (Josephus, *B.J.* 7.320– 389). It is true that he sympathises most with the Essenes and their life (*B.J.* 2.119–161). At all events, he is full of empathy for different Jewish groups. And at the same time he understands the Romans, having experienced a deep break in his life when he was captured as

---

[27] Cf. S. Mason, *Flavius Josephus on the Pharisees: A Compositional Critical Study* (Leiden: Brill, 1991).

a Jewish general in Galilee. Josephus also had a Jewish and a Roman identity, an identity as a Pharisee and rebellious Jew. Josephus and Paul may be exceptions in their time but both show the possibility of a pluralistic life and a plural identity as early as in those times.

However, the best witness is Paul himself. He describes himself in a way which shows a plural identity. In 1 Cor 9:19–23 he expresses an awareness of a multifaced and plurimorph life:

> For though I am free with respect to all,
> I have made myself a slave to all,
> so that I might win more of them.
> To the Jews I became as a Jew,
> in order to win Jews.
> To those under the law I became as one under the law
> (though I myself am not under the law)
> so that I might win those under the law.
> To those outside the law
> I became as one outside the law
> (though I am not free from God's law but am under Christ's law).
> To the weak I became weak,
> so that I might win the weak.
> I have become all things to all people,
> that I might by all means save some.
> I do it all for the sake of the gospel,
> so that I may share in its blessings.

In antiquity a person with such an ability to adapt to other persons and to assimilate to them would be called a flatterer with dubious motifs.[28] But Paul is no flatterer. He is a person with the ability to activate at least four internal personalities according to his own words: a Jew under the law, a Gentile outside the law, a strong man with religious liberty and a weak man with religious anxiety. If Paul himself describes his person in such a plural way, we do not distort his person in an anachronistic way

---

[28] P. Marshall, *Enmity in Corinth: Social Conventions in Paul's Relations with the Corinthians* (Tübingen: Mohr Siebeck, 1987), esp. ch. 3: "The Character of the Flatterer."

by doing so. He experienced more than one transformation in his biography. All the personalities of the past survive in him.

To sum up: Paul writes the letter to the Romans knowing that his life is endangered when he travels to Jerusalem. He is writing his theological testament. In this testament we are listening to a dialogical self, writing to the Roman congregation in dialogue with a pluralistic Judaism and Christianity. Through his biography Paul was acquainted with a pluralistic Judaism. He himself had a plural Jewish identity. And as a Christian missionary he had founded many congregations of Christians with different cultural heritage. In his testament he does justice to a multifaced Judaism and Christianity in his time and in his personality—as far as limited persons can do justice to the religious and cultural world they are living in.

Misquoting Manuscripts?
The Orthodox Corruption
of Scripture Revisited

Tommy Wasserman
Norwegian School of Leadership and Theology

Introduction

The view that doctrinal alterations have affected the text of the New Testament was first proposed by Johann Jakob Wettstein, who formulated the following canon of criticism: "Of two variant readings that which seems more orthodox is not immediately to be preferred."[1] On the other hand, the well-known Cambridge scholar F. J. A. Hort rejected this principle and stated that, "[E]ven among the numerous unquestionably spurious readings of the New Testament there are no signs of deliberate falsification of the text for dogmatic purposes."[2] More recently, several other scholars have treated the subject.[3] In my own research I have encountered some peculiar readings in the textual transmission of the Greek New Testament, some of which most likely reflect the theology, not of the New

---

[1] "Inter duas variantes lectiones ea, quae magis orthodoxa videtur, non est protinus alteri praeferenda" (J. J. Wettstein, ed., *Novum Testamentum Graecum* [2 vols.; Amsterdam: Dommerian, 1751–1752], 2:864). The canon in question was formulated already in 1730 in his *Prolegomena ad Novi Testamenti graeci editionem accuratissimam*, which was later republished along with the critical edition.

[2] B. F. Westcott and F. J. A. Hort, *The New Testament in the Original Greek* (2 vols.; London: Macmillan, 1881–1882), 1:282.

[3] K. W. Clark, "Textual Criticism and Doctrine," *Studia Paulina: In Honorem Johannis de Zwaan* (Haarlem: De Erven F. Bohn, 1953), 52–65; idem, "The Theological Relevance of Textual Variation in Current Criticism of the Greek New Testament," *JBL* 85 (1966): 1–16; E. J. Epp, *The Theological Tendency of Codex Bezae Cantabrigiensis in Acts* (Cambridge: Cambridge University Press, 1966); H. Eshbaugh, "Textual Variants and Theology: A Study of the Galatian Text of Papyrus 46," *JSNT* 3 (1979): 60–72; M. C. Parsons, "A Christological Tendency in P75," *JBL* 105 (1986): 463–79; P. M. Head, "Christology and Textual Transmission: Reverential Alterations in the Synoptic Gospels," *NovT* 35 (1993): 105–29.

Testament authors, but of the scribes who changed the text.[4] The fact that scribes did alter the text of the New Testament for dogmatic reasons seems to be accepted by most scholars today.[5] However, there are considerably different opinions as to the degree to which this phenomenon has affected the textual transmission. Many scholars, including myself, see this phenomenon as relatively limited, either to certain MSS (e.g., $\mathfrak{P}^{72}$ or codex Bezae) or to some isolated passages.[6]

On the other hand, the well-respected New Testament scholar and textual critic Bart Ehrman has proposed that significant parts of the New Testament text have been corrupted by Christian scribes for dogmatic reasons. Ehrman presented his challenging thesis in the monograph *The Orthodox Corruption of Scripture*, and more recently in the popularized version, *Misquoting Jesus*, which appeared on the New York Times bestseller list during a long period in 2005–2006.[7]

Ehrman takes as a starting point Walter Bauer's view of the Christian movement during the first centuries. In Bauer's classic study, *Rechtgläubigkeit und Ketzerei im ältesten Christentum*, Bauer rejected the traditional view that early Christianity was made up of a single "orthodox" type of Christianity, from which various heretical minorities developed.[8] Instead a number of divergent groups with

---

[4] T. Wasserman, "Papyrus 72 and the Bodmer Miscellaneous Codex," *NTS* 51 (2005): 137–54; idem, *The Epistle of Jude: Its Text and Transmission* (Stockholm: Almqvist & Wiksell International, 2006), 30–72; idem, "Theological Creativity and Scribal Solutions in Jude," in *Textual Variation: Theological and Social Tendencies* (ed. H. A. G. Houghton and D. C. Parker; Piscataway: Gorgias Press, 2008), 75–83.

[5] As an example of contemporary application of this pinciple, see B. M. Metzger, *A Textual Commentary on the Greek New Testament* (2d ed.; Stuttgart: Deutsche Bibelgesellschaft, 1994). The committee frequently refers to possible theological motivation behind textual variants.

[6] Cf. Head, "Christology," 129: "The 'improvements' examined here have not affected the general reliability of the transmission of the text in any significant matter."

[7] B. D. Ehrman, *The Orthodox Corruption of Scripture: The Effect of Early Christological Controversies on the Text of the New Testament* (Oxford: Oxford University Press, 1993); idem, *Misquoting Jesus: The Story of Who Changed the Bible and Why* (San Francisco: Harper, 2005). More recently Ehrman was followed by his student, W. C. Kannaday, *Apologetic Discourse and the Scribal Tradition Evidence of the Influence of Apologetic Interests on the Text of the Canonical Gospels* (Leiden: Brill, 2004). When this essay was completed, a second edition of Ehrman's *The Orthodox Corruption of Scripture* was published (Oxford University Press, 2011). However, the new edition remained virtually unchanged apart from an additional survey on the work done in textual criticism since the first edition.

[8] W. Bauer, *Rechtgläubigkeit und Ketzerei im ältesten Christentum* (Tübingen: Mohr Siebeck, 1907).

competing ideas and practices appeared very early on, none of which was in majority. Bengt Holmberg has aptly called Bauer's model of early Christianity a scenario of "centerless multiplicity," i.e., "a movement characterized by great variety and no obvious center that defines the whole."[9] According to Bauer, the "proto-orthodox" Christian group gained dominion in the third century and eventually succeeded to marginalize other groups. Hence, what was later stamped as "heresy" could in some regions be earlier forms of Christianities that were pushed back. Bauer's view of the early Christian movement has become influential among scholars of early Christianity, especially in the recent decades ever since the English translation of his work appeared in 1971.[10] Holmberg explains this success with the fact that Bauer's refutal of previous historical models has fit well into the emerging post-modern climate.[11] On the other hand, Bauer's thesis has received severe critique, ever since the publication of his work.[12]

Building on Bauer's work, Ehrman places the scribes of the New Testament within this historical framework and calls them "the orthodox corruptors of scripture."[13] He suggests that the diversification of groups within early Christianity with their distinct social structures, beliefs and practices corresponds to the spectrum of individuals who copied the manuscripts. Early on, the text of the New Testament was affected by scribes who, according to their theological persuasion, made conscious changes in the documents they reproduced, making them *say* what they were already thought

---

[9] B. Holmberg, "Understanding the First Hundred Years of Christian Identity," in *Exploring Early Christian Identity* (ed. B. Holmberg; Tübingen: Mohr Siebeck, 2008), 1–32, esp. 10. In his critique of Bauer's view, Holmberg poses a resulting question that remains unanswered, *viz.* how and when this alleged explosion from a movement with a one-person origin into a plethora of wildly divergent Christ-believing groups took place (ibid., 12–13).

[10] W. Bauer, *Orthodoxy and Heterodoxy in Earliest Christianity* (trans. R. A. Kraft and G. Krodel; Philadelphia: Fortress, 1971).

[11] Ibid., 11.

[12] The most detailed critical analysis, which sums up previous critiques, is offered by T. A. Robinson, *The Bauer Thesis Examined: The Geography of Heresy in the Early Christian Church* (Lewiston: Mellen, 1988). For a more recent critique and further references, see Holmberg, *Understanding Christian Identity*, 10–16.

[13] Ehrman, *Orthodox Corruption*, 274.

to *mean*. Hence, the orthodox gained control, not only over the church and its doctrines, but over the sacred text itself. Nevertheless, it is still possible for the modern critic to detect the various changes that have crept into the textual tradition. Hence, Ehrman presents an impressive number of examples of "orthodox corruption" affected by early Christological controversies. He groups them under four main headings:

> Anti-Adoptionistic Corruptions of Scripture
> Anti-Separationist Corruptions of Scripture
> Anti-Docetic Corruptions of Scripture
> Anti-Patripassianist Corruptions of Scripture[14]

Space does not permit me to go through all of Ehrman's examples in a systematic fashion. In the following I will therefore restrict myself to a selection of passages treated by Ehrman in one of the largest chapters of his monograph, those passages that, according to his claims, reflect anti-adoptionistic corruption. Nevertheless, I believe that the result of this survey, based on a relatively large number of passages is quite representative. I will demonstrate that Ehrman's interpretation of the textual evidence in these passages is seriously defective. I should emphasize that my aim is not to prove that the New Testament textual tradition is unaffected by "orthodox corruption," although I think this factor plays a minor role. Instead I attempt to prove that, on a closer inspection, many of Ehrman's examples do not apply to the issue at all, and that often there are other, more plausibe explanations for the textual variation.

Anti-Adoptionistic Corruption

Under various subheadings in the chapter entitled "Anti-Adoptionistic Corruptions of Scripture," Ehrman treats passages that he thinks scribes changed in order to avoid the notions that Jesus

---

[14] Ibid., ix.

had a human father, or that he came into existence at his birth, or that he was adopted to be the Son of God at his baptism. Conversely, he attempts to demonstrate how the scribes changed other passages in order to emphasize Jesus' divinity, his pre-existence and the fact that his mother was a virgin.[15] In this chapter, however, Ehrman also cites examples of what he views as adoptionistic corruption, similarly reflecting the battle between various early Christian groups over the sacred text. As I refer to Ehrman's examples of orthodox corruption in selected passages, I will indicate the alternative reading(s) in each passage, one of which is identified by Ehrman as the primary reading. Occasionally, however, I have omitted some poorly attested variant readings since they do not affect the discussion. For convenience sake, I will not specify all the textual witnesses that support the printed text of NA[27] in a given passage, unless Ehrman claims that it contains an adoptionistic/anti-adoptionistic corruption.

1. Jesus the Unique Son of God—
The Orthodox Affirmation of the Virgin Birth

Since the battle against the adoptionists centered on the doctrine of the virgin birth, Ehrman identifies several examples of orthodox corruption in the birth narratives in the first two chapters of Matthew and Luke.

Luke 2:22
adoptionistic corruption: ἀνήγαγον οἱ γονεῖς τὸ παιδίον Ἰησοῦν (X Θ^mg 4 50 64 273 1071 GrNy)

alternative reading: ἀνήγαγον αὐτόν (NA[27])

Luke 2:27
anti-adoptionistic corruption: omit τοὺς γονεῖς (245 1347 1510 2643)

alternative reading: τοὺς γονεῖς (NA[27])

---

[15] Ibid., 47–118.

Luke 2:33
anti-adoptionistic corruption: (ὁ) Ἰωσὴφ καὶ ἡ μήτηρ (A Δ Θ Ψ *f*¹³
28 33 180 565 579 700 892 1006 1010 1241 1292 1342 1424 1505
𝔐 a aur b β c e f ff² l q r¹ vg^mss sy^p.h.pal mss bo^pt eth^TH)

alternative readings: ὁ πατὴρ αὐτοῦ καὶ ἡ μήτηρ (NA²⁷) / Ἰωσὴφ ὁ
πατὴρ αὐτοῦ καὶ ἡ μήτηρ (157 [eth^pp])

Luke 2:41
anti-adoptionistic corruption: ὅ τε Ἰωσὴφ καὶ ἡ Μαριά(μ) (1012 a b
g¹ l r¹) / "Joseph and Mary, his mother (c ff²) / "His kinfolk" (sy^s.p)

alternative reading: οἱ γονεῖς αὐτοῦ (NA²⁷)

Luke 2:42
adoptionistic corruption: ἀνέβησαν οἱ γονεῖς αὐτοῦ ἔχοντες αὐτόν
(D d e [c r¹])

alternative readings: ἀναβάντων αὐτῶν (Γ Δ Θ *f*¹·¹³ 28 157 245 700
1424 𝔐) / ἀναβαινόντων αὐτῶν (NA²⁷)

Luke 2:43
anti-adoptionistic corruption: Ἰωσὴφ καὶ ἡ μήτηρ αὐτοῦ (A C K N Γ
Δ Ψ 0130 *f*¹³ 28 245 565 1071 1424 𝔐 b c f ff² l q r¹ sy^p.h bo^pt)

alternative reading: οἱ γονεῖς αὐτοῦ (NA²⁷)

Because of the similar nature of the variants in these six passages in
Luke 2:22–43 where we find abundant references to Jesus' parents,
I will comment on them together. I have collected the evidence in
various witnesses, in order to demonstrate first of all that no witness
has been consistently changed throughout this stretch of text, and,
secondly, that some witnesses actually display opposite tendencies,
which, again, disproves the notion of theologically motivated
corruption.

	Luke 2:22	Luke 2:27	Luke 2:33
ℵ	ἀνήγαγον αὐτόν	τοὺς γονεῖς	ὁ πατὴρ αὐτοῦ καὶ ἡ μήτηρ
A	ἀνήγαγον αὐτόν	τοὺς γονεῖς	ὁ Ἰωσὴφ καὶ ἡ μήτηρ (anti-adoptionistic)
B	ἀνήγαγον αὐτόν	τοὺς γονεῖς	ὁ πατὴρ αὐτοῦ καὶ ἡ μήτηρ
D	ἀνήγαγον αὐτόν	τοὺς γονεῖς	ὁ πατὴρ αὐτοῦ καὶ ἡ μήτηρ
X	ἀνήγαγον οἱ γονεῖς τὸ παιδίον Ἰησοῦν (adoptionistic)	τοὺς γονεῖς	ὁ Ἰωσὴφ καὶ ἡ μήτηρ (anti-adoptionistic)
245	ἀνήγαγον αὐτόν	omit (anti-adoptionistic)	ὁ Ἰωσὴφ καὶ ἡ μήτηρ (anti-adoptionistic)
c	(ἀνήγαγον αὐτόν)	(τοὺς γονεῖς)	(ὁ Ἰωσὴφ καὶ ἡ μήτηρ) (anti-adoptionistic)

	Luke 2:41	Luke 2:42	Luke 2:43
ℵ	οἱ γονεῖς αὐτοῦ	ἀναβαινόντων αὐτῶν	οἱ γονεῖς αὐτοῦ
A	οἱ γονεῖς αὐτοῦ	ἀναβαινόντων αὐτῶν	Ἰωσὴφ καὶ ἡ μήτηρ αὐτοῦ (anti-adoptionistic)
B	οἱ γονεῖς αὐτοῦ	ἀναβαινόντων αὐτῶν	οἱ γονεῖς αὐτοῦ
D	οἱ γονεῖς αὐτοῦ	ἀνέβησαν οἱ γονεῖς αὐτοῦ ἔχοντες αὐτόν (adoptionistic)	οἱ γονεῖς αὐτοῦ
X	οἱ γονεῖς αὐτοῦ	ἀναβάντων αὐτῶν	Ἰωσὴφ καὶ ἡ μήτηρ αὐτοῦ (anti-adoptionistic)
245	οἱ γονεῖς αὐτοῦ	ἀναβάντων αὐτῶν	Ἰωσὴφ καὶ ἡ μήτηρ αὐτοῦ (anti-adoptionistic)
c	(Ἰωσὴφ καὶ Μαριὰμ ἡ μήτηρ αὐτοῦ) (anti-adoptionistic)	(ἀνέβησαν οἱ γονεῖς αὐτοῦ ἔχοντες αὐτόν) (adoptionistic)	(Ἰωσὴφ καὶ ἡ μήτηρ αὐτοῦ) (anti-adoptionistic)

What we see from these examples is that no witness display a consistent pattern of what could be perceived as adoptionistic/anti-adoptionistic changes.[16] On the contrary, some witnesses display opposite tendencies. In the case of Luke 2:42 Ehrman actually identifies adoptionistic corruption only in codex Bezae (D d), not in the other witnesses that share the reading (c e r¹), because here he chooses to relate it to the context and the previous reading in v. 41 (he apparently overlooked the fact that the Old Latin MS e shares both readings with Bezae):

> It should be noted that precisely the opposite pattern of corruption occurs in the text of Luke 2:42, where codex Bezae and several Old Latin manuscripts change the text from "they went up to the feast" to read "his parents went up to the feast, taking him with them." In this case the change [presumably in c and r¹] was apparently not made for theological but for literary reasons, simply to clarify what is assumed in the rest of the pericope, that Jesus accompanied his parents on the occasion. Because the scribe of codex Bezae [and e] reads γονεῖς in verse 41, there can be no question of his importing an adoptionistic tone to the account.[17]

So when Ehrman detects an "opposite pattern of corruption" in Bezae he apparently attempts to downplay one of the tendencies and look for an alternative explanation ("literary reasons"). If Ehrman would have followed this line of reasoning consistently, being sensitive to the attestation in all six examples combined, he might have drawn very different conclusions. A question that remains concerning this particular passage in Luke 2:42 is whether it is defensible to assume that the reading reflects an adoptionistic corruption only in Bezae (and presumably e), and not in the other Old Latin witnesses to the same reading. Does Ehrman think that the reading arose independently, and was theologically motivated in just these two "Western" witnesses?

---

[16] Ehrman admits, apparently with some surprise, that the changes "occur randomly in various textual witnesses, not at all with the kind of consistency one might expect" (ibid., 56). Nevertheless, he fails to realize the negative implication of this observation for his thesis.

[17] Ibid., 103 n. 59.

An alternative explanation is to see the variation mainly as a question of stylistic preference on the part of the scribes. In light of the inconsistent pattern of variation, I do not think the affirmation of the Virgin birth is the issue here. The scribes knew fully that Joseph was not Jesus' biological father—there was no need to prove it by altering the text.

John 6:42
anti-adoptionistic corruption: ὅτι οὖτός ἐστιν Ἰησοῦς ὁ υἱὸς Ἰωσήφ (𝔓⁶⁶* saᵐˢ)

alternative reading: οὐχ οὖτός ἐστιν Ἰησοῦς ὁ υἱὸς Ἰωσήφ (NA²⁷)

Ehrman suggests that the readings of 𝔓⁶⁶ in vv. 42 and 44 reflect a clear attempt to heighten the irony of the unbelievers' misperception that Jesus was the son of Joseph and Mary.[18] He explains that the reading in v. 42 cannot be an adoptionistic change because of the corresponding change in v. 44 (see below). He fails to consider that the latter change is absent from the Sahidic manuscript (is the change in v. 42 adoptionistic in that witness then?), while it is found in a few other MSS that conversely lack this change in v. 42. In my opinion, this is another instance when Ehrman overinterprets textual minutiae. He should have indicated that the former reading is in fact corrected in 𝔓⁶⁶, possibly by the original scribe. In any case, I agree with Royse who regards the original reading in v. 42 with ὅτι as a harmonization to the context: "the scribe simply continued ελεγον with οτι (see vs. 42b: λεγει οτι), a construction that indeeds [sic] makes perfectly good sense." [19]

John 6:44
anti-adoptionistic corruption: ὁ πατήρ μου (𝔓⁶⁶ G 157)

alternative reading: ὁ πατήρ (NA²⁷)

---

[18] Ibid., 57.

[19] See J. Royse, *Scribal Habits in Early Greek New Testament Papyri* (Leiden: Brill, 2008), 453 n. 305. Elsewhere, Royse points out that Ehrman finds doctrinal significance in other readings of 𝔓⁶⁶* but he always cites them simply as "𝔓⁶⁶" (p. 459).

Ehrman connects this textual variant to the preceding one in v. 42. Since the scribe of 𝔓⁶⁶ displays a tendency to omit short words rather than to add them, Ehrman suggests that μου is a deliberate addition in order to "reinforce the 'correct' [orthodox] construal of the passage."[20] He does not discuss the presence of the pronoun in other witnesses. Ehrman's case, combining the corrected reading of 𝔓⁶⁶ in v. 42 with its reading here, is built on sand. A more natural explanation for the change in all witnesses is to regard it as a harmonization to the common phrase in the Gospel of John, ὁ πατήρ μου (5:17; 6:32; 8:54; 10:29; 14:23; 15:1, 8).[21] Moreover, Gordon Fee has in fact identified a tendency in 𝔓⁶⁶ to add the possessive pronoun after πατήρ and μαθηταί when looking at differences from the basic tradition of 𝔓⁶⁶.[22]

2. The Orthodox Opposition to an Adopted Jesus

Ehrman proposes that the scribes changed some places in order to avoid the notion that Jesus was adopted to be the Son of God at his baptism.[23]

Luke 3:22
anti-adoptionistic corruption: σὺ εἶ ὁ υἱός μου ὁ ἀγαπητός, ἐν σοὶ εὐδόκησα (𝔓⁴ ℵ A B L W Δ Θ Ψ 070 0233ᵛⁱᵈ f¹·¹³ 33 579 1241 𝔐 aur e q vg syʰ sa boᵖᵗ armᵐˢˢ eth geo slav Aug NA²⁷)

alternative reading: υἱός μου εἶ σύ, ἐγὼ σήμερον γεγέννηκά σε (D a [b] c d ff² l r¹ Ju, Cl [add ἀγαπητός after σύ] Meth Eus Ambst Hil Tyc Latin mssᵃᶜᶜ· ᵗᵒ ᴬᵘᵍ Cyr)

This is the first instance that Ehrman identifies a corruption in the text adopted in NA²⁷. The passage is also one of four highlighted

---

[20] Ehrman, *Orthodox Corruption*, 57, 104 n. 64. It should be noted that 𝔓⁶⁶ has a very slight tendency to omit more often than to add (Royse, *Scribal Habits*, 544).

[21] The phrase occurs four times in the other Gospels (Matt 15:3; 16:17; 18:35; Luke 5:17). According to Royse, harmonization is frequent in 𝔓⁶⁶ and there are several examples of singular readings reflecting harmonization to Johannine usage, e.g., 17:3, 6, 24; 18:37; 21:6b (ibid., 542–4). Royse does not treat this particular passage since it is not a singular reading.

[22] G. D. Fee, *Papyrus Bodmer II (𝔓⁶⁶): Its Textual Relationships and Scribal Characteristics* (Salt Lake City: University of Utah Press, 1968), 51.

[23] Ehrman, *Orthodox Corruption*, 61–62.

examples of anti-adoptionistic corruption that receive extensive treatment under separate headings (Mark 1:1; Luke 3:22; John 1:18; 1 Tim 3:16).[24] Ehrman rightly points out that the external attestation of the second reading in Luke 3:22, which he thinks is original, has been discounted too easily in some treatments.[25] The reading is indeed well attested in the early period. In my opinion, however, Ehrman exaggerates the weight of the evidence in favor of it.

First, he states that among sources of the second and third centuries, it is virtually the only reading to be found, and "except for the third-century manuscript 𝔓[4], there is no certain attestation of the other reading [adopted in NA[27]], the reading of our later manuscripts, in this early period."[26] In fact, the most recent research on 𝔓[4] suggests that it belongs in the second century.[27] Moreover, Clement of Alexandria attests to a conflated reading (including ἀγαπητός), so it is clear that both readings are very early. Furthermore, Ehrman does not mention the important remark by Augustine that the most ancient Greek MSS do not attest to the second reading.[28]

His appeal to sources like the *Gospel according to the Hebrews*, the *Didascalia*, and the *Gospel according to the Ebionites* is

---

[24] Because of the limited space I will only treat three of these passages (Luke 3:22; John 1:18; 1 Tim 3:16). An examination of Mark 1:1 will be published elsewhere. It suffices to say that new textual evidence has come to light since the publication of Ehrman's monograph that strengthens the possibility of an accidental omission of the phrase "Son of God" (υἱοῦ θεοῦ) in Mark 1:1, interpreted by Ehrman as a deliberate anti-adoptionistic omission (*Orthodox Corruption*, 75). In addition to the evidence presented by Ehrman, the following Byzantine MSS omit the phrase: 530 582* 820* 1021 1436 1692 2430 2533 *l*2211 (K. Aland and B. Aland, eds., *Text und Textwert der griechischen Handschriften des Neuen Testaments. IV.1: Die Synoptischen Evangelien: Das Markusevangelium* [2 vols.; Berlin: de Gruyter, 1998], 2:2). Hence, Ehrman's statement that an accidental omission is "rendered yet more difficult by the circumstance that the same error, so far as our evidence suggests, was not made by later scribes of the Byzantine tradition" is now obsolete (*Orthodox Corruption*, 73).

[25] Ibid., 62.

[26] Ibid. Cf. idem, *Lost Christianities: The Battles for Scripture and Faiths We Never Knew*. (Oxford: Oxford University Press, 2003), 222: "In the oldest surviving witnesses to Luke's Gospel, however, the voice instead quotes the words of Psalms 2:7."

[27] For the latest discussion, see S. D. Charlesworth, "T. C. Skeat, P64+67 and P4, and the Problem of Fibre Orientation in Codicological Reconstruction," *NTS* 53 (2007): 582–604.

[28] Ehrman is clearly aware of the passage in *Cons.* 2.14 since he refers to it in order to demonstrate that Augustine knew both readings (*Orthodox Corruption*, 107 n. 92), but he omits the crucial remark about the MSS that were available to Augustine: "*Illud uero quod nonnulli codices habent secundum Lucam, hoc illa uoce sonuisse quod in Psalmo scriptum est: Filius meus es tu, ego hodie genui te: quamquam in antiquioribus codicibus Graecis non inueniri perhibeatur . . .* " (CSEL 43:132).

questionable, since we do not know exactly which source or sources they depend on. It is likely that some traits of these accounts derive from an apocryphal source. The most significant trace is found already in Justin, who says that after Jesus had gone into the water "a fire was kindled in the Jordan" (*Dial.* 88). The *Gospel of the Ebionites* apparently knew the same tradition (here it stands in direct conjunction with the words from Ps 2:7; see *Pan.* 30.8.7), as did probably the *Diatessaron* and several later writers.[29] Interestingly, the tradition is also attested in some "Western" witnesses to the Matthean account of the baptism in Matt 3:15.[30]

Ehrman thinks there can be little doubt that Justin refers to the text of Luke, since he states that the Holy Spirit descended upon Jesus in the "form" (εἴδει) of a dove, the word being unique to Luke. I maintain, however, that Justin or someone else before him has harmonized several sources to include synoptic as well as apocryphal elements.[31] The particular passage in *Dial.* 88 is introduced with the words, καὶ ἐλθόντος τοῦ Ἰησοῦ ἐπὶ τὸν Ἰορδάνην (Luke does not mention that the baptism took place at the Jordan). Justin refers to the occasion in *Dial.* 103 too, and there it is mentioned in direct connection with the temptation that follow in Matthew and Mark (not Luke).

Ehrman's reference to Origen is directly misleading, since there is nothing in the context that suggests that Origen is citing Luke 3:22 in *Comm. Jo.* 1.32.[32] On the contrary, one gets the impression that Origen is citing Ps 2:7. Hence, what can be safely said of all these sources, apart from the MSS, is that they all witness to the early tradition that connected the words of Ps 2:7 (LXX), υἱός μου εἶ σύ ἐγὼ σήμερον γεγέννηκά σε, with Jesus (cf. Acts 13:33; Heb 1:5; 5:5), and at least four sources connect the words to Jesus' baptism (*Gos. Heb., Gos. Eb.,* Justin, Clement, and most

---

[29] Cf. Metzger, *Textual Commentary*, 8–9.

[30] Between Matt 3:15 and 16 the Latin codices Vercellensis (a) and Sangermanensis (g¹) add: *et cum baptizaretur Iesus* (om. *Iesus* a) *lumen magnum fulgebat* (*lumen ingens circumfulsit* a) *de aqua, ita ut timerent omnes qui erant* (*advenerant* a).

[31] Justin is cited in support of the reading in NA²⁷ and UBS⁴ but the attestation must, nevertheless, be critically evaluated.

[32] Ehrman erroneously refers to *Comm. Jo.* 1.29, see *Orthodox Corruption*, 107 n. 91.

probably the *Didascalia*), and may be dependent on Luke 3:22.

As for transcriptional probabilities, Ehrman points out that both readings can be viewed as scribal harmonizations, either to Mark 1:11 or to Ps 2:7. However, he finds it more likely that a scribe will harmonize a Gospel text to another parallell in the Gospels than to a passage in the Old Testament. In my opinion, it is important in this case, where harmonization can go in both directions, to pay attention to Hort's famous dictum, "knowledge of documents should precede final judgment on readings."[33] The second reading is attested chiefly by "Western" witnesses. Significantly, harmonization, including the expansion of Old Testament quotations, is a hallmark of the "Western" text, whereas it occurs rarely among Alexandrian witnesses.[34] In fact, when we turn to Acts 13:33, where the same words from Psalm 2:7 are cited, Bezae and some other witnesses add Ps 2:8! Another hallmark of the Western text, besides harmonizing, is the introduction of material about Jesus from extra-canonical sources.[35]

Ehrman is correct in pointing out that the second reading could be doctrinally offensive to later scribes. On the other hand, the argument can be turned around: the harmonization to Ps 2:7 in some witnesses may ultimately derive from an apocryphal source (from adoptionistic circles), in which the story was modified to include the full citation of Ps 2:7.[36] As in Matt 3:15, this extra-canonical source affected some corners of the New Testament textual tradition.

1 John 5:18

anti-adoptionistic corruption A: ἡ γέννησις τοῦ Θεοῦ (1127 1505 1852 2138 latt syʰ bo)

alternative reading: ὁ γεννηθεὶς ἐκ τοῦ θεοῦ (NA²⁷)

---

[33] Westcott and Hort, *The New Testament*, 1:31.

[34] G. Zuntz, *The Text of the Epistles: A Disquisition upon the Corpus Paulinum* (London: Oxford University Press, 1953), 171–2.

[35] D. C. Parker, *Codex Bezae: An Early Christian Manuscript and Its Text* (Cambridge: Cambridge University Press, 1992), 279.

[36] Cf. the further development in the accounts of *Gos. Eb.* and *Gos. Heb.* that the Spirit entered into Jesus, or came to rest in him.

anti-adoptionistic corruption B: τηρεῖ ἑαυτόν (‭א‬ Aᶜ P Ψ 5 6 33 81 322 323 436 442 468 1243 1739 1881 𝔐 Did Or PsOec)

alternative reading: τηρεῖ αὐτόν (NA²⁷)

Ehrman identifies two readings as orthodox corruptions: first, the replacement of the participle γεννηθείς with the noun γέννησις and, secondly, the replacement of the personal pronoun αὐτόν with the reflexive pronoun ἑαυτόν.[37] Ehrman thinks ὁ γεννηθείς refers to Christ, and that the two variant readings represent attempts to avoid this adoptionistic interpretation. The UBS committee, on the other hand, thinks that both variants arose, not because of theological considerations, but because of an "ambiguity of reference intended by the words ὁ γεννηθεὶς ἐκ τοῦ θεοῦ," which prompted scribes to clarify the meaning.[38]

First, it should be noted that the two "corruptions" are in fact interrelated; the Greek and Latin MSS that attest to ἡ γέννησις naturally also will attest to αὐτόν, "The birth from God keeps him" (the reflexive pronoun, "himself," would not make sense). Ehrman rightly rejects this reading, but he then should also discount the attestation of these witnesses in the latter variation-unit, which he does not.[39] In fact, the only significant witnesses that remain in support for the text that Ehrman thinks is original, αὐτόν, are A* and B². However, both the original scribes of Alexandrinus and Vaticanus actually wrote AYTON without breathing and accent and could therefore have intended both αὐτόν and αὑτόν (=ἑαυτόν).[40] Moreover, even the personal pronoun can actually be understood

---

[37] Ehrman, *Orthodox Corruption*, 70. (Ehrman wrongly indicates the masculine article in the first reading.)

[38] Metzger, *Textual Commentary*, 650.

39 "Thus . . . one can conclude that the personal pronoun, as attested in manuscripts A* B and a range of other Greek and versional witnesses, must be original" (*Orthodox Corruption*, 71).

[40] Cf. the UBS⁴ apparatus. In 1 John 5:10, the ECM has correctly noted that the original scribes of Alexandrinus and Vaticanus who copied AYTΩ can suppport either the personal or the reflexive pronoun. I have proposed to the editors that this be noted in 5:18 too. In several places a later scribe of Vaticanus has added a rough breathing (e.g., Mark 5:26 and Jude 16) indirectly supporting the reflexive pronouns (these examples are not noted in NA²⁷).

in the reflexive sense in the first place (cf. Luke 23:13; Acts 8; Heb 5:3; Rev 8:6; 18:7). In light of the very slim support, it is reasonable that the new Editio Critica Maior (ECM) has abandoned the reading previously printed in NA²⁷, i.e., the same reading that Ehrman thinks is original.[41] The UBS committee apparently did not realize how weak the support was for this variant, partly because they, like Ehrman, did not consider how it relates to the previous variation unit.

Further, Ehrman thinks Johannine style supports ὁ γεννηθεὶς . . . τηρεῖ αὐτόν, since γεννάω is always in the perfect passive when designating believers in 1 John (eight times).[42] However, the aorist passive is actually used to refer to believers in John's Gospel (e.g., 1:13). Moreover, γεννάω never designates Christ elsewhere in 1 John.[43] The aorist may have been used here for stylistic reasons (to avoid repetition). Finally, the passage in 1 John 3:3 offers a good parallell to the use of a verb with reflexive pronoun referring to the believer's sanctification. Hence, we arrive at the following translation of this passage as it stands in the *ECM*: "We know that everyone who is born of God does not sin, but the one who has been born of God keeps himself."

3. Jesus, Son of God before His Baptism

Since the adoptionists connected Jesus' sonship to his baptism, Ehrman identifies several references to Jesus as the Son of God before the time of his baptism that reflect textual corruption.

Matthew 1:18
anti-adoptionistic corruption: ἡ γέννησις οὕτως ἦν (L *f*¹³ 33 𝔐 Ir Or)

---

[41] The reflexive pronoun will be adopted in Nestle-Aland 28th edition (which will include all changes to the critical text adopted in the ECM).

[42] Ehrman indicates nine times but one occurance in 1 John 5:1 (which is in the aorist) cannot be counted since it does not refer to the believer.

[43] There is an occurance in John 18:37, ἐγὼ εἰς τοῦτο γεγέννημαι (perfect passive), but, significantly, without textual variation. In any case, one would have expected ἐκεῖνος here in 1 John 5:18, as in 2:6; 3:3, 5, 7, 16; 4:17.

alternative reading: ἡ γένεσις οὕτως ἦν (NA²⁷)

Both γένεσις and γέννησις can mean "birth," but, as Ehrman points out, the former noun can also denote "creation," "beginning," and "origination," and therefore he thinks that scribes replaced it in order to avoid the notion that this was the moment in which Jesus Christ came into being.[44] He does not think this was a "simple slipup" due to the orthographic and phonetic similarity of the nouns, since both readings are widely attested. However, if we look at the passage in Luke 1:14, where the angel announces the birth of John the Baptist to Zechariah, we find the same variation between the two synonyms in the MSS. In that case Ehrmann apparently thinks that later scribes harmonized the noun to the verb γεννάω used in the preceding verse.[45] But this could well have happened here in Matthew too, since the verb γεννάω features even more prominently in this context, both in the previous genealogy and in the following account of Jesus' birth. The fact that Matthew uses γένεσις in a somewhat different sense in v. 1 ("origin"), may also have led to the preference of the synonym γέννησις on the part of the scribes.[46]

Luke 2:43
anti-adoptionistic corruption: "The boy, the Lord Jesus" (sy^pal)

alternative reading: Ἰησοῦς ὁ παῖς (NA²⁷)

Apparently, the Palestinian Syriac identifies the twelve-year-old Jesus as "the Lord" (ὁ κύριος) at this point.[47] Ehrman regards this as another example of anti-adoptionistic corruption reflecting an exalted view of Jesus prior to his baptism.[48] He is apparently

---

[44] Ehrman, *Orthodox Corruption*, 76.

[45] Ibid., 111 n. 146.

[46] Cf. Metzger, *Textual Commentary*, 7.

[47] The reading is found in all three lectionary witnesses to the Palestinian Syriac in slightly different forms. See A. L. Smith and M. D. Gibson, *The Palestinian Syriac Lectionary of the Gospels, Re-Edited from Two Sinai MSS. and from P. de Lagarde's Edition of the Evangeliarium Hierosolymitanum* (London: K. Paul, Trench, Trubner & Co., 1899), 259.

[48] Ehrman, *Orthodox Corruption*, 75.

unfamiliar with the character of the version, and its limitations in representing the Greek *Vorlage,* from which it was translated.[49] One of the curious features of the Syriac versions in general is that they occasionally render (ὁ) Ἰησοῦς with *maran* ("our Lord").[50] In fact, in the Palestinian Syriac version (ὁ) Ἰησοῦς is almost invariably rendered by *mare Isus*, "the Lord Jesus", corresponding to Syriac ecclesiastical idiom![51] Hence, this reading has absolutely nothing to do with anti-adoptionistic corruption. Instead, such an ascription rather reflects Ehrman's deficient methodology, disregarding the particular context and nature of individual variant readings.

4. Jesus the Divine: The Orthodox Opposition to a Low Christology

Ehrman suggests that the most common kind of anti-adoptionistic corruption in the New Testament involve "the orthodox denial that Jesus was a 'mere man'."[52] He thinks these corruptions move in two directions: either they heighten Jesus' divine character, or they minimize his human limitations.

John 1:18
anti-adoptionistic corruption: μονογενὴς θεός (𝔓⁶⁶ ℵ* B C* L *pc* syʰᵐᵍ geo² Orᵖᵗ Did Cyrᵖᵗ NA²⁷) / ὁ μονογενὴς θεός (𝔓⁷⁵ ℵ¹ 33 bo Clᵖᵗ Clᵉˣ ᵀʰᵈᵖᵗ Orᵖᵗ Eusᵖᵗ GrNy Eph)

alternative readings: ὁ μονογενὴς υἱός (A C³ Wˢ Θ Ψ *f*¹·¹³ 𝔐 a aur b c e f ff² vg syᶜ·ʰ·ᵖᵃˡ arm eth geo¹ slav Irˡᵃᵗ ᵖᵗ Clᵖᵗ Clᵉˣ ᵀʰᵈᵖᵗ Hipp Orˡᵃᵗ ᵖᵗ Eusᵖᵗ Ath Basᵖᵗ Chr Cyrᵖᵗ Thret Tert Ambst Hilᵖᵗ Ambrᵖᵗ Hier Aug) /

---

[49] See S. P. Brock, "Limitations of Syriac in Representing Greek," in *The Early Versions of the New Testament* (ed. B. M. Metzger; Oxford: Clarendon Press, 1977), 83–98.

[50] F. C. Burkitt, *Evangelion da-Mepharreshe* (2 vols.; Cambridge: Cambridge University Press, 1904), 2:97–9.

[51] Brock, "Limitations," 87. Cf. the comment to Rom 3:26 in Metzger, *Textual Commentary*, 449. It is unfortunate that the IGNTP apparatus cites the Palestinian Syriac version in support of κύριος in Luke 2:43, since it apparently has the potential of misleading users to draw wrong conclusions of what was in the Greek *Vorlage*.

[52] Ehrman, *Orthodox Corruption*, 77.

μονογενὴς υἱὸς θεοῦ (q Ir^(lat pt) Ambr^(pt vid)) / ὁ μονογενής (vg^(ms))

The reading θεός, with or without the article, has strong support by the best witnesses. On the other hand, the attestation is mainly limited to Alexandrian witnesses, whereas the main rival reading υἱός is more widely attested. Ehrman prefers the latter reading on the basis of internal evidence. Firstly, it conforms with Johannine usage; μονογενής and υἱός are used in conjunction in John 3:16, 18 and 1 John 4:9; and, secondly, μονογενὴς θεός is "virtually impossible to understand within a Johannine context."[53] Ehrman suggests that the reading with θεός may reflect a harmonization to the context where θεός occurs some seven times, υἱός never. Under all circumstances, he thinks there was a theological motivation to do so: "The variant was created to support a high Christology in the face of widespread claims... that Christ was not God but merely a man, adopted by God."[54] One may well question whether it is at all possible to detect an anti-adoptionistic motivation behind a harmonization within a context where the Logos is understood to be God right at the outset (v. 1).

Ehrman goes on to state that the sense of the reading μονογενὴς θεός is impossible, suggesting that Jesus is the *unique* God, since in John, the Father is also God. At the same time, he rejects the alternative interpretation of the adjective μονογενής as substantival, standing in apposition with θεός, "(the) unique one, God," since he thinks that the use of an adjective as a substantive, when it precedes a noun of the same gender, number and case, is impossible: "No Greek reader would construe such a construction as a string of substantives, and no Greek writer would create such an inconcinnity."[55] Apparently, Ehrman is wrong. Daniel Wallace has cited a number of examples of such a construction just from the New Testament (Luke 14:13; 18:11; John 6:70; Acts 2:5; Rom 1:30; Gal 3:9; Eph 2:20; 1 Tim 1:9; 1 Pet 1:1; 2 Pet 2:5).[56] Admittedly, this construction is syntactically

---

[53] Ibid., 79.

[54] Ibid., 82.

[55] Ibid., 81.

[56] D. B. Wallace, "The Gospel according to Bart: A Review Article of *Misquoting Jesus* by Bart Ehrman," *JETS* 49 (2006): 327–49, esp. 345.

difficult, but, at the same time, that fact in itself speaks in favor of its originality (*lectio difficilior potior*). It should also be noted that μονογενής is used as a substantive four verses earlier in John 1:14.[57]

Furthermore, the variation between μονογενὴς θεός and ὁ μονογενὴς θεός is, in my opinion, signficant for the overall evaluation of the passage. The only comment Ehrman offers in this regard is that "if external support is considered decisive, the article is probably to be preferred" because "𝔓⁷⁵ is generally understood to be the strongest" and "𝔓⁶⁶, which supports the shorter text, is notoriously unreliable when it comes to articles and other short words."[58] It is true that 𝔓⁶⁶ (like 𝔓⁷⁵) shows a tendency to omit articles,[59] but in this case the reading of 𝔓⁶⁶ is shared by other prominent Alexandrian manuscript witnesses (ℵ* B C* L), so there is a strong reason to believe that there was no article in the exemplar. The anarthrous use of θεός is more primitive, and, as the UBS committee observes, "There is no reason why the article should have been deleted, and when υἱός supplanted supplanted θεός it would certainly have been added."[60] Hence, the reading μονογενὴς θεός best explains the rival readings ὁ μονογενὴς θεός and ὁ μονογενὴς υἱός. The latter reading may reflect scribal harmonization to the Johannine collocation μονογενὴς υἱός (John 3:16, 18; 1 John 4:9). In any case, it seems difficult to detect an anti-adoptionistic motivation on the part of the scribes in a passage that already reflects a high Christology, regardless of what textual decision we make.

1 Tim 3:16

anti-adoptionistic corruption: θεὸς ἐφανερώθη ἐν σαρκί (ℵᶜ Aᶜ C² D² Ψ 1739 1881 𝔐 vgᵐˢ GrNy Chr Thret)

---

[57] Wallace points out that the substantival function of μονογενής in patristic authors was commonplace (ibid., 346). See *PGL*, s.v. μονογενής B 7.

[58] Ehrman, *Orthodox Corruption*, 80, 112 n. 163.

[59] Royse's study of the papyrus witnesses demonstrates that among the 109 significant singulars (not counting the corrections), 𝔓⁶⁶ is found to add the article on one occasion and omit it six times, whereas 𝔓⁷⁵ adds the article six times and omits it fourteen times. See Royse, *Scribal Habits*, 507, 511, esp. n. 588 (𝔓⁶⁶); 660, 662 (𝔓⁷⁵).

[60] Metzger, *Textual Commentary*, 169.

alternative readings: ὃς ἐφανερώθη ἐν σαρκί (NA²⁷) / ὃ ἐφανερώθη ἐν σαρκί (D* lat Hil Ambst Pel Aug Qu)

There is little doubt that the reading ὃς ἐφανερώθη ἐν σαρκί is to be preferred. Witnesses that read the pronoun in the neuter (bringing it in conformity with the antecedent μυστήριον) indirectly support ὅς. As for the reading θεός, it is quite likely that it first arose due to the confusion of OC with the *nomen sacrum,* Θ͞C. Ehrman, however, remarks that the corrections in four uncials show that the change was not an accident; "it did not creep into the tradition unawares."[61] Here I think it is important to make a distinction between the *origin* of a reading, and its subsequent *transmission.* I agree with Ehrman insofar as these corrections show that subsequent changes to θεός in some MSS were not done by accident; the scribes/correctors knew the reading θεός and preferred it, either because it supplied a subject for the six following verbs, or because of dogmatic reasons (or both).[62] This does not exclude the possibility that the variant initially arose by accident.

Ehrman goes on to state that the change must have been early, at least from the third century given its widespread attestation in the fourth century.[63] In an accompanying footnote he explains that of all witnesses of either variant, only Origen antedates the fourth century. (Origen's witness is apparently found in a fourth-century Latin translation of his works, reflecting ὅς). First, it should be pointed out that the earliest attestation of θεός in an actual Greek MS is the correction in C (04), probably dating from the sixth century, whereas the earliest attestation of ὅς is in ℵ* (01) dating from ca. 350 C.E.[64] Furthermore, attestations of θεός in patristic writers are not found until the last third of the fourth century (Gregory

---

[61] Ibid., 78.

[62] Cf. Metzger, *Textual Commentary,* 574.

[63] Ehrman, *Orthodox Corruption,* 78.

[64] Some scholars have proposed that codex Alexandrinus reads Θ͞C, but this is not generally accepted. See F. H. A. Scrivener, *A Plain Introduction to the Criticism of the New Testament for the Use of Biblical Students* (ed. E. Miller; 2 vols; 4th ed.; London: Deigton, 1894), 2:391–2. Codex B (03) does not preserve 1 Tim.

of Nyssa, Apollinaris, John Chrysostom)—half a century after the Council of Nicaea.[65] This silence during the first phases of the Christological and Trinitarian controversies is strange, since the reading, if it existed in the third century or earlier, would indeed have been very attractive to use as prime evidence for Jesus' divinity.

5. Christ as Divine: The Exchange of Predicates

Ehrman points out that it was common for proto-orthodox Christians of the second and third centuries to "exchange predicates" in which attributes and activities of God were predicated of Christ, and vice versa, as reflected in writers like Ignatius, Melito and Tertullian. On the other hand, he points out that they were "cautious not to identify Christ and God in such a way as to eliminate any distinctions between them."[66] Correspondingly, he suggests that this "balancing act" is reflected in textual changes in the MSS.

1 Cor 10:5
anti-adoptionistic corruption: εὐδόκησεν, κατεστρώθησαν γὰρ ἐν τῇ ἐρήμῳ (81 *pc*)

alternative reading: εὐδόκησεν ὁ θεός, κατεστρώθησαν γὰρ ἐν τῇ ἐρήμῳ (NA[27])

The passage in 1 Cor 10 contains a Christian interpretation of the account of Israel's experience in the wilderness. The words ὁ θεός are omitted in codex 81 (and a few other MSS), so that the subject of the verb εὐδόκησεν is ὁ Χριστός from v. 4; "He (Christ) was not pleased with most of them, and they were struck down in the wilderness."[67] Ehrman points out that the christological focus

---

[65] Liberatus Diaconus of Cartaghe (6th cent.) in *Brevarium* 19 (PL 68:1033–1034) records a narrative, according to which Macedonius II, Patriarch of Constantinople (496–511 C.E.) was deprived by Emperor Anastasius for having corrupted the Scriptures, and that he was the inventor of this very reading, θεός, in 1 Tim 3:16. The narration only proves that the two readings ὅς and θεός were known in the early sixth century.

[66] Ehrman, *Orthodox Corruption*, 87.

[67] Besides codex 81, Ehrman cites Clement and Irenaeus for the omission of ὁ θεός, probably

already present in the passage is extended through this omission, so as to attribute to Christ the execution of divine wrath.[68] I think this subsingular reading should rather be viewed as an accidental omission. Significantly, Ehrman does not note that the same valuable Alexandrian witness, codex 81, is among the very few witnesses that read θεόν in v. 9 (A 81 *l*883) instead of the better attested readings Χριστόν and κύριον.[69] It seems to me that θεόν in v. 9 would be the least expected reading to find in a witness alleged to heighten the Christology of the passage.

1 Cor 10:9
anti-adoptionistic corruption: μηδὲ ἐκπειράζωμεν τὸν Χριστόν (𝔓[46] D F G Ψ 1739 1881 𝔐 latt sy[p.h] co geo[1] slav Ir[lat] Or[1739mg] Eus Ambst Ambr Pel Aug NA[27])

alternative readings: μηδὲ ἐκπειράζωμεν τὸν κύριον (ℵ B C P 33 104 326 365 1175 2464 *pc* sy[hmg.pal] arm geo[2] Epiph Hes) / μηδὲ ἐκπειρά ζωμεν τὸν θεόν (A 81 *l*883)

The reading Χριστόν has early and diverse attestation including the oldest Greek manuscript of the Pauline corpus (𝔓[46]). According to the UBS committee, it is the reading that best explains the origin of the other readings; the notion that the ancient Israelites tempted Christ in the wilderness was too difficult for some scribes, who substituted "either the ambiguous κύριον or the unobjectionable θεόν."[70] Caroll D. Osburn is also in favor of Χριστόν and he thinks that the change to κύριον was possibly made for theological reasons in the end of the third century by some Eastern Father, influenced by the Antiochene

---

depending on the patristic textual data indicated in Tischendorf's eight edition (1869) of *Novum Testamentum Graece*. However, I have not been able to identify any citations in either Clement and Irenaeus that can be used for text-critical purposes, according to modern standards of evaluating patristic evidence (neither reference is included in NA[27]).

[68] Ehrman, *Orthodox Corruption*, 89.

[69] A genealogical relationship is known to exist between A and 81. Recent research in the Catholic Epistles has somewhat unexpectedly shown that the later minusclue 81 has a predominantly older textual state than the uncial 02 (see above). This is most probably the case in the Pauline epistles too.

[70] Metzger, *Textual Commentary*, 494.

school that stressed a literal interpretation.[71] As for intrinsic evidence, both the committee and Osburn points to Paul's analogous reference to Christ in v. 4, ἡ πέτρα δὲ ἦν ὁ Χριστός.[72] However, Ehrman does not find these arguments persuasive. First, most Christians did believe that Christ was actively involved in the Old Testament and would not have perceived the reading Χριστόν as difficult. Secondly, the reading κύριον is found in Alexandrian witnesses (ℵ B C 33 et al.) which speaks against an Antiochene origin. Thirdly, although Paul understood Christ to be present in the wilderness to sustain the Israelites, he attributed their judgment solely to God, as seen in v. 5. Thus, Ehrman regards κύριον as the original reading, and thinks that the text was changed to Χριστόν by proto-orthodox scribes in order to combat adoptionistic Christology.[73]

I question whether it is really necessary to ascribe this "exchange of predicates" in one direction or the other to theological motivation on the part of "proto-orthodox scribes," made in order to combat specific opponents. I think there are many possible explanations for this type of variation, and in each case the full context has to be considered. Sometimes the changes in divine names and titles may be explained on palaeographic grounds (i.e., the confusion of *nomina sacra*); other changes reflect a concern for clarification (e.g., the specification of ambiguious κύριος); still others are due to harmonization or lectionary influence; but some changes, I suspect, are simply due to a free and unreflected attitude on the part of the scribes to interpret what is already implied in the text. In fact, Ehrman himself captures this point well in an earlier discussion of the very similar context in Jude 5, where there is variation concerning whether it was "the Lord," "Jesus" or "God" who brought the people out of Egypt and later destroyed those who did not believe. He says that these "variations . . . are all explicable from the Old Testament narratives themselves and from early Christian

---

[71] Cf. C. D. Osburn, "The Text of 1 Corinthians 10:9," in *New Testament Textual Criticism: Its Significance for Exegesis—Essays in Honour of Bruce M. Metzger* (ed. J. Epp and G. D. Fee; Oxford: Clarendon, 1981), 201–12, esp. 211–12.

[72] Metzger, *Textual Commentary*, 494; Osburn, "The Text of 1 Corinthians 10:9," 208.

[73] Ehrman, *Orthodox Corruption*, 90.

understandings of them, at least as intimated in 1 Cor 10."[74]
Significantly, if we look at the textual variation between significant
manuscripts that are extant in 1 Cor 10:4–5, 9 and Jude 5, referring
to the pre-existent Christ, who saves, sustains and judges the
people, we find no clear pattern concerning divine names and titles:

	Jude 5	1 Cor 10:5	1 Cor 10:9
ℵ	κύριος	ὁ θεός	κύριον
A	Ἰησοῦς	ὁ θεός	θεόν
B	Ἰησοῦς	ὁ θεός	κύριον
C	ὁ θεός (C²ᵛⁱᵈ)	ὁ θεός	κύριον
Ψ	κύριος	ὁ θεός	Χριστόν
81	Ἰησοῦς	omit (Χριστός implied subject)	θεόν
1739	Ἰησοῦς	ὁ θεός	Χριστόν
𝔐	ὁ κύριος	ὁ θεός	Χριστόν

In conclusion, the textual transmission does not reflect any
discernable tendency on the level of text-types or individual
manuscript witnesses. The evidence speaks directly against Ehrman's
notion of conscious alterations made by proto-orthodox scribes for
dogmatic purposes in order to combat adoptionistic Christology.

Conclusion

We have analysed seventeen selected examples of orthodox
corruption, brought forth by Bart Ehrman in his influential work
on the orthodox corruption of Scripture. Ehrman's optimism
regarding the ability of modern textual criticism, not only to identify
corruption, but to reconstruct the initial text in these passages may
come as a surprise. As we have seen, Ehrman accepts the initial

---

[74] Ibid., 86. In this instance, I agree with Ehrman that 𝔓⁷² reflects proto-orthodox corruption stating
that it was "God Christ" (θεὸς Χριστός) who brought the people out of Egypt, and I agree with
Ehrman in this judgment.

text as adopted in NA^{27} with very few exceptions (Mark 1:1; Luke 3:22; John 1:18; 1 Cor 10:9).[75] My examination, however, has demonstrated several problems with his procedure as he identifies various variant readings as examples of "orthodox corruption."

The first problem with Ehrman's text-critical analysis is the mixed nature of the sample that he uses. It seems to me that he has harvested the entire textual tradition in order to find data to support his preconceived thesis, without crossexamining the possible tendencies of *individual witnesses*. It will become clear that, on the level of the individual witness, it is very difficult to detect any consistent theological tendency. On the contrary, individual witnesses will often reflect directly opposite tendencies (e.g., adoptionistic/anti-adoptionistic).

The second and more serious problem with Ehrman's procedure is the mechanical character of his treatment of *individual passages*. Whenever there is textual variation in a passage that somehow relates to Christology, Ehrman too easily identifies one reading as the original and another as "orthodox corruption." Ehrman's philological and text-critical groundwork is unsatisfactory, in that he lacks a sensitivity to the particular context and nature of the variation in the individual passage.

In a classic essay on "The Application of Thought to Textual Criticism," Alfred E. Housman proposed that "every problem which presents itself to the textual critic must be regarded as possibly unique."[76] This sound view of textual criticism excludes every mechanical application of a single canon of criticism to a passage, e.g., to prefer the least orthodox reading whenever there is a grain of suspicion that a passage may have been tampered with for doctrinal reasons. Instead, the textual critic should attempt at each point to seek the most plausible explanation for the textual variation, weighing external and internal evidence and utilizing whatever principles that may apply to the individual problem.

---

[75] It should be noted that the ratio in favor of NA^{27} would in fact be significantly higher if we counted all of Ehrman's examples in this chapter on anti-adoptionistic corruption, and in the whole monograph.

[76] A. E. Housman, "The Application of Thought to Textual Criticism," *Proceedings of the Classical Association* 18 (1921): 67–84, esp. 69.

If the criteria are found to be in conflict, which is often the case, the textual critic has to decide when to give greater consideration to one criterion and less to another. As I have attempted to demonstrate in my treatment of these examples, a balanced judgment will often require knowledge of the pecularities of individual manuscripts and their scribe(s), the citation habits of church fathers, and a familiarity with the character of a particular version and its limitations in representing the *Vorlage* from which it was translated.[77]

Indeed, this close examination of a significant number of passages has confirmed the judgment of Gordon Fee who in a review of Ehrman's work points out that, "too often [Ehrman] turns mere *possibility* into *probability*, and *probability* into *certainty*, where other equally viable reasons for corruption exist."[78]

---

[77] Hence, we are reminded again of Hort's dictum, "knowledge of documents should precede final judgment on readings" (Westcott and Hort, *The New Testament*, 1:31).

[78] G. D. Fee, review of B. D. Ehrman, *The Orthodox Corruption of Scripture*, CRBR 8 (1995): 203–66, esp. 204.

The Judaism Paul Left Behind Him[1]

Stephen Westerholm
McMaster University

Introduction

Little can be said about my topic that will not, by some, be deemed controversial, but my title at least is not meant to be so. Whether we think that Paul, in turning his back on what he once considered "gains" so that he might "gain Christ,"[2] was abandoning Judaism *tout court* or merely exchanging one form of Judaism for another, it is clear that he abandoned *something*. That *something*—or, more precisely, what Paul as an apostle writes about that *something*[3]—is the topic of this paper.

That *something* which he himself once practiced but later abandoned was also *something* that he believed non-Christian[4] Jews

---

[1] This article is dedicated, with my admiration and best wishes, to Bengt Holmberg, a friend and former fellow-student in the seminars of Birger Gerhardsson.

[2] The language is that of Phil 3:7–8.

[3] Paul calls it "Judaism" (Gal 1:13–14), providing the warrant for the usage of the term in this paper. Cf. J. M. G. Barclay, "Paul Among Diaspora Jews: Anomaly or Apostate?" *JSNT* 60 (1995): 89–120, esp. 113, n. 43. "Judaism" in this context appears to refer to life under the Sinaitic covenant and its laws, a "slavery" from which Paul claims believers have been delivered (4:21–5:1; see the discussion below). But what nomenclature best designates the way of life Paul abandoned will not be debated here.

[4] Though, to repeat, nomenclature is not the focus of this paper, some justification for using the terms "non-Christian," "pre-Christian," and "Christian" may well be in order, given their conspicuous absence from Paul's writings, and given that the use of these familiar terms may indeed obscure significant differences between first century believers in Christ and their twenty-first century counterparts. Pragmatic considerations count for something, and these terms are convenient and simple when compared with the clumsiness of proposed alternatives. They are, moreover, hallowed by long established and popular usage, which, as a general rule, is stubbornly resistant to scholarly attempts at innovation and purification (a general rule for which, as a general rule, we may give much thanks). Beyond pragmatic justifications of this kind, we may note that the term "Christian," while not used by Paul, does have roots in the first century (see B. Holmberg, "The Life in the Diaspora Synagogues: An Evaluation," in *The Ancient Synagogue: From its Origins until 200 C.E.* [ed. B. Olsson and M. Zetterholm; Stockholm: Almqvist & Wiksell International, 2003], 219–32, esp. 226–8), and serves to identify, and to distinguish from others, a group of people whom Paul himself regarded as readily identifiable and distinguishable from others, though not one for which he had a handy designation (cf. E. P. Sanders, *Paul, the Law, and the Jewish People* [Philadelphia: Fortress, 1983],

continued to practice. Note, for example, his claim in Phil 3:9 that he himself had quit the pursuit of "a righteousness of [his] own that comes from the law" in order to seek "the righteousness from God" that is "based on faith." The same language recurs in Rom 9:30–10:13, where it is "Israel" that is said to strive for a righteousness based on the law (Rom 9:31; 10:5), in ignorance of "the righteousness that comes from God" (10:3) and is based on faith (10:6). Paul could (as we say) "relate" to zealous non-Christian Jews because he had once been one himself (compare Rom 10:2 with Gal 1:14; Phil 3:6). We may therefore expand the evidential base on which we draw for Paul's understanding of his former way of life to include passages that describe the way of life of non-Christian Jews in general.[5]

When Paul speaks of his pre-Christian days in Phil 3, his point is that believers in Philippi should not heed those who advocate physical circumcision and (presumably) observance of other distinctively Jewish practices (Phil 3:2). To reinforce his point, Paul notes that he himself once journeyed along the path that such people promote, but had left it for the greater good of knowing Christ (3:4–11). By implication, then, it would be foolish for Christians in Philippi to take up a life that Paul had seen fit to reject. It is likely that the same

---

175): it overlaps entirely with those he labels "believing ones" (e.g., 1 Cor 1:21; Gal 3:22; 1 Thess 1:7; 2:10); "those who are being saved" (1 Cor 1:18; 2 Cor 2:15); "saints" (1 Cor 1:2; 6:1–2; Phil 4:22); "those who belong to Christ (Jesus)" (1 Cor 15:23; Gal 5:24); "the church" (1 Cor 12:28; Phil 3:6) or "church(es) of God" (1 Cor 10:32; 11:16, 22; 15:9) or "of Christ" (Rom 16:16), etc., all regarded as part of an increasingly worldwide "brotherhood" ("in the Lord" [Phil 1:14; cf. 1 Thess 4:10; 5:25–27]). Furthermore, the term draws attention to the (not insignificant) commonalities between first-century believers in Christ and those of later centuries, as well as to what distinguished first-century believers in Christ, as it has distinguished later believers, from those outside their communities: baptism as an initiation rite; celebration of "the Lord's supper" (to use Paul's terminology [1 Cor 11:20]) as an ongoing observance; faith in Jesus as Messiah, the Son of God, whose death and resurrection are the divinely appointed means of salvation; and a recognition of all who share in these observances and convictions, wherever found and whatever their ethnic background, as one's "brothers and sisters in Christ." These common features, fundamental to the self-understanding of first-century believers in Christ no less than to that of Christians in later centuries, are obscured—as the proverbial elephant in the room is somehow lost to view—when the title "Christian" is refused to first-century believers in Christ. Cf. the comments of Bengt Holmberg in "Understanding the First Hundred Years of Christian Identity," in *Exploring Early Christian Identity* (ed. B. Holmberg; Tübingen: Mohr Siebeck, 2008), 1–32, esp. 3–5. For an alternative view, see the article in the same volume (59-92) by (my McMaster colleague and friend) Anders Runesson ("Inventing Christian Identity: Paul, Ignatius, and Theodosius I").

[5] In particular, Rom 2–3, 9–11; 2 Cor 3.

implication lies behind Paul's talk in Galatians about his "onetime life in Judaism."[6] Teachers who followed Paul into Galatia have told the believers to get circumcised and adopt other practices prescribed by the Mosaic law. In effect Paul is saying already in chapter 1 that he knew that way of life well and had outstripped others in its practice; but he had abandoned it when God revealed to him his Son (Gal 1:13–16). Why, then, should the Galatians now adopt it?

If Paul sees a parallel between his former life in Judaism and the path advocated by his opponents[7] in Galatia, then his arguments against them in Galatians provide further evidence of his understanding of the Judaism he had left behind him. To be sure, the immediate issue is not what the Galatians are to think about Judaism as such, but whether they, as Gentile believers in Christ, should be circumcised. Yet circumcision could only have been urged upon the Galatians as part of a bigger picture, i.e., as a requirement for membership in the people of God—a people marked by their adherence to the Mosaic covenant. It is worth noting, in this context, that Paul's opponents saw no conflict between the requirement for circumcision and a recognition of Jesus as Messiah.[8] Indeed, if the term "Judaism" is used to mean life lived under the Mosaic covenant and its laws, then these teachers came to Galatia to promote a sect that had recently begun to take shape *within Judaism,* distinguished from other Jews precisely by its faith in Jesus as Messiah. In the view of these teachers, the framework within which all God's people were to live remained that of the Mosaic law and covenant.

That such was his opponents' line of argument appears clear from Paul's response to it. The Galatians, as *he* perceived their situation, were eager to be "under law" (4:21), the very law to which he, as a believer in Christ, had died (2:19) but under which non-Christian

---

[6] Cf. K-W. Niebuhr, *Heidenapostel aus Israel: Die jüdische Identität des Paulus nach ihrer Darstellung in seinen Briefen* (Tübingen: Mohr Siebeck, 1992), 20–21.

[7] It is sometimes suggested that the teachers who followed Paul into Galatia may not have thought they were opposing Paul. But to my mind the peculiar emphases of Gal 1 and 2 are best understood as a response to a deliberate attempt to undermine Paul's claims to apostolic commissioning and authority.

[8] So much is implied by Gal 6:12.

Jews continued to live (cf. 1 Cor 9:20). The Galatians were thus on the verge of entering the same covenant (that of Mount Sinai), and thereby experiencing the same "slavery," as that known by "the present Jerusalem" (4:21–5:1). They, like the pre-Christian Paul of Philippians 3, and like the non-Christian Jews of Rom 9:30–10:13, would be pursuing a righteousness based on the law (Gal 5:4; cf. Rom 9:31; Phil 3:9)—a righteousness that Paul contrasts with that of faith in Galatians (3:11–12; cf. also 2:16) just as he does in Philippians and Romans. Thus, though his opponents thought faith in Christ itself required faithfulness to the laws of God's covenant with Israel, Paul saw adoption of their position as a complete severing of one's ties with Christ (5:4) and an entering upon the very way of life which he, in embracing God's revelation of his Son, had abandoned. The Epistle to the Galatians thus provides us with indispensable evidence for how Paul, as apostle, had come to view the Judaism he left behind him.

Such, then, is the evidence on which the following depiction will be based: Paul's accounts of his own life before his encounter with Christ, his portrayal of the life of non-Christian Jews, and his arguments against those who were advocating what (in his view) amounted to the same way of life as he had once practiced and as was now lived by non-Christian Jews. Before we turn to the depiction, however, three preliminary points should be noted.

1. My focus throughout this paper is on Pauline thought, *not* on (any form of) first-century Judaism *per se*. What Paul writes about his "onetime life in Judaism" is the product of Christian theologizing; it represents, at best, *indirect* evidence of the way he viewed his old way of life while still immersed in it, and of the way non-Christian Jews in the first century perceived their own life and practice. But my concern here is to explore that for which Paul's writings provide *direct* evidence: his views *as an apostle of Jesus Christ* of the Judaism he once practiced but later came to reject—and, given that he came to reject it, on what explanations he provides of its inadequacies. That has its own interest, and it is the purpose of this paper to illuminate it.

2. Part of what distinguishes Paul's Christian from his pre-Christian view of his old way of life is that he has come to describe the latter in terms designed to highlight a contrast with (how he understands) his present life: he has now, e.g., been redeemed from the curse that hangs over all whose claim to righteousness is based on the "works of the law" (Gal 3:10–13; cf. 4:5).[9] Yet while it is true that Paul's descriptions of his pre-Christian life (and of the life of non-Christian Jews) are shaped by his understanding of what it means to be a believer in Christ, it is also true that they thereby illuminate the self-identity Paul possesses precisely *as a believer*. In what follows, attention will be paid to this latter aspect of my topic as well.

3. Though any attempt at a composite picture of the Judaism Paul left behind him must collect and weigh the evidence from each of his letters before proceeding with generalizations, limitations of space require that I confine this presentation to the resulting composite picture. I am of course aware of the risk involved in a systematic presentation of evidence detached from its original context. Nonetheless, where points are made which seem consistent with Pauline emphases in all his epistles, the evidence will simply be cited without comment. Where points are made that seem dependent on the distinctive argumentation of a particular epistle, that will also be noted. The result, I trust, will be faithful to Paul's thought while still reflecting the occasional nature of the writings in which we encounter it.

---

[9] It must, however, be conceded that a sharp contrast between Judaism as he knew it and the Christian faith he came to adopt was present in Paul's mind even *before* he abandoned the former for the latter: he cites his persecution of the church as a mark of his devotion to Judaism (Gal 1:13; cf. Phil 3:6; and note John 16:2). Cf. T. L. Donaldson, *Paul and the Gentiles: Remapping the Apostle's Convictional World* (Minneapolis: Fortress, 1997), 284–92.

"Under Law"

I begin with the smashingly obvious. Paul sees the piety of the Judaism he left behind him, and of non-Christian Jews in general, as centered on Torah and its observance.

In the autobiographical section of Galatians 1, Paul recalls his past in these terms: "I progressed in Judaism beyond many of my peers among my people, for I was far more zealous for the traditions of my forefathers" (Gal 1:14). To what "traditions" is he referring? Josephus tells us that the Sadducees recognized as valid only prescriptions written in the law of Moses, whereas the Pharisees "transmitted to the people certain regulations handed down from the fathers" (*A.J.* 13.297). In Matthew and Mark as well, Pharisees criticize Jesus' disciples for their failure to observe the (extrabiblical) "tradition of the elders" (Matt 15:2; Mark 7:5). Since Paul himself was a Pharisee (Phil 3:5), it is tempting to see distinctively Pharisaic, extrabiblical traditions behind his claim that, in his "onetime life in Judaism," he showed great zeal for "the traditions of [his] forefathers."

But such is too narrow a reading of his words. When Josephus speaks of the "ancestral laws" and "customs" of the Jews, he is clearly thinking of the (written) Torah.[10] Paul himself may have observed the law in its Pharisaic interpretation and with Pharisaic amplifications. But he was fully aware that the Pharisees were not the only Jews devoted to the Mosaic code.[11] And since he speaks of his zeal for the ancestral traditions as the standard for measuring his progress "in Judaism,"[12] the traditions in question are presumably such as all religious Jews observed. These, then, are the laws of the Pentateuch, the laws of Moses: to show zeal for God "in

---

[10] See my *Jesus and Scribal Authority* (Lund: Gleerups, 1978), 15–16.

[11] Philippians 3:5 implies as much. When Paul writes that "as to the law," he was "a Pharisee," he means that, among the various ways of construing and observing the law found among Jews, it was the Pharisaic interpretation that he followed. The implication appears to be, however, that Pharisees were well known for the strictness of their interpretations and the rigor of their practice. Cf. A. I. Baumgarten, "The Name of the Pharisees," *JBL* 102 (1983): 411–28; E. P. Sanders, *Judaism: Practice and Belief 63 BCE–66 CE* (London: SCM, 1992), 420–21.

[12] Pharisees would not have been Pharisees if they had not thought the Pharisaic construal of the law was the best on offer. Nonetheless they would not have equated the term "Judaism" with a distinctively Pharisaic way of life. Cf. Sanders, *Judaism,* 448–51.

Judaism" means to show zeal for God's laws. Paul claims that in his pre-Christian days he outshone his compatriots in this regard.

Faithfulness to Torah was the measure, not only of one's progress "in Judaism," but also of one's righteousness (i.e., before God). As noted above, Paul characterizes both his own pre-Christian life and the life of non-Christian Jews as a pursuit of a righteousness based on observance of the Mosaic law (Phil 3:9; Rom 9:31).[13] That Paul can also speak of such righteousness as his "own" (Phil 3:9), and that of non-Christian Jews as "their own" (Rom 10:3), does not mean that, even as an apostle, he thought of it negatively as (what we call) "self-righteousness." The point is simply that one's righteousness depended on one's ("own") observance of the law:[14] "It is not the hearers of the law who are righteous before God, but the doers of the law who will be justified [= found righteous]" (Rom 2:13).[15] This is very much in keeping with the language of Deut 6:25: "And it will be righteousness for us, if we are careful to do all this commandment before the Lord our God, as he has commanded us."[16]

Observance of the Mosaic laws was, of course, one's obligation,

---

[13] Though (as noted above) the focus of this paper is on Paul's retrospective understanding of the Judaism he left behind him, not on first-century Judaism *per se,* Paul's observation that non-Christian Jews pursue a righteousness based on law is not without interest in the context of a current debate about the nature of Second Temple Judaism. Critics of E. P. Sanders are wont to question the universality, among Jews of the period, of the piety he labels "covenantal nomism"; they point out that whole strands of Jewish literature (particularly wisdom and apocalyptic texts) from the period make little or no reference to the covenant or laws of Sinai; see, e.g., the references in my *Perspectives Old and New on Paul: The "Lutheran" Paul and His Critics* (Grand Rapids: Eerdmans, 2004), 344, n. 8; and in my "Paul's Anthropological 'Pessimism' in its Jewish Context," in *Divine and Human Agency in Paul and His Cultural Environment* (ed. J. M. G. Barclay and S. Gathercole; London: T & T Clark, 2006), 71–98, esp. 87–8, n. 49. Assuming that what the authors of these texts did not write about did not concern them, Sanders's critics argue that there were groups of Jews in antiquity for whom Sinai held little significance. Against this the obvious counterargument is that what got included in such texts was determined rather by their genre than by the limitations of their authors' interests. Without pursuing that discussion here, we may at least note that Paul shows no awareness of a Judaism that did not center on Sinai. Judaism, as one widely travelled, well informed, intensely religious, first-century Jew knew it, was devoted to the laws of Moses and expressed its devotion to God by obeying them.

[14] If one could be "blameless" by the standard of "righteousness under the law" (Phil 3:6), then such "righteousness" was clearly measured by one's conduct. On the verse, see the discussion in my *Perspectives,* 272, n. 26; 402–3.

[15] Cf. my *Perspectives,* 262–73.

[16] Cf. also Ezek 18:5–9, where *individual* righteousness, based on one's own observance of God's commands, is (programmatically) in view.

as a Jew, under the covenant that Israel had entered with God at Mount Sinai (Exod 19:3–8; 24:3–8). Paul makes clear that the obligation was entailed in one's circumcision, understood as one's entry-point into that covenant (cf. Gal 5:3). Under the sanctions of that covenant, those who disobeyed its laws were cursed (Gal 3:10), whereas obedience brought "life" in God's favor. Paul can thus sum up the defining principle of the "righteousness based on law" in the words of Lev 18:5: "The one who does these things [i.e., who observes these commandments] will live by them" (so Gal 3:12; Rom 10:5; cf. Deut 30:15–20).

Paul can thus speak of those bound by the Mosaic covenant and its obligations as "under law." The situation, he believed, carried with it negative consequences; but the expression itself can be used without any such connotations simply to distinguish Jews (who are "under law") from non-Jews (who are not; cf. 1 Cor 9:20–21; and note that Christ himself, as a Jew, was born "under law," according to Gal 4:4). Negative connotations are present first when those contrasted with Jews ("under law") are not Gentiles (who are without the law), but Christians, who are "not under law, *but under grace*" (Rom 6:14–15; cf. Gal 4:4–5; 5:18).

And, to be sure, Paul does find points of contrast between all that has been said about Jewish life (and his own past) "under law," on the one hand, and the life of Christians (including his own) on the other. His erstwhile zeal for the law and for the "gains" that he would secure by its observance has been replaced by (and its "gains" dismissed as mere "garbage" in comparison with) a desire to "gain Christ and be found in him" (Phil 3:4–11). If zeal for the law once found expression in his persecution of the church, he "now proclaimed the faith that he once tried to destroy" (Gal 1:13, 23). Pursuit of his "own" righteousness, based on his observance of the law, has been replaced by a prizing of the righteousness that is his as a gift from God, received by faith (Phil 3:9; cf. Rom 5:17). The operative principle for his new life is not "The one who does these commandments will live by them," but "The one who is righteous *through faith* shall live" (and, for its part, "the law is not based on faith"; Gal 3:11–12).[17] The covenant under which Christians live is not that of Mount Sinai—from the "slavery" of which they have been set free (4:24; 5:1)—but that promised to Abraham and to all who, by sharing Abraham's faith in the gospel message, have become Abraham's true offspring (3:7–9, 15–18, 29; 4:21–5:1). Freed ("redeemed") from the "curse" of the law (3:13), they have been "called" into a state of "grace" (1:6; cf. Rom 5:2; Gal 5:4). For them, God's will is to be discerned, not (as in Rom 2:18) through the prescriptions of Torah, but by the judgment of their renewed minds (Rom 12:2) and the direction of the divine Spirit in which they are to "walk" and whose "fruit" they are to bear (Gal 5:16–25). They are under no obligation to obey the law's commandments as such: having "died" to the law,[18] they are free from its sphere of authority ("not under law")[19]—though the good they are to do (as the "fruit of the Spirit") is such that no law will condemn (Gal 5:22–23).

---

[17] Note also the pointed assertion that the righteousness of faith is "apart from law" in Rom 3:21–22.

[18] Rom 7:6; Gal 2:19. Surely Paul the apostle never wrote anything more contrary to the whole ethos of the Judaism he left behind him than when he claimed that he had to "die to the law" in order to "live to God" (Gal 2:19).

[19] Rom 6:14–15; 7:6; 1 Cor 9:20; Gal 4:5; 5:18. Cf. my *Perspectives,* 431–3. Albert Schweitzer argued, on the basis of 1 Cor 7:17, 20, that, for Paul, precisely *because* the law is no longer valid for believers, they must show the utter insignificance of such externalities by maintaining the state they were in (the "status quo") when they became believers. Hence, Jewish Christians should continue to live by the law, though non-Jews must not submit to its regulations; see *The Mysticism of Paul the Apostle* (London: A. & C. Black, 1931), 192–6. But Rom 14 shows clearly that Paul thought it appropriate for believers (whether or not they were Jews is not a factor in the discussion) with a "strong" conscience (like his own) to treat all days the same and to eat any food they liked. (For the latter point, see also 1 Cor 10:23–11:1, where, again, ethnicity plays no part in instructions pertaining to food that are given to a church that included both Jewish and Gentile believers.) Just as clearly Paul indicates in 1 Cor 9:20–21 that he lived "without the law" when among Gentiles though, for strategic (missionary) purposes, he lived by the law when among Jews. Of this text, and Paul's claim that, among Jews, he "*became as* a Jew," C. K. Barrett writes pointedly: "But Paul . . . was a Jew. He could *become* a Jew only if, having been a Jew, he had ceased to be one and become something else. His Judaism was no longer of his very being, but a guise he could adopt or discard at will" (*The First Epistle to the Corinthians* [2d ed.; London: Adam & Charles Black, 1971], 211). (The perspective of this verse [like that, e.g., of 1 Cor 10:32, where "the church of God" is treated as a separate category from "Jews" and "Greeks"] must be balanced, though not displaced, by texts like Rom 9:3; 11:1, where Paul asserts his kinship ["according to the flesh"] with the Jewish people.) Moreover, much of what he says (in claims that are *never* qualified by reference to ethnicity, though, if anything, they have particular relevance precisely for *Jewish* believers) would lose its force if he imagined believers as still bound to observe a law which he claims they are no longer "under," to which he says they have "died," and from which, as from the Sinaitic covenant of which the law is a part, they have been "set free." The "commandments" that Paul, in 1 Cor 7, envisages believers obeying explicitly exclude circumcision

"In the Flesh"

Paul can use the term "flesh" in a neutral way of the embodied existence of human beings, including both his own as an apostle (Gal 2:20) and that of Christ himself (Rom 8:3; 9:5). But his more distinctive usage of the term designates humanity as hostile to God, or even the hostility itself.[20] Ever since Adam's act of disobedience, human beings have not been born into the innocence of Eden, where perfect communion with their Creator was enjoyed, but into a race estranged from God, entertaining illusions of autonomy, and marked in its behavior by an "ungodliness and unrighteousness" that provoke God's wrath (Rom 1:18). Its fundamental sin of refusing to give God due acknowledgement and thanks (1:21) finds expression in multifarious derivative sins, to the committing and consequences of which God has "given them up" (1:24, 26, 28). Humanity lives "under [the power of] sin" (3:9), or "in sin" (6:1), or as "slaves of sin" (6:16–23). It does not find it within itself to submit to God's law (8:7). Such is the state of humanity "in the flesh"; "in the flesh" nothing "good" (i.e., nothing untouched by sin) is to be found (7:18).

(which is treated as a matter of indifference), and they are explicitly to be obeyed *whether or not one is circumcised* (7:19). There is thus no justification for generalizing Paul's words in 1 Corinthians 7 to indicate (what Paul in the passage does *not* indicate) a continuing obligation on the part of Jewish Christians to observe the commandments of the Mosaic law. See D. G. Horrell, "'No Longer Jew or Greek': Paul's Corporate Christology and the Construction of Christian Community," in *Christology, Controversy and Community: New Testament Essays in Honour of David R. Catchpole* (ed. D. G. Horrell and C. M. Tuckett; Leiden: Brill, 2000), 321–44, esp. 337–9. Nor (*contra* P. J. Tomson, *Paul and the Jewish Law: Halakha in the Letters of the Apostle to the Gentiles* [Minneapolis: Fortress, 1990], 67–8) does Gal 5:3 suggest such an obligation. Circumcision marks the entry point into the Sinaitic covenant; should the Galatians become circumcised, they would then (as Paul observes in Gal 5:3) be obligated to obey all the laws of that covenant. But such an obligation no longer applies to Christians who have been "set free" from the "slavery" of that covenant and have "died" to its laws (2:19; 4:21–5:1). That Paul expected Jewish Christians *not* to observe Jewish dietary laws at the common meals of Christians is noted by Sanders, *Paul, the Law,* 177–9; B. Holmberg, "Jewish *Versus* Christian Identity in the Early Church?" *RB* 105 (1993): 397–425. In general, however, and without qualifying his statements of freedom from the law, Paul does think obedience to particular statutes is very much in order (again, whether one is Jew or Gentile is not a factor) if required by the scruples of one's sensitive ("weak") conscience (Rom 14:2, 5, 14, 23), or by the need to avoid either offending others (14:13–22; cf. 1 Cor 8:7–13) or undermining one's attempts to proclaim to them the gospel message (1 Cor 9:20).

[20] Cf. J. M. G. Barclay, *Obeying the Truth: Paul's Ethics in Galatia* (Minneapolis: Fortress, 1991), 194–209; J. D. G. Dunn, *The Theology of Paul the Apostle* (Grand Rapids: Eerdmans, 1998), 62–70.

The point to be made here is that Paul sees the life of Jews "under the law," in this respect, as no different from that of Gentiles "without the law": the law was given to, and is lived under by, people who are "in the flesh."[21] Hence the dilemma of Rom 7:14–25, for what happens when sinful flesh encounters God's law—however "holy, righteous, and good" the commandments themselves may be[22]—is inevitable. The rebelliousness inherent in human beings (i.e., the "sin" of Rom 7:8–11) lies dormant until confronted with a command against which it can rebel; but such a confrontation brings out its true character (sin is shown to be "exceedingly sinful through the commandment" [7:13]). Even where there is an acknowledgement that the law is good (7:16, 22; Paul may well be thinking here of his own erstwhile zeal for the law, and that of other pious Jews), it is evil that continues to be done (7:15–25).[23] The weakness of the flesh prevents the law from conveying the life it promises (8:3; cf. 7:10). "The mindset of the flesh is one of hostility toward God. It does not submit to God's law, nor can it do so. Those who are in the flesh cannot please God" (8:7–8).

The same conclusion is reached in the discussion of universal sinfulness that opens the letter to the Romans. Jews, informed by the law they have been given, can instruct Gentiles about their mutual obligation to do what is good (2:17–20). But, essentially, there is no difference between Jew and Gentile either in what God requires of them (2:6–11) or in their response to that requirement. Jews sin under the law, Gentiles sin apart from the law, and both,

---

[21] Note, e.g., that for Galatian believers to submit to the law was to attempt to complete "with the flesh" what was begun "with the Spirit" (Gal 3:3). To list the ways in which one complied with the law's requirements is to give expression to one's "confidence in the flesh" (Phil 3:3–6).

[22] Rom 7:12. It appears that Paul's primary purpose in including what is essentially an extended parenthesis between Rom 7:6 and 8:1 is to show how the law itself can be good, even though its encounter with sinful humanity only serves to exacerbate human sinfulness (5:20) and to highlight "the sinfulness of sin" (7:13). Earlier passing remarks in the letter (3:20; 5:20; 6:14; 7:5) required such an explanation. Cf. W. G. Kümmel, *Römer 7 und das Bild des Menschen im Neuen Testament* (Munich: Christian Kaiser, 1974 [summarized in my *Perspectives,* 135–46]).

[23] Paul must have found the supreme example of this phenomenon in the way his very zeal for the law led him to persecute "the church of God" (Gal 1:13–14; Phil 3:6). Cf. S. J. Chester, *Conversion at Corinth: Perspectives on Conversion in Paul's Theology and the Corinthian Church* (London: T & T Clark, 2003), 185–6.

because of their sin, face condemnation (Rom 2:12; cf. 3:22–23). Jews and Gentiles alike are explicitly said to live "under sin" (Rom 3:9). Hence Jews (under the Sinaitic covenant) no less than Gentiles (outside it) need to be "saved" (i.e., from the wrath to come; so Rom 10:1; 11:14; 1 Cor 9:20–22; cf. 1:18–25).[24]

This aspect, too, of Paul's depiction of non-Christian Jews contrasts sharply with what he says about believers[25] who have "died with Christ" to the old way of life and have begun, with Christ, a new (Rom 6:1–11; 2 Cor 5:17; Gal 2:19–20). The latter are no longer "in the flesh" (in the negative sense of the term; Rom 8:9); indeed, "those who belong to Christ Jesus have *crucified the flesh*" (Gal 5:24). Similarly, having died, with Christ, to sin, they are no longer under its power: they no longer live—they *must* not any longer live—"in sin" (Rom 6:1–23). Once alienated from God as God's "enemies," they have now been reconciled to God by the death of God's Son (Rom 5:10). They await the appearance of God's Son and, with it, deliverance from the wrath to come (1 Thess 1:10; 5:9).

The human drama of sin and redemption can, for Paul, be told as a story of two persons, Adam and Christ (Rom 5:12–21; cf. 1 Cor 15:21–22). Adam's sin made people sinners, and it brought them under the power of sin and death. Christ's act of righteousness makes people righteous, the recipients of God's gift of righteousness, and the beneficiaries of overflowing grace. Depicted in these terms,

---

[24] "The crucial point is that Paul applied the entrance requirement 'faith in Jesus Christ' to Jews as well as to Gentiles. Even Peter and Paul, who had lived as righteous Jews, had to do *something else* in order to be members of the people of God; they had to have faith in Christ (Gal. 2:15f.)" (Sanders, *Paul, the Law,* 172 [see 171–9]; cf. T. L. Donaldson, "Jewish Christianity, Israel's Stumbling and the *Sonderweg* Reading of Paul," *JSNT* 29 [2006]: 27–54, esp. 44–7; B. Longenecker, "On Israel's God and God's Israel: Assessing Supersessionism in Paul," *JTS* 58 [2007]: 26–44, esp. 26–35).

[25] It also represents a reconfiguration of what, as a zealous Jew, he perceived to be humanity's plight: "It was only the revelation of Christ as the saviour of all that convinced him that all men, both Jew and Gentile, were enslaved to sin. Before then, he must have distinguished between Jews, who were righteous (despite occasional transgressions) and 'Gentile sinners' (Gal 2:15)" (E. P. Sanders, *Paul and Palestinian Judaism* [Philadelphia: Fortress, 1977], 499). On the other hand, a negative portrayal of Israel's persistent behavior under the covenant and of the consequences of their waywardness was certainly at hand, ready to be drawn upon, in both biblical and postbiblical traditions; it was hardly an *ex nihilo* creation of the apostle. Cf. F. Thielman, *From Plight to Solution: A Jewish Framework for Understanding Paul's View of the Law in Galatians and Romans* (Leiden: Brill, 1989), and M. A. Elliott, *The Survivors of Israel: A Reconsideration of the Theology of Pre-Christian Judaism* (Grand Rapids: Eerdmans, 2000).

distinctions between Jews and Gentiles vanish; indeed, neither Abraham nor Moses has a determining role to play in the drama. Moses (i.e., the Mosaic *law*) is allowed only the very secondary role of exacerbating, and thus highlighting the depths of, human sinfulness (Rom 5:20). As for Abraham, he—like Paul himself, zealous Jew though he was—is among the "ungodly" for whom justification is only possible by faith (4:3–5; 5:6). In short, Jews, for all the privileges granted them, belong, like Gentiles, to a creation infested and marred by sin; and it is beyond the power of the law to transform the "present evil age" (Gal 1:4) or to make sinners righteous (2:21; 3:21).

The "Ministry of Death"

Yet privileged they were: the Sinaitic covenant and laws under which Jews lived were divinely instituted, and their institution was accompanied by a display of divine glory.

Admittedly, when Paul, in Galatians, wants to persuade his readers *not* to take on the obligations of that covenant, its negative aspects alone are highlighted. Righteousness, Paul declares, is simply not attainable under the law (Gal 2:16, 21; 3:21); indeed, all whose claim to righteousness depends on observance of the "works of the law" are subject to the curse that the law pronounces on its transgressors (3:10).[26] Paul goes on to stress that the law was not even given until 430 years after God gave promises to Abraham, and that it by no means displaced those promises (3:15–17). Nor was the law's validity, once given, to last longer than until the appearance of Christ, the object of the Abrahamic promise (3:19). The latter was conveyed directly by God to Abraham, whereas the law was left to be passed on through subordinates (3:18–20). Though not opposed to the promise, the law served only to supervise the imprisonment of people "under sin" until, with the "coming" of "faith," they would be set free (3:21–25). The covenant of Mount Sinai brought enslavement

---

[26] On the interpretation of this verse, see my *Perspectives*, 375 n.66.

to its subjects (4:24).[27] It is easy to forget, while reading Galatians, that the law and covenant of Mount Sinai *were* divine institutions.[28]

That point is made explicitly in 2 Corinthians and Romans; still, the plight of those living under the law remains very much what it was in Galatians.

God's glory (Paul reminds the Corinthians) was revealed when God's law was given; so great was the glory on Moses' face that the people of Israel could not bear to see it (2 Cor 3:7). Yet the service ("ministry") of God that it introduced could be summed up as one of "condemnation" (3:9) and "death" (3:7): even though the law promised life and blessing to those who obeyed it at the same time as it threatened those who disobeyed it with death and cursing, only the latter outcome is realized among human beings who are, as we have seen, "in the flesh" (cf. the exclusively negative outcome cited in Gal 3:10).[29] And as in Galatians, the law is

---

[27] The nature of Paul's argument in these chapters should be carefully noted. He opposes the notion that the Galatian Christians should be circumcised, *not* because this part of a still valid Mosaic economy is inapplicable in their case, *nor* because the whole of a still valid Mosaic economy is not meant for Gentiles, *nor* because the advocates of circumcision for Gentiles have distorted the Mosaic economy along ethnocentric lines. Paul's opponents, he believes, were not wrong in thinking that the Mosaic economy required circumcision, but in failing to realize that the Mosaic economy itself had lost its validity. At the best of times righteousness was simply not achievable by means of the Mosaic economy. Lacking the means to justify sinners, it could only curse and enslave them. In the plan of God, the economy and laws of Mount Sinai played an important but temporary role as guardian of God's people until Messiah should come and deliver them. For Gentile believers in Christ to be circumcised now would be a disaster, not because they would be unnecessarily taking on requirements binding only on Jews, but because they would be abandoning Christ, whose death is the sole means by which Jews and Gentiles alike can find righteousness; and they would be embracing life under a covenant that can only condemn its (inevitably sinful) subjects.

[28] That they were divine in origin can nonetheless be read between the lines even in Galatians. The fundamental principle of the Sinaitic covenant and law is spelled out in a quotation from sacred Scripture (3:12, citing Lev 18:5). The love commandment (Lev 19:18) is said (in Gal 5:14) to sum up the whole law, and to be something that believers should "fulfill." It is, moreover, *God's* purpose in giving the law that is summed up in the words "because of transgressions" in 3:19; and God's design for the limited temporal validity of the law is in view when Paul adds "until the offspring should come to whom the promise had been made." And if transgression of the law brings a divine curse (3:10), then its terms must articulate divine demands.

[29] At no point in Paul's letters does he pause to consider the claim, axiomatic among Jews, that the law provides for the atonement of sins inevitably and regrettably committed even by those otherwise oriented toward serving God. Had he thought the subjects of the covenant were guilty merely of particular indiscretions, then the provisions of the Mosaic covenant for their atonement might have been an issue. But if the subjects of the covenant are incorrigible sinners, as Paul believes they are, then no Jew of his day would have denied Paul's further claim that the Mosaic covenant condemns

conceded only a temporary validity (2 Cor 3:11; Gal 3:19, 23–25).

In Romans, as noted above, Paul goes to considerable lengths to defend the goodness of the law and its commandments (7:7–25); but he is compelled to do so because the lot of those living under the law is depicted no differently than in Galatians and 2 Corinthians. Righteousness under the law is not possible (3:20); what the law brings is "knowledge" of sin (3:20; 7:7), a provocation to sin (7:5, 7–8), an exacerbation of sin (5:20), a legal foundation for the punishment of sin (4:15). That being the case, the effective purpose of the law is merely to highlight the profundity of human alienation from God.

If the "ministry" introduced by Moses brought "condemnation" and "death," that of the new covenant under which Paul serves is one of "righteousness"[30] and "life" (2 Cor 3:7–9). The opening chapters of Romans supply the thinking behind these claims. In brief:

1. All human beings are subject to the divine demand to do what is good (Rom 2:6–11).
2. The universal requirement finds paradigmatic expression when God gives his law to a favoured people (Rom 2:17–20).
3. Israel's failure to observe the law brought upon themselves its condemnation and death, as the "ungodliness and unrighteousness" of all humankind evoke God's wrath (2 Cor 3:7, 9; Rom 1:18; 2:12; 3:9–20).
4. Into a situation in which Jews and non-Jews alike have failed to attain righeousness by meeting God's demands, God has "now" intervened to make "righteousness" and "life" possible "apart from law" (Rom 3:21–22; 2 Cor 3:7–9): a righteousness and life made possible by the death of Christ that atoned for sins (Rom 3:24–26), and granted

---

them. Paul thus differs from other Jews not so much in his understanding of the requirements of the covenant as in his assessment of human sinfulness. Cf. M. Winninge, *Sinners and the Righteous: A Comparative Study of the Psalms of Solomon and Paul's Letters* (Stockholm: Almqvist & Wiksell International, 1995), 264, 306–7; T. Laato, *Paul and Judaism: An Anthropological Approach* (Atlanta: Scholars Press, 1995); and my "Anthropological 'Pessimism.'" The point, then, of saying that "no flesh will be justified by works of the law" (Gal 2:16) is that God's favor cannot be enjoyed by *sinners* under a covenant that demands compliance with its laws.

[30] The term, in this context, effectively means "acquittal"; cf. Rom 5:16, 18.

extraordinarily to sinners who respond in faith to the good news of salvation (3:21–26).

The "Weakness of the Law"

In Rom 8:3, Paul, summing up the dilemma depicted in 7:7–25, identifies the "weakness of the law" as its inability to cope with "sin in the flesh." Though itself "holy (7:12) and "spiritual" (7:14), when it encounters those who are "flesh-ly" and "sold under sin," it demonstrates rather than overcomes the "surpassing sinfulness of sin" (7:13–14). The latter is first overcome in One who, in the very "likeness of sinful flesh," nonetheless lived righteously, and who, again in that very flesh, died "for sin" (8:3; cf. 5:18–19). His is not, however, an isolated triumph, but one that opens to others—those who, by sharing in his "death to sin," are no longer "in the flesh" (6:6, 10–11; 8:9)—the possibility of living, not "according to the flesh," but "according to the Spirit": in them the law is "fulfilled" (8:4).

Interpreters of Paul have frequently suggested that the apostle identifies the failure of those living "under the law" as their *distortion* of the law's true nature and purpose. Jews (on one such reading[31]) turn the law's demand for obedience into an invitation to win God's recognition *by their achievements* in observing the law: a law that calls for radical submissiveness before God is thus distorted into an opportunity for self-assertion. Or (on another such reading[32]) Jewish ethnocentrism misunderstands God's gift of the law to Israel as signaling a privileged status that exempts Jews from judgment; and it leads them to invest too much of their identity in their distinctiveness from Gentiles. Against such readings, it is remarkable how Paul persists in speaking, not so much of Jewish misunderstandings of the law as of the inability of the law itself to convey righteousness (Rom 3:20; Gal 2:16, 21; 3:21) or life (Gal 3:21) to human beings "under sin." Not, of course, that God's

---

[31] That of Rudolf Bultmann; see my summary of his work, with references, in *Perspectives,* 150–54.

[32] That of James D. G. Dunn; see my summary, with references, in *Perspectives,* 183–92.

law is seen as the problem: human sinfulness is the problem. But Paul repeatedly makes the point that the law is not the tool to overcome the problem. Far from misunderstanding the law, (the pre-Christian Paul, and) Jews who pursue a righteousness based on observance of its commands are shown as following the path spelled out in the law itself (Rom 10:5; Gal 3:12, citing Lev 18:5). But that road to righteousness is closed to sinners.[33] For sinners, righteousness can only be found "apart from law" (Rom 3:21).

Such I take to be the gravamen of what Paul writes about the Judaism he left behind him. Two other points, however, merit mention.

1. Though Moses himself prescribed "doing" the commandments (Rom 10:5), the coming of Christ marks "the end of the law" as a path to righteousness (a path that, indeed, was never viable for sinners) and the effective revelation of the "righteousness of God," available to all who believe (3:21–22; 10:3–4, 6:13). Paul thus sees Jews who *continue* to pursue the old path to righteousness, believing righteousness can be attained by "works" rather than by "faith," as acting in ignorance or defiance of "the righteousness of God" (9:32; 10:3, 19–21).

2. In principle, if one *could* be righteous by doing righteous deeds, one *would* have something to boast of;[34] but such boasting can have no place before God (cf. 1 Cor 1:26–31). Appropriately, then, the righteousness God grants to sinners who believe excludes all boasting (Rom 3:27).

---

[33] Such, Paul believes, was the situation before as well as after Christ came (indeed, it was the situation that necessitated Christ's coming). The righteousness of even an Abraham or a David was not the result of their (righteous) "works" in compliance with the law, but a gift of divine forgiveness (so Rom 4:1–8).

[34] So Rom 4:2. The passage does not, however, indicate that those zealous for the law have a particular propensity for such boasting. This may, however, be implicit in Phil 3:3–6. See the discussion in L. Thurén, *Derhetorizing Paul: A Dynamic Perspective on Pauline Theology and the Law* (Tübingen: Mohr Siebeck, 2000), 165–78.

"Beloved on Account of the Fathers"

Finally, we must recall that, for the Paul of Rom 9–11, there is more to Israel's story than its present condition reveals.

Israel, the objects of God's blessings (Rom 9:4–5), has now "stumbled" in unbelief (i.e., in the gospel; 9:32–33; 11:11, 20, 23); because of unbelief, many *physical* descendants of Abraham have been cut off like branches from the "olive tree" of God's people (11:17–22). Nonetheless, Israel remains "beloved on account of the fathers" to whom God's promises were given (11:28). And God's promises, once given, cannot fail (9:6); the "calling" of God is "irrevocable" (11:29). Somehow (Paul does not venture to say how) Israel's unbelief—in which they must not "remain" if they are to find their place again as God's people (11:23)—will give way to faith;[35] Israel's "ungodliness"—which necessarily makes them the objects of God's wrath (1:18)—will be "banished" (11:26); and then, in spite of their current "disobedience"—while non-Jews, by believing in the gospel, find mercy—they will themselves experience God's mercy (11:32). "And so all Israel will be saved" (11:26). This climax to the story of Israel Paul labels a "mystery" (11:25); but he finds it as inevitable as it is incomprehensible, and for the same reason: Israel's ultimate salvation is included in the purposes of a God whose ways transcend all human understanding (11:33–36).

---

[35] Cf. Sanders, *Paul, the Law,* 195; Donaldson, "Sonderweg," 51.

"Will the Real Gentile-Christian Please Stand Up!" Torah and the Crisis of Identity Formation

Magnus Zetterholm
Lund University

Introduction

Compared to the long and extensive interest in "Jewish Christianity" among New Testament scholars,[1] the phenomenon of "Gentile Christianity" has not yet attracted any substantial interest.[2] This is probably due to the fact that most scholars dealing with the development of "early Christianity" have not been overly interested in the distinction between Jews and non-Jews within the early Jesus movement. It is a fair conjecture that the interest in "Jewish-Christianity," at least partly, can be explained by the assumed heretical nature of this group. In Christian scholarship the label "Jewish-Christianity" has often had quite pejorative connotations.[3] While Paul, together with some other Jews and non-Jews, generally is considered to have (rightly) promoted a common religious identity among adherents to Jesus based on the movement's radical break with Judaism in general and with the Torah in particular, "Jewish-

---

[1] See e.g. the bibliographies in these volumes: M. A. Jackson-McCabe, ed., *Jewish Christianity Reconsidered: Rethinking Ancient Groups and Texts* (Minneapolis: Fortress, 2007); O. Skarsaune, *In the Shadow of the Temple: Jewish Influences on Early Christianity* (Downers Grove: InterVarsity Press, 2002); O. Skarsaune and R. Hvalvik, eds., *Jewish Believers in Jesus: The Early Centuries* (Peabody: Hendrickson, 2007).

[2] See, however, T. L. Donaldson, *Paul and the Gentiles: Remapping the Apostle's Convictional World* (Minneapolis: Fortress, 1997); B. Kahl, *Galatians Re-Imagined* (Minneapolis: Fortress, 2010); D. C. Lopez, *Apostle to the Conquered: Remapping Paul's Mission* (Minneapolis: Fortress, 2008).

[3] See J. Carleton Paget, "The Definition of the Terms *Jewish Christian* and *Jewish Christianity* in the History of Scholarship," in *Jewish Believers in Jesus: The Early Centuries* (ed. O. Skarsaune and R. Hvalvik; Peabody: Hendrickson, 2007), 22–52, for an overview of the use of the term in the history of research.

Christians" still assumed (wrongly) that Jews who believed Jesus to be the Messiah of Israel should continue to observe the Torah.

According to this paradigm, non-Jews within "Pauline Christianity" had merged together with the Jews in the community, developing into a third race of sorts, a new religious entity, neither Jewish, nor Gentile. The "Christian church," or "early Christianity" was thus characterized by a far-reaching theological and ritual conformity and the identity of non-Jewish adherents to the Jesus movement became less interesting. Together with Jesus-believing Jews, non-Jewish followers of Jesus were simply "Christians," and their original ethnic identity was effectively eradicated in many scholarly reconstructions. A classic formulation of this idea is found in E. P. Sanders's *Paul the Law and the Jewish People*:

> Paul's own view was that, with regard to access to membership in the people of God, Jew and Gentile were on equal ground and both had to join what was, in effect, a third entity.[4]

As a result of this idea, very few scholars in the middle of the 20th century pondered the problem of "Christian identity". The majority simply assumed that "Christians" were involved in a conflict with Judaism, which gave rise to a "Christian identity." Rudolf Bultmann, for instance, maintained that the debate with Judaism developed "in purely theoretical fashion the principle of Christian faith in antithesis to the principle of the Jewish Torah-religion."[5] Moreover, Ernst Käsemans's (in)famous statement that Paul's "message of justification is a fighting doctrine, directed against Judaism,"[6] aptly captures the *Zeitgeist* of most Pauline scholarship during the larger part the 20th century.

---

[4] E. P. Sanders, *Paul, the Law, and the Jewish People* (Minneapolis: Fortress, 1983), 172.

[5] R. Bultmann, *Theology of the New Testament* (2 vols.; Waco: Baylor University Press, 2007), 1:109.

[6] E. Käsemann, *Perspectives on Paul* (Philadelphia: Fortress, 1971), 70.

Paul and Christian Identity

The idea of "Christians" as a *tertium genus* is still very common, and embraced by scholars from various traditions.[7] In some studies from the end of the 20th century there is, however a clear tendency to present a more complex picture, and to their credit such studies are often stripped of the rather flagrant anti-Semitism, which characterized much previous scholarship. For instance, in his methodologically sophisticated study of the emergence of the religion of "the earliest churches," Gerd Theissen claims that Paul remained Jewish in his self-understanding even though he abandoned Torah observance.[8] The renunciation of circumcision and food regulations eventually led to a break between Jews and Christians in the generation after Jesus—yet the two groups still belonged closely together. In Theissen's view attempts from traditionalistic groups who wanted "to maintain the tie with Judaism by adopting the marks of Jewish identity,"[9] led Paul to the conclusion that Torah observance had to be abandoned altogether, but the final rejection of Judaism occurred only later, as he claims is evident from the Gospels.[10]

James D. G. Dunn, representing the so-called New Perspective on Paul and highly influenced by E. P. Sanders's groundbreaking revision of ancient Judaism,[11] also offers a more complex picture of the relation between Jews and non-Jews within the early Jesus movement. Dunn offers an alternative to the idea of a merging together of the ethnic identities, "Jew" and "Gentile," suggesting that Paul created a new, shared identity by redefining "Israel" to

---

[7] See e.g. D. Boyarin, *A Radical Jew: Paul and the Politics of Identity* (Berkeley: University of California Press, 1994); B. Holmberg, "Jewish *Versus* Christian Identity in the Early Church," *RB* 105 (1998): 397–425; D. Horrell, "'Becoming Christian': Solidifying Christian Identity and Content," in *Handbook of Early Christianity: Social Science Approaches* (ed. A. J. Blasi, et al.; Walnut Creek: AltaMira, 2002), 309–35; H. Räisänen, *The Rise of Christian Beliefs: The Thought World of Early Christians* (Minneapolis: Fortress, 2010).

[8] G. Theissen, *The Religion of the Earliest Churches: Creating a Symbolic World: A Theory of Primitive Christian Religion* (Minneapolis: Fortress, 1999), 231.

[9] Theissen, *Religion of the Earliest Churches*, 209.

[10] Ibid., 169–70.

[11] E. P. Sanders, *Paul and Palestinian Judaism: A Comparison of Patterns of Religion* (Minneapolis: Fortress, 1977),

mean "the called of God." In Dunn's view, the ethnic categories, "Jew" and "Gentile," remain to some extent and "Israel," should not yet be understood as the "new Israel."[12]

A similar idea is found in Philip Eslers's study, *Conflict and Identity in Romans* (2003).[13] Using various social-scientific theories, Esler claims that Paul was trying to solve ethnic conflicts in the Roman community, by urging the community to embrace a common identity "in Christ" without obliterating the identity of either subgroup, thus explicitly trying to maintain the original identities of the Jews and non-Jews in the movement. Thus, preserving the original ethnic identities, "Jew" and "Gentile," was an important aspect of developing Christian identity in Eslers's view.[14]

However, both Dunn and Esler agree that Paul's Jewish identity, especially regarding Torah observance, was significantly affected by his belief in Christ. In Dunn's view, Paul found nothing wrong with the Torah, except those parts that created a barrier between Jews and non-Jews, that is, identity markers such as circumcision, food laws and purity regulations.[15] Similarly, according to Esler the only problem with the Torah from Paul's point of view was its failure to achieve what it was designed to do: "The law, in short, was not strong enough for the dirty job God gave it."[16]

Recently, scholars, also influenced by Sanders's study of Palestinian Judaism, have reached quite different conclusions regarding Paul's relation to Judaism. This tradition, influenced by the works of scholars like Krister Stendahl, John J. Gager, and Lloyd Gaston,[17] emphasizes

---

[12] J. D. G. Dunn, *The Theology of Paul the Apostle* (Grand Rapids: Eerdmans, 1998), 504–9.

[13] P. F. Esler, *Conflict and Identity in Romans: The Social Setting in Paul's Letter* (Minneapolis: Fortress Press, 2003).

[14] Esler does not use the term "Jew" but translates Ἰουδαῖοι as "Judeans" stressing the territorial connotations of the designation, see *Conflict and Identity*, 62–8.

[15] See e.g., J. D. G. Dunn, "The New Perspective on Paul," *BJRJ* 65 (1983): 95–122; idem, *The Partings of the Ways: Between Christianity and Judaism and Their Significance for the Character of Christianity* (London: SCM Press, 1991), 117–139; idem, "Who Did Paul Think He Was? A Study of Jewish-Christian Identity," *NTS* 45 (1999): 174–93.

[16] Esler, *Conflict and Identity*, 361, 364.

[17] J. G. Gager, *Reinventing Paul* (Oxford: Oxford University Press, 2000); L. Gaston, *Paul and the Torah* (Vancouver: University of British Columbia Press, 1990); K. Stendahl, *Paul among Jews and Gentiles, and Other Essays* (London: SCM Press, 1977).

Paul's Jewish identity in a more radical way. Some scholars, like Mark Nanos,[18] even assume that Paul continued observing the Torah after his involvement with the Jesus movement. In William S. Campbell's view, Paul does not convert to "Christianity," nor does he breake with Judaism. While both Jewish and non-Jewish identities undergo a transformation of sorts, this does not imply the emergence of a common "Christian" identity, according to Campbell. Rather, the two groups, Jews and non-Jews, retain their original identities.[19]

This recent development within Pauline studies affects not only our view of the apostle, but also the reconstructions of the development of the early Jesus movement as a whole and its transition into what later became known as the Christian church. If Paul can be viewed as being part of Judaism rather than in conflict with Judaism, and at least as Torah observant as any other Jew in the Diaspora, his relation to certain key players within the early Jesus movement has to be fundamentally reconsidered.

Firstly, if the major dividing line between different factions of Jewish followers of Jesus was not the issue of whether the Torah was still valid for Jews, there must be a different reason for the fierce conflicts within the movement. Secondly, perspectives on Paul, which emphasize his Jewish identity, make attempts at defining "Jewish-Christianity" less relevant. If Jews within the early Jesus movement in general agreed that Jewish followers of Jesus should continue to express their relation to the God of Israel by observing the Torah, the traditional ideological constructions of "Jewish" versus "Gentile" Christianity has to be called into question.

I tend to believe that different views on the inclusion of non-Jews in the eschatological people of God among Jewish adherents to the Jesus movement, is a more likely explanation of the controversies within the movement. Thus, various, often conflicting, ideas of how non-Jewish followers of Jesus should relate to Israel, to

---

[18] See e.g. M. D. Nanos, *The Mystery of Romans: The Jewish Context of Paul's Letter* (Minneapolis: Fortress, 1996); idem, *The Irony of Galatians: Pauls' Letter in First Century Context* (Philadelphia: Fortress, 2001); idem, "Paul and Judaism: Why Not Paul's Judaism?" in *Paul Unbound: Other Perspectives on Paul* (ed. M. Given; Peabody: Hendrickson, 2010), 117–60.

[19] W. S. Campbell, *Paul and the Creation of Christian Identity* (London: T&T Clark, 2006).

Israel's God, to the Torah, and to the people of Israel, co-existed and constituted the main problem within the movement. One major problem for all Jews who socialized with non-Jews was the Jewish notion that non-Jews were considered morally impure, primarily because of their involvement in what from a Jewish perspective was considered idolatry.[20] This means that it was not, as previously assumed, different opinions of the *general* validity of the Torah that distinguished different Jewish Jesus-oriented groups from each other, but whether or not the Torah was a suitable tool for creating a holy and pure people out of profane, impure, idolatrous *non-Jews*. On these issues there seems to have existed multiple Jewish opinions.

Jewish Attitudes Toward Non-Jews

Although there was probably a certain Jewish reluctance to socialize with non-Jews, there can be no doubt that social relations between Jews and non-Jews were common, especially in the Diaspora. It is true that Jews at some places were confined to certain areas, like in Rome[21] and Alexandria,[22] but as for Antioch-on-the Orontes, the sources do not conclusively show that Jews lived in certain Jewish areas.[23] In any event, the mere existence of large Jewish populations in the great ancient cities makes it almost impossible to imagine that Jews did not interact with the non-Jewish population.

In his extensive study on Jewish patterns of universalism, Terrence Donaldson distinguishes between several kinds of Jewish attitudes to non-Jews. Firstly, he deals with evidence of non-Jews

---

[20] See C. E. Hayes, *Gentile Impurities and Jewish Identities: Intermarriage and Conversion from the Bible to the Talmud* (Oxford: Oxford University Press, 2002); J. Klawans, "Notions of Gentile Impurity in Ancient Judaism," *AJSR* 20 (1995): 285–312; idem, *Impurity and Sin in Ancient Judaism* (Oxford: Oxford University Press, 2000); M. Zetterholm, "Paul and the Missing Messiah," in *The Messiah: In Early Judaism and Christianity* (ed. M. Zetterholm; Minneapolis: Fortress, 2007), 33–55.

[21] J. M. G. Barclay, *Jews in the Mediterranean Diaspora: From Alexander to Trajan (323 BCE–117 CE)* (Edinburgh: T&T Clark, 1996).

[22] S. Gambetti, *The Alexandrian Riots of 38 CE and the Persecution of the Jews: A Historical Reconstruction* (Leiden: Brill, 2009).

[23] M. Zetterholm, *The Formation of Christianity in Antioch: A Social-Scientific Approach to the Separation between Judaism and Christianity* (London: Routledge, 2003), 87–88.

who in different ways express sympathy with Judaism.[24] This could take various forms, such as non-Jews honoring the temple, attending synagogue services, adopting Jewish customs, or acknowledging the God of Israel as the supreme deity.[25] Jewish attitudes to non-Jewish sympathizers were typically positive, according to Donaldson:

> [T]he impression is given that Gentiles who engaged in monotheistic worship, who recognized the divine origin of Israel's law, and who adopted a Jewish way of life to a certain extent were thereby fulfilling everything that God expected of them as Gentiles.[26]

Occasionally, of course, sympathizers went all the way and became Jews meaning that the proselyte henceforth was expected to exclusively worship the God of Israel, and to observe the Torah. According to Donaldson this was normally considered as something positive—converts were welcomed and "enjoyed the same relationship with God as did native-born Israelites."[27] Furthermore, Donaldson makes a distinction between "exclusive monotheism," characterizing groups, which rejected all monotheistic beliefs except their own, and "generous monotheism," characterizing groups, which showed a positive attitude towards those who worshipped the one creator God. With some Jewish authors this could mean presenting the Jewish law as a general monotheistic ethic principle, or equating the Torah with Greek philosophy, which sometimes meant downplaying the specific Jewish identity markers.[28] In sum: there is ample evidence of a positive Jewish attitude towards non-Jews who sympathized with Judaism, or who converted to Judaism. Furthermore, Jews sometimes presented the Torah as a universalistic ethical principal suitable also for non-Jews.

There are some dissenting voices, however. Some texts from

---

[24] See also S. J. D. Cohen, *The Beginnings of Jewishness: Boundaries, Varieties, Uncertainties* (Berkeley: University of California Press, 1999), 140–74.

[25] T. L. Donaldson, *Judaism and the Gentiles: Patterns of Universalism (to 135 CE)* (Waco: Baylor University Press, 2007), 471.

[26] Donaldson, *Judaism and the Gentiles*, 481.

[27] Ibid., 491.

[28] Ibid., 493–5.

the intertestamental period take up the theme that the non-Jewish nations will be destroyed or subordinated to Israel found in the Hebrew Bible.[29] In these texts conversion does not seem to be an option. In *1 En.* 91:9, for example, the author states that:

> All that which is (common) with the heathen shall be surrendered; their towers shall be inflamed with fire, and be removed from the whole earth. They shall be thrown into the judgment of fire, and perish in wrath and in the force of eternal judgment.[30]

Donaldson points out that some authors describe God as waiting for the nations to turn to him even though this waiting is fruitless and the non-Jews ultimately face destruction.[31] As for the possibility of conversion to Judaism the author of *Jubilees* (15:26) takes the most extreme position making conversion virtually impossible:

> And anyone who is born whose own flesh is not circumcised on the eighth day is not from the sons of the covenant which the Lord made for Abraham since (he is) from the children of destruction.[32]

As Nina Livesey states, the author of *Jubilees* substantially strengthens the command to circumcise every male in Gen 17:12 and "permits no deviation from this temporal requirement: to avoid circumcision results in death."[33] Only males circumcised on the eight day are elected for salvation.

While most Jews apparently had a positive attitude toward sympathizers and believed that non-Jews could convert to Judaism and become included in Israel, others evidently had a less favorable view of non-Jews in general, and to the possibility of conversion to Judaism.

---

[29] See e.g. Amos 1:3–2:3; Isa 13:1–19:15; Jer 46:1–50; Ezek 25:1–30:26. On the eschatological status of non-Jews see also Zetterholm, *Formation of Christianity*, 136–40.

[30] Trans. E. Isaac (*OTP*). See also e.g. Bar. 4:25, 31–35; *Jub.* 22:20–22; *Sib. Or.* 3:669–701; *T. Mos.* 10:7.

[31] E.g. *Apoc. Abr.* 31:6, see Donaldson, *Judaism and the Gentiles*, 510 n. 3.

[32] Trans. O. S. Wintermute (*OTP*).

[33] N. E. Livesey, *Circumcision as a Malleable Symbol* (Tübingen: Mohr Siebeck, 2010), 18. See also Donaldson, *Paul and the Gentiles*, 52–53.

Interestingly, these opposing attitudes toward non-Jewish involvement in Judaism and Torah observance are found also in slightly later texts. In the so-called R. Ishmael midrashim, representing a particular rabbinic school of interpretation, we clearly encounter a universalistic tendency, according to which it is good for non-Jews to observe the Torah. This is stated, for instance in *Mekilta de R. Ishmael* (Bahodesh 1), in an interpretation of Exod 19:2. The midrash reads:

> *They encamped in the wilderness [Exod 19:2].* The Torah was given in public, openly in a free place. For had the Torah been given in the land of Israel, the Israelites could have said to the nations of the world: You have no share in it. But now that it was given in the wilderness publicly and openly in a place that is free for all, everyone wishing to accept it could come and accept it.[34]

Similarly, in *Sipra* on Lev 18:1–5, a non-Jew "doing" Torah is compared to the high priest:

> *You shall keep my laws and my rules, and by doing them man* [אדם] *shall live* [Lev 18:5]. Rabbi Jirmia used to say: "How do we know that even a non-Jew who 'does Torah' [עושה תורה] is like the high priest? Scripture says, *by doing [this] man shall live* [Lev 18:5]. Priests, Levites, and Israelites it does not say here [rather Scripture says 'man']. And likewise it says, *this is the Torah of man* [וזאת תורת האדם] [2 Sam 7:19]. Priests, Levites, and Israelites it does not say here. And likewise it says, *Open the gates, and let …* [Isa 26:2]. Priests, Levites, and Israelites it does not say here, rather, *Open the gates, and let a righteous nation* [גוי צדיק] *enter, [a nation] that keeps faith* [Isa 26:2]."[35]

By stressing that the biblical text does not specifically mention the categories that make up "Israel"—priests, Levites, and Israelites—and by connecting Lev 18:5 to Isa 26:2, the author clearly indicates that Torah observance leads to life also for non-Jews who engage

---

[34] Trans. Lauterbach (2:198).

[35] Quoted from K. Hedner Zetterholm, *Jewish Interpretation of the Bible: Ancient and Contemporary* (Minneapolis: Fortress, 2012).

in observing God's law—Torah is not restricted only to Jews. As pointed out by Marc Hirshman, nothing indicates that the non-Jew mentioned in the midrash is involved in *studying* the Torah. The comparison is made between the high priest and a non-Jew *observing* the Torah. Moreover, nothing implies a conversion context—the non-Jew is not a proselyte but a Torah observant non-Jew.[36] Thus, according to these texts the Torah is given to all mankind including non-Jews, who, without converting to Judaism,[37] may have a share in the Torah and in the world to come.

However, other texts, such as *m. Avot* 3:14, reveal a completely different attitude towards non-Jewish involvement in the Torah:

> He [R. Akiva] would say, "Precious is the human being, who was created in the image [of God]. It was an act of still greater love that it was made known to him that he was created in the image [of God], as it is said, For in the image of God he made man [Gen 9:6]. Precious are Israelites, who are called children to the Omnipresent. It was an act of still greater love that they were called children to the Omnipresent, as it is said, You are the children of the Lord your God [Deut 14:1]. Precious are Israelites, to whom was given the precious thing. It was an act of still greater love that it was made known to them that to them was given that precious thing with which the world was made, as it is said, For I give you a good doctrine. Do not forsake my Torah [Prov 4:2]."[38]

This text emphasizes that the Torah is the exclusive property of the Jewish people. The same is true of the following passage from *Sipre* to Deuteronomy (§ 345), where non-Jewish involvement in the Torah is compared to adultery:

> [T]he Torah is betrothed to Israel and is like a married woman with respect to the nations of the world. And so it says, "Can a man rake embers into bosom without burning his clothes? Can a man walk on

---

[36] See M. Hirshman, "Rabbinic Universalism in the Second and Third Centuries," *HTR* 93 (2000): 101–115, esp. 108.

[37] Hirshman, "Rabbinic Universalism," 114–115.

[38] Trans. J. Neusner.

live coals without scorching his feet? It is the same with one who sleeps with his fellow's wife; none who touches her will go unpunished."[39]

These two opposing attitudes toward non-Jewish involvement in Torah business are often associated with two rabbinic "schools."[40] The more universalistic attitude is attributed to R. Ishmael's school while the latter, more particularistic one, to the school of R. Akiva. Even if those ideas cannot be traced back to the historical figures, R. Ishmael and R. Akiva, with any certainty, the existence of "schools" in the sense of "distinct and recognizable interpretative practices, assumptions, and terms" has been reasserted in recent scholarship.[41]

This means that two opposing attitudes to non-Jews, one universalistic and one more particularistic, can be found in the Hebrew Bible, in the intertestamental literature and in early rabbinic literature. This strongly indicates the existence of two distinctive intellectual traditions that originated early on and developed over time. There are, for instance, indications that the R. Ishmael "school" was dependent on earlier wisdom traditions like those found in Ben Sira.[42] The existence of these different approaches to non-Jews is, in my view, highly relevant when reconstructing the history of the early Jesus movement.

Non-Jews and the Synagogue

The fact that a wide range of Jewish literature from the Hebrew Bible to early tannaitic midrashim deal with how to relate properly to non-Jews is, of course, in itself a strong evidence of social interaction between Jews and non-Jews. Also, as is well known, and thus hardly controversial, there is overwhelming evidence of non-Jewish participation in Jewish religious life. Josephus, for instance,

---

[39] Cited from S. D. Fraade, *From Tradition to Commentary: Torah and Its Interpretation in the Midrash Sifre to Deuteronomy* (Albany: State University of New York Press, 1991), 57.

[40] Hirshman, "Rabbinic Universalism."

[41] A. Yadin, *Scripture as Logos: Rabbi Ishmael and Ther Origins of Midrash* (Philadelphia: University of Pennsylvania Press, 2004), xi.

[42] Yadin, *Scripture as Logos*, 162–5.

specifically states regarding Antioch that the Jewish communities had a special attraction for the non-Jewish population. The Jews were according to Josephus "constantly attracting to their religious ceremonies multitude of Greeks, and these they had in some measure incorporated with themselves" (*B.J.* 7.45).[43] In another famous statement Josephus explicitly mentions that this connection to Judaism involved a certain adaptation to a Jewish life-style (*C. Ap.* 2.282):

> The masses have long since shown a keen desire to adopt our religious observances; and there is not one city, Greek or barbarian, nor a single nation, to which our custom of abstaining from work on the seventh day has not spread, and where the fasts and the lighting of lamps and many of our prohibitions in the matter of food are not observed.[44]

Although it is evident that Josephus has no intention of presenting an objective view on this matter, the fact that Greco-Roman authors, like Seneca, and Epictetus, also reveal knowledge of non-Jewish symphatization with Judaism, means that we can be quite certain that the phenomenon was common in antiquity.[45]

Thus, during the first century c.e. we know that non-Jews participated as guests in some Diaspora synagogues. They had consequently developed personal relationships with Jews, and had indeed adopted Jewish religious customs. They were probably rather well-informed about the ideological background to Jewish traditions. We have to admit that these people could be described, at least to some extent, as partly Torah observant non-Jews. In fact, as argued by Shaye Cohen, *some may even have called themselves Jews.*[46]

What may the reason be for this non-Jewish involvement with Judaism? If one attempts to relate non-Jewish interest in Judaism to the Jewish patterns of universalism as defined by Donaldson,

---

[43] Trans. Thackery (LCL).

[44] Trans. Thackery (LCL).

[45] See e.g. Seneca, *Ep.* 108.22; Plutarch, *Superst.* 166A. See also Donaldson, *Judaism and the Gentiles*, 363–409; M. Murray, *Playing a Jewish Game: Gentile Christian Judaizing in the First and Second Centuries CE* (Waterloo: Wilfred Laurier University Press, 2004), 11–27.

[46] Cohen, *Beginnings*, 66–68.

it appears rather evident that non-Jews interacted with Jews who looked favorable upon their interest in Jewish traditions. Jewish attitudes to non-Jewish sympathizers were typically positive we recall from above. It is not a far-fetched conjecture that those Jews who interacted with non-Jewish sympathizers in the synagogues of the Diaspora were influenced by a universalistic ideology with roots in the Hebrew Bible and present in the intertestatmental literature and early midrashim. Thus, the reason as to why non-Jews observed parts of the Torah is most likely because they were inspired to do so by Jews embracing a universalistic ideology with regard to Torah observance.

I have argued elsewhere that it is sociologically most likely that those non-Jews who joined the Jesus movement were recruited from groups who had previously been in contact with Judaism, that is, Torah observant sympathizers.[47] From a sociological standpoint non-Jewish Torah observance also make sense: as pointed out by Rodney Stark there is a strong tendency among converts to conform to the behavior in the new group.[48] Even though "conversion" in the sense of leaving one religion for another does not apply to the situation in antiquity, the general mechanism is still is applicable.

Non-Jews interested in Judaism would quite naturally be prone candidates for finding a theology attractive that explicitly gave them a place within Jewish soteriology. Through the death and resurrection of Jesus-the-Messiah, non-Jews were guaranteed a place in the world to come, and were also protected against the spiritual rulers and powers which posed a constant threat to people in antiquity. As Reuven Kimelman aptly puts it:

> It is also possible that those pagans initially interested in Judaism converted to Christianity upon encountering a form of Judaism, as it were, more acceptable to their Roman sensibilities. What could be better than getting written scriptures, antiquity, morality,

---

[47] Zetterholm, "Missing Messiah," 44–45.

[48] R. Stark, *The Rise of Christianity: How the Obscure, Marginal Jesus Movement Became the Dominant Religious Force in the Western World in a Few Centuries* (San Francisco: HarperCollins, 1997), 18.

and monotheism, along with the salvific power of a divine man.[49]

Their interest in Judaism in the first place may have been motivated precisely by such concerns and by imitating a Jewish life style non-Jews may have tried to gain righteousness in the eyes of the God of Israel, the God and ruler of the entire universe.

Non-Jews in the Early Jesus movement

If we accept these assumptions, we reach the conclusion that *the first non-Jews who joined the Jesus movement most likely were Torah-observant.* Furthermore, we need to accept that during the first century, the general trend among non-Jews who associated themselves with Jews, whether being followers of Jesus or not, was *toward* observing the Torah. Nothing indicates that the Jesus movement initially took a different position. On the contrary, Acts' version of the so-called Apostolic Council reveals that there were forces within the movement advocating Torah observance for non-Jews:

> Then certain individuals came down from Judea and were teaching the brothers, "Unless you are circumcised according to the custom of Moses, you cannot be saved." . . . But some believers who belonged to the sect of the Pharisees stood up and said, "It is necessary for them to be circumcised and ordered to keep the law of Moses."[50]

Even though the event as such is narrated in a highly idealized way, there is no reason to question the historicity of the idea that non-Jews should observe the Torah, in this case after having converted to Judaism. The existence of "Jewish Christians" is, of course, a striking proof of the existence of Jewish groups who to various degrees advocated a Jewish life style for non-Jewish adherents to

---

[49] R. Kimelman, "Identifying Jews and Christians in Roman Syria-Palestine," in *Galilee through the Centuries: Confluence of Cultures* (ed. E. M. Meyers; Winona Lake: Eisenbrauns, 1999), 301–33, esp. 307.

[50] Acts 15:1, 5.

the Jesus movement. However, while "Jewish Christianity" often has been thought of as an anomaly, a heretic misconception of the true nature of "Christianity,"[51] I would assume that this way of connecting non-Jews to the Torah, even allowing for formal conversions, was the natural, possibly even the dominant approach to non-Jewish followers of Jesus.[52]

According to recent scholarship, the community that produced the Gospel of Matthew took precisely the position Luke claims that "certain individuals" did, arguing that salvation and Jewish identity were intertwined. According to scholars embracing this view, Matthew's community could be described as a secteristic Jewish messianic group, demanding conversion, including male circumcision of non-Jews who wanted to join the community.[53] David Sim, for instance, states:

> Any members of Matthew's community who were not Jewish by birth must have been Jewish by conversion. That is to say, any people of non-Jewish origin in this community had become (Christian) Jewish proselytes in order to join it. As proselytes they enjoyed the privileges of the Jewish people and they were obliged to uphold the Torah.[54]

Apparently, the Matthean community seems to have embraced the same universalistic pattern as the one mentioned by Donaldson above: Jews who encouraged non-Jews to convert to Judaism and welcomed those who did so.

However, a less strict version of this form of universalistic pattern also seems represented within the Jesus movement. This approach

---

[51] A perspective highly emphasized by F. C. Baur, "Die Christuspartei in Der Korinthischen Gemeinde, Der Gegensatz Des Petrinischen Und Paulinischen Christenthums in Der Ältesten Kirche, Der Apostel Petrus in Rom," *Tübingen Zeitschrift für Theologie* 4 (1831): 61–206. See also Carlton Paget, "Definition," 48–52.

[52] See J. D. G. Dunn, *Acts of the Apostles* (Valley Forge: Trinity Press, 1996), 198: "it is hard to deny the strength of their case."

[53] See e.g. J. A. Overman, *Matthew's Gospel and Formative Judaism: The Social World of the Matthean Community* (Minneapolis: Fortress, 1990); A. J. Saldarini, *Matthew's Christian-Jewish Community* (Chicago: Chicago University Press, 1994); D. C. Sim, *The Gospel of Matthew and Christian Judaism: The History and Social Setting of the Matthean Community* (Edinburgh: T&T Clark, 1998).

[54] Sim, *Gospel of Matthew*, 247–8.

seems more in line with positive attitudes toward non-Jews who without converting to Judaism express sympathy by socializing with Jews, participating in Jewish religious life, and by engaging in eclectic Torah observance as Josephus bears witness to: "in some measure incorporated with themselves."[55] *Didache* 6:2–3 possibly indicates such an alternative:

> For if you can bear the entire yoke of the Lord [ὅλον τὸν ζυγὸν τοῦ κυρίου], you will be perfect [τέλειος ἔσῃ]; but if you cannot, do as much as you can. And concerning food, bear what you can. But especially abstain from food sacrificed to idols; for this is a ministry to dead gods.

This addition to the Two Ways section is generally considered to represent a Jewish address to non-Jewish followers of Jesus. However, as with much of the material in the *Didache*, it is hard to know at what stage in the redaction process this section was added, or what its original *Sitz im Leben* was. It seems likely that this section was added to the Two Ways instruction in a context where the Torah was observed by Jewish followers of Jesus and the section therefore probably does not belong to the latest layers in the redaction process.[56]

It seems reasonable to assume that the "yoke of the Lord" refers to the Torah,[57] even though this specific combination never occurs in other Jewish literature in which expressions like "yoke of the kingdom" or "yoke of Heaven" are common. All occurrences in the New Testament except one refer to the Torah.[58] However, if the phrase "yoke of the Lord" were understood as referring to the Torah *as interpreted by Jesus*,[59] the expression would make sense, especially in relation to Matt 11:29–30: "Take my yoke [ζυγός] upon you, and

---

[55] *B.J.* 7.45.

[56] H. van de Sandt and D. Flusser, *The Didache: Its Jewish Sources and Its Place in Early Judaism and Christianity* (Minneapolis: Fortress, 2002), 29.

[57] J. A. Draper, "Torah and Troublesome Apostles in the Didache Community," *NTS* 33 (1991): 347–72, esp. 362; Sandt and Flusser, *Didache*, 269. Cf., however, the discussion in K. Niederwimmer, *The Didache: A Commentary* (Minneapolis: Fortress, 1998), 121–3.

[58] In Matt 11:29, 30; Acts 15:10; Gal 5:1 and Rev 6:5 ζυγός refers to the Torah. The exception is 1 Tim 6:1.

[59] Draper, "Troublesome Apostles," 362.

learn of me; for I am meek and lowly in heart: and ye shall find rest unto your souls. For my yoke [ζυγός] is easy, and my burden is light."[60]

In *Did.* 6:2 "perfection" is thus connected to Torah observance, but nowhere is "perfection" defined in terms of "becoming Jewish," even if the possibility that this is what is meant should not be ruled out. By connecting *Did.* 6:2 to the call to live as to be found perfect in the end time in *Did.* 16:2, Jonathan Draper, for instance, argues that the community indeed expected non-Jewish adherents to convert to Judaism and that they only by doing so could be regarded as "perfect."[61] But given the universalistic patterns describe by Donaldson and the probability that Jews in ordinary synagogues inspired non-Jews to observe the Torah, another possibility is to see the *Didache's* attitude toward non-Jews as a common Jewish approach to non-Jews. Thus, I would assume that the title of the *Didache* ("the teaching of the Lord ... to the nations"), in *Did.* 6:2–3 implies that the community allowed non-Jews to remain non-Jewish but continued to admonish them to observe the Torah according to the halakha of Jesus.

So far we have seen that two attitudes toward non-Jews within "common Judaism" are also found within the Jewish Jesus movement. Some Jews, like those of the community of Matthew, believed that it was a good thing for non-Jews to convert to Judaism and thus to observe the Torah. Others, as possibly reflected in the *Didache*, considered preserved ethnic identity in combination with Torah observance to be a suitable approach. What about the more negative view of the non-Jew, conversion, and Torah observance seen in the *Jubilees* and the R. Akiva midrashim for instance? Does this approach also find its counterpart within the early Jesus movement?

Regardless of what position scholars take on the question of Paul's own relation to the Torah, the fact that he vigorously objected to non-Jewish involvement in the Torah is universally recognized. The traditional explanation for this is that Paul had realized that the

---

[60] W. D. Davies and D. C. Allison, *A Critical and Exegetical Commentary on the Gospel According to Matthew* (3 vols.; London: T&T Clark: 1991), 2:289–90.

[61] Draper, "Troublesome Apostles," 368.

Torah had failed to do what it was intended to do,[62] or, as Rudolf Bultmann put it: "*mans's effort to achieve his salvation by keeping the Law only leads him to sin, indeed this effort itself in the end is already sin*."[63] Such very distinct Lutheran interpretations of Paul have recently been modified—we recall, for example, Dunn's idea that Paul only rejected those parts of the Torah that separate Jews from non-Jews—but the idea of a general opposition between Paul and Judaism, indeed between Judaism and Christianity, is still the dominant paradigm governing the interpretation of Paul.

However, if we embrace a perspective on Paul that allows him to remain fully Jewish, "ethnically, culturally, religiously, and theologically,"[64] and also taking into account the various attitudes toward non-Jews prevalent within "common" Judaism, a different picture emerges. A "Lutheran" Paul fits poorly into the thought worlds of Second Temple Judaism and while truly unique ideas occasionally do emerge from nothing, more often than not they are dependent on ideas already prevalent in the cultural matrix. Accordingly, I believe it to be more methodologically sound to interpret Paul in relation to a reconstruction of the symbolic world of first-century Judaism than against the background of ideas emerging from the Reformation.

Many Jews obviously believed that non-Jews would be included in the eschatological salvation and Paul seems to have been among them.[65] As the apostle to the Gentiles, he believed that he had a special responsibility to "bring about the obedience of faith among all the Gentiles" (Rom 1:5). Evidently he did not see this as involving conversion to Judaism (like Matthew's community did). Instead, Paul advocated preserved ethnic identities (like the *Didache* community) and opposed conversions to Judaism by non-Jewish adherents to the Jesus movement (or Jews becoming "Greeks" for that matter): "Was anyone at the time of his call already circumcised? Let him not seek to remove the marks of circumcision. Was anyone at the

---

[62] Esler, *Conflict and Identity*, 361.

[63] Bultmann, *Theology of the New Testament*, 1:264.

[64] P. Eisenbaum, *Paul Was Not a Christian: The Original Message of a Misunderstood Apostle* (New York: HarperOne, 2009), 9.

[65] Donaldson, *Judaism and the Gentiles*, 499–505; Zetterholm, *Formation of Christianity*, 138–9.

time of his call uncircumcised? Let him not seek circumcision" (1 Cor 7:18). But unlike the *Didache*, and probably the majority of Jews in the Diaspora, Paul clearly disapproved of non-Jews observing the Torah in the same way Jews did, thereby presumably claiming a certain privileged status before the God of Israel.

Above I suggested that the first non-Jews who joined the Jesus movement most likely were Torah-observant, meaning that those non-Jews Paul encountered in the synagogues of the Diaspora had been encouraged to observe the Torah, which they also gladly did while remaining non-Jews. Was Paul inspired by an ideology similar to the one we encountered in the tannaitic midrashim? Did he, unlike the author of the *Didache*, believe that the Torah was the precious gift to the *Jewish* people only? Did he consider non-Jewish Torah observance comparable to adultery? If so, this less universalistic approach discernible in Second Temple Judaism, but fully developed only in early tannaitic literature, is also represented within the early Jesus movement. Paul strove forcefully to correct a very common behavior in the Diaspora that he believed to be wrong, not because there was something wrong with the Torah as such or because Paul had left Judaism for Christianity, but simply because he did nor believe Torah observance (or conversion to Judaism) was for non-Jews. Paul's view is still rather unique: on the one hand he certainly believed that non-Jews had a place in the world to come, on the other hand, salvation could neither be achieved by conversion to Judaism, nor by non-Jewish Torah observance. In Paul's view, non-Jews could be saved only by the faithfulness of Jesus-the-Messiah and he thus combines a particularistic view of the relation between the non-Jew and the Torah with a universalistic view of the salvation of the nations.

Conclusion

Not without considerable difficulties and under constant renegotiations, mainstream Christianity eventually succeeded in creating a fairly well-defined Christian identity. An important prerequisite for this process was to solve the problem of the two categories, Jews and non-Jews, which was eventually achieved by simply eliminating the former category. This radical solution, a virtual inversion of the balance of power as compared to the situation during the first century, was a new invention unlike anything during the early phase of the Jesus movement. Meanwhile, various Jesus oriented Jewish groups continued to struggle with the issue of ethnicity within the movement. Some ways seem never to have parted or have parted very late.[66]

During the major part of the first century the problem of how to relate to non-Jews dominated the Jesus movement. This essay suggests that the various strategies embraced by different Jesus oriented groups were dependent on the overarching ideology of the individuals who exercised influence on the actual group. Thus, Jews who had a positive attitude to non-Jews, who rejoiced over non-Jews who appropriated specific Jewish traits, continued to relate to non-Jews in the same way after being involved with the Jesus movement. Jews, who believed that non-Jews would benefit from conversion to Judaism, would continue to favor that position also within the context of the Jesus movement. Finally, Jews who believed the Torah to be God's most precious gift to the people of Israel, would vigorously try to get non-Jews to stop expressing their relation to the God of Israel through imitating parts of a Jewish life style, most probably against their will.

Thus, during most of the first century it is quite hard to define a real "Gentile-Christian." It could mean someone, who after joining the Matthean community had converted to Judaism, thus becoming a Torah observant *Jewish* disciple of Jesus. Or it could

---

[66] See the various contributions in A. H. Becker and A. Y. Reed, eds., *The Ways That Never Parted: Jews and Christians in Late Antiquity and the Early Middle Ages* (Tübingen: Mohr Siebeck, 2003), and Kimelman, "Identifying Jews and Christians."

mean someone who without changing his or her ethnic status observed as much of the Torah as possible, thereby becoming "perfect." And, of course, it could mean someone who perhaps against his or her will had been forced to cease expressing his or her loyalty to the God of Israel by Torah observance.

I doubt there ever existed a *tertium genus*, a third race, consisting of former Jews and non-Jews, other than as a hope and a dream: "For he is our peace; in his flesh he has made both groups into one and has broken down the dividing wall, that is, the hostility between us" (Eph 2:14).

Bibliography

A Patristic Greek Lexicon. Edited by G. W. H. Lampe. Oxford: Oxford University Press, 1968.

Abegg, M. G. "The Covenant of the Qumran Sectarians." Pages 81–98 in *The Concept of the Covenant in the Second Temple Period.* Edited by S. E. Porter and J. C. R. de Roo. Atlanta: Society of Biblical Literature, 2003.

Abramowski, L. "Die 'Erinnerungen der Apostel' bei Justin." Pages 341–53 in *Das Evangelium und die Evangelien: Vorträge vom Tübinger Symposium 1982.* Edited by P. Stuhlmacher. Tübingen: Mohr Siebeck, 1983.

Ådna, J., and H. Kvalbein, eds. *The Mission of the Early Church to Jews and Gentiles.* Tübingen: Mohr Siebeck, 2000.

Aland, K., and B. Aland, eds. *Text und Textwert der griechischen Handschriften des Neuen Testaments. IV.1: Die Synoptischen Evangelien. Das Markusevangelium.* 2 vols. Berlin: de Gruyter, 1998.

Alexander, L. "Memory and Tradition in the Hellenistic Schools." Pages 113–53 in *Jesus in Memory: Traditions in Oral and Scribal Perspectives.* Edited by W. H. Kelber and S. Byrskog. Waco: Baylor University Press, 2009.

Alon, G. *Jews, Judaism, and the Classical World: Studies in Jewish History in the Times of the Second Temple and Talmud.* Jerusalem: Magness Press, 1977.

Anderson, A. A. *The Book of Psalms.* 2 vols. Grand Rapids: Eerdmans, 1972.

Anderson, B. R. *Imagined Communities.* London: Verso, 1983.

Arnal, W. *The Symbolic Jesus: Historical Scholarship, Judaism and the Construction of Contemporary Identity.* London: Equinox, 2005.

Arnim, H. von. *Leben und Werke des Dio von Prusa.* Berlin: Weidmannsche Buchhandlung, 1898.

Arnold, R. C. D. *The Social Role of Liturgy in the Religion of the Qumran Community.* Leiden: Brill, 2006.

Ascough, R. S. "'A Place to Stand, A Place to Grow': Architectural and Epigraphic Evidence for Expansion in Greco-Roman Associations." Pages 76–98 in *Identity and Interaction in the Ancient Mediterranean: Jews, Christians and Others. Festschrift for Stephen G. Wilson*. Edited by Z. Crook and P. Harland. Sheffield: Sheffield Phoenix Press, 2007.

—, *Paul's Macedonian Associations: The Social Context of Philippians and 1 Thessalonians*. Tübingen: Mohr Siebeck, 2003.

Ascough, R. S., ed. *Religious Rivalries and the Struggle for Success in Sardis and Smyrna*. Waterloo: Wilfrid Laurier University Press, 2005.

Aune, D. E. "The Prophetic Circle of John the Patmos and the Exegesis of Revelation 22.16." *JSNT* 37 (1989): 103–16.

—, "The Social Matrix of the Apocalypse of John." *BR* 26 (1981): 16–32.

—, *Revelation 1-5*. Dallas: Word Books, 1997. Cambridge: Cambridge University Press, 1993.

Aviam, M. "Distribution Maps of Archaeological Data from the Galilee: An Attempt to Establish Zones Indicative of Ethnicity and Religious Affiliation." Pages 115–32 in *Religion, Ethnicity, and Identity in Ancient Galilee*. Edited by J. Zangenberg, H. W. Attridge, and D. B. Martin. Tübingen: Mohr Siebeck, 2007.

—, "Neutestamentliche Hinweise auf halakhische Regelungen." Pages 449–62 in *Nuovo Testamento: Teologie in dialogo culturale: Scritti in onore di Romano Penna nel suo 70° compleanno*. Edited by N. Ciola and G. Pulcinelli. Bologna: Edizioni Dehoniane, 2008.

—, *Antijudaismus im Galaterbrief?: Exegetische Studien zu einem polemischen Schreiben und zur Theologie des Apostels Paulus*. Göttingen: Vandenhoeck & Ruprecht, 1999.

Bammel, C. "Die erste lateinische Rede gegen die Christen." *ZKG* 104 (1993): 295–311.

Barclay, J. M. G. "Constructing Judean Identity after 70 C.E.: A Study of Josephus's *Against Apion.*" Pages 99–112 in *Identity & Interaction in the Ancient Mediterranean: Jews, Christians and Others.* Edited by Z. A. Crook and P. A. Harland. Sheffield: Phoenix Press, 2007.

—, "Paul Among Diaspora Jews: Anomaly or Apostate?" *JSNT* 60 (1995): 89–120.

—, "Paul's Story: Theology as Testimony." Pages 133–56 in *Narrative Dynamics in Paul: A Critical Assessment.* Edited by B. W. Longenecker, Louisville: Westminster John Knox Press, 2002.

—, *Against Apion.* Vol. 10 of *Flavius Josephus Translation and Commentary.* Edited by S. Mason. Leiden: Brill, 2007.

—, *Jews in the Mediterranean Diaspora: From Alexander to Trajan (323 BCE–117 CE).* Edinburgh: T&T Clark, 1996.

—, *Obeying the Truth: Paul's Ethics in Galatia.* Minneapolis: Fortress, 1991.

Baron, S. W. *A Social and Religious History of the Jews: Vol. 1: To the Beginning of the Christian Era.* New York: Columbia University Press, 1952.

Barrett, C. K. *A Commentary on the First Epistle to the Corinthians.* New York: Harper & Row, 1968.

—, *The Acts of the Apostles.* 2 vols. Edinburgh: T&T Clark, 1994.

—, *The First Epistle to the Corinthians.* 2d ed. London: Adam & Charles Black, 1971.

Barth, F. "Introduction." Pages 9–38 in *Ethnic Groups and Boundaries.* Edited by F. Barth. Oslo: Universitetsforlaget, 1969.

Barth, M. *Ephesians: Introduction, Translation, and Commentary.* 2 vols. New York: Doubleday, 1974.

Bauckham, R. J. "Apocalypses." Pages 135–87 in *Justification and Variegated Nomism: Vol 2: The Complexities of Second Temple Judaism.* Edited by D. A. Carson, P. T. O'Brien, and M. A. Seifrid. Tübingen: Mohr Siebeck, 2001.

Bauer, W. *Orthodoxy and Heterodoxy in Earliest Christianity.* Translated by R. A. Kraft and G. Krodel. Philadelphia: Fortress, 1971.

—, *Rechtgläubigkeit und Ketzerei im ältesten Christentum.* Tübingen: Mohr Siebeck, 1907.

Bauer, W., F. W. Arndt and F. W. Gingrich. *Greek-English Lexikon of the New Testament and Other Early Christian Literature.* 3d ed. Chicago, University of Chicago Press, 2001.

Baumgarten, A. I. "The Name of the Pharisees." *JBL* 102 (1983): 411–28.

Baur, F. C. "Die Christuspartei in der korinthischen Gemeinde, der Gegensatz des petrinischen und paulinischen Christenthums in der ältesten Kirche, der Apostel Petrus in Rom." *Tübingen Zeitschrift für Theologie* 4 (1831): 61–206.

Beall, T. S. *Josephus' Description of the Essenes Illustrated by the Dead Sea Scrolls.* Cambridge: Cambridge University Press, 1988.

Beck, R. "On Becoming a Mithraist: New Evidence for the Propagation of the Mysteries," Pages 175–94 in *Religious Rivalries in the Early Roman Empire and the Rise of Christianity.* Edited by L. E. Vaage. Waterloo: Wilfrid Laurier University Press, 2006.

Becker, A. H. and A. Y. Reed. *The Ways that Never Parted: Jews and Christians in Late Antiquity and the Early Middle Ages.* Tübingen: Mohr Siebeck, 2003.

Becker, J. *Paul: Apostle to the Gentiles.* Louisville: John Knox, 1993.

Bellinzoni, A. J. *The Sayings of Jesus in the Writings of Justin Martyr.* Leiden: Brill, 1967.

Belzen, J. A. "Culture, Religion and 'the Dialogical Self': Roots and Character of a Secular Cultural Psychology of Religion." *Archiv für Religionspsychologie und Seelenführung* 25, (2003): 7–24.

Benko, S. "Pagan Criticism of Christianity During the First Two Centuries," *ANRW* 2.23:1055–118. Part 2, *Principat*, 2.23. Edited by H. Temporini and W. Haase. New York: de Gruyter, 1989.

Benvenisti, M. *Sacred Landscape: The Buried History of the Holy Land since 1948.* Berkeley: University of California Press, 2000.

Betz, H. D. *Galatians: A Commentary on Paul's Letter to the Churches in Galatia.* Minneapolis: Fortress, 1979.

Beutler, J. *Die Johannesbriefe.* Regensburg: Verlag Friedrich Pustet, 2000.

Biema, D. van. "The Pope's Favorite Rabbi." *Time* (May 24, 2007)

Bilde, P. *Flavius Josephus Between Jerusalem and Rome.* Sheffield: JSOT, 1988.

Black, M. "The Use of Rhetorical Terminology in Papias on Mark and Matthew." *JSNT* 37 (1989): 31–41.

Blanck, H. *Wiederverwendung alter Statuen als Ehrendenkmähler bei Griechen und Römern.* Rome: L' Erma di Bretschneider, 1969.

Blanton, T. R. *Constructing a New Covenant: Discursive Strategies in the Damascus Document and Second Corinthians.* Tübingen: Mohr Siebeck, 2007.

Bleich, J. D. "Teaching Torah to Non-Jews." *Tradition: A Journal of Orthodox Jewish Thought* 2 (1980): 192–211.

Blum, H. *Die antike Mnemotechnik.* Hildesheim: Georg Olms Verlag, 1969.

Bockmuehl, M. *The Epistle to the Philippians.* London: A&C Black, 1997.

Boismard, M.-E. "'Je ferai avec vous une alliance nouvelle.'" *LumVie* 8 (1953): 94–109.

—, "La connaissance dans l'alliance nouvelle, d'après la première lettre de saint Jean." *RB* 56 (1949): 365–91.

Bosch, D. *Transforming Mission: Paradigm Shifts in Theology of Mission.* Maryknoll: Orbis Books, 1991.

Böttrich, C. *Das slavische Henochbuch.* Gütersloh: Gütersloher Verlagshaus, 1995.

—, *Weltweisheit–Menschheitsethik–Urkult: Studien zum slavischen Henochbuch.* Tübingen: Mohr Siebeck, 1992.

Boyarin, D. *A Radical Jew: Paul and the Politics of Identity.* Berkeley: University of California Press, 1994.

Bradshaw, P. F., M. E. Johnson and L. E. Phillips. *The Apostolic Tradition: A Commentary.* Minneapolis: Fortress, 2002.

Brock, S. P. "Limitations of Syriac in Representing Greek." Pages 83–98 in *The Early Versions of the New Testament.* Edited by B. M. Metzger. Oxford: Clarendon Press, 1977.

Brown, P. "Late Antiquity." Pages 235–312 in *A History of Private Life from Pagan Rome to Byzantium.* Edited by P. Veyne. Cambridge: Harvard University Press, 1987.

Brown, R. E. and J. P. Meier. *Antioch and Rome: New Testament Cradles of Catholic Christianity.* London: Chapman, 1983.

Brown, R. E. *The Epistles of John.* Garden City, New York: Doubleday, 1982.

—, *The Gospel According to John.* 2 vols. Garden City, New York: Doubleday, 1966–1970.

Bruneau P., and J. Ducat. *Guide de Délos.* 3d ed. Paris: Boccard, 1983.

Buell, D. K. *Why This New Race*: *Ethnic Reasoning in Early Christianity.* New York: Columbia University Press, 2005.

Bultmann, R. *Theology of the New Testament* Waco: Baylor University Press, 2007 [1951–1955 in German].

Burkitt, F. C. *Evangelion da-Mepharreshe.* 2 vols. Cambridge: Cambridge University Press, 1904.

Burridge, R. A. *What are the Gospels? A Comparison with Graeco-Roman Biography.* 2d ed. Grand Rapids: Eerdmans, 2004.

Byrskog, S. "A New Quest for the *Sitz im Leben*: Social Memory, the Jesus Tradition and the Gospel of Matthew." *NTS* 52 (2006): 319–36.

—, "Christology and Identity in the Gospels: The Glory of Adam in the Narrative Substructure of Paul's Letter to the Romans." Pages 1–18 in *Identity Formation in the New Testament.* Edited by B. Holmberg and M. Winninge. Tübingen: Mohr Siebeck, 2008.

—, "Memory and Identity in the Gospels: A New Perspective." Pages 33–57 in *Exploring Early Christian Identity.* Edited by B. Holmberg. Tübingen: Mohr Siebeck, 2008.

—, "Performing the Past: Gospel Genre and Identity Formation in the Context of Ancient History Writing." Pages 28–44 in *History and Exegesis: New Testament Essays in Honor of Dr. E. Earle Ellis for His Eightieth Birthday.* Edited by S.-W. Son. New York: T&T Clark, 2006.

—, "The Early Church as a Narrative Fellowship: An Exploratory Study of the Performance of the *Chreia.*" *TTKi* 78 (2007): 207–26.

—, "The Transmission of the Jesus Tradition." Pages 1465–94 in vol. 2 of *The Handbook of the Study of the Historical Jesus.* 4 vols. Edited by T. Holmén and S. E. Porter. Leiden: Brill, 2011.

—, "When Eyewitness Testimony and Oral Tradition Become Written Text." *SEÅ* 74 (2009): 41–53.

—, *Jesus the Only Teacher: Didactic Authority and Transmission in Ancient Israel, Ancient Judaism and the Matthean Community.* Stockholm: Almqvist & Wiksell International, 1994.

—, Review of Rudolf Bultmann, *The History of the Synoptic Tradition. JBL* 122 (2003): 549–55.

—, *Story as History—History as Story: The Gospel Tradition in the Context of Ancient Oral History.* Tübingen: Mohr Siebeck, 2000.

Cadbury, H. J. "Names for Christians and Christianity in Acts." Pages 375–92 in *Additional Notes to the Commentary.* Edited by K. Lake and H. J. Cadbury. Vol. 5 of *The Beginnings of Christianity: Part I. The Acts of the Apostles.* Edited by F. J. Foakes-Jackson and K. Lake. London: Macmillan, 1933.

Campbell, R. A. *The Elders: Seniority within Earliest Christianity.* Edinburgh: T&T Clark, 1994.

Campbell, W. S. "Divergent Images of Paul and His Mission." Pages 187–211 in *Reading Israel in Romans*: *Legitimacy and Plausibility of Divergent Interpretations.* Edited by C. Grenholm and D. Patte. Harrisburg: Trinity Press International, 2000.

—, "I Rate All Things as Loss: Paul's Puzzling Accounting System: Judaism as Loss or the Re-Evaluation of All Things in Christ." Pages 39–61 in *Celebrating Paul: Festschrift in Honor of Jerome Murphy-O'Connor, O.P., and Joseph A. Fitzmyer, S.J.* Edited by P. Spitaler. Washington D.C.: Catholic Biblical Association of America, 2011.

—, "Unity and Diversity in the Church: Transformed Identities and the Peace of Christ in Ephesians." *Transformation* 25 (2008): 15–31.

—, *Paul and the Creation of Christian Identity.* London: T&T Clark, 2006.

Cancik, H., and H. Schneider. *Der neue Pauly: Enzyklopädie der Antike.* 16 vols. Stuttgart: Metzler, 1996–2003.

Cappelletti, S. *The Jewish Community of Rome from the Second Century BCE to the Third Century CE.* Leiden: Brill, 2006.

Carey, G. *Elusive Apocalypse: Reading Authority in the Revelation of John.* Macon: Mercer University Press, 1999.

Carleton Paget, J. "Jewish Proselytism at the Time of Christian Origins: Chimera or Reality?" *JSNT* 62 (1996): 65–103.

—, "The Definition of the Terms *Jewish Christian* and *Jewish Christianity* in the History of Scholarship." Pages 22–52 in *Jewish Believers in Jesus: The Early Centuries.* Edited by O. Skarsaune and R. Hvalvik. Peabody: Hendrickson, 2007.

Carlsson, L. *Rounds Trips To Heaven: Otherworldly Travelers in Early Judaism and Christianity.* Lund: Department of History and Anthropology of Religions, Lund University, 2004.

Carter, W. *Matthew and the Margins: A Socio-Political and Religious Reading.* London: T&T Clark, 2000.

Chancey, M. *The Myth of a Gentile Galilee.* Cambridge: Cambridge University Press, 2002.

Charlesworth, S. D. "T. C. Skeat, P64+67 and P4, and the Problem of Fibre Orientation in Codicological Reconstruction." *NTS* 53 (2007): 582–604.

Chennattu, R. M. *Johannine Discipleship as a Covenant Relationship.* Peabody: Hendrickson, 2006.

Chester, S. J. *Conversion at Corinth: Perspectives on Conversion in Paul's Theology and the Corinthian Church.* London: T&T Clark, 2003.

Clark, K. W. "Textual Criticism and Doctrine." Pages 52–65 in *Studia Paulina: In Honorem Johannis de Zwaan.* Haarlem: De Erven F. Bohn, 1953.

—, "The Theological Relevance of Textual Variation in Current Criticism of the Greek New Testament." *JBL* 85 (1966): 1–16.

Clarke, G. W. "The Historical Setting of the *Octavius* of Minucius Felix." *JRH* 4 (1967): 268–86.

Cohen, S. J. D. *The Beginnings of Jewishness: Boundaries, Varieties, Uncertainties.* Berkeley: University of California Press, 1999.

Collins A. Y., and J. J. Collins. *King and Messiah as Son of God: Divine, Human, and Angelic Messianic Figures in Biblical and Related Literature.* Grand Rapids: Eerdmans, 2008.

Collins, A. Y. "Christian Messianism and the First Jewish War with Rome." Pages 222–43 in *Biblical Traditions in Transmission: Essays in Honor of Michael A. Knibb.* Edited by C. Hempel and J. M. Lieu; Leiden: Brill, 2006.

—, "The Origin of Christian Baptism," *Studia Liturgica* 19 (1989): 28–46. Repr. pages 35–57 in *Living Water, Sealing Spirit: Readings on Christian Initiation* (ed. M. E. Johnson; Collegeville: Liturgical Press, 1995)

—, *Cosmology and Eschatology in Jewish and Christian Apocalypticism.* Leiden: Brill, 1996.

—, *Crisis and Catharsis: The Power of the Apocalypse.* Philadelphia: Fortress, 1984.

—, *Mark: A Commentary.* Minneapolis: Fortress, 2007.

Collins, J. J. *Between Athens and Jerusalem: Jewish Identity in the Hellenistic Diaspora*. New York: Crossroad, 1983.

Conzelmann, H. *1 Corinthians: A Commentary.* Philadelphia: Fortress, 1975.

—, *Acts of the Apostles: A Commentary*. Philadelphia: Fortress, 1987.

Cotter, W. "The Collegia and Roman Law: State Restrictions on Voluntary Associations." Pages 74–89 in *Voluntary Associations in the Graeco-Roman World.* Edited by J. S. Kloppenborg and S. G. Wilson. London: Routledge, 1996.

Couture, P. "The Teaching Function in the Church of 1 John (2:20, 27)." Ph.Diss., Pontifical Gregorian University, 1967.

Cribiore, R. *Writing, Teachers, and Students in Graeco-Roman Egypt*. Atlanta: Scholars Press, 1996.

Cromhaut, M. *Jesus and Identity: Reconstructing Judean Ethnicity in Q*. Eugene: Wipf & Stock, 2007.

Crüsemann, F. *Kanon und Sozialgeschichte: Beiträge zum Alten Testament.* Gütersloh: Chr.Kaiser/Gütersloher Verlaghaus, 2003.

Dahl, N. *Studies in Ephesians: Introductory Questions, Text- & Edition-Critical Issues, Interpretation of Texts and Themes*. Edited by D. Hellholm, V. Blomqvist, and T. Fornberg. Tübingen: Mohr Siebeck, 2000.

Danker, F. W. *Benefactor: Epigraphic Study of a Graeco-Roman and New Testament Semantic Field*. St. Louis: Clayton, 1982.

Davies W. D., and D. C. Allison. *A Critical and Exegetical Commentary on the Gospel According to Matthew*. 3 vols. T&T Clark: London, 1991.

Devalle, S. B. C. *Discourses of Ethnicity: Culture and Protest in Jharkand*. London: Sage Publications, 2002.

Dodd, C. H. "Note on John 21,24," *JTS* 4 (1953): 212–13.

Donaldson, T. L. "Jewish Christianity, Israel's Stumbling and the *Sonderweg* Reading of Paul." *JSNT* 29 (2006): 27–54.

—, *Judaism and the Gentiles: Patterns of Universalism (to 135 CE)*. Waco: Baylor University Press, 2007.

—, *Paul and the Gentiles: Remapping the Apostle's Convictional World.* Minneapolis: Fortress, 1997.

Donaldson, T. L., ed. *Religious Rivalries and the Struggle for Success in Caesarea Maritima.* Waterloo: Wilfrid Laurier University Press, 2000.

Donfried, K. P., and P. Richardson, eds., *Judaism and Christianity in First Century Rome.* Grand Rapids: Eerdmans 1998.

Draaisma, D. *Metaphors of Memory: The History of Ideas about the Mind.* Cambridge: Cambridge University Press, 2000.

Draper, J. A. "Torah and Troublesome Apostles in the Didache Community." *NTS* 33 (1991): 347–72.

Duling, D. "Ethnicity, Ethnocentrism, and the Matthean E*thnos*." *BTB* 35 (2005): 125–43.

Dunn, J. D. G. "The Justice of God: A Renewed Perspective on Justification by Faith." *JTS* 43 (1992): 1–22.

—, "The New Perspective on Paul." *BJRL* 65 (1983): 95–122.

—, "Who Did Paul Think He Was? A Study of Jewish-Christian Identity." *NTS* 45 (1999): 174–93.

—, "Yet once more—'The Works of the Law.'" *JSNT* 46 (1992): 99–117.

—, *Jesus Remembered.* Grand Rapids: Eerdmans, 2003.

—, *Jesus, Paul and the Law: Studies in Mark and Galatians.* Louisville: Westminster John Knox Press, 1990.

—, *The Acts of the Apostles.* Valley Forge: Trinity Press, 1996.

—, *The Partings of the Ways: Between Christianity and Judaism and their Significance for the Character of Christianity.* London: SCM Press, 1991.

—, *The Theology of Paul the Apostle.* Grand Rapids: Eerdmans, 1998.

Edanad, A. "The New-Covenant Perspectives of 1 John: An Exegetical and Theological Study of 1 John and Its Vision of Christian Existence as the Realization of the Eschatological Covenant." Ph.Diss., Pontifical Gregorian University, 1967.

Edwards, D. R. and C. Th. McCollough, eds. *The Archaeology of Difference: Gender, Ethnicity, Class and the "Other" in Antiquity: Studies in Honor of Eric M. Meyers*. Boston: ASOR, 2007.

Edwards, M., M. Goodman and S. Price, eds. *Apologetics in the Roman Empire: Pagans, Jews, and Christians.* Oxford: Oxford University Press, 1999.

Edwards, R. B. *The Johannine Epistles*. Sheffield: Sheffield Academic Press, 1996.

Ehrensperger, K. *Paul and the Dynamics of Power: Communication and Interaction in the Early Christ-Movement*. London: T&T Clark, 2007.

Ehrman, B. D. *Lost Christianities: The Battles for Scripture and Faiths We Never Knew*. Oxford: Oxford University Press, 2003.

—, *Misquoting Jesus: The Story of Who Changed the Bible and Why*. San Francisco: Harper, 2005.

—, *The Orthodox Corruption of Scripture: The Effect of Early Christological Controversies on the Text of the New Testament*. Oxford: Oxford University Press, 1993.

Eisenbaum, P. *Paul Was Not a Christian: The Original Message of a Misunderstood Apostle*. New York: HarperOne, 2009.

Elliott, J. H. "Jesus the Israelite was Neither a 'Jew' nor a 'Christian': On Correcting Misleading Nomenclature." *JSHJ* 5 (2007): 119–54.

Elliott, M. A. *The Survivors of Israel: A Reconsideration of the Theology of Pre-Christian Judaism*. Grand Rapids: Eerdmans, 2000.

Engberg-Pedersen, T. "Philo's De Vita Contemplativa as a Philosopher's Dream." *JSJ* 30 (1999): 40–64.

—, "The Relationship with Others: Similarities and Differences Between Paul and Stoicism." *ZNW* 85 (2004): 36–60.

Epp, E. J. *The Theological Tendency of Codex Bezae Cantabrigiensis in Acts*. Cambridge: Cambridge University Press, 1966.

Epstein, L. J. "Why the Jewish People Should Welcome Converts." *Judaism* 43 (1994): 302–12.

Eriksen, T. H. Us and Them in Modern Societies: Ethnicity and Nationalism in Mauritius, Trinidad, and Beyond. Oslo: Scandinavian University Press, 1992.

Erlemann, K. "1 Joh und der jüdisch-christliche Trennungsprozess." *TZ* 55 (1999): 285–302.

Eshbaugh, H. "Textual Variants and Theology: A Study of the Galatian Text of Papyrus 46." *JSNT* 3 (1979): 60–72.

Esler, P. F. "Paul and Stoicism: Romans 12 as a Test Case." *NTS* 50 (2004): 106–24.

—, *Community and Gospel in Luke-Acts: The Social and Political Motivations of Lucan Theology*. Cambridge: Cambridge University Press, 1987.

—, *Conflict and Identity in Romans: The Social Setting in Paul's Letter*. Minneapolis: Fortress, 2003.

Evans, C. E. "Covenant in the Qumran Literature." Pages 55–80 in *The Concept of the Covenant in the Second Temple Period*. Edited by S. E. Porter and J. C. R. de Roo. Atlanta: Society of Biblical Literature, 2003.

Falk, D. "Psalms and Prayers." Pages 35–56 in *Justification and Variegated Nomism*: *Vol.1*: *The Complexities of Second Temple Judaism*. Edited by D. A. Carson, P. T. O'Brien andM. A. Seifrid. Tübingen: Mohr, 2001.

Faust, A. *Israel's Ethnogenesis: Settlement, Interaction, Expansion and Resistance*. London: Equinox, 2007.

Fee, G. D. *Papyrus Bodmer II ($\mathfrak{P}^{66}$): Its Textual Relationships and Scribal Characteristics*. Salt Lake City: University of Utah Press, 1968.

—, Review of B. D. Ehrman, *The Orthodox Corruption of Scripture*, *CRBR* 8 (1995): 203–6.

Feldman L., and M. Reinhold. *Jewish Life and Thought Among Greeks and Romans*. Philadelphia: Fortress, 1996.

—, "The Portrayal of Pinehas by Philo, Pseudo-Philo and Josephus." *JQR* 92 (2002): 315–45.

—, *Jew and Gentile in the Ancient World: Attitudes and Interactions From Alexander to Justinian*. Princeton: Princeton University Press, 1993.

Fieger, M. *Im Schatten der Artemis: Glaube und Ungehorsam in Ephesus*. Bern: Peter Lang, 1998.

Fisk, B. M. "Synagogue Influence and Scriptural Knowledge among the Christians of Rome." Pages 157–85 in *As It Is Written: Studying Paul's Use of Scripture*. Edited by S. E. Porter and C. D. Stanley. Atlanta: Society of Biblical Literature, 2008.

Fitzmyer, J. *Romans: A New Translation with Introduction and Commentary*. New York: Doubleday 1993.

Fjärstedt, B. *Missionen skiftar ansikte: Missionsteologi i tiden*. Stockholm: Verbum, 1991.

Flemming, R. *Medicine and the Making of Roman Women: Gender, Nature, and Authority from Celsus to Galen*. Oxford: Oxford University Press, 2000

Flusser, D. "The 'Flesh-Spirit' Dualism in the Qumran Scrolls and the New Testament." *Judaism of the Second Temple Period: Vol. 1: Qumran and Apocalypticism*. Grand Rapids: Eerdmans, 2006.

—, *Jesus*. 2d ed. Jerusalem: Magnes Press, 1998.

Fraade, S. D. *From Tradition to Commentary: Torah and its Interpretation in the Midrash Sifre to Deuteronomy*. Albany: State University of New York Press, 1991.

Francis, J. A. *Subversive Virtue: Asceticism and Authority in the Second-Century Pagan World*. University Park: Pennsylvania State University Press, 1995.

Fredriksen, P. "Mandatory Retirement: Ideas in the Study of Christian Origins Whose Time Has Come to Go." *SR* 35 (2007): 231–46.

Frey, J. "Das Judentum des Paulus." Pages 5–43 in: *Paulus : Leben – Umwelt – Werk – Briefe*. Edited by Oda Wischmeyer. Tübingen: UTB, 2006.

—, "Paul's Jewish Identity." Pages 285–321 in *Jewish Identity in the Greco-Roman World*. Edited by J. Frey, D. R. Schwartz, and S. Gripentrog. Leiden: Brill 2007.

Freyne, S. *Galilee and the Gospels: Collected Essays*. Tübingen: Mohr Siebeck, 2000.

—, *Galilee from Alexander the Great to (Hadrian: 323 BCE to 135 CE)*. Wilmington: Glazier, 1980.

—, *Galilee, Jesus and the Gospels*. Dublin: Gill and MacMillan, 1988.

—, *Jesus: A Jewish Galilean*. London: T&T Clark, 2004.

Furnish, V. P. "The First Letter of Paul to the Corinthians." Pages 1932–34 in *The HarperCollins Study Bible: New Revised Standard Version, with the Apocryphal/Deuterocanonical Books with Concordance*. Edited by H. W. Attridge. San Francisco: HarperSanFrancisco with the SBL, 2006.

Gaca, K. L. *The Making of Fornication: Eros, Ethics and Political Reform in Greek Philosophy and Early Christianity*. Berkeley: University of California Press, 2003.

Gager, J. G. *Reinventing Paul*. Oxford: Oxford University Press, 2000.

Gambetti, S. *The Alexandrian Riots of 38 CE and the Persecution of the Jews: A Historical Reconstruction*. Leiden: Brill, 2009.

Garroway, J. "Neither Jew nor Gentile, but Both: Paul's "Christians" as "Gentile-Jews." Ph.D. diss., Yale University, 2008.

Gasparro, G. S. "Asceticism and Anthropology: *Enkrateia* and 'Double Creation' in Early Christianity." Pages 127–46 in *Asceticism*. Edited by V. Wimbush and R. Valantasis. Oxford: Oxford University Press, 1998.

Gaston, L. *Paul and the Torah*. Vancouver: University of British Columbia Press, 1990.

Gaventa, B. R. *Our Mother Saint Paul*, Louisville: Westminster John Knox Press, 2007.

Geertz, C. "The Integrative Revolution: Primordial Sentiments and Civil Politics in the New States." Pages 105–57 in *Old Societies and New States*. Edited by C. Geertz. New York: Free Press, 1963.

Gerhardsson, B. "If We Do Not Cut the Parables out of Their Frames." *NTS* 37 (1991): 321–35.

—, "Illuminating the Kingdom: Narrative Meshalim in the Synoptic Gospels." Pages 266–309 in *Jesus and the Oral Gospel Tradition*. Edited by H. Wansbrough, Macon: Mercer University Press, 1991.

—, "The Earthly Jesus in the Synoptic Parables." Pages 49–62 in *Christology, Controversy and Community: Festschrift for David R. Catchpole*. Edited by D. G. Horrell and C. M. Tuckett. Leiden: Brill, 2000.

—, "The Narrative Meshalim in the Synoptic Gospels: A Comparison with the Narrative Meshalim in the Old Testament." *NTS* 34 (1988): 339–63.

—, *Memory and Manuscript: Oral Tradition and Written Transmission in Rabbinic Judaism and Early Christianity.* Lund: Gleerup, 1964 [1961].

Gilbert, G. "Roman Propaganda and Christian Identity in the World-View of Luke-Acts." Pages 233–56 in *Contextualizing Acts. Lukan Narrative and Greco-Roman Discourse*. Edited by T. Penner and C. Vander Stichele. Atlanta: Scholars Press, 2003.

Gilman, S. L. *The Jew's Body.* New York: Routledge, 1991.

Glare, P. G. W., ed. *The Oxford Latin Dictionary*. Oxford: Clarendon Press, 1968–1982.

Goldhill, S. *Foucault's Virginity: Ancient Erotic Fiction and the History of Sexuality*. Cambridge: Cambridge University Press, 1995.

Goldmann, S. "Statt Totenklage Gedächtnis: Zur Erfindung der Mnemotechnik durch Simonides von Keos." *Poetica* 21 (1989): 43–66.

Goodman, M. "Nerva, the *fiscus Judaicus* and Jewish Identity," *JRS* 79 (1989), 40–44.

—, *Mission and Conversion: Proselytizing in the Religious History of the Roman Empire.* Oxford: Clarendon, 1994

Gräbe, P. J. Der neue Bund in der frühchristlichen Literatur unter Berücksichtigung der alttestamentlich-jüdischen Voraussetzungen. Würzburg: Echter Verlag, 2001.

Griffith, T. *Keep Yourselves from Idols.* Sheffield: Sheffield Academic Press, 2002.

Günther, M. *Die Frühgeschichte des Christentums in Ephesus.* Frankfurt am Main: Peter Lang, 1995.

Haacker, K. "Der Werdegang des Apostels Paulus. Biographische Daten und ihre theologische Relevanz." *ANRW* 26.2:815–938. Part 2, *Principat*, 26.2. Edited by H. Temporini and W. Haase. New York: de Gruyter 1995.

—, "Paul's Life." Pages 19–33 in *The Cambridge Companion to St Paul.* Edited by J. D. G. Dunn. Cambridge: Cambridge University Press, 2003.

—, *Paulus: Der Werdegang eines Apostels.* Stuttgart: Kath. Bibelwerk, 1997.

Habicht, Chr. *Altertümer von Pergamon VIII 3: Die Inschriften des Asklepieions.* Berlin: de Gruyter, 2000.

Haenchen, E. *The Acts of the Apostles: A Commentary.* Philadelphia: Westminster,: 1971.

Hall, R. G. "The Ascension of Isaiah: Community Situation, Date, and Place in Early Christianity." *JBL* 109 (1990): 289–306.

Hallam, A. F. *Concurrences between Dio Chrysostom's First Discourse and the New Testament.* Capitalist Press, 1985.

Harink, D. "Paul and Israel: An Apocalyptic Reading." *ProEccl* 16 (2007), 359–380.

Harland, P. A. *Associations, Synagogues and Congregations: Claiming a Place in the Ancient Mediterranean Society.* Minneapolis: Fortress, 2003.

Harrington, H. K. *The Purity Texts.* London: T&T Clark, 2004.

Hartman, L. "Baptism." Pages 583–94 in vol. 1 of *The Anchor Bible Dictionary.* Edited by D. N. Freedman. 6 vols. New York: Doubleday, 1992.

Haslam, S. A., and M. J. Platow. "Your Wish is Our Command: The Role of Shared Identity in Translating a Leader's Vision into Followers' Action." Pages 213–28 in *Social Identity Processes in Organizations*. Edited by M. A. Hogg and D. J. Terry. New York: Psychology Press, 2001.

Hatch, E. *The Organization of the Early Christian Churches*. London: Longmans, 1888.

Hayes, C. E. *Gentile Impurities and Jewish Identities: Intermarriage and Conversion From the Bible to the Talmud*. Oxford: Oxford University Press, 2002.

Hays, R. B. *The Faith of Jesus Christ: The Narrative Substructure of Galatians 3:1-4:11*. 2d ed. Grand Rapids: Eerdmans, 2002

Head, P. M. "Christology and Textual Transmission: Reverential Alterations in the Synoptic Gospels." *NovT* 35 (1993): 105–29.

Heckel, T. K. *Vom Evangelium des Markus zum viergestaltigen Evangelium*. Tübingen: Mohr Siebeck, 1999.

Hedner Zetterholm, K. *Jewish Interpretation of the Bible: Ancient and Contemporary*. Minneapolis: Fortress, 2012.

Heinrici, G. "Die christengemeinden Korinths und die religiösen Genossenschafen der Griechen." *ZWT* 19 (1876): 465–526.

Hemer, C. J. *The Letters to the Seven Churches of Asia in their Local Setting*. Sheffield: JSOT Press, 1981.

Hengel, M. (in collaboration with Roland Deines) "Der vorchristliche Paulus." Pages 177–293 in *Paulus und das antike Judentum*. Edited by M. Hengel and U. Heckel. Tübingen: Mohr, 1991.

—, *The Four Gospels and the One Gospel of Jesus Christ*. Harrisburg, Trinity Press International, 2000.

Hermans, H. H. M., and H. J. G. Kempen. *The Dialogical Self: Meaning and Movement*. San Diego: Academic Press, 1993.

Heschel, S. *The Aryan Jesus: Christian Theologians and the Bible in Nazi Germany*. Princeton: Princeton University Press, 2008.

Hill, C. E. *The Johannine Corpus in the Early Church*. Oxford: Oxford University Press, 2006.

Hirshman, M. "Rabbinic Universalism in the Second and Third Centuries." *HTR* 93 (2000): 101–15.

Hofius, O. "Das Evangelium und Israel: Erwägungen zu Römer 9–11." *ZTK* 83 (1986): 297–324.

Holmberg, B. "Jewish *Versus* Christian Identity in the Early Church." *RB* 105 (1998): 397–425.

—, "The Life in the Diaspora Synagogues: An Evaluation." Pages 219–32 in *The Ancient Synagogue: From its Origins until 200 C.E.* Edited by B. Olsson and M. Zetterholm. Stockholm: Almqvist & Wiksell International, 2003.

—, "The Methods of Historical Reconstruction in the Scholarly 'Recovery' of Corinthian Christianity." Pages 255–71 in *Christianity at Corinth: The Quest for the Pauline Church.* Edited by E. Adams and D. G. Horrell. Louisville: Westminster John Knox, 2004.

—, "Understanding the First Hundred Years of Christian Identity." Pages 1–32 in *Exploring Early Christian Identity.* Edited by Bengt Holmberg. Tübingen: Mohr Siebeck, 2008.

—, *Paul and Power: The Structure of Authority in the Primitive Church as Reflected in the Pauline Epistles.* Lund: CWK Gleerup, 1978. Repr., Minneapolis: Fortress, 1990.

—, *Sociology and the New Testament: An Appraisal.* Minneapolis: Fortress, 1990.

Holmberg, B., ed. *Exploring Early Christian Identity.* Tübingen: Mohr Siebeck, 2008.

Hornblower, S., and A. Spawforth, eds. *Oxford Classical Dictionary.* 3d ed. Oxford: Oxford University Press, 1996.

Horrell, D. G. "'Becoming Christian': Solidifying Christian Identity and Content." Pages 309–35 in *Handbook of Early Christianity: Social Sciences Approaches.* Edited by A. J. Blasi, J. Duhaime and P.-A. Durcotte. Oxford: Altamina, 2002.

—, "'No Longer Jew or Greek': Paul's Corporate Christology and the Construction of Christian Community." Pages 321–44 in *Christology, Controversy and Community: New Testament Essays in Honour of David R. Catchpole.* Edited by D. G. Horrell and C. M. Tuckett. Leiden: Brill, 2000.

—, "The Label *Christianos*: 1 Peter 4:16 and the Formation of Christian Identity." *JBL* 126 (2007): 383–91.

—, *The Social Ethos of the Corinthian Correspondence: Interests and Ideology from 1 Corinthians to 1 Clement.* Edinburgh: T&T Clark, 1996.

Horsley, R. *Galilee, History, Politics, People.* Valley Forge: Trinity, 1995.

Housman, A. E. "The Application of Thought to Textual Criticism." *Proceedings of the Classical Association* 18 (1921): 67–84.

Hunter, D. G. *Marriage, Celibacy, and Heresy in Ancient Christianity: The Jovinian Controversy.* Oxford: Oxford University Press, 2007.

Hurtado, L. W. *Lord Jesus Christ: Devotion to Jesus in Earliest Christianity.* Grand Rapids: Eerdmans, 2003.

—, *One God, One Lord: Early Christian Devotion and Ancient Jewish Monotheism.* Philadelphia: Fortress, 1988.

Hvalvik, R. "Jewish Believers and Jewish Influence in the Roman Church until the Early Second Century." Pages 179–216 in *Jewish Believers in Jesus: The Early Centuries.* Edited by O. Skarsaune and R. Hvalvik. Peabody: Hendrickson, 2007.

Hyldahl, N. Om retfærdighed og syndfrihed: En fortolkning af de tre Johannesbreve. Copenhagen: University of Copenhagen, 2007.

Iustinus Martyris. *Dialogus cum Tryphone.* Edited by M. Marcovich. Berlin: de Gruyter, 1997.

Jackson-McCabe, M. A., ed. *Jewish Christianity Reconsidered: Rethinking Ancient Groups and Texts.* Minneapolis: Fortress, 2007.

Jaensson Wallander, C. "Debatt kring stadgar mot fundamentalism," *Kyrkans Tidning* 41 (2007): 10.

James, W., *Varieties of Religious Experience*. London: Fontana, 1960.

Jewett, R. *Romans: A Commentary*. Minneapolis: Fortress, 2007.

Johnson Hodge, C. *If Sons, Then Heirs: A Study of Kinship and Ethnicity in the Letters of Paul*. Oxford: Oxford University Press, 2007.

Jones, C. P. *The Roman World of Dio Chrysostom*. Cambridge: Harvard University Press, 1978.

Jones, S. *The Archaeology of Ethnicity: Constructing Identities in the Past and Present*. London: Routledge, 1997.

Judge, E. A. "Judaism and the Rise of Christianity: A Roman Perspective." *TynBul* 45 (1994): 355–68.

—, "The Roman Base of Paul's Mission." Pages 553–67 in *The First Christians in the Roman World: Augustan and New Testament Essays*. Edited by J. R. Harrison Tübingen: Mohr Siebeck 2008.

—, "The Social Identity of the First Christians: A Question of Method in Religious History." *JRH* 11 (1980): 201–17.

Juhl Christiansen, E. *The Covenant in Judaism and Paul: A Study of Ritual Boundaries as Identity Markers*. Leiden: Brill, 1995.

Juster, J. *Les Juifs dans l'empire romain: Leur condition juridique, économique et sociale: Tome premier*. Paris: Geunther, 1914.

Kahl, B. *Galatians Re-Imagined*. Minneapolis: Fortress, 2010.

Kannaday, W. C. *Apologetic Discourse and the Scribal Tradition Evidence of the Influence of Apologetic Interests on the Text of the Canonical Gospels*. Leiden: Brill, 2004.

Käsemann, E. *Commentary on Romans*. Grand Rapids: Eerdmans, 1980.

—, *Perspectives on Paul*. Philadelphia: Fortress, 1971 [1969 in German].

Kennedy, H. A. A. "The Covenant Conception in the First Epistle of St. John." *ExpTim* 28 (1916–1917): 23–26.

Killebrew, A. *Biblical Peoples and Ethnicity: An Archaeological Study of Egyptians, Canaanites, Philistines, and Early Israel 1300–1100 B.C.E.* Atlanta: Society of Biblical Literature, 2005.

Kimelman, R. "Identifying Jews and Christians in Roman Syria-Palestine." Pages 301–33 in *Galilee through the Centuries: Confluence of Cultures.* Edited by E. M. Meyers. Winona Lake: Eisenbrauns, 1999.

King, R. A. H. *Aristotle and Plotinus on Memory.* Berlin: de Gruyter, 2009.

Kittel, G., and G. Friedrich, eds. *Theological Dictionary of the New Testament.* Translated by G. W. Bromiley. 10 vols. Grand Rapids: Eerdmans, 1964–1976.

Klauck, H-J. *The Religious Context of Early Christianity: A Guide to Graeco-Roman Religions.* Minneapolis: Fortress, 2000.

—, *Die Johannesbriefe.* Darmstadt: Wissenschafliche Buchgesellschaft, 1991.

Klauck, H.-J., and B. Bäbler. *Dion von Prusa: Olympische Rede oder über die erste Erkenntnis Gottes, eingeleitet, übersetzt und interpretiert von Hans-Josef Klauck, mit einem archäologischen Beitrag von Balbina Bäbler.* Darmstadt: Wissenschaftliche Buchgesellschaft, 2000.

Klawans, J. "Notions of Gentile Impurity in Ancient Judaism." *AJSR* 20 (1995): 285–312.

—, *Impurity and Sin in Ancient Judaism.* New York: Oxford University Press, 2000.

Kloppenborg, J. "*Evocatio Deorum* and the Date of Mark." *JBL* 124 (2005): 419–50.

—, "Judaeans or Judaean Christians in James?" Pages 113–35 in *Identity & Interaction in the Ancient Mediterranean: Jews, Christians and Others.* Edited by Z. A. Crook and P. A. Harland. Sheffield: Phoenix Press, 2007.

Koester, H. "Ephesos in Early Christian Literature." Pages 119–40 in *Ephesos, Metropolis of Asia: An Interdisciplinary Approach to Its Archaeology, Religion, and Culture*. Edited by H. Koester. Valley Forge: Trinity, 1995.

Koolmeister, K., T. Tallmeister, and J. F. Kindstrand. *An Index to Dio Chrysostomus*. Stockholm: Almqvist & Wiksell International, 1981.

Kraemer, R. S. *Her Share of the Blessings: Women's Religions among Pagans, Jews, and Christians in the Greco-Roman World*. Oxford: Oxford University Press, 1992.

Kümmel, W. G. *Römer 7 und das Bild des Menschen im Neuen Testament*. Munich: Christian Kaiser, 1974.

Kürzinger, J. "Die Aussage des Papias von Hierapolis zur literarischen Form des Markusevangeliums." *BZ* 21 (1977): 245–64.

Laato, T. *Paul and Judaism: An Anthropological Approach*. Atlanta: Scholars Press, 1995.

Lake K., and H. J. Cadbury, eds. *English Translation and Commentary*. Vol 4 of *The Beginnings of Christianity: Part I. The Acts of the Apostles*. Edited by F. J. Foakes Jackson and K. Lake. London: Macmillan 1933.

Lampe, P. "The Roman Christians of Romans 16." Pages 216–30 in *The Romans Debate*. Edited by K. P. Donfried. Peabody: Hendrickson, 1991.

—, *From Paul to Valentinus: Christians at Rome in the First Two Centuries*. London: Continuum, 2003.

Lang, B. "Israels Religionsgeschichte aus ethnologischer Sicht." *Anthropos 101* (2006): 99–109.

Lawrence, J. D. *Washing in Water: Trajectories of Ritual Bathing in the Hebrew Bible and Second Temple Literature*. Leiden: Brill, 2006.

Levick, B. "Women, Power, and Philosophy at Rome and Beyond." Pages 133–55 in *Philosophy and Power in the Graeco-Roman World. Essays in Honour of Miriam Griffin*. Edited by G. Clark and T. Rajak. Oxford: Oxford University Press, 2002.

Levin, C. *Die Verheissung des neuen Bundes in ihrem theologiegeschichtlichen Zusammenhang ausgelegt.* Göttingen: Vandenhoeck & Ruprecht, 1985.

Levine, A.-J. *The Misunderstood Jew.* New York: HarperOne, 2007.

Levinskaya, I. *The Book of Acts in its Diaspora Setting.* Vol. 5 of *The Book of Acts in Its Ancient Literary Setting.* Edited by B. W. Winter. Grand Rapids: Eerdmans, 1996.

Lichtenberger, H. "Jews and Christians in Rome in the Time of Nero: Josephus and Paul in Rome", *ANRW* 2.26:2142–76. Part 2, *Principat*, 2:26. Edited by H. Temporini and W. Haase. New York: de Gruyter, 1989.

—, "Alter Bund und neuer Bund." *NTS* 41 (1995): 400–414.

Liddell, H. G., R. Scott, H. S. Jones. *A Greek-English Lexicon.* 9th ed. Clarendon Press: Oxford, 1996.

Lieu, J. M. Image and Reality: The Jews in the World of the Christians in the Second Century. Edinburgh: T&T Clark, 1996.

—, "The Audience of Apologetics: The Problem of the Martyr Acts." Pages 205–23 in *Contextualising Early Christian Martyrdom.* Edited by J. Engberg, U. Holmsgaard Eriksen and A. Klostergaard Petersen. Frankfurt am Main: Peter Lang, 2011.

—, "The Race of the God-fearers," *JTS* 46 (1995): 483–501.

—, "What Was from the Beginning: Scripture and Tradition in the Johannine Epistles." *NTS* 39 (1993): 458–77.

—, *Christian Identity in the Jewish and Graeco-Roman World.* Oxford: Oxford University Press, 2004.

—, *Neither Jew nor Greek? Constructing Early Christianity.* Edinburgh: T&T Clark, 2002.

—, *The Theology of the Johannine Epistles.* Cambridge: Cambridge University Press, 1991.

Linder, A. *The Jews in Roman Imperial Legislation: Edited with Introductions, Translations, and Commentary.* Detroit: Wayne State University Press, 1987.

Livesey, N. E. *Circumcision as a Malleable Symbol.* Tübingen: Mohr Siebeck, 2010.

Locker, G. W. "So ändern sich die Zeiten: Das Jesusbuch in reformierter Lesart." Pages 53–67 in *Ein Weg zu Jesus: Schlüssel zu einem tieferen Verständnis des Papstbuches.* Edited by T. Söding. Freiburg im Breisgau: Herder, 2007.

Longenecker, B. "On Israel's God and God's Israel: Assessing Supersessionism in Paul." *JTS* 58 (2007): 26–44.

Lopez, D. C. *Apostle to the Conquered: Remapping Paul's Mission.* Paul in Critical Contexts. Minneapolis: Fortress, 2008.

Luckritz Marquis, T. "At Home or Away: Travel and Death in 2 Corinthians 1-9." Ph.D. diss., Yale University, 2008.

Lüdemann, G. "Eine peinliche Entgleisung." No pages. Cited 8 March 2008. Online: http://www.spiegel.de/wissenschaft/mensch/0,1518,479636,00.html

Luz, U. *Matthew 8–20.* Minneapolis: Fortress, 2001.

Mack, B. L., and V. K. Robbins. *Patterns of Persuasion in the Gospels.* Sonoma: Polebridge Press, 1988.

Malatesta, E. *Interiority and Covenant.* Rome: Biblical Institute Press, 1978.

Malherbe, A. J. *Paul and the Popular Philosophers.* Minneapolis: Fortress, 1989.

Malina, B. J. *The New Testament World: Insights from Cultural Anthropology.* Atlanta: John Knox Press, 1981.

Marshall, I. H. *A Critical and Exegetical Commentary on the Pastoral Epistles.* Edinburgh: T&T Clark, 1999.

Marshall, P. *Enmity in Corinth: Social Conventions in Paul's Relations with the Corinthians.* Tübingen: Mohr Siebeck, 1987.

Martin, D. B. *The Corinthian Body.* New Haven: Yale University Press, 1995.

Martin, R. P. *Reconciliation: A Study in Paul's Theology.* Philadelphia: Fortress 1977.

Martin, T. "Apostasy to Paganism: The Rhetorical Stasis of the Galatian Controversy." Pages 73–94 in *The Galatians Debate: Contemporary Issues in Rhetorical and Historical Interpretation*. Edited by M. D. Nanos, Peabody: Hendrickson 2002.

Martyn, J. L. *Galatians.* New York: Doubleday, 1997.

Mason, S. "Jews, Judeans, Judaizing, Judaism: Problems of Categorization in Ancient History." *JSJ* 38 (2007): 457–512.

—, "The Contra Apionem in Social and Literary Context: An Invitation to Judean Philosophy." Pages 187–228 in *Josephus' Contra Apionem: Studies in its Character and Context with a Latin Concordance to the Portion Missing in Greek*. Edited by L. Feldman and J. R. Levinson. Leiden: Brill, 1996.

—, *Flavius Josephus on the Pharisees: A Compositional Critical Study*. Leiden: Brill, 1991.

McDonald, M. Y. *Early Christian Women and Pagan Opinion: The Power of the Hysterical Woman*. Cambridge: Cambridge University Press, 1996.

McGowan, A. "Eating People: Accusations of Cannibalism against Christians in the Second Century." *JECS* 2 (1994): 413–42.

McKnight, S. *A Light Among the Gentiles: Jewish Missionary Activity in the Second Temple Period.* Minneapolis: Fortress, 1991.

Meeks, W. A. *The First Urban Christians: The Social World of the Apostle Paul*. New Haven: Yale University, 1983.

Meier, J. P. "*Presbyteros* in the Pastoral Epistles." *CBQ* 35 (1973): 323–45.

—, *A Marginal Jew: Rethinking the Historical Jesus: Volume One: The Roots of the Problem and the Person*. New York: Doubleday, 1991.

Meskell, L. *Archaeology under Fire: Nationalism, Politics and Heritage in the Eastern Mediterranean and Middle East*. London: Routledge, 1998.

Metzger, B. M. *A Textual Commentary on the Greek New Testament.* 2d ed. Stuttgart: Deutsche Bibelgesellschaft, 1994.

Meyer, B. F. *The Early Christians: Their World Mission and Self-Discovery.* Wilmington: Glazier, 1986.

Meyers, E. M. "The Cultural Setting of Galilee: The Case of Early Judaism." *ANRW* 19.1:686–701. Part 2, *Principat*, 19.1. Edited by H. Temporini and W. Haase. New York: de Gruyter, 1979.

—, "Archaeology and Nationalism in Israel: Making the Past Part of the Present." Pages 64-77 in *Zeichen aus Text und Stein: Studien auf dem Weg zu einer Archäologie des Neuen Testaments.* Edited by S. Alkier, and J. Zangenberg. Tübingen: Francke, 2003.

—, "Galilean Regionalism as a Factor in Historical Reconstruction." *BASOR* 21 (1976): 93–101.

—, "Jesus and His World. Sepphoris and the Quest for the Historical Jesus." Pages 185–97 in *Saxa Loquentur: Studien zur Archäologie Palästinas/Israels.* Edited by C. G. den Hertog, U. Hübner and S. Münger. Münster: Ugarit, 2003.

—, "The Problem of Gendered Space in Syro-Palestinian Domestic Architecture: The Case of Roman-Period Galilee." Pages 44–69 in *Early Christian Families in Context.* Edited by D. L. Balch and C. Osiek. Grand Rapids: Eerdmans, 2003.

Milgrom, J. *Leviticus 1-16.* New York: Doubleday, 1991.

Misztal, B. A. *Theories of Social Remembering.* Maidenhead: Open University Press, 2003.

Mitchell, M. M. *Paul and the Rhetoric of Reconciliation: An Exegetical Investigation of the Language and Composition of 1 Corinthians.* Louisville: Westminster John Knox Press, 1991.

—, *The Heavenly Trumpet: John Chrysostom and the Art of Pauline Interpretation.* Tübingen: Mohr Siebeck, 2000.

Momigliano, A. *Claudius: The Emperor and his Achievement.* Oxford: Clarendon, 1934.

Moreland, M. "The Inhabitants of Galilee in the Hellenistic and Early Roman Periods." Pages 33–59 in *Religion, Ethnicity, and Identity in Ancient Galilee.* Edited by J. Zangenberg, H. W. Attridge, and D. B. Martin. Tübingen: Mohr Siebeck, 2007.

Morrison, M. D. *Who Needs a New Covenant? Rhetorical Function of the Covenant Motif in the Argument of Hebrews.* Eugene: Pickwick, 2009.

Mount, C. *Pauline Christianity: Luke-Acts and the Legacy of Paul.* Leiden: Brill, 2002.

Moxnes, H. "Identity in Jesus' Galilee – From Ethnicity to Locative Intersectionality," *BibInt* 18(2010): 390–416.

—, "Jesus som europeer? Jesus-forskningen og Europas problemer i det 19. Århundre." *DTT* 69 (2006): 62–78

—, "Renan's Vie de Jésus as Representation of the Orient." Pages 85–108 in *Jews, Antiquity, and the Nineteenth-century Imagination.* Edited by H. Lapin and D. B. Martin. Bethesda: University Press of Maryland, 2003.

—, "The Construction of Galilee as a Place for the Historical Jesus." *BTB* 31 (2001): 26–37, 64–77.

—, "The Historical Jesus: From Master Narrative to Cultural Context." *BTB* 28 (1999): 135–49.

—, "The Quest for Honor and the Unity of the Community in Romans 12 and in the Orations of Dio Chrysostom." Pages 203–30 in *Paul in His Hellenistic Context.* Edited by T. Engberg-Pedersen. Edinburgh: T&T Clark, 1994.

—, *Jesus and the Rise of Nationalism. A New Quest for the Nineteenth Century Historical Jesus.* London: I. B. Tauris, 2012.

Müller, K. *Tora für die Völker: Die Noachidischen Gebote und Ansätze zu ihrer Rezeption im Christentum.* Berlin: Institute Kirche und Judentum, 1994.

Müller, M. "The Hidden Context: Some Observations to the Concept of New Covenant in the New Testament." Pages 649–58 in *Texts and Contexts: Biblical Texts in Their Textual and Situational Contexts.* Edited by T. Fornberg and D. Hellholm. Oslo: Scandinavian University Press, 1995.

Munier, C. *L'Apologie de Saint Justin Philosophe et Martyr.* Fribourg: Éditions Universitaires Fribourg Suisse, 1994.

Murphy- O'Connor, J. *Paul: A Critical Life.* Oxford: Clarendon, 1996.

Murray, M. *Playing a Jewish Game: Gentile Christian Judaizing in the First and Second Centuries CE.* Waterloo: Wilfred Laurier University Press, 2004.

Mussies, G. *Dio Chrysostom and the New Testament: Parallels Collected.* Leiden: Brill, 1972.

Mußner, F. "Ein Buch der Beziehungen." Pages 87–98 in *Ein Weg zu Jesus: Schlüssel zu einem tieferen Verständnis des Papstbuches.* Edited by T. Söding. Freiburg im Breisgau: Herder, 2007.

Mutschler, B. *Das Corpus Johanneum bei Irenäus von Lyon: Studien und Kommentar zum dritten Buch von Adversus haereses.* Tübingen: Mohr Siebeck, 2006.

Nanos, M. D. "Paul and Judaism: Why Not Paul's Judaism?" Pages 117–160 in *Paul Unbound: Other Perspectives on Paul.* Edited by M. Given. Peabody: Hendrickson, 2010.

—, *The Irony of Galatians: Pauls' Letter in First Century Context.* Philadelphia: Fortress, 2001.

—, *The Mystery of Romans: The Jewish Context of Paul's Letter.* Minneapolis: Fortress, 1996.

Nauck, W. *Die Tradition und der Charakter des ersten Johannesbriefes.* Tübingen: Mohr Siebeck, 1957.

Neusner, J. "Einzigartig in 2000 Jahren. Die neue Wende im jüdisch-christlichen Dialog." Pages 71–90 in *Ein Weg zu Jesus: Schlüssel zu einem tieferen Verständnis des Papstbuches.* Edited by T. Söding. Freiburg im Breisgau: Herder, 2007.

—, "My Argument with the Pope." *Jerusalem Post* (Maj 29, 2007).

—, "Who needs 'The Historical Jesus'? An Essay Review." *BBR* 4 (1994): 113–26.

—, 1993. *A Rabbi Talks with Jesus: An Intermillenial Interfaith Exchange.* New York: Doubleday, 1993.

Niebuhr, K.-W. *Heidenapostel aus Israel: Die jüdische Identität des Paulus nach ihrer Darstellung in seinen Briefen.* Tübingen: Mohr Siebeck, 1992.

Niederwimmer, K. *The Didache: A Commentary.* Minneapolis: Fortress, 1998.

Noack, B. "The Day of Pentecost in Jubilees, Qumran, and Acts." *ASTI* 1 (1962): 73–85.

Nock, A. D. *Conversion: The Old and the New in Religion from Alexander the Great to Augustine of Hippo.* Oxford: Clarendon, 1933.

Nolland, J. *The Gospel of Matthew: A Commentary on the Greek Text.* Grand Rapids: Eerdmans, 2005.

Nostra Aetate: Declaration on the Relation of the Church to Non-Christians: Proclaimed by Pope Paul VI, October 28, 1965. No pages. Cited 24 March 2008. Online: http://www.vatican.va/archive/hist_councils/ii_vatican_council/documents/vat-ii_decl_19651028_nostra-aetate_en.html

O'Brien, P. T. *Commentary on Philippians.* Grand Rapids: Eerdmans, 1991.

Oakman, D. E. *Jesus and the Peasants.* Eugene: Cascade Books, 2008.

Oberlinner, L., and A. Vögtle. *Anpassung oder Widerspruch? Von der apostolichen zur nachapostolischen Kirche.* Freiburg: Herder, 1992.

Oestigaard, T. *Political Archaeology and Holy Nationalism: Archaeological Battles over the Bible and Land in Israel and Palestine from 1967–2000.* Gothenburg: Göteborg University, 2007.

Öhler, M. "Römisches Vereinsrecht und christliche Gemeinden." Pages 51–71 in *Zwischen den Reichen: Neues Testament und Römisches Reich.* Edited by M. Labahn and J. Zangenberg; Tübingen: Francke, 2002.

Olsson, B. "När pingstfestens dag kom förnyades förbundet." Pages 157–170 in *Så som det har berättats för oss: Om bibel, gudstjänst och tro.* Edited by G. Samuelsson and T. Hägerland. Örebro: Libris, 2007.

—, *Första Petrusbrevet.* Stockholm: EFS-förlaget 1982.

—, *Johannesbreven.* Stockholm: EFS-förlaget, 2008.

—, *Structure and Meaning in the Fourth Gospel: A Text-Linguistic Analysis of John 2:1–11 and 4:1–42.* Lund: Gleerup, 1974.

Osburn, C. D. "The Text of 1 Corinthians 10:9." Pages 201–12 in *New Testament Textual Criticism: Its Significance for Exegesis—Essays in Honour of Bruce M. Metzger*. Edited by E. J. Epp and G. D. Fee. Oxford: Clarendon, 1981.

Overman, J. A. *Matthew's Gospel and Formative Judaism: The Social World of the Matthean Community*. Minneapolis: Fortress, 1990.

Painter, J. *1, 2, and 3 John*. Collegeville: Liturgical Press, 2002.

Parker, D. C. *Codex Bezae: An Early Christian Manuscript and Its Text*. Cambridge: Cambridge University Press, 1992.

Parsons, M. C. "A Christological Tendency in P75." *JBL* 105 (1986): 463–79.

Pauly, A. *Paulys Realencyclopädie der classischen Altertumswissenschaft*. New edition G. Wissowa. 49 vols. Munich, 1980.

Penn, R. "Performing Family: Ritual Kissing and the Construction of Early Christian Kinship." *JECS* 10 (2002): 151–74.

Pepper, S. C. *World Hypotheses: A Study in Evidence*. Berkeley: University of California Press, 1942.

Peterman, G. W. *Paul's Gift from Philippi: Conventions of Gift-Exchange and Christian Giving*. Cambridge: Cambridge University Press, 1997.

Petersen, W. L. "Textual Evidence of Tatian's Dependence upon Justin's Apomnemoneumata." *NTS* 36 (1990): 512–34.

Pfohl, G., ed. *Griechische Inschriften als Zeugnisse des privaten und öffentlichen Lebens*. München, Heimeran, 1965.

Pilch J. J. and B. J. Malina. *Biblical Social Values and Their Meaning: A Handbook*. Peabody: Hendrickson, 1993.

Porter, S. E. and J. C. R. de Roo, eds. *The Concept of the Covenant in the Second Temple Period*. Atlanta: Society of Biblical Literature, 2003.

Porter, S. E., and C. D. Stanley, eds. *As It Is Written: Studying Paul's Use of Scripture*. Atlanta: Society of Biblical Literature, 2008.

Pryor, J. W. *John: Evangelist of the Covenant People*. Downers Grove: InterVarsity Press, 1992.

Qimron, E. and J. H. Charlesworth, "Rule of the Community." Pages 1–51 in *The Dead Sea Scrolls. Hebrew, Aramaic, and Greek Texts with English Translation: Vol 1*. Edited by J. H. Charlesworth. Tübingen: Mohr Siebeck, 1994.

Rader, W. *The Church and Racial Hostility: A History of Interpretation of Ephesians 2:11–22*. Tübingen: Mohr Siebeck, 1978.

Räisänen, H. "Römer 9–11: Analyse eines geistigen Ringens." *ANRW* 25.4: 2891–929. Part 2, *Principat*, 25.4. Edited by H. Temporini and W. Haase. New York: de Gruyter 1987.

—, *Paul and the Law*. 2d ed. Tübingen: Mohr Siebeck, 1987.

—, *The Rise of Christian Beliefs: The Thought World of Early Christians*. Minneapolis: Fortress, 2010.

Rajak, T. and D. Noy. "*ARCHISYNAGOGOI*: Office, Title and Social Status in the Graeco-Jewish Synagogue." *JRS* 83 (1993): 75–93.

Ratzinger, J. (Benedict XVI). "Glaube, Vernunft und Universität: Erinnerungen und Reflexionen." No pages. Cited 8 March 2008. Online: http://www.epub.uni-regensburg.de/406/.

—, (Benedikt XVI). *Jesus von Nazareth: Erster Teil: Von der Taufe im Jordan bis zur Verklärung*. Freiburg im Breisgau: Herder, 2007.

Reasoner, M. *The Strong and the Weak: Romans 14.1–15.13 in Context*. Cambridge: Cambridge University Press, 1999.

Reed, J. L. *Archaeology and the Galilean Jesus*. Harrisburg: Trinity, 2000.

Reicher, S. "The Context of Social Identity: Domination, Resistance and Change." *Political Psychology* 25 (2004): 921–45.

Reinhartz, A. "Rodney Stark and 'the Mission to the Jews.'" Pages 197–212 in *Religious Rivalries in the Early Roman Empire and the Rise of Christianity*. Edited by L. E. Vaage. Waterloo: Wilfrid Laurier University Press, 2006.

Renan, E. *Vie de Jésus*. Paris: Michel Lévy frères, libraires éditeurs, 1863.

Richardson, P. "Augustan-Era Synagogues in Rome." Pages 17–29 in *Judaism and Christianity in First-Century Rome.* Edited by K. P. Donfried and P. Richardson; Grand Rapids: Eerdmans, 1998.

Riches, J. "Matthew's Missionary Strategy in Colonial Perspective." Pages 128–42 in *The Gospel of Matthew in its Roman Imperial Context.* Edited by J. Riches and D. C. Sim; London: T&T Clark, 2005.

Riesner, R. *Paul's Early Period: Chronology, Mission Strategy, Theology.* Grand Rapids: Eerdmans, 1998.

Robinson, T. A. *The Bauer Thesis Examined: The Geography of Heresy in the Early Christian Church.* Lewiston: Mellen, 1988.

Royse, J. *Scribal Habits in Early Greek New Testament Papyri.* Leiden: Brill, 2008.

Ruiten, J. van. "The Covenant of Noah in *Jubilees* 6.1–38." Pages 167–90 in *The Concept of the Covenant in the Second Temple Period.* Edited by S. E. Porter and J. C. R. de Roo. Atlanta: Society of Biblical Literature, 2003.

Runesson, A. "Architecture, Conflict, and Identity Formation: Jews and Christians in Capernaum From the 1th to the 6th Century." Pages 231–57 in *Religion, Ethnicity, and Identity in Ancient Galilee: A Region in Transition.* Edited by J. Zangenberg, H. W. Attridge and D. B. Martin. Tübingen: Mohr Siebeck, 2007.

—, "Inventing Christian Identity: Paul, Ignatius, and Theodotius I." Pages 59–92 in *Exploring Early Christian Identity.* Edited by B. Holmberg. Tübingen: Mohr Siebeck, 2008.

—, "Particularistic Judaism and Universalistic Christianity? Some Critical Remarks on Terminology and Theology." *Journal of Greco-Roman Christianity and Judaism* 1 (2000): 120–44.

—, "Re-Thinking Early Jewish–Christian Relations: Matthean Community History as Pharisaic Intragroup Conflict." *JBL* 127 (2008): 95–132.

—, "The Synagogue at Ancient Ostia: The Building and its History from the First to the Fifth Century." Pages in 29–99 in *The Synagogue of Ancient Ostia and the Jews of Rome: Interdisciplinary Studies.* Edited by B. Olsson, D. Mitternacht, and O. Brandt. Stockholm: Paul Åström, 2001.

Runesson, A., D. D. Binder and B. Olsson. *The Ancient Synagogue From its Origins to 200 C.E.: A Source Book.* Leiden: Brill, 2008

Rusam, D. *Die Gemeinschaft der Kinder Gottes.* Stuttgart: Kohlhammer, 1993.

Rutgers, L. V. "Roman Policy toward the Jews: Expulsions from the City of Rome during the First Century C.E." Pages 93–116 in *Judaism and Christianity in First-Century Rome.* Edited by K. P. Donfried and P. Richardson. Grand Rapids: Eerdmans, 1998.

Saldarini, A. J. *Matthew's Christian-Jewish Community.* Chicago: Chicago University Press, 1994.

Salmeri, G. "Dio, Rome, and the Civic Life of Asia Minor." Pages 53–92 in *Dio Chrysostom. Politics, Letters, and Philosophy.* Edited by S. Swain. Oxford: Oxford University Press, 2000.

Sanders, E. P. "Jesus' Galilee." Pages 3–41 in *Fair Play: Diversity and Conflicts in Early Christianity: Essays in Honour of Heikki Räisänen.* Edited by I. Dunderberg, C. Tuckett, K. Syreeni. Leiden: Brill, 2002.

—, *Jesus and Judaism.* Philadelphia: Fortress, 1985.

—, *Judaism: Practice and Belief 63 BCE-66CE.* London: SCM, 1992.

—, *Paul and Palestinian Judaism: A Comparison of Patterns of Religion.* London: SCM, 1977.

—, *Paul, the Law, and the Jewish People.* Minneapolis: Fortress, 1983.

Sandnes, K. O. "Imitatio Homeri? An Appraisal of Dennis R. MacDonald's 'Mimesis Criticism.'" *JBL* 124 (2005): 715–32.

—, "Revised Conventions in Early Christian Paraenesis—'Working Good' in 1 Peter as an Example." Pages 373-403 in *Early Christian Paraenesis in Context*. Edited by J. Starr and T. Engberg-Pedersen. Berlin: de Gruyter, 2004.

—, *The Challenge of Homer: School, Pagan Poets, and Early Christianity*. London: T&T Clark 2009.

Sandt, H. van de and D. Flusser. *The Didache: Its Jewish Sources and its Place in Early Judaism and Christianity*. Minneapolis: Fortress, 2002.

Sauer, E. *The Archaeology of Religious Hatred in the Roman and Early Medieval World*. Stroud: Tempus, 2003.

Schaller, B. "Christus, 'der Diener der Bescheidung…, auf ihn werden die Völker hoffen': Zu Charakter und Funktion der Schriftzitate in Röm 15,7–13." Pages 261–85 in *Das Gesetz im frühen Judentum und im Neuen Testament: Festschrift für Christoph Burchard zum 75. Geburtstag*. Edited by D. Sänger and M. Konradt. Göttingen: Vandenhoeck & Ruprecht, 2006.

Scheid, J. "Le sens des rites. L'exemple romain." Pages 39–71 in *Rites et croyances dans les religions du monde romain: huit exposés suivis de discussions: Vandœuvre-Genève, 21-25 août 2006*. Edited by J. Scheid. Genève: Fondation Hardt, 2007.

—, "Religions in Contact." Pages 112–26 in *Religions of the Ancient World: A Guide*. Edited by S. I. Johnston. Cambridge: Harvard University Press, 2004.

Schenker, A. Das Neue am neuen Bund und das Alte am alten: Jer 31 in der hebräischen und griechischen Bibel. Göttingen: Vandenhoeck & Ruprecht, 2006.

Schlarb, E. *Die Gesunde Lehre: Häresie und Wahrheit im Spiegel der Pastoralbriefe*. Marburg: N. G. Elwert, 1990.

Schmithals, W. *Paul and James*. London: SCM, 1965.

Schnabel, E. J. *Early Christian Mission*. 2 vols. Downers Grove: Intervarsity Press, 2004.

Schneider, S. M. "The Raising of the New Temple: John 20:19-23 and Johannine Ecclesiology." *NTS* 52 (2006): 337–55.

Schnelle, U. *Paul: His Life and Theology.* Grand Rapids: Baker Academic, 2005.

—, *The History and Theology of the New Testament Writings.* London: SCM, 1994.

Schönborn, C. K. 2007. "Der Papst auf der Agora: Über einen Anspruch den allein Gott stellen kann." Pages 43–52 in *Ein Weg zu Jesus: Schlüssel zu einem tieferen Verständnis des Papstbuches.* Edited by T. Söding. Freiburg im Breisgau: Herder, 2007.

Schröter, J. "Ratzinger und seine Suche nach dem historischen Jesus." *Die Kirche, Evangelische Wochenzeitung* (May 20, 2007).

Schürer, E. *The History of the Jewish People in the Age of Jesus Christ: Revised and edited by G. Vermes and F. Millar.* 4 vols. Edinburgh: T&T Clark, 1973–1987.

Schütz, J. H. *Paul and the Anatomy of Apostolic Authority.* Louisville: Westminster John Knox, 2007 [1975].

Schweitzer, A. *Geschichte der Leben-Jesu-Forschung.* 4th ed. Tübingen: Mohr Siebeck, 1926.

—, *The Mysticism of Paul the Apostle.* London: A&C Black, 1931.

Schwemer, A. M. "Paulus in Antiochien." *BZ* 42 (1998): 161–80.

Scrivener, F. H. A. *A Plain Introduction to the Criticism of the New Testament for the Use of Biblical Students.* Edited by E. Miller. 2 vols. 4th ed. London: Deigton, 1894.

Sen, A. K. *Reason Before Identity.* Oxford: Oxford University Press, 1999.

Sherwin-White, A. N. *Roman Society and Roman Law in the New Testament.* Oxford: Clarendon, 1963.

Silberman, N. A. *Between Past and Present: Archaeology, Ideology, and Nationalism in the Modern Middle East.* New York: Doubleday, 1990.

Sim, D. *The Gospel of Matthew and Christian Judaism: The History and Social Setting of the Matthean Community.* Edinburgh: T&T Clark, 1998.

Simondon, M. *La mémoire et l'oubli dans la pensée grecque jusqu'à la fin du Ve siècle avant J.-C: Psychologie archaïque, mythes et doctrines.* Paris: Belles Lettres, 1983.

Skarsaune, O. and R. Hvalvik, eds., *Jewish Believers in Jesus: The Early Centuries.* Peabody: Hendrickson, 2007.

Skarsaune, O. *In the Shadow of the Temple: Jewish Influences on Early Christianity.* Downers Grove: InterVarsity Press, 2002.

Small, J. P. *Wax Tablets of the Mind: Cognitive Studies of Memory and Literacy in Classical Antiquity.* London: Routledge, 1997.

Smallwood, E. M. *The Jews under Roman Rule from Pompey to Diocletian.* Leiden: Brill, 1981.

Smith, A. L. and M. D. Gibson. *The Palestinian Syriac Lectionary of the Gospels, Re-Edited from Two Sinai MSS. and from P. de Lagarde's Edition of the Evangeliarium Hierosolymitanum.* London: K. Paul, Trench, Trubner & Co., 1899.

Sollors, W. *Beyond Ethnicity: Consent and Descent in American Culture.* New York: Oxford University Press, 1986.

Sorabji, R. *Aristotle on Memory.* (2d ed. London: Duckworth, 2004.

Spence, S. *The Parting of the Ways: The Roman Church as a Case Study.* Leuven: Peeters, 2004.

Spieckermann, H. "'Barmherzig und gnädig ist der Herr ...'" *ZAW* 102 (1990): 1–18.

—, "God's Steadfast Love: Towards a New Conception of Old Testament Theology." *Bib* 81 (2000): 305–27.

Spilka, B., P. Shaver, and L. A. Kilpatrick. "A General Attribution Theory for the Psychology of Religion." *JSSR* 24 (1985): 1–20.

Spilka, B., R. W. Hood, B. Hundsberger and R. Gorsuch. *The Psychology of Religion: An Empirical Approach.* 3d ed. New York: Guilford Press, 2003.

Spilsbury, P. "Josephus." Pages 241–60 in *Justification and Variegated Nomism: Vol .1: The Complexities of Second Temple Judaism.* Edited by D. A. Carson, P. T. O'Brien, and M. A. Seifrid. Tübingen: Mohr, 2001.

Standhartinger, A. "Der Papst und der Rabbi: Anmerkungen zum christlich-jüdischen Dialog im Jesusbuch Benedikt XVI." Pages 146–157 in *Ein Weg zu Jesus. Schlüssel zu einem tieferen Verständnis des Papstbuches*. Edited by T. Söding Freiburg im Breisgau: Herder, 2007.

Stark, R. *The Rise of Christianity: How the Obscure, Marginal Jesus Movement Became the Dominant Religious Force in the Western World in a Few Centuries*. San Francisco: HarperCollins, 1997.

Stegemann, E. "'Kindlein, hütet euch vor den Götterbildern!'" *TZ* 41 (1985): 284–94.

Stegemann, E. W., and W. Stegemann. *The Jesus Movement: A Social History of Its First Century*. Edinburgh: T&T Clark, 1999.

Stendahl, K. *Paul Among Jews and Gentiles, and other Essays*. London: SCM Press, 1977.

Stern, M. ed. *Greek and Latin Authors on Jews and Judaism: Edited with Introductions, Translations and Commentary*. 3 vols. Jerusalem: Israel Academy of Sciences and Humanities, 1974–1984.

Stowers, S. K. *A Rereading of Romans: Justice, Jews, and Gentiles*. New Haven: Yale University Press, 1994.

Straub, J. "Identität." Pages 277–303 in *Handbuch der Kulturwissenschaften: Vol. 1: Grundlagen und Schlüsselbegriffe*. Edited by F. Jaeger and B. Liebsch. Stuttgart: Metzler, 2004.

Strecker, G. *The Johannine Letters: A Commentary on 1, 2, and 3 John*. Minneapolis: Fortress, 1996.

Strelan, R. *Paul, Artemis and the Jews in Ephesus*. Berlin: de Gruyter, 1996.

Tajfel, H. *Human Groups and Social Categories: Studies in Social Psychology*. Cambridge: Cambridge University Press, 1981.

Taylor, J. E. *Jewish Women Philosophers of First Century Alexandria: Philo's Therapeutae Reconsidered*. Oxford: Oxford University Press, 2003.

Taylor, V. *The Gospel According to St. Mark.* London: Macmillan, 1952.

Tcherikover, V. *Hellenistic Civilization and the Jews.* Philadelphia: Jewish Publication Society of America, 1959.

Tellbe, M. *Christ-Believers in Ephesus: A Textual Analysis of Early Christian Identity Formation in a Local Perspective.* Tübingen: Mohr Siebeck, 2009.

—, *Paul between Synagogue and State: Christians, Jews, and Civic Authorities in 1 Thessalonians, Romans and Philippians.* Stockholm: Almqvist & Wiksell International, 2001.

Thatcher, T. "Why John Wrote a Gospel: Memory and History in an Early Christian Community," Pages 79–97 in *Memory, Tradition, and Text: Uses of the Past in Early Christianity.* Edited by A. Kirk and T. Thatcher. Atlanta: Society of Biblical Literature, 2005.

The Jewish People and Their Sacred Scriptures in the Christian Bible. Boston: Pauline Books & Media, 2002.

Theissen, G. *A Theory of Primitive Christian Religion.* London: SCM, 1999.

—, *The Religion of the Earliest Churches: Creating a Symbolic World: A Theory of Primitive Christian Religion.* Minneapolis: Fortress, 1999.

Thielman, F. *From Plight to Solution: A Jewish Framework for Understanding Paul's View of the Law in Galatians and Romans.* Leiden: Brill, 1989.

Thiessen, W. *Christen in Ephesus: Die historische und theologische Situation in vorpaulinischer und paulinischer Zeit und zur Zeit der Apostelgeschichte und der Pastoralbriefe.* Tübingen: Francke, 1995.

Thiselton, A. *The First Epistle to the Corinthians.* Grand Rapids: Eerdmans, 2000.

Thornton, C.-J. "Justin und das Markusevangelium," *ZNW* 84 (1993): 93–109.

Thurén, L. *Derhetorizing Paul: A Dynamic Perspective on Pauline Theology and the Law.* Tübingen: Mohr Siebeck, 2000.

Thyen, H. "Johannesbriefe." Pages 186–200 in vol. 17 of *Theologische Realenzyklopädie*. Edited by G. Krause and G. Müller. 36 vols. Berlin: de Gruyter, 1977–.

Timmer, D. "Sinai 'Revisited' Again: Further reflections on the Appropriating of Exodus 19 – Numbers 10 in 1QS." *RB* 115 (2008): 481–98.

Tomson, P. J. *Paul and the Jewish Law: Halakha in the Letters of the Apostle to the Gentiles*. Minneapolis: Fortress, 1990.

Trebilco, P. *Jewish Communities in Asia Minor.* Cambridge: Cambridge University Press, 1991.

—, *The Early Christians in Ephesus from Paul to Ignatius*. Tübingen: Mohr Siebeck, 2004.

Trevett, C. "The Other Letters to the Churches of Asia: Apocalypse and Ignatius of Antioch." *JSNT* 37 (1989): 117–35.

Turner, J. C., with M. A. Hogg, P. J. Oakes, S. D. Reicher, and M. S. Wetherell. *Rediscovering the Social Group: A Self-Categorization Theory*. Oxford: Blackwell, 1987.

Vaage, L. E. "Ancient Religious Rivalries and the Struggle for Success: Christian, Jews, and Others in the Early Roman Empire." Pages 3–19 in *Religious Rivalries in the Early Roman Empire and the Rise of Christianity.* Edited by L. E. Vaage. Waterloo: Wilfrid Laurier University Press, 2006.

Vaage, L. E., ed. *Religious Rivalries in the Early Roman Empire and the Rise of Christianity*. Waterloo: Wilfrid Laurier University Press, 2006.

VanderKam, J. C. "Shavu'ot". Pages 871–2 in vol. 2 of *Encyclopedia of the Dead Sea Scrolls*. 2 vols. Edited by L. H. Shiffman and J. C. VanderKam. Oxford: Oxford University Press, 2000.

—, *The Book of Jubilees*. Sheffield: Sheffield Academic Press, 2001.

Vaux, R. de. *Ancient Israel.* 2 vols. New York: McGraw-Hill, 1961.

Vermes, G. "Ratzinger and Not the Pope." *The Times* (May 19, 2007).

—, *Jesus the Jew: A Historian's Reading of the Gospels*. London: Collins, 1973.

Veyne, P. *Bread and Circuses: Historical and Political Pluralism.* London: Penguin Books, 1992.

Wagner J. R. *Heralds of the Good News: Isaiah and Paul in Concert in the Letter to the Romans.* Leiden: Brill, 2003.

Wahlde, U. C. von. *The Johannine Commandments: 1 Joh and the Struggle for the Johannine Tradition.* New York: Paulist Press, 1990.

Wallace, D. B. "The Gospel according to Bart: A Review Article of *Misquoting Jesus* by Bart Ehrman." *JETS* 49 (2006): 327–49.

Waltzing, J.-P. *Études historique sur les corporations professionnelles chez les Romains.* 4 vols. Leiden: Peeters, 1895–1900. Repr., Hildesheim: George Olms, 1970.

Walzer, R. *Galen on Jews and Christians.* London: Oxford University Press, 1949.

Wander, B. *Gottesfürchtige und Sympathisanten: Studien zum heidnischen Umfeld von Diasporasynagogen.* Tübingen: Mohr Siebeck, 1998.

Ware, J. P. *The Mission of the Church in Paul's Letter to the Philippians in the Context of Ancient Judaism.* Leiden: Brill, 2005.

Wasserman, T. "Papyrus 72 and the Bodmer Miscellaneous Codex." *NTS* 51 (2005): 137–54.

—, "Theological Creativity and Scribal Solutions in Jude." Pages 75–83 in *Textual Variation: Theological and Social Tendencies.* Edited by H. A. G. Houghton and D. C. Parker. Piscataway: Gorgias Press, 2008.

—, *The Epistle of Jude: Its Text and Transmission.* Stockholm: Almqvist & Wiksell International, 2006.

Watson, F. *Paul, Judaism and the Gentiles.* 2d ed. Cambridge: Cambridge University, 2007.

Westcott, B. F., and F. J. A. Hort. *The New Testament in the Original Greek.* 2 vols. London: Macmillan, 1881–1882.

Westerholm, S. "Paul's Anthropological 'Pessimism' in its Jewish Context." Pages 71–98 in *Divine and Human Agency in Paul and His Cultural Environment.* Edited by J. M. G. Barclay and S. Gathercole. London: T&T Clark, 2006.

—, *Jesus and Scribal Authority.* Lund: Gleerups, 1978.

—, *Perspectives Old and New on Paul: The "Lutheran" Paul and His Critics.* Grand Rapids: Eerdmans, 2004.

Wettstein, J. J., ed. *Novum Testamentum Graecum.* 2 vols. Amsterdam: Dommerian, 1751–1752.

White, L. M. *From Jesus to Christianity: How Four Generations of Visionaries & Storytellers Created the New Testament and Christian Faith.* San Francisco: HarperOne, 2004.

—, *The Social Origins of Christian Architecture: Volume I: Building God's House in the Roman World: Architectural Adaptation Among Pagans, Jews, and Christians.* Valley Forge: Trinity Press International, 1990.

Whittaker, M. *Jews and Christians: Graeco-Roman Views.* Cambridge: Cambridge University Press, 1984.

—, *Tatian* Oratio ad Graecos *and Fragments.* Oxford: Clarendon Press, 1982.

Williams, M. H. *The Jews Among the Greeks and Romans: A Diaspora Source Book.* London: Duckworth, 1998.

Winninge, M. *Sinners and the Righteous: A Comparative Study of the Psalms of Solomon and Paul's Letters.* Stockholm: Almqvist & Wiksell International, 1995.

Winter, B. W. "Acts and Roman Religion: The Imperial Cult." Pages 93–103 in *The Book of Acts in its Graeco-Roman Setting.* Edited by D. W. Gill and C. Gempf. Vol 2 of *The Book of Acts in Its First Century Setting.* Edited by B. W. Winter. Grand Rapids: Eerdmans, 1994.

—, "Rehabilitating Gallio and his Judgement in Acts 18:14–15." *TynB* 57 (2006): 291–308.

—, "The Public Honouring of Christian Benefactors Rom 13.3–4 and 1 Peter 2.14–15." *JSNT* 34 (1988): 87–103.

—, *After Paul Left Corinth: The Influence of Secular Ethics and Social Change*. Grand Rapids: Eerdmans, 2001.

—, *Philo and Paul among the Sophists*. Grand Rapids: Eerdmans, 2002.

—, *Seek the Welfare of the City: Christians as Benefactors and Citizens*. Grand Rapids: Eerdmans, 1994.

Wintermute, O. S. "Jubilees." Pages 35–142 in *The Old Testament Pseudepigrapha, Volume 2: Expansions of the 'Old Testament' and Legends, Wisdom and Philosophical Literature, Prayers, Psalm, and Odes, Fragments of Lost Judeo-Hellenistic Works*. Edited by J. H. Charlesworth. New York: Doubleday, 1985.

Witetschek, S. *Ephesische Enthüllungen 1: Frühe Christen in einer antiken Großtadt. Zugleich ein Beitrag zur Frage nach den Kontexten det Johannesapokalypse*. Leuven: Peeters, 2008.

Wolff, C. *Jeremia in Frühjudentum und Urchristentum*. Berlin: Akademie-Verlag, 1976.

Wolter, M. "Wo bleibt der Eigensinn der Evangelien?" *Rheinischer Merkur* (May 24, 2007).

Wurm, A. *Die Irrlehrer im ersten Johannesbrief*. Freiburg: Herdersche Verlagshandlung, 1903.

Yadin, A. *Scripture as Logos: Rabbi Ishmael and ther Origins of Midrash*. Philadelphia: University of Pennsylvania Press, 2004.

Zahn, T. *Geschichte des Neutestamentlichen Kanons*. 2 vols. Erlangen and Leipzig: A. Deichert'sche Verlagsbuchh, 1889.

Zangenberg, J. "A Region in Transition: Introducing Religion, Ethnicity and Identity in Ancient Galilee." Pages 1–10 in *Religion, Ethnicity, and Identity in Ancient Galilee*. Edited by J. Zangenberg, H. W. Attridge, and D. B. Martin. Tübingen: Mohr Siebeck, 2007.

Zangenberg, J., H. W. Attridge and D. B. Martin, eds. *Religion, Ethnicity, and Identity in Ancient Galilee*. Tübingen: Mohr Siebeck, 2007.

Zetterholm, M. "Paul and the Missing Messiah." Pages 33–55 in *The Messiah: In Early Judaism and Christianity*. Edited by M. Zetterholm. Minneapolis: Fortress, 2007.

—, *The Formation of Christianity in Antioch: A Social-Scientific Approach to the Separation between Judaism and Christianity*. London: Routledge, 2003.

Ziegler, K. J. F., W. Sontheimer and H. Gärtner, eds. *Der kleine Pauly: Lexikon der Antike*. 5 vols. München: Druckenmüller, 1964–1975.

Zuntz, G. *The Text of the Epistles: A Disquisition upon the Corpus Paulinum*. London: Oxford University Press, 1953.

Index of Passages

Christian Literature

Apostolic Constitutions and Canons